ASSIMILATE

# ASSIMILATE

A Critical History of Industrial Music

S. ALEXANDER REED

OXFORD
UNIVERSITY PRESS

# OXFORD
UNIVERSITY PRESS

Oxford University Press is a department of the University of Oxford. It furthers the University's objective of excellence in research, scholarship, and education by publishing worldwide.

Oxford   New York
Auckland   Cape Town   Dar es Salaam   Hong Kong   Karachi
Kuala Lumpur   Madrid   Melbourne   Mexico City   Nairobi
New Delhi   Shanghai   Taipei   Toronto

With offices in
Argentina   Austria   Brazil   Chile   Czech Republic   France   Greece
Guatemala   Hungary   Italy   Japan   Poland   Portugal   Singapore
South Korea   Switzerland   Thailand   Turkey   Ukraine   Vietnam

Oxford is a registered trade mark of Oxford University Press in the UK and certain other countries.

Published in the United States of America by
Oxford University Press
198 Madison Avenue, New York, NY 10016

Library of Congress Cataloging-in-Publication Data
Reed, S. Alexander.
Assimilate : a critical history of industrial music / S. Alexander Reed.
   pages cm
ISBN 978-0-19-983258-3 (hardcover : alk. paper) — ISBN 978-0-19-983260-6 (pbk. : alk. paper)
1. Industrial music—History and criticism. I. Title.
ML3528.7.R44 2013
781.64809—dc23      2012042281

3   5   7   9   8   6   4   2

Printed in the United States of America on acid-free paper

Publication for this book was supported by the AMS 75 PAYS Endowment of the American Musicological Society, funded in part by the National Endowment for the Humanities and the Andrew W. Mellon Foundation.

# Contents

# Acknowledgments

Invaluable commentary, questions, and suggestions throughout this project came from several anonymous readers and also from my fellow scholars Ian Reyes, Marsha Bryant, Daphne Carr, Robert Fink, Mary Lewis, Andrew Weintraub, Rebekah Ahrendt, Philip Tagg, Zarah Ersoff, and Galen Brown. Helpful discussions and opinions were offered by attendees at conferences where earlier versions of this book's chapters were presented. Amy Gorelick, Lee Hendricks, and Phil Sandifer also inspired, advised, and cooked good food. Vital early manuscript guidance came courtesy of Jane Behnken. Thomas Finnegan provided detailed and witty copy editing. Suzanne Ryan is to thank for believing in this book enough to bring it to Oxford University Press.

Thanks to all of those who granted interviews or whose incidental conversations made their way into this book; whether you're quoted directly or not in these pages, you helped to shape them. I'm also grateful to those who helped me with archival research and with helping me find some obscure sources: James "Ned" Kirby, Kelly Litzenberger, and Walt Miller deserve mention here by name. Thanks also to my army of volunteer transcribers: Daniel Siepmann, Amber Braun, Leslie McCluskey-Eissing, John Aho, Stefanie Acevedo, James Young, Donovan Howe, Andria Poiarkoff, Amanda Swenson, Morgan Rich, Sarah Bushey, Adam Scott Neal, Lindsey O'Brien, and Holly Ray.

My colleagues at the University of Florida and New York University have been immensely supportive throughout the writing of this book. Especially vital has been the trusting encouragement of John Duff, Paul Richards, Paul Koonce, James Paul Sain, Leslie Odom, Jennifer Thomas, Silvio Dos Santos, Margaret Butler, Mutlu Çitim-Kepic, and Amanda Mayberry. The University of Florida Fine Arts Scholarship Enhancement Fund assistance in my 2011 research travel. Penelope Collins, Aiva Veinberga, Sarah Manvel, and Koen, Annette, and Jaap Brand were wonderfully hospitable during these expeditions. Further funding for this book was provided by the AMS 75 PAYS Endowment of the American Musicological Society.

Thanks to the countless people around the world who have made, written about, and contextualized this music. Those who personally helped me know, enjoy, and think critically about it are too many to name, but they include my sisters, Robyn and Karen, Kurt Thorn, Doug Morse, Chris Boone, Ian Struckhoff, Rosemary Ledesma, Jacob Racusin, Brian Ales, Rik Millhouse, Aaron Fuleki, and Jeremy Long. I am particularly grateful to my parents for tolerating my lifelong immersion in this music. Finally, I owe special thanks to my wife, Meredith Collins, whose love, patience, proofreading, academic camaraderie, encouragement, and smart conversation make writing, thinking, and music better every day.

# Foreword

A brief word of warning. I have to confess to a level of discomfort when the term *industrial* is put to me. As a musician and producer who, it would seem, had more than a passing flirtation with what the media and music consumers broadly label "industrial music," or "industrial beats," I tend to bristle a little. As a founding member of Cabaret Voltaire, a group who hail from a northern British industrial city, it seems I can offer little defense, though. We made music that was often sonically brutal, we challenged ideas of authority and control, we toyed with moody and often taboo imagery, we were simultaneously intellectual and anti-intellectual, we thought ourselves iconoclastic, and we wore raincoats sometimes; in our defense it was the north and it did rain occasionally.

Perhaps the initial reaction is justifiable, as "industrial" was never a term we applied to ourselves. Wary of being burdened with a media definition, we felt a natural fear of having a spectrum of work reduced to a single classification. There was also an issue of courtesy. Throbbing Gristle, with a commensurate serving of gravitas and mischievousness, tagged their record label *Industrial Music for Industrial People*. As friends and peers, we were honored to have releases on the label, but understandably we avoided any identity conflict out of respect.

In truth it has to be said that the muted response to being called "industrial" is much more complex. Fearful of becoming a self-fulfilling prophecy, we did not find the idea that we would become a short-lived sonic reification of our city's monocultural identity appealing. Similarly, we felt under no obligation to answer for a whole subsequent genre as the media began to box it up. Like all artists, we felt responsible for ourselves alone, and as the industrial banner unfurled to incorporate disparate protagonists, some too singular in ideology for our tastes, a diplomatic distance was put in place. But perhaps for many who are invested in the meaning of the "I-word," particularly in the context of the dominant rock modality, this arm's-length riposte has put "industrial" outside the general music discourse or academic reflection for too long. Many of the implications, connections, and consequences of the music made in its name have been overlooked, denied proper scrutiny.

It should be recognized that music movements are in large part externally constructed and driven; they are convenient labels to help market and shelve. In truth, music and the creative process do not work in isolation or mutual exclusion but are part of a much more complex series of associations and connections. There is clearly a need to progress beyond classification to unpack the rich complexity contained inside. It is important and appropriate to look at the wider contexts in order to appraise the etymology, processes, ideologies, and legacies of what we term industrial. This book addresses the industrial cultural spectrum from esoteric to populist, presenting evidence of the diverse and dispersed roots of the industrial story and its sonic, text-based, visual, and performance heritage.

Music, as ever, proves to be a medium that translates and disseminates ideas quickly and effectively. The industrial narrative is not exclusively one of music, but the immediacy of popular sound has enabled it to progress and articulate its ideas. We can see here the industrial account is one that has remained in constant flux, has multiple trigger points and infinite destinations, and has carried along pathways that continue to resonate. On a macro level, the ideological challenges to social and cultural control—and our tacit compliance—that the key protagonists who are identified here threw down were truly prescient; we ignore their commentary at our own peril. On a more discrete level, the actual sounds and processes on which the industrial templates were drawn continue to echo through contemporary urban sounds of dubstep, grime, and electronic dance music and are evident in work by noise and sound artists. In addition, the accompanying imagery, which forms a large part of the industrial narrative, continues to provide a benchmark for the gritty realism or dystopian futures in television and film production.

The industrial story, at least for me, acknowledges the importance of time and place. At the beginning of the 1980s, the defining period, there was a fusion of raw elements: readily available technology, postpunk ideology, a vibrant DIY ethos, burgeoning Reaganomics, and a whiff of insurrection in the air. Speaking a little of my own industrial credentials, those boxes were clearly ticked. To those of us living and making sounds in a northern English city, there was unavoidable synergy between the place and its output. Everyone was collaterally implicated. The city's sounds during the 1980s were both a considered response and a practical resolution to the industrial atrophy that was well under way by this time. Against a backdrop of Thatcherite fiscal policy and regional confrontation, Sheffield's regeneration was in every sense postindustrial. Built upon the bones of its once-thriving steel and cutlery production, the abandoned offices, workshops, and factories proved useful to would-be musicians, producers, and artists who would come to occupy these lost properties. Cultural redemption came to those who were happy to exploit Youth Employment schemes and the cheap council housing of the time to provide their own solutions to southern capital abandonment. However, as much as the geography was helping configure the sounds that began to emanate—Clock DVA, Hula, Human League, BEF, et al.—many of a northern disposition feared entrapment, the conviction being that music was an agent of escape, an effective means of transcending those very spaces and signifiers that shaped or confined you.

From a creative perspective, this conflict between day-to-day reality and otherness offered a useful tension central to what was produced. The shiny modernity of technology, an escape route to an idealized future, was in turn anchored in the more subversive dirt of reality. The pyschogeography of the city was an indelible stain on us, as I'm sure it was for others. Drop hammers, fiery furnaces, and steel forges—the clichéd sounds and sights of heavy industry were part of the sonic deal being made. In many cases, this filtering was pretty literal. In our case, the first gig we ever played, which had some dynamic consequences, was perhaps inflamed by the use of a tape loop of a steam hammer (from Ostend, as Richard proudly pronounced) as the rhythm track. "Nag Nag Nag," a more successful Cabs single, made sure that it wasn't to be emasculated by claims of rank commercialism; percussion fills came courtesy of bashing metal keyboard legs. Some of our earlier machines were ex-government tape recorders, dangerously heavy and built, it would seem, to withstand nuclear attack. For our part, we walked the walk.

The inspiration of Dada offered a guidebook of how to go about deconstructing a world that did not adequately represent the one we actually inhabited. Suitably driven by Duchamp, Tzara, and other past pugnacious artists, this was a sincere if somewhat naïve attempt to tear up the plans and devise new strategies. Process meant the rejection of traditional methods and instrumentation. The recording studio became the most valuable writing tool; tape machines, effected voices, "treated" instruments, tape loops, and drum machines. Song structures and linear arrangements were abandoned; the logocentric norm of most contemporary music was dismissed for a sonic democracy. The music was intended to be primal, visceral, and provocative. Noise, for us a Sheffield birthright, was the most effective tool in the box. Although most at the time were unaware of many of the readings into the inherent political and social power of noise, it was clearly a language of subversion. Noise defied order and control. It was a musical taboo. Sonic belligerence. It could destabilize. This was not entertainment, but it was fun. The BBC Radiophonic Workshop and Lou Reed's *Metal Machine Music* worked, for us, in perfect . . . well, perhaps not harmony.

To understand the thinking behind the sounds, there needs to be some recognition also of the images that were processed. It can be argued that an expanding media meant the post-1960s were primarily visually driven. Bombarded with television and film images, much of the music that was produced under the industrial banner sought to align sounds with other media. Music was in effect a translating medium. For many bands at the time, inspired by Velvet Underground and the dark psychedelia of Warhol's Exploding Plastic Inevitable, the thinking was to encourage immersion into a total experience. Multimedia and text were an important component, an attack on all fronts; like others, we filtered, collated, and cut up visuals in true Gysin style to accompany gigs and later produce video releases. Still, rather than anodyne, psychedelic textures and colors, punk had conditioned most into the power of representation the shock tactics of realism. This was a generation seeped in the imagery of the Cold War, the inheritors of Oppenheimer's nightmare. As an example, for British players the vision was made startlingly real by the disturbing footage in Peter Watkins's 1965 documentary-drama *War Games* that followed the buildup and aftermath of a Soviet nuclear attack on a UK city. The sights and sounds were strange pre-echoes of the Burroughs-esque dystopian world we inhabited. As a group, we continued to draw on this imagery. Our 1984 video for "Sensoria" was shot in the abandoned hospital where the postnuclear apocalypse *Threads* had been filmed.

Although never perceiving this as any kind of movement or collective, there was a clear sense of connection. Throbbing Gristle, as mentioned, were key agents and offered a gateway for a number of kindred spirits—23 Skidoo, David Tibet, Last Few Days, et al. On a wider scale, the importance cannot be overstated of Vale at RE/Search Publications, whose San Franciscan North Beach apartment became an important transit point and destination during the late 1970s and 1980s for musicians, writers, and an array of general nonconformists. Vale's seatless VW Beetle was industrial by default, and collaborator Mark Pauline, artist and inventor extraordinaire, made kinetic art that encapsulated the zeitgeist perfectly. Vale and RE/Search's connections to the City Lights bookshop around the corner added extra cachet, linking those passing through the North Beach hub to America's postwar renegade literati. Across the water, Chrome were a big influence at the time, and we had our home-grown companions— Hula, Clock DVA, and Workforce, to name a few. It is interesting to note that at this point, as a shared sense of identity was beginning to emerge, the fear of being trapped or simply standing still meant that most looked to their own map to find an interesting path to the next destination. Other people had joined the conversation. When Cabaret Voltaire moved to Some Bizzare Records, there was a growing sense of collective spirit, but one (it must be said) that had no name and no slogan—just attitude and ideas. The label, whose rise was colorful and whose ultimate demise was a divisive and cautionary tale, drew together a roster that included two of the toughest kids on the block, Einstürzende Neubauten and Test Dept., who literally played with the detritus of industry. These together with Coil, Psychic TV, and Jim "Foetus" Thirlwell ensured that the label was defining its own aesthetic, leading rather than being led.

There was also acknowledgement of changing dynamics during the mid-to-late 1980s, particularly from the east coast of the United States, where perceptions of beats and dance floor cultures were being transformed. The industrial ethos, which sought to configure body and mind, was being remodeled by fresh rhythms that equally made play with social and cultural themes in nocturnal spaces. The embryonic hip-hop and electro sounds emanating from that side of the Atlantic Ocean were making an impact on embedded understandings of race, gender, and the body. It seems that British audiences who had already absorbed soul and Jamaican rhythms into their sonic lexicon assimilated these beats and cultures more readily. With changing drug practices as a timely accelerant, it was only a matter of time before the tougher beats of Detroit techno would form an affinity with places like Sheffield and Düsseldorf. As is often the case with game-changing music, this became a loose cartel of second-tier cities, places away from the moneyed business capitals that shaped their cultural identity through manufacturing, ancillary trades, and pastimes. In the late 1980s, Richard Kirk and I worked in Chicago recording with house producer Marshall Jefferson, but also spending time with Al Jourgensen and Chris Connelly making the Acid Horse twelve inch for the pivotal WaxTrax! label. As outsiders, it seemed natural—no conflict of ideology or technologies, just simple shifts of emphasis. The sounds evolve. Sheffield made its own adjustments, integrated its cultural idiosyncrasies. Warp Records became the city's first real label, and significantly, with a track by the seemingly industrial sounding Forgemasters, the label would also become known for Sweet Exorcist's and LFO's onomatopoeic "bleep" releases. Although not part of the industrial canon, nevertheless the sound of industry was made corporeal.

At this point, as we shift gears toward the connecting tissue of the web, the fractal changes of sounds, rhythms, and shall we say attendant practices become difficult to map. The micro cultures and myriad splinters become ever more impenetrable as they eventually move and in many cases dissipate online. Perspectives become a little more subjective in a digital domain, and we enter a kind of Möbius strip of meaning: reference points and destinations endlessly feeding back on themselves as we search for patterns in the complexity in order to compartmentalize and find meaning. Back to our start point: we have to acknowledge the reductionist nature of music taxonomy. Like all genre descriptions, "industrial" can potentially be misunderstood through no fault of those who contribute, but rather the consequences of trying to shoehorn disparate elements into one tidy space.

However, as this volume eloquently details, away from these exhausted formulas, the notion of industrial, although diverse and often conflicting, is inclusive, rich, and complex. It presents a nucleus around which sounds, images, words, processes, and ideas fly. This is not simply a case of a literal translation of terms but rather requires the mapping of sources, pathways, and possibilities. Industrial music should not be seen as the mere mimicking of sounds, signifiers, and attitudes but considered as part of a much wider conversation. We have progressed from the celebration of machines and power for their own sake that characterized the early Futurists to a much broader discourse that addresses the technologies, processes, implications, and consequences of industry, technology, and mass production. It is important that the discourse continue. The tacit and explicit control exerted through current online and digital technologies are rooted in the state and corporate cultures of the recent past, during which all things industrial thrived. Perhaps it is a significant time to appraise the work of musicians, writers, and artists whose combative stances challenge the dominant ideologies and practices that surround them.

Stephen Mallinder
September 3, 2012

# ASSIMILATE

# Introduction:
# The Front Lines

## 1. A Fading Vision Lost in Time

It was April 5, 1991, and Gary Levermore was worried. He'd spent thousands flying the band Front Line Assembly from Vancouver to London for a concert he was promoting that night at the Venue, a seventy-year-old stone building in New Cross. "It wasn't in the center of town where you'd think it would be easy for people to get to. Instead it was a few miles further south; not on an underground line," he remembers.[1] The first time Front Line Assembly had played London, in July 1989, the turnout was disastrously low—just twenty or thirty fans, according to one concertgoer.[2] On the band's live LP from that night, the recorded sound of the crowd cheering had to be edited and recycled from track to track just to give the sonic illusion of a packed room.

Levermore blamed that dismal debut on a national strike, "the first since 1926," as he recalls.[3]✿ Whatever the cause, though, he needed Front Line Assembly to succeed this time around, not just because he was promoting the show but because they were signed to Third Mind Records, his own label that he'd launched as a teenager in 1982, an outgrowth of his self-published zine *Tone Death*. Third Mind had grown a bit over the years, but in the early 1990s it was still a small operation, and a good crowd at this show would mean important sales.

When Levermore arrived at the old theater, though, it was clear there would be no repeat of 1989's miserable show. Wrapped in a long queue down Clifton Ride were some three hundred industrial fans, dressed in black. "I knew that was a significant event," he says.[4] When the band took the stage, they opened and closed their set with the singles "Iceolate" and "Mental Distortion," respectively—both hard, electronic dance songs that UK music rag *Melody Maker* had crowned "single of the week" the previous year.

Front Line Assembly, and with them industrial music as a whole, was on the popular ascendant. Members Bill Leeb and Rhys Fulber had honed a formula of

---

✿ The summer 1989 strikes included London Underground and bus workers, dock workers, passport office personnel, and air traffic controllers.

mechanized dance music that fused together manic narratives of high technology, global warfare, emotional suffering, and the uneasy promise of transhumanism. In 1991, plugged-in concertgoers all over Europe and America heard this music as exhilarating and dangerous: the sound of the present crashing into the future.

Industrial music, of course, did not begin in the nineties. Depending on whom you ask, the genre goes back at least to 1975, and its preconditions were set in place much earlier, as the first chapters of this book will explore. That having been said, Front Line Assembly's early 1990s output is a potent starting place for an exploration of the genre because it clearly illustrates some of the conflicts central to most so-called industrial music of the last thirty years. Take the track "Mindphaser," which was the first new song they released after playing that memorable 1991 show. The single propelled sales of *Tactical Neural Implant*, the album it promoted, to more than seventy thousand copies—not enough to crack the pop charts by any stretch, but more than enough to cement it as a classic among clubgoers, DJs, and musicians even now, some two decades later.

"Mindphaser" pits two potentially opposing hearings against one another. The first way to listen focuses our attention on the song's strange timbres and collage-based construction, its foreboding vision of the future, and Leeb's dictatorial bark, all the stuff of Cold War agitprop. "Mindphaser" here resembles political action, even if the ideology, movement, or state that it stands for is undefined. Lyrically, the song paints a war between machines and humanity—like something out of *The Terminator* or *The Matrix*—but the recording's compelling cybernetic throb and vocal processing make it hard to know which team we're supposed to root for.

In using the signifiers of political critique like this without clearly articulating their politics, Front Line Assembly is knowingly operating within and even exemplifying industrial music's intellectual heritage. "Mindphaser" is welded together from disparate sources, recontextualizing media fragments with limited care about their recognizability—a creative hallmark of the genre handed down from the literary "cut-up" experiments that authors Brion Gysin and William S. Burroughs pioneered in 1959 and beyond. For example, Front Line Assembly's singer and founding member Leeb lifts a few lyrics directly from the 1988 industrial club hit "The Hacker," by UK act Clock DVA: "Digital murder, the language of machines." Entering amidst an ever-changing instrumental palette at just over three minutes into the song is the sound of sheet metal percussion, a musical slogan for the genre, instantly recognizable to anyone who's heard Kraftwerk's 1977 proto-industrial anthem "Metal on Metal." Pervading "Mindphaser" are samples of dialogue from the cyberpunk-inspired film *Robocop 2*. Beyond this, the music video for the song, directed by Robert Lee, inserts footage of Front Line Assembly smoothly into a montage edited together from clips of the 1989 Japanese sci-fi movie *Gunhed*. Even the track's title originated elsewhere: in 1976, Klaus Schulze (formerly of Tangerine Dream) released a twenty-five-minute electronic composition called "Mindphaser," and perhaps more significantly, Whitehouse, an English industrial noise band (whose style is often called "power electronics") released their own "Mindphaser" in 1980—a featureless brick of buzzing feedback and groaning sadomasochistic lyrics. This couldn't have been news to Leeb, who in mid-1980s Vancouver had been known to own the deepest industrial record collection in town.

As we'll discuss later, this kind of reappropriation has some important aesthetic, political, and philosophical implications, but beyond using industrial music's cut-up blueprints in the song's structure and creative process, Front Line Assembly chooses building blocks—Clock DVA, Kraftwerk, *RoboCop 2*, *Gunhed*, and Whitehouse—that all exist within the world of ideas, images, sounds, and associations that industrial music traffics in and connotes. At both its deep and outermost levels, then, the song is in dialogue with the industrial genre's trajectory and routines; with a certain self-awareness, "Mindphaser" summarizes and remixes its own historical context.

This sort of erudite assessment is common in writing about industrial music. Scholar Jason Hanley argues, "Industrial musicians, journalists, and fans worked to construct an active, self-conscious history for themselves in a subculture that viewed musical sound as a form of political action."[5] Postpunk journalist Simon Reynolds writes not quite incredulously that industrial music is frequently "portrayed as the most content-heavy and intent-heavy form of music ever."[6]✿ But Hanley and Reynolds are talking about how the music is *viewed* and *portrayed*, not whether in unguarded moments it's made and enjoyed with such monumental gravity. Surely even the stoniest true believers in the genre's purported "information war" against authority at least occasionally take pleasure in the music as an end unto itself.

This matters because the second way to listen to "Mindphaser" is as a catchy tune. *Melody Maker* called *Tactical Neural Implant* "melodious and accessible," and it's true that "Mindphaser" follows pretty standard pop logic: built on a 4/4 dance rhythm, its two-chord verses and major-key chorus foreground a coherent lyric whose shoot-em-up narrative is exciting and kinetic, if a little grim. The song would be recognizable if performed "unplugged," and Mark Dery's book *Escape Velocity: Cyberculture at the End of the Century* calls it "cyberpunk rock," suggesting a closer kinship with the blues origins of rock and roll than

---

✿ Reynolds then adds in his blog, "(in that sense, for all its refusal of rock'n'roll as sound, the most rockist form of music ever?)."

with the melting formlessness that characterizes so much early industrial music.[7] The aforementioned promotional clip of "Mindphaser" even won Best Alternative Video at MuchMusic's 1992 Canadian Music Video Awards. Leeb himself certainly advocates for this pop hearing of the song, laughing with feigned chagrin in a 1992 interview, "I think there are actually a few real songs on [the album]. They have choruses and verses! Yes, I know!"[8] In these ways, it's a departure from industrial music's past, and its flirtations with wider popularity seem at first glance to have done little to tear down political control systems or to prepare us for its "war of technology [that] threatens to ignite."

The tension between these two hearings of "Mindphaser" extends to whole eras of the genre, in fact. Go out to an industrial club today and you'll hear tunes that more closely resemble pissed off Pet Shop Boys than twenty-first-century Dada. There are plenty who believe that industrial music lost its way at some crossroads between the esoteric lo-fi noise of the late-1970s band Throbbing Gristle and the radio-ready singles of mid-1990s Nine Inch Nails, and indeed it's pretty easy to construct a simple decline-and-fall narrative, no doubt invoking the idea of "selling out" at some point. Arguments of that sort have certainly been made about punk music and hip-hop (interestingly, over nearly the exact same time period).

But this sort of narrative mourns a supposed loss of integrity without really questioning what that integrity was in the first place, or whom it mattered to and why, or whether the music's changes over time might be more than just dilution or soul selling. It also reinforces the silly cultural assumption that inaccessible music and art somehow bears a special rectitude. The pages that follow look deeply at issues of this sort, and ultimately they offer an understanding of industrial music that reveals otherwise hidden connections over its lifespan.


## 2. Industrial Politics and the Pan-Revolutionary

Jason Hanley writes that industrial musicians "create particular modernist aesthetics that attempt to comprehend and comment on what came to be known as the 'modern crisis' of the twentieth century."[9] First things first: modernism, largely arising from western educated society, is a worldview that sharply critiques its own culture's traditional moral and artistic values of truth, unity, order, and a supposedly self-evident (but rarely voiced) hierarchy of peoples, pleasures, and behaviors. Scholars James Naremore and Patrick Brantlinger characterize modernism as "Aggressively individualistic, contemptuous of bourgeois realism, and sometimes nostalgic for preindustrial society . . . at once reactionary and new."[10]

That said, the crisis Hanley is talking about has to do with a certain cultural self-awareness that both fueled and was fueled by modernism early in the twentieth century. Take for instance anthropology's revelation of the world's vastly diverse practices of music, religion, economics, social politics, gender, and sex. By presenting so many alternatives to the European and American baselines of post-Enlightenment capitalism, Christianity, and heternormativity, scholars chipped away at the position of privilege that western culture had assumed in its own eyes, revealing the simple but remarkable truth that there were *other ways to be*. Linguists got in on the action too, once they saw that other cultures' languages seemed to reflect and encode worldviews different from their own. Implicit in all this research was the nagging question of whether we in the west might be merely another people among many, with languages, social rituals, and economic structures that reflect systemic, culturally relative values so pervasive as to seem invisible, so deeply assumed as to resist articulation.

And in fact, Karl Marx and Friedrich Engels had suggested something along these lines in the previous century, indicating that wealthy, powerful social classes tend toward tyranny, not because they're evil but because their unchecked cultural power all but necessarily blinds them to the perspectives and even the existence of others whom they unknowingly subjugate under their own worldview. This line of thinking suggests not only that we in the west might be largely ignorant of our own behaviors but also that these behaviors themselves might seem wicked once we view them from the outside. At the same time, it distressingly suggests that our worldviews and even our free will might not really be our own, but could instead be handed down from past and present bodies of authority. The image of an agent blind to himself, unwittingly acting out both destruction and enslavement, certainly resonated later during the Cold War era of brainwashing paranoia and conspiracy theories.

So to a certain sensibility within modernist thinking, no single nation or economic class was to blame for western culture's biggest troubles and identity crises, but instead the central problem lay in the act of cultural programming itself, revealing the mind of the individual as a new battlefield. Unsettled by this reality, some artists and activists with a contrarian streak and a poet's desire for absolute freedom began to perceive western culture's most fundamental institutions as infections to be purged.✿ Industrial music's ideologues and their

---

✿ Author Jennifer Shryane posits that industrial music's eye toward the destruction of social structures makes it more nihilistic than revolutionary: it "did not strive to subvert society but to pervert it."[11] This reduction, however, takes the music's nihilistic moments at face value, granting neither the potential of this perversion to awaken the individual from society's collectivism nor the music's possible function as the processing and purging of waste in clearing the toxic way to some unthinkably distant freedom.

intellectual allies didn't just want to discard capitalism or Christianity, but they in fact saw themselves as *pan-revolutionary*: language, gender identity, beauty, the ego, and logic itself were all prime for the chopping block. These entities are, according to pan-revolutionary thought, insidiously transparent filters that shape our perceptions and identities, doing so with our silent complicity. As the Australian industrial band SPK wrote in 1981, "Control is no longer a sinister plot by 'them' vs. 'us'—a paranoid delusion. It is internalized and operates via *consent* to remain a balanced/integrated/cooperating citizen."[12] Their argument here is that we in fact have the power to free ourselves from this conditioning, and only by *deprogramming* can we really know our true selves and act with free will.

But how does one rid oneself of language? How can a person live in North America or Western Europe and genuinely escape capitalism? Worse yet, isn't any apparent path out of these ubiquitous, invisible determiners just a feature of their very structures? In their anti-everything insurgency, some would-be revolutionaries have taken to direct political engagement or terrorism as methods of change, but considered respectively, the notion of "working within the system" can seem a euphemism for surrender, and real physical violence often proves ethically unacceptable or ultimately ineffective. These difficulties, probed by social theorists such as Gilles Deleuze and Félix Guattari, make clear that deprogramming isn't easy. We can understand Throbbing Gristle's 1979 declaration that "we need some discipline here" as both a send-up of control structures' power over people and also a dead serious reminder of just how hard it is to divorce oneself from those structures—that it takes real discipline to maintain the void left by deprogramming.

For this reason, radical twentieth-century art has repeatedly pointed toward the *irrational* as a promising aesthetic and political path. This unreason broadly encompasses surrealism, Dada, discordianism, chaos magick, cyberpunk, and the alternative histories of what author Adam Parfrey calls "Apocalypse Culture." It helps explain the rigidly arbitrary strangeness that some radical thinkers have embraced in their anti-hierarchical attempts to fill the vacuum left by deprogramming—usually as a preemptive conceptual placeholder, but sometimes as the genuine adoption of some alternative way of being, newly availed. Examples include the oddly regimented public clowning of proto-Throbbing Gristle art troupe COUM Transmissions; the practice of orthographically constrained writing—*OuLiPo*—to which Belgian band Front 242's lead singer Jean-Luc De Meyer has dedicated himself in recent years; or the bizarre, Pepsi-obsessed thematics of Negativland's 1997 album *Dispepsi*. These little reprogrammings highlight their own arbitrary nature, making them safer, more transparent practices than "normal" or "rational" behavior, which otherwise masquerades as identity and absolute truth. The irrational is most easily articulated through art, because art isn't subject to the practical, ethical, and economic expectations of other kinds of cultural work. Art also has the bonus of affording low commitment and plausible deniability for the casual or merely curious noncomformist.

Different artistic approaches can serve the pan-revolutionary drive. A common tack within industrial music involves the use of noise, which a lot of musicians and scholars believe is emancipatory, destabilizing, and able to overload and undercut our perceptions of order—Einstürzende Neubauten's ear-splitting 1993 "Headcleaner" serves as a good example here both in sound and in name. Within industrial music, noise is essential as both a sonic and a conceptual building block. Artists can also symbolically disrupt order by erasing the lines that govern certain kinds of meaning, as with the basic division between subject and object—the self and other—upon which western identity is predicated. Some dedicated artists have achieved this in anatomically transgressive ways, notably the genital self-mutilation themes in the work of Rudolf Schwarzkogler and Bob Flanagan, or the Pandrogyne project of Genesis and Lady Jaye Breyer P-Orridge; the goal of destroying the ego similarly lies at the heart of certain drug practices embraced by freethinkers such as Terence McKenna.[13]

All this is the intellectual tree in which industrial musicians and audiences over time consistently claim lineage. The genre uses menacing aesthetics to embrace the combative fringes of twentieth-century thought, but it almost always does so out of longing for a certain utopia that can be found only before the beginning and after the end of control.

## 3. Theory and Practice

To gauge how industrial music has historically embodied or deviated from these pan-revolutionary notions, a few concepts are worth articulating at this point. In terms of translating radical twentieth-century ideas into real-world change, an especially useful figure to know about is Guy Debord, who was a postwar artist, vandal, author, and social theorist. Leader of the Parisian group the Situationist International, he studied surrealism and Marxism to arrive at a peculiar set of strategies that went well beyond academic theorizing. Through his book *The Society of the Spectacle* and through the actions of the Situationist International, Debord was crucial in instigating the May 1968 Paris Uprising, which nearly overthrew the French government. Although the Situationists fell short of revolution, the events of 1968 were a testament to the anticontrol power that Debord and his followers had learned to harness; few have come so close to a modern cultural revolt in a stable western nation, especially with an agenda so artistically rooted.

Two of the Situationist International's most important tactics were *dérive* and *détournement*. Dérive is a process of exposing the hidden influences in one's immediate surroundings by instinctually and intuitively responding to a space— a city, a room, a forest, or even a conceptual environment. Simultaneously dominating and surrendering to this "psychogeography," dérive manifests in Europe's squatter culture of the 1970s, and more recently in the "Occupy" movements. The practice is a way to identify and traverse what philosophers Deleuze and Guattari dub "lines of flight"—escape routes. The other important Situationist technique is détournement, which is the act of turning the words, symbols, and actions of authorities back on themselves, recontextualized. As we'll see, this is a primary behavior of industrial music. It also manifests in hip-hop sampling, *Adbusters* style artwork, and the aforementioned cut-up techniques of both Gysin and Burroughs. Because Debord's historical sympathies of anarchism, Marx, and surrealism all align with industrial music's self-declared lineage, and because his practices not only describe certain behaviors of industrial music but are also historically effective as revolutionary tools, dérive and détournement will recur as ideas throughout this book.

Being the very operating system of western culture, the *spectacle* (as Debord calls it) is our collective, mediated perception of the world, filtered through language, economics, government, technology, and religion. These forces shape our identity and predetermine a range of our possible actions. One reason they collectively have this power is that they are so big and so ubiquitous as to seem invisible, like water to a fish; they masquerade as "the way things are." A good word to use here is *hegemony*, which refers to the surrounding social structures held in place by tacit consensus.

Because hegemony's control over people is wrapped up in its silent invisibility, Situationist and industrial logic demands that to free ourselves from unwritten rules, we first have to reveal them—and this is done by breaking those rules, provoking their enforcement, and broadcasting the identity and brutality of their agents to all. Debord's approaches are subtle and irrational in some ways, but they're effective methods in instigating the glitch, the crash that reveals the operating system's presence. As scholar Mark Nunes writes, "error signals a path of escape from the predictable confines of informatic control: an opening."[14] This is part of why a lot of industrial music revels in shocking, transgressive imagery and subject matter: where there is transgression, there is law, and where we reveal law, we reveal external control. In the eyes and ears of many artists, fans, and scholars, one idealized goal of industrial music is to expose tyranny's face and true nature, hoping to render revolt and systemic implosion all but inevitable.

Systems of power adapt, though, even when the people who helm them cannot; it's what Debord calls the recuperation of the spectacle, and it's an ongoing process. An example from within recent music would be the taming of punk rock into new wave and its subsequent repackaging in the 1990s as "alternative." Recuperation is one of a handful of reasons industrial music can sometimes seem less transgressive than it purports to be: it's difficult to remain the front lines of this anti-everything struggle for any period of time. It's certainly the case that once-shocking records like Clock DVA's paranoid "The Connection Machine" and Die Form's kinky "Shaved Girls" carry a little less punch in a world where *The X Files* and online porn are yesterday's news. It also bears acknowledging that the genre's reputation for transgression sometimes outpaces its audiovisual reality, because for many artists and audiences ugliness and noise are more appealing as badass personal identity traits than as musical features.

## 4. What Is This Book?

All this intellectualizing isn't just some after-the-fact, egghead interpretation of the music; as we'll see throughout this book, countless industrial musicians and fans readily plug themselves into these ideas and their literary heritage. Subculture historian V. Vale, who edited 1983's landmark *The Industrial Culture Handbook*, emphasizes that in the days of the genre's formation, "everyone actually read books, and we knew who was hip. Everyone I know was a huge Burroughs fan, and I turned them on to J. G. Ballard. . . . We were into the French theorists."[15] Indeed, Burroughs himself took Cosey Fanny Tutti and Genesis P-Orridge of Throbbing Gristle under his wing, and Al Jourgensen of the band Ministry looked up to Timothy Leary as a personal mentor.❀ The Slovenian band Laibach has collaborated with philosopher Slavoj Žižek, and SPK's Dominic Guerin casually namedrops the likes of Deleuze and Guattari in interviews. Both from within and outside the industrial community, the claims

❀ With the conceptualization in 2003 of the gender-deconstructing Pandrogyne project, Genesis Breyer P-Orridge has been the artist's preferred name, Breyer being the given last name of Jacqueline "Lady Jaye" Breyer P-Orridge, whom Genesis married in 1993. This book uses the previous name Genesis P-Orridge and a corresponding male pronoun when discussing the artists's pre-2003 work.

that this music is knowingly more than mere personal expression and public entertainment are innumerable, earnest, and specific. But in the same way that "Mindphaser" functions as pop, we must not forget industrial music is something that people dance to, make friendships over, and talk about aesthetically—not just politically. For all its anticapitalist positioning, this music is something people buy and sell, and they use it to buy and sell other things, too. Indeed, to what degree can we really suppose that Gary Levermore and Front Line Assembly hoped to dismantle capitalism while worrying about selling enough tickets to pay for a transatlantic flight?

Part of what makes industrial music's story compelling is the tension between all its theoretically rich ideology and the way that people have really engaged with it. This tension is at the heart of debates over what industrial music is and isn't, what it means, who listens to it, and why. There are lots of musical and historical features of industrial music worth discussing—and this book digresses into plenty of them—but a dialectic approach allows us to see how the cracks that spider outward from the collision of theory and practice don't neatly divide makers, fans, and scholars into factions, but instead cut each of us down the middle. It's the reason we can swell with an urgent promise of the pan-revolutionary while simultaneously rocking out to sampled guitars and huge, distorted drums. The idea here is to understand both the finer points of industrial music's most articulate theorizing and also the more personal, anecdotal, and even anthropological side of the music and its communities.

This book is foremost a history of industrial music, which means that there's ample information of the who-did-what-when sort concerning Cabaret Voltaire, Einstürzende Neubauten, Skinny Puppy, Nine Inch Nails, Haujobb, and VNV Nation. There are a lot of songs mentioned in the pages that follow, and so finding a way to listen to them will make the book a more rewarding read. There are plenty of ways to do this online. But a history of industrial music goes beyond playlists; it's also a history of ideas and identity, and so this book looks at the how the music was born, the reasons behind its changes over time, and its past, present, and future effects on the surrounding world.

This history is called *Assimilate* because as we'll see, how industrial music and this surrounding world of hegemonies play off of one another is at once a conflict and a mutual absorption. Throughout the book are musical interpretations that demonstrate the forms of this assimilation. Assimilation also describes the kind of pleasures that the genre's fans experience: self-consciously, the music assimilates listeners and their bodies in a spectacle of control. Just think of the titular commands given in industrial club classics such as Nitzer Ebb's 1987 "Let Your Body Learn," Cyber-Tec Project's 1995 "Let Your Body Die," and Combichrist's 2006 "Get Your Body Beat." At the same time, listeners assimilate the music too: paying attention to the abstract noise of Throbbing Gristle, NON, Brighter Death Now, or Whitehouse can mean trying—even inadvertently—to rein the sound in to some understandable, meaningful form. As with the sadomasochism that industrial music has thematically invoked from its earliest days, there's a lingering question here of who's really in control of whom. It's also worth mentioning that "Assimilate," a 1985 dance track by the Canadian band Skinny Puppy, is one of the most recognizable songs in the genre's history.

To be sure, some artists, topics, labels, regions, and eras receive less attention than others throughout this text. Sometimes this is because other authors have already written incisively and extensively on certain subjects—for example, this book doesn't attempt to compete with Simon Ford's exhaustive account of the band Throbbing Gristle in *Wreckers of Civilisation*; Alexei Monroe's tome on the Slovenian industrial act Laibach, *Interrogation Machine*; or Jennifer Shryane's careful theorizing in *Blixa Bargeld and Einstürzende Neubauten: German Experimental Music*. In other parts of the present book, it's doubtless that the authorial biases of leftism, of having grown up in the United States, and of having come to love industrial music early in the 1990s have indubitably colored perceptions of what's historically important. The scholarly bias of this book also means that there's a fair bit of prehistory in the first few chapters; readers who'd prefer to cut to the chase are welcome to skip ahead to Chapter 4. At any rate, it's hoped that any gaps in history or understanding here will be filled by others in the future.

## 5. The "I-Word"

A critical history of industrial music starts with the problematic question, What is industrial music? Though some purists might think it's ideal to study in isolation only music that is indisputably "industrial"—releases by the label Industrial Records, 1976–1981—the undeniable reality is that there has existed for three decades since then a body of work referred to as industrial music by fans, marketers, and musicians alike. Taken together, this music constellates a reasonably consistent sound palette, a compatible set of visual aesthetics, a commonly understood lyrical code, and the self-declared lineage already discussed.

It's necessary to say all this because with unnerving frequency many canonical "industrial" artists deny having anything to do with industrial music. "I'm so industrial that I'm not industrial," boasts a spoof article in the Sonic Boom e-zine, but the caricature is amazingly accurate.[16] Consider the 1992 press release for Skinny Puppy's *Last Rights*, which claims the record "surpass[es] and redefin[es] what the ignorant still call 'Industrial.'"[17] Or take Bon Harris of Nitzer Ebb, who flatly states, "I never really felt like we fit with the industrial label," despite naming an album *Industrial Complex*.[18] Cabaret Voltaire's Richard Kirk insists that his band doesn't belong alongside Throbbing Gristle and other first-wave "industrial" acts, stating that the term "was a reference to them, not us."[19] With more frustration, one famous interviewee for this book refers to the genre's name as the "I-word," saying, "I don't want to be associated with it. It's like a millstone around my fucking neck."[20] Taking another approach, Paul Lemos of the Long Island–based act Controlled Bleeding dismisses the whole category, saying, "I don't know what 'industrial' means . . . such stereotypical categorizations hurt music of any form."[21] Einstürzende Neubauten percussionist N. U. Unruh similarly declares, "I don't believe in industrial or whatever."[22]

Despite all this, in most accepted narratives acts such as Einstürzende Neubauten and Skinny Puppy are the textbook exemplars of industrial, luminaries of the genre. So what gives? If all these artists aren't industrial, then who is? And if they are all so voluntarily specific in their resistance to being industrial, then what is the opposing cultural force that seeks to include them among all things industrial, and whose side of the story should we listen to?

We can understand this inclusionist cultural force with thoroughness and perhaps a little sympathy if we think about how genre works.

First, one of music's main functions is in affirming or suggesting identity traits (either real or potential) to listeners; the more successfully these traits line up with or steer a listener's sense of who she or he wants to be at that moment, the more likely she or he is to identify with and respond positively to the music. These identity traits—ideas like "cool," "misunderstood," "cultured," "dangerous," "British," "sexy," or "mourning"—are socially constructed; they have to do with how people see themselves and one another. When people agree on a repertory or a set of musical ideas as offering a reliably predictable array of identity traits that they can consistently tap into, then they have at once isolated a genre and its genre community. Thus when *The Wire* editor Chris Bohn says industrial "can only ever be a broad umbrella term which lost its credentials once it included the likes of Nine Inch Nails and Skinny Puppy," he is distancing himself not merely from certain bands but from the people who listen to them and call them industrial.[23] This attitude declares, "I would rather cast off the remainder of the genre's output than try to account for any connection between me and *those people*."

Regardless of how any one person uses a piece of music—even if it's the composer—genres are socially constructed, just like personal identity. *No one person or entity gets to categorize a musical performance, recording, gesture, or idea unilaterally into a genre*; instead, as scholars Jennifer Lena and Richard

Peterson argue, genres are "systems of orientations, expectations, and conventions that bind together an industry, performers, critics, and fans in making what they identify as a distinctive sort of music."[24] These orientations, expectations, and conventions are part of what musicologist Jeffrey Kallberg calls the "generic contract," and they could take the form of a repeated quarter-note kick at 140 bpm in trance techno, or the assumption that rap artists write their own lyrics, or that a band called Cannibal Corpse is not a barbershop quartet.[25]

The boundaries of a genre tend to be both hazy and changing over time. Genre in any medium is neither a prescriptive set of features nor is it a circularly defined body of works, canonized and fixed; instead, it's perpetually negotiated by artists, by fans and commentators, by marketers and media, and by archivists and academics.✿ Roughly analogous to these four voices in a genre's development are (according to Lena and Peterson) the four stages that genres tend to pass through over time: from avant-garde to scene-based to industry-based to traditionalist.[26]✿✿ These stages have to do with how music is used—aesthetic experimentation versus social engagement versus corporate economy versus cultural preservation—and by whom.

In the case of industrial music, it certainly began at what Lena and Peterson call the avant-garde stage: "quite small, having no more than a dozen participants. . . . Members play together informally in an effort to create a genre ideal for the group."[27] This was true with the first generation of English industrial musicians. Beyond that, it certainly spawned scenes, and as this book goes on to assert, with this expansion came a shift in the matter of who determined what is and isn't industrial—itself an important social process among fans and journalists, as it grants subcultural power and defines aesthetic preferences. Whether industrial music ever fully became an industry-based genre is perhaps debatable, but the music and its communities have at least flirted with—some would say hopped into bed with—both the corporate and the curatorial traditionalists. To see this, one need only look respectively to the boom of American pseudo-industrial rock in the mid and late 1990s (like Stabbing Westward and Linkin Park) and to the emergence of "classic" style Electronic Body Music (EBM) in recent years (like the band Autodafeh, or the 2011 workshop given by Front 242's Patrick Codenys, "How to Build an EBM Track"[28]).

---

✿ See the writing of film theorist Rick Altman.

✿✿ Lena and Peterson grant that other paths are possible. It's noteworthy that every genre they study at some point passes through a "scene-based" iteration; this absolutely supports the notion of genre as an organic social construction. As an aside, the use of "avant-garde" here is idiosyncratic to them; an important footnote in Chapter 3 of this book will address the general term in greater depth.

Importantly for the future, the people who negotiate the generic contract also have the power to kick-start a genre back into a "previous" stage, though from the outside this usually looks like a music's death and rebirth. So given industrial music's strongly anticorporate agenda, and given that across the stages of genre trajectory musicians progressively cede control over their work's uses—from private, to public, to corporate, finally landing in the embalmer's hands at the traditionalist stage—can it really be a surprise that some musicians feel as though the "industrial" tag has been co-opted, even irreversibly poisoned?

Genres also serve the practical function of introducing subcultural artists and communities to one another. For example, the band PTI tells of handing out their 2003 demo CD on a city street to enthusiastic strangers simply by saying "Chicago Industrial," instantly aligning themselves with a specific genre. But even if genre labeling can build an audience for upstarts like PTI, it can become an economic constraint to acts whose audience potentially extends beyond that genre's community; hence the journalistic eyeroller that a band "transcends the genre."

Industrial fanzine *Tanz Der Rosen* asserted in 1996 that "even a 3 year old is mature enough to understand the simple chaotic gap between industrial, its later subcultures and noise music,"[29] and indeed it's important to differentiate among these manifestations and to recognize the difference between, say, SPK circa 1982 and Rotersand circa 2009. This book certainly grants that there are real differences in the artistic intent, musical features, and public use of the music discussed in pages to come; nevertheless the broad label of "industrial" has served to group this cultural repertoire over time, and it's a more honest history to admit and study this phenomenon than to dismiss entire musical practices that are obviously meaningful to people all over the world, even if the generic contract of later industrial dance music might be differently codified from that of the genre's pioneering moments.

In the case of industrial music specifically, the divide between the rigidly exclusive view of the music and the more inclusive one carries with it some important conceptual baggage directly related to the earlier question of industrial music's political agenda. Essentially, what's at stake is whether industrial music was a single event in history or an ongoing cultural project. This idea will get a deeper treatment later, but for the time being, let's explore—rather than constrain—what has been called industrial music.

Looking at the genre's wider chronology like this allows us to see some interesting realities. For example, the incestuous nature of industrial musicians' social communities has oftentimes led to artists who emerged in the music's early days, such as Adi Newton (of Clock DVA), Richard Kirk (of Cabaret Voltaire), and Tom Ellard (of Severed Heads), appearing much later on albums with younger, poppier acts such as Haujobb, Acid Horse, and Seabound, respectively. And for that matter, the last years of the 2000s saw a revival of interest in industrial music's experimental early days with rereleases on Frank Maier's Vinyl on Demand label, a boom of new music in the so-called minimal wave scene, and a growing notion that the blogosphere had begun to recapitulate (without nostalgia) the practices of industrial music's nearly forgotten tape trading communities of the early 1980s.

In its propensity to cut up culture and make meaning anew, industrial music is best understood in relation to people, politics, technology, and other music. As such, we'll be listening for the echoes that reverberate between industrial music and totalitarianism, war, punk rock, performance art, techno, and technology.

Keep your ears open—it's about to get noisy.

# Part I

# TECHNOLOGY AND THE PRECONDITIONS OF INDUSTRIAL MUSIC

EARLY IN THE TWENTIETH CENTURY, "INDUSTRIAL MUSIC" MEANT THE MUSIC played for or performed by workers to facilitate their labor.[1] In its broadest definitions, industrial music could refer to dustbowl field songs and maritime shanties, but by the mid-1930s it especially denoted recorded music, piped through loudspeakers by such corporations as Muzak, RCA, and General Electric, into already noisy factories.[2] At the height of World War II, *The Musical Quarterly* boasted, "In facilitating the all-out war production effort, music has been found a valued ally, judging by the phenomenal increase of plants, arsenals, and shipyards using it. . . . On the assembly line, music is applied to such prosaic objectives as speeding output, relieving fatigue, reducing accidents and absenteeism, bolstering morale."[3] In the same article, workers noted, "if you are on a bad job, the music most certainly helps you to forget it and stops you from grumbling."[4] It was so effective that industrial music was in fact declared by the English government as mandatory fare in military factories, and so the BBC themselves pumped out the tunes, ranging from foxtrots to Viennese waltzes to Brahms.

This was a functional music, not consumed as art but disseminated to streamline workers' efficiency, decrease their emotion, increase reliability, and promote unity among them. In short, it was played to make humans as machinelike as possible: no mistakes, no dissent, no slowing down. Any irony that modern "industrial music" casts on this original "industrial music" is intentional. In seeking to reveal the coglike role that people play in a larger system of control, the likes of Throbbing Gristle and Cabaret Voltaire saw technology as both a component of hegemony and an easy metaphor for it.

The next few chapters demonstrate how and why this came to be. Specifically, industrial music's perspective on humankind's relationship to technology has historical roots that reach back over three centuries, but whose most relevant articulations arrived with the revolutionary technophilia of Italian Futurism and the antiauthoritarian techno-paranoia of American author William S. Burroughs. The understanding of technology, art, and power that Futurism and Burroughs together convey are two sides of the same coin, comprising an intellectual *precondition* for industrial music's belief systems. As we'll see, the literary and philosophical ideas behind industrial music often matter to musicians and fans of the genre at least as much as any sonic forebear; this is evident in that the variety of sounds encompassed by this thing called industrial music is far more wide-ranging than its attitudes. Finally, concluding this conceptual prehistory are a few pages devoted to the important question of just what—if anything—industrial and "classical" art music have to do with one another.

# Italian Futurism

## 1. The Aesthetics of the Machine

The first organized movement dedicated to the technologization of art and humanity was called Futurism, and it was articulated in a 1909 manifesto by Filippo Tommaso Marinetti.✿ The Futurists were a group mostly of Italian artists who were disgusted with representational art's limits and its clichés—right angles, landscapes, the nude. Marinetti and the Futurists were determined to "destroy the cult of the past, the obsession with the ancients, pedantry and academic formalism. Totally invalidate all kinds of imitation. Elevate all attempts at originality, however daring, however violent."[1] Beyond severing all ties with the morality and forms of the past, Futurism's determination to explore the new was intolerant even of the present (hence the movement's name). Instead, it focused on the impact of the present against the future: the eternal, instantaneous cutting edge. Futurists were artistically obsessed with swift, explosive action as an aesthetic: sounds, images, and forms that perpetually propelled into newness. Struggle and penetration were central themes in Futurist art, which sometimes took on a violent guise; the movement's admiration of war and brutality, tied in with its peculiar Italian nationalism, led many of its adherents ultimately to Fascism. Futurists even reveled in the antagonism between themselves and their audiences: "We will . . . bear bravely and proudly the smear of 'madness' with which they try to gag all innovators."[2]

This longing for confrontation, novelty, and speed found a potent metaphor in technology. Marinetti called Futurism "the aesthetics of the machine," and indeed, the signification of the machine as an idea resonated with Futurist thinking on at least two important levels. First, machines were themselves capable, in theory anyway, of the ceaseless motion that so fascinated Marinetti and his followers—the "eternal, omnipresent speed."[3] Machines could unsentimentally enact a combustion that bespoke vitality itself. Second, in the early

---

✿ Writings of Marinetti's that may be considered Futurist in nature date back at least to 1905, and the Futurists themselves partially stemmed from the Florentine Movement, which dates back at least to 1896.

twentieth century, the machine was an ever-evolving, ever-improving symbol of modernity. Progress—without regard to Old World aesthetics or morality—drove mankind's development of the machine, and as workers organized into systematic assembly lines to weld metal on metal, they mimicked the very technology they built. And so it was that mechanization was central to Futurism. By embracing the art made possible by machines, these brash Italian artists were themselves at the vanguard of new human sensory experience.

Perhaps the most famous document of twentieth-century technophilia is Luigi Russolo's 1913 Futurist manifesto *The Art of Noises*. Enamored with the musical possibilities inherent in recorded sound, Russolo envisions a symphony of clanging metal, creaking wood, scraped dishes, howling animals, and running water. He bellows that

> by selecting, coordinating and dominating all noises we will enrich men with a new and unexpected sensual pleasure. Although it is characteristic of noise to recall us brutally to real life, the art of noise must not limit itself to imitative reproduction. It will achieve its most emotive power in the acoustic enjoyment, in its own right, that the artist's inspiration will extract from combined noises.[4]

Russolo's conceptual attempt to separate pure sounds from the connotations of their sources was what differentiated his "Futurist orchestra" from earlier incorporations of noise into music, which had been mere novel amusements.

Russolo not only laid the theoretical foundation for sampling as both an associative practice and a purely sonic listening experience—what the French pioneer of *musique concrète* Pierre Schaeffer called "reduced hearing"—but he enacted it too. For the year or two that followed "The Art of Noises," Russolo and fellow Futurist Ugo Piatti constructed hand-cranked musical instruments called *Intonarumori*, building up a large ensemble with which they hissed, cracked, and clattered for dubiously receptive audiences. In the grand tradition of Igor Stravinsky's brutal *The Rite of Spring*, Russolo and Marinetti incited a riot at their debut performance in Rome, April 1914. Crowds in London begged the musicians to stop playing, leading Marinetti, ever confrontational and sensationalistic, to consider the exhibitions a tremendous success.[5]

The image of high-concept artists terrorizing British audiences with noise music is eerily prescient of the legendary early performances of Throbbing Gristle, who in the mid-1970s took the same scandalous glee in confounding popular aesthetics and morality. This contrarian streak isn't merely incidental in Futurism and industrial music alike. Just as Marinetti asserts, "Except in struggle, there is no more beauty. No work without an aggressive character can be a masterpiece. Poetry must be conceived as a violent attack,"[6] industrial music too has inherent themes of physical exertion, struggle, and war.

The connection across sixty-five years of artistic movements from Futurism to the dawn of industrial music is far from academic speculation; Futurism is explicitly cited in the music of bands like Spahn Ranch, Nurse With Wound, and Pornotanz, among others. First-wave industrialist Monte Cazazza took part in a 1975 performance in San Francisco, *A Futurist Sintesi*, that attempted to revive the movement's spirit, and German industrial legends Einstürzende Neubauten not only pay lyrical tribute to Marinetti in their 2007 song "Let's Do It Dada," but their 1993 video for "Blume" uses a physical replica of Russolo's *Intonarumori* as both set and props. Brian Williams, the man behind ambient industrial act Lustmord and a musician with collaborations in the scene ranging from SPK to Chris & Cosey to Clock DVA to Monte Cazazza, wrote in 1996, "Over the last two decades terms such as 'industrial' . . . have been applied to an ever increasing and ever more bewildering array of musicians. . . . It is appropriate to attribute the actual origin of modern sonic experimentation to the writing of the Futurist manifesto 'The Art of Noises' by Luigi Russolo."[7]

## 2. Crash

More than just a point of explicit reference, Futurism pervades industrial music symbolically. Consider the music video for Revolting Cocks' 1988 "Stainless Steel Providers." The clip begins with a montage of industrial tools machining parts for a motorcycle, and then a leather-clad young woman drives the motorcycle in dizzyingly sped up motion through night traffic. The band members then douse the motorcycle in gasoline, set it ablaze with a blowtorch, and throw it off a building.

Marinetti begins his original manifesto with a rhapsodic worship of "the famished roar of automobiles": "And on we raced, hurling watchdogs against doorsteps, curling them under our burning tires like collars under a flatiron. Death, domesticated, met me at every turn, gracefully holding out a paw, or once in a while hunkering down, making velvety caressing eyes at me from every puddle."[8] Shortly after in his narrative, Marinetti crashes his car while swerving to avoid two bicyclists—symbols of outdated ignorance. We might read this as an illustration that sympathy for the outmoded destroys progress, but Marinetti, in crashing, also experiences a new Futurist joy: the revelation of the collision, the violent thrill that comes when speed, technology, and motion outgrow the surrounding world. Thus the high-velocity crash—the explosion— is a means of expanding the constraints against which art, in the eyes of the

Futurists, must struggle, regardless of how self-destructive its effects. This was a powerful idea that resurfaced in the work of the Vienna Aktionists in the 1960s and most famously in J. G. Ballard's 1973 novel *Crash*, where car wrecks literally become the subject of sexual fetish.

This helps us better understand the progress throughout the "Stainless Steel Providers" video, where Futurism's tropes are presented in progressively radical forms: the band builds the technology, tests and enjoys its speed, and then destroys it redundantly, with the gasoline dousing shot repeated, suggesting a perpetual violence through fire and its crash off the rooftop. All of this is set to the backdrop of singer Chris Connelly's feverish chanting:

> It bleeds efficiency
> The way I feel on stainless steel,
> And all it does to me
> Stainless steel providers
>
> Another tire
> Let it catch on fire
> A metal motor mantra
> Makes you waste the time of day
> You'll sit on a timebomb, forever and ever

The Futurist compatibilities of the song become more striking when we see the reappearance of the fishnet-clad woman and her motorcycle a year and a half

*Figure 1.1: A video still from "Stainless Steel Providers" by Revolting Cocks and the album cover of* Chicks & Speed: Futurism *by Lead Into Gold starkly echo Futurist themes. Video directed by Eric Zimmerman and photographed by Eric S. Koziol; album cover photograph by Brian Shanley; model/driver: Judy Pokonosky.*

ASSIMILATE

later, emblazoning the cover of an EP by Lead Into Gold, a band whose every last member (Al Jourgensen, Paul Barker, and William Rieflin) also played in Revolting Cocks. The name of this EP is *Chicks & Speed: Futurism*, and its lead single was called "Faster Than Light."

Drawing so many explicit connections between industrial music and Futurism may belabor the point of their connectedness, but it serves another significant purpose: it demonstrates that the individuals making this music were not merely tapping into a mind-set that was incidentally similar to an important artistic movement in the past, but were themselves literarily aware of Futurism, of artistic philosophy, of critical theory. One reason, then, why it's important to consider industrial music so high-mindedly is that the genre itself is at least on occasion consciously engaged in literary discourse. This can happen even at its trashiest moments, of which more than a few belong to Revolting Cocks.

# 2.
# William S. Burroughs

## 1. Junkie

If industrial music is one part optimistic techno-fetishism, its other indubitable twentieth-century precondition is every bit as literary as Futurism, if more cynical.

William S. Burroughs, a techno-paranoid American author often grouped with the beat movement, contributed two ideas to industrial music specifically. First was the alignment of authority figures and controlling agencies into one metaphorical identity of the machine, and second was an artistic means of exposing, questioning, and subverting humankind's mechanized enslavement to this machine.

Burroughs's fiction is generally interpreted less as storytelling than as sociology, tactics, and philosophy. Burroughs's outspoken distrust of tradition, authority, and order has roots and manifestations in his life prior to and beyond his writing, and indeed much of his oeuvre is essentially autobiographical. For these reasons, we'll want to cover some facts about him before discussing his writing.

Born in St. Louis in 1914, less than a year after Russolo published "The Art of Noises," Burroughs attended the Los Alamos Ranch School in New Mexico, later annexed by the U.S. government for the purpose of developing the atomic bomb. Early in life, he was surrounded by technology and privilege—his grandfather patented an adding machine and brought the family significant wealth.

A Harvard dropout, Burroughs was a social misfit, both effeminate and violent. His evasion of military service during World War II, his homosexuality, his drug-addiction in the 1940s and 1950s, and his expatriation to Mexico all bespoke a seedy unfitness to dwell in the day's whitewashed America. His most unsavory moment came in 1951, when he killed his common-law wife, Joan Vollmer, in what was allegedly a bizarre accident. Vollmer, a unique exception to his sexual preference, was playing "William Tell" with Burroughs at a party in Mexico City; firing his gun while drunk, Burroughs missed the water glass she'd balanced atop her head, and shot her in the skull. As he was awaiting trial, his brother bailed him out and he left the country. He was found guilty *in ab-*

*sentia* but never served time. (For what very little it's worth now, Burroughs would express constant repentance and sadness over the incident for the rest of his life.)

All this happened before Burroughs wrote his first novel, the 1953 autobiographical *Junkie*. The ideas that he articulates in the book and especially in its dizzyingly schizophrenic successors make the most sense when we understand them as reflections of the particular political moment that framed the sordidness of his early life. Once we understand that the inherited worldview of industrial music has its origins in the actual historical world whose norms of acceptability and taste Burroughs found himself so grossly violating, then not only do we see his writings as preconditional but we can better understand industrial music as part of a meaningful response to real events and attitudes.

As an illustration of the world in which—and against which—Burroughs lived, consider the American panic in the early and mid-1950s over brainwashing, a process by which it was widely thought that decent citizens could be subconsciously conditioned to carry out acts of war, espionage, and treason. Within the day's popular understanding, these secret soldiers wouldn't even need to know of their own hidden allegiance but might instead be sleeper agents, trained to activate when a signal was given.

Edward Hunter, the American agent and journalist who coined the term, described brainwashing as "a planned confusion of the mind where shadow takes form and form becomes shadow."[1] Note in this description how the line between shadow and form erodes, and thus the host and parasite entwine in one another until they're indistinguishable. Whether penetrative brainwashing really occurred during Joseph McCarthy's Red Scare or not, it framed the traditional means and ends of conflict—diplomacy and resources, for example—as merely metaphors or tokens, and instead it acknowledged humans themselves as the targets, weapons, and prizes in any real bid for domination. Individual citizens were incited to doubt their very identities in the face of monolithic authority.

To politically critical westerners, the individual powerlessness insinuated by the threat of communist brainwashing was only half of the equation: the so-called free countries that warned of reprogramming's unprovable dangers were similarly conditioning their own citizens into fearful obedience. The anticommunist witch hunt spearheaded by McCarthy in the name of freedom had the effect of branding any nonconformity as anti-American, and so it's not merely in the pages of *Junkie* that one saw a "tie-up between narcotics and Communism"; indeed, all of decent western culture cast suspicion on "other"-ness of any sort as evidence of moral, economic, governmental, industrial, and military infiltration.[2]

This left Burroughs and any other leftist, gay, drug-using, art-creating, non-white, or otherwise "undesirable" citizen trapped in a matrix that reinforced a distrust of authority both at home and abroad. In England, among the most tragic cases to reify the metaphors of the machine, government, and sexuality was the apparent suicide in 1954 of Alan Turing, pioneer of computing and artificial intelligence, who was accused of homosexuality—a charge that brought with it the implicit suspicion of embodying "the myth of the homosexual traitor," as his biographer David Leavitt explains.[3]

## 2. The Control Machines

Seemingly beleaguered for his every move (rightly or not), Burroughs fostered a paranoia toward authority in all its guises, and he began assembling an idiosyncratic theory of control. In his post-*Junkie* work, he uses the term *control machines* to refer to technology, religion, government, and language. The control machine as an idea can be seen as a peculiar version of Debord's spectacle, or of what Marx calls "the whole superstructure," or of philosopher Theodor Adorno's notion of "the culture industry." These models all vary in their specifics, but they identify an overarching set of invisible connections between hegemonically ubiquitous cultural entities.✽

To Burroughs, control machines occupy conceptual spaces, defining and overtaking them, ultimately supplanting whatever neutrality they might once have had. For example, he believed that language and technology had come to occupy a broadly human space and that their subsequent stranglehold over modern life was no less insidious and enslaving than the heroin addiction with which he personally struggled; it's what he calls "the algebra of need."

These metaphors may seem a little mixed up—with rapidity, Burroughs invokes the ideas of language as a virus, control images, and cultural imperialism—but such haphazard depictions effectively reveal a sinister interchangeability among control machines: they were all out to get him, whoever *they* were. Thus, in his post-*Junkie* output, gods, beasts, corporations, nations, chemicals, and radio waves literally morph into one another throughout scatologically over-ripe, nonlinear orgies of space aliens, third-world prostitution, cowboy mythol-

---

✽ Both industrial musicians and those who write about industrial music variously use a range of critical approaches to talk about more or less the same thing; each of these ideas is a distinct and detailed theoretical model, but they nonetheless graft onto each other with enough basic commonality to accommodate industrial music's hazy worldview, expressed as much in the form of a gut feeling as a clear rubric.

ogies, and mind-scrambling drugs. In the 1991 film adaptation of his 1959 book *The Naked Lunch*, typewriters are sexual appendages, giant sentient bugs, and undercover federal agents all at once.

Importantly, this fluidity doesn't just serve to conflate control machines; it also combats them. In order to hold dominion, a control machine needs to inhabit a stable domain, and so the gross nonsense of Burroughs's writing denies the control machine any kind of stable space. Just as the addict needs the drug, the drug is useless without the addict, or as literary theorist David Seed puts it, the machine "cannot be imagined in separation from the agencies that exercise it."[4] Burroughs's claim that the pages of *The Naked Lunch* could be read in any order wasn't just a gimmick, then, but a move to tear down the structure that houses the machine—the organism and ego to which is it parasitic. He attempts to bypass the authorities of language and thought to which prose and readers alike are hosts, unbeknownst and addicted.

This particular conception of power and its conflation is exceedingly important to the industrial mind-set. Let's get back to the music now to see how Burroughs's ideas play out.

## 3. Mediatic Verses

The band KMFDM, whose name is an acronym for Kein Mehrheit Für Die Mitleid—an intentionally confusing rearrangement of "Kein Mitleid Für Die Mehrheit" ("no sympathy for the majority")—places itself by virtue of the name outside of the aforementioned majority and is thus "othered." In "A Drug Against War," the opening song from 1993's *Angst*, the band's lead singer Sascha Konietzko shouts in a one-note melody a litany of what Burroughs would call "control machines," his message to a presumably adolescent audience hitting closer to home with each line: "Television, religion, social destruction. Sex and drugs . . . Parental advice leads to mental erosion."

This all happens over a 322 bpm heavy metal-influenced backing track that commences with a sample of what one presumes is a military man, ordering, "Bomb the livin' bejeebers out of those forces." Not only do the sample and the repeated lyrical references to war and "empty shells fall[ing] to the ground" imbue the song with clear martial signification, but the music itself encodes this too. In the introduction and the chorus, Doppler effect sounds of falling bombs gently glide over the racket; the piercingly unrealistic drum machine snare straddles a convenient resemblance between a marching band and a machine gun. At 322 bpm, the eighth-note snare fills at the end of verses fire at about eleven rounds every second—the same rate as an AK-47. Once this is juxtaposed in proximity with what appears to be an actual sample of gunfire just over a minute into the track, the connection is clear. On one level then, media, religion, sex, drugs, and parents are invoked, all literally on the same note, and thereby flattened into a monolithic unit of authority. But beyond that, the military—and by extension the government (note the sample at 1:09, "what you're advocating is a bigger war," employing the rhetoric of politics)—are similarly faces of the very same agents of "mental erosion."

Just as KMFDM's name bizarrely swaps acronymic word placement, the band inverts the Nixon-Reagan language of the War on Drugs to serve their purposes as a self-declared Drug Against War. In doing so, they upend the violent signification of their music, for despite the panicked sample at the song's end, insisting that we "kill everything," the same authority figure whose commands to bomb began the track replies calmly "That's not enough," taking what may have been plausibly readable as the band's reveling in militarism to a level of droll absurdity. Indeed, KMFDM's incessant name checking, ironic use of gospel backup singers, and comic book style cover art by illustrator Aidan "Brute!" Hughes all wink knowingly to fans. This rejection of genuine military ideology relegates martial authority to the ranks of the lyrics' aforementioned television and religion, and Konietzko makes that clear when he sneers about "cremation of senses in a friendly fire," stepping out of the war that he otherwise might be accused of egging on. While the sound effects pervading the recording literally resemble the sounds of war, Konietzko tells us in the second verse that he brings "sonic bombardment," effectively defanging any connection of these recorded bombs to real ones: they remain sounds. KMFDM's music refuses to take part in supporting the power structures whose interchangeability it reveals.

The Burroughsian practice of equating power structures and authorities until they're all gears of the same machine appears again and again in industrial music. In 1989, the Belgian duo à;GRUMH…, who were early players in the dance-oriented subgenre called Electronic Body Music (or more commonly, EBM), released the A-side "Ayatollah Jackson." Like KMFDM, à;GRUMH… conflates military force, religion, and government as they chant, "The sacred book on Sunday, the machine gun every day . . . Oran para la dictadura, el processo de la democracia [Pray to the dictatorship, the process of democracy]." The song's lyrics alternate from verse to verse between French, English, and Spanish, offering up manifestolike tirades in each, and in the process squashing even different languages into one communicative mechanism where any tongue is interchangeable with another. There's even a little nod of self-awareness of this in a lyrical phrase near the song's end, "Mediatic verses," which acknowledges that this linguistic switching is itself as much a part of the song as the words

| Duration (measures) | Section | Language | Musical Events | Pitch |
|---|---|---|---|---|
| 3 | Intro | | Drums enter | |
| 6 | | | Bass enters | B♭ |
| 6 | Verse 1: "Les fous de Dieu..." | French | | |
| 4 | Postverse 1: "The sacred book on Sunday..." | English | | |
| 12 | Break | | Backbeat enters | |
| 12 | Verse 2: "Los mercenarios de Dios..." | Spanish | | |
| 8 | Verse 3: "La pyramide humaine..." | French | | |
| 3 | Postverse 2: "Agobiar el cuerpo..." | Spanish | | E♭ |
| 4 | Break | | | B♭ |
| 6 | Verse 1 repeat | French | Lead synth enters | |
| 13 | Break | | | |
| 3 | Postverse 1 repeat | English | | |
| 8 | Chorus: "The fools of God..." | | | E♭ |
| 3 | Break | | | B♭ |
| 8 | Verse 3 repeat | French | | |
| 7 | Postverse 3: "Fánatic excess..." | English | | |
| 4 | Chorus repeat | | | E♭ |
| 4 | | | | B♭ |
| 4 | Chorus repeat | | | E♭ |
| 4 | | | | B♭ |
| 2 | Break | | | |
| 4 | Chorus repeat (incomplete, with lyric change) | | | E♭ |
| 4 | | | | F |
| 1 | Cadence | | Lead synth out | B♭ |

Figure 2.1: Song structure of "Ayatollah Jackson" by à;GRUMH...

sung in each language—a tidy encapsulation of the theorist Marshall McLuhan's famous assertion that "the medium is the message."[5] And of course, the song title's juxtaposition of a religious authority's name alongside a pop idol's again brings television and the mechanisms of celebrity into a conceptual tangle that now includes warfare, religion, totalitarianism, democracy, and language itself.

The harmonies of "Ayatollah Jackson" also support the free interplay of these signs. At the song's heart is a one-measure-long synthesizer bassline whose rhythm is unchanging atop a steady 128 bpm dance beat. The bass pattern is played chiefly in B-flat minor but shifts up to E-flat minor a handful of times as the song continues, and although this is a common move in pop harmony, its occurrence is peculiarly timed against the lyrics. To understand this better, take a look at the structure of the song (Figure 2.1).

Although we can easily connect E-flat as a bass pitch with the song's chorus, instead of differentiating the lyrical content of the song, this move highlights the interchangeability both of language and of power structures invoked lyrically.

Here's how: in the opening verse of "Ayatollah Jackson," à;GRUMH... sings of "Les fous de Dieu [The fools of God]." Then, when the song hits what is nominally the chorus (as indicated by its repetition and chord change), its subject is also (this time in English) "The fools of God." If the song's harmonic motion to the chorus is to mean anything at all, then why would it underlie a simple lyrical restatement—the only one in the song? The answer to this question is not to be found in the interplay of the languages sung; English is used plenty over a B-flat bass in addition to the chorus E-flat, and E-flat is neither exclusive to the chorus nor to English, since it's the chord over which the line "Agobiar el cuerpo es un mensaje de amor [the oppression of the body is a message of love]" is previously sung.

This may all seem a bit dizzying, but in short, the sameness of lyrical meaning in both verse and chorus, with B-flat and E-flat centers alike, tends to collapse any difference we might derive from the song's internal parts.[6] This is why listening to the song feels like a plateau with no peak; it resists traditional differentiations of structure.

Adding to the confusion still are the perplexing durations of the track's internal sections. Across western pop genres, the overwhelming tendency is for the lengths of musical phrases and indeed whole verses and choruses to be four, eight, or sixteen measures long; our ears and our bodies are attracted to rhythmic powers of two. The leftmost column of the chart above not only reveals a tendency toward awkward sectional lengths, especially in the first half of the song, but also shows that corresponding sections—the three verses, their post-verses, and the several breaks—lack consistency even unto themselves. Verse lengths are six, twelve, and eight measures, while postverse lengths are three, four, and seven measures. The patterns one expects to find in the relationships between lyrics and music in a song are clouded here by a nearly arbitrary set of internal dimensions. Differentiated, discrete spaces in a piece of music help us make sense of the whole, but when the sung subverts the structural hallmarks that musically and linguistically govern how, for example, dictatorship, democracy, God, the body, and Michael Jackson all differ from one another, then the music aligns these subjects into an amorphous mixture of power entities: the machine is de-institutionalized.✿

Neither a metaphorical trick nor arbitrary, these metamorphoses are in fact the goals in Burroughs's algebra of need. He writes, "The ultimate purpose of cancer and all virus is to replace the host," and so, for example, in *The Naked Lunch*, when a man is through experimentation somehow "de-anxietized," Burroughs reveals that the paranoia lifted from him was in fact the virus on which

---

✿ One important contributor to the strange scaffolding of a song like "Ayatollah Jackson" is the technology with which it was created. As will be discussed in Chapter 8, the ease with which a pattern could loop resulted in phrase and sectional durations that had more to do with the musicians' improvisatory and performative whim than with a careful pre-compositional plan. Similarly, transposing a synthesizer line was very easy with a sequencer, and so industrial music often features direct transposition of keyboard parts (sometimes by strange intervals) instead of harmonic changes with more traditional voice leading. A good example of this is Throbbing Gristle's 1979 "Hot on the Heels of Love."

ASSIMILATE

his humanity relied; it had invisibly replaced its host.[7] Now free of it, the character "turns to viscid, transparent jelly that drifts away in green mist, unveiling a monster black centipede."[8]

More famous and perhaps most significant in Burroughs's writing is the literal equation of language with disease, mentioned earlier: "the written word was literally a virus that made the spoken word possible. The word has not been recognized as a virus because it has achieved a state of stable symbiosis with the host."[9] Thought without words is nearly impossible; humans and language are defined in relation to one another. Concerned in his boundless paranoia that language itself is an agent of enemy control, Burroughs sought to liberate humanity and literature from the assumptions and constraints that language imposes, and in doing so he laid the second of his two principal foundations for industrial music.

## 5. The Cut-Up

Film scholar Anne Friedberg exposes in the writings of Burroughs the response to the word-as-virus situation. Quoting his book *The Ticket That Exploded*, Friedberg explains, "Within the viral metaphor, 'inoculation can only be effected through exposure.' Words and images must be used, but only in recombinative patterns."[10]

Burroughs achieved this inoculation through what he and co-author Brion Gysin called the "cut-up" method of recontextualizing and remixing signs. The story goes that Gysin, a writer, painter, and friend of Burroughs, began experimenting in the summer of 1959 with cutting pages of text into vertical columns, and then rearranging these long strips of paper in random order. The effect, as they discovered, was that the essential linguistic character of the original text in many cases remained, but the strange phrases and fragments that resulted from reading what was no longer a linear text offered entirely new images and meanings. Burroughs recommends mixing texts and repeating the process—"As many Shakespeare Rimbaud poems as you like"—in order to "produce the accident of spontaneity."[11] Mechanization becomes the text's author. It samples and digitizes raw artifacts from the surrounding world and from the machinist's mind.

Gysin and Burroughs acknowledged that Dadaist Tristan Tzara may have been the first to experiment with this idea, when, onstage in 1916, he caused a ruckus by reading random words drawn from a hat, declaring that he was thereby creating a new poem on the spot. However, the key innovation this time around lay in Gysin and Burroughs's belief that the cut-up possessed real power to disrupt the textual worlds from which it derived. Having quickly applied the method to tape recording and photography, Burroughs wrote, "I have frequently observed that this simple operation—make recordings and take pictures of some location you wish to discommode or destroy, now play recordings back and take more pictures—, will result in accidents, fires, removals."[12] If this viral inoculation could work to shut down a business or cause a traffic jam, then by cutting up and reordering the sounds of industry, authority, religion, commerce, and war, those held under their sway might be deprogrammed as the control machines sputter and reveal their own evil; this is the glitch described in this book's introduction. Burroughs and Gysin called the new meanings and effects that result from the juxtaposition of texts (or the collaboration of individuals) the *third mind*—a powerful narrative voice whose own forceful will does not come from a single text or author, nor even their sum, but is discursive, autonomous, even sentient.✿

Although collage has been a technique in pop music production since the mid-1950s (first used in Buchanan and Goodman's 1956 hit "The Flying Saucer"), the cut-up as a means of producing seemingly random internal juxtapositions from within a starting text shares a particular and deep kinship with industrial music. Unlike collage, the cut-up is specifically imbued with an agenda: it is a method of détournement that, in the words of Guy Debord, asserts "indifference toward a meaningless and forgotten original"—indifference that is especially pronounced and political when the original demands allegiance.[13]

It's not just this anti-author(ity) sentiment and power that attracts industrial music to the cut-up; in fact there have been specific historical connections that both instructed and reinforced the genre's use of the technique. Demonstrating and contributing to the cut-up's industrial kinship is the personal and creative relationship between Burroughs and Genesis P-Orridge, founder of Throbbing Gristle and of Industrial Records, the label from which the entire genre takes its name. P-Orridge writes of meeting Burroughs for the first time in 1971:

> He took the remote and started to flip through the channels, cutting up programmed TV. I realized he was teaching me. At the same time he began to hit stop and start on his Sony TC cassette recorder, mixing in "random" cut-ups of prior recordings. These were overlaid with our conversation, none acknowledging the other, an instant holography of information and environment. I was already being taught. What Bill explained to me then was pivotal to the unfolding of my life and art:

---

✿ *The Third Mind* is the title of Burroughs and Gysin's collaborative cut-up manual. It is also from this notion that the aforementioned Third Mind Records takes its name.

Everything is recorded.✿ If it is recorded, then it can be edited. If it can be edited then the order, sense, meaning and direction are as arbitrary and personal as the agenda and/or person editing.[14]✿✿

P-Orridge goes on: "If reality consists of a series of parallel recordings that usually go unchallenged, then reality only remains stable and predictable until it is challenged and/or the recordings are altered, or their order changed."[15] This outlook is compatible not only with P-Orridge's somewhat idiosyncratic magical perspective but also with the cyberpunk and hacker-oriented ideas and imagery that would saturate and characterize industrial music later in the 1980s and 1990s.

P-Orridge's tutelage under and championing of Burroughs and Gysin led to the release of a collection of Burroughs's 1959–1978 cut-up archives through Industrial Records—the 1981 LP *Nothing Here Now but the Recordings*—and to his co-curating the autumn 1982 "Final Academy" multiperformance event at the Ritzy Cinema in Brixton, South London, which featured both Burroughs and Gysin as well as the first performance by P-Orridge's spin-off group Psychic TV. This extravaganza is remembered by many as a high point in the history of industrial thought and music.

## 6. Process as Composition

Cut-up techniques have propelled songs to popularity in industrial circles during every era of the genre; Front 242's 1988 "Welcome To Paradise," the Evolution Control Committee's 1998 "Rocked By Rape," and Boole's 2002 "America Inline" are good examples. However, P-Orridge's literally religious fervor toward the practice suggests Throbbing Gristle's music as an especially potent case study. Though the next chapter will explore the band's music in greater depth, for now consider Throbbing Gristle's track "Still Walking."

"Still Walking" appears on both the 1979 album *20 Jazz Funk Greats* and 1980 *Heathen Earth*, which is a recording of a live in-studio performance. In its original 1979 incarnation, driving the song is a sputtering, reverberated

---

✿ In P-Orridge's worldview, heavily influenced by occultic philosophy, reality is a loose consensus of perception and is thus in no way absolute. Therefore, for anything at all to exist meaningfully, it must be perceived. Hence, his use of "recorded" here applies not merely to technological media but also epistemologically.

✿✿ Burroughs's owning a remote control in 1971 is not a misremembering; P-Orridge says it was "the first I ever saw."

sixteenth-note pulse of a low-pitched analogue synthesizer, panned cyclically between right and left channels, with drum machine snares and clinks doubling the rhythms. Amidst this flanged clattering—all run through a low-frequency oscillator called the "Gristleizer," built by band member Chris Carter—are guitar groans (played by Cosey Fanni Tutti) and violin shrieks (courtesy of P-Orridge), processed to sound more like circular saws than stringed instruments. The song enacts an obsessive arbitrariness: no pitch, no moment, no process takes center stage as the sounds career about the stereo field in static agitation.

Listening carefully, however, reveals a peculiar nonlinear lyric, spoken by each of the band's four members, starting at different moments and taken at differing paces. In his study of *20 Jazz Funk Greats*, musician and scholar Drew Daniel writes, "The oblique lyrical snippets hint at a resolution, a domestic, occult scenario kept just out of sight . . . one is being given too much information, and yet the band is also holding something back."[16] Indeed the text, which band member Peter "Sleazy" Christopherson acknowledges as having cut-up origins, bears the abstraction of Burroughs as well as the oddly nondescript capacity to mean both nothing and anything—like a "contentless scene" acting exercise.[17]

> this end
> or all of us
> he said
> all of us do it
> each time asleep
> each time he said
> especially again
> especially item

But the cut-up process becomes a formal element of "Still Walking" not merely through the text's genesis; it is the random juxtapositions and phasing of the text when spoken by the band's members that bring it into dialogue with itself. Every word and phrase that we discern beneath the noise is called to meaning against every previous speech and speaker in the song.

A better understanding of "Still Walking" can be gleaned when we consider not only the 1979 album version but also the 1980 rendition from *Heathen Earth*.

The song's title and duration are the same, but at first glance that's where the similarities end. In the 1980 recording, the only instrumental feature is a quiet bass swelling that gently breathes in a slow rhythm, like the swinging of a pendulum or the beating of a heart. Gone are the screeching strings and the ugly drum machine chattering. The text spoken throughout the song is an entirely different, too. The 1979 "Still Walking" text, in addition to its blank banality, makes reference to ritual, totem, water, and a "spell of semen"; P-Orridge calls it a magical text and Christopherson relates its origins to P-Orridge's fascination with occultist Austin Osman Spare.[18] In contrast, the 1980 text, divided between Christopherson and Tutti, comes across more as prostitution than ritual. Christopherson recalls, "Cosey and I used to do this sort of thing spontaneously. It was almost like we were having a separate conversation with somebody else, but the combination of alternating lines between us produced a third mind."[19] In this version, Christopherson incessantly offers awkward lines such as "You walkin' on that way? 'Cos uh, I've got to get on this way as well" and "I've got everything that we need; we could just go"—lines that might be conceivably innocent at first were it not for Tutti's world-weary utterances of "You make it a bit too obvious" and "A little bit later, maybe." This text's identity as a failed pickup is one of many "third minds" that arise from its internal possibilities. What keeps us from hearing the performance as just a two-minded dialogue is that Christopherson and Tutti's lines are never in response to one another, but they instead overlap: they are two simultaneous monologues. The suggested world of the speakers is not contiguous in time or perception but is cut up. And like the 1979 "Still Walking," a contentlessness hovers uneasily in mysterious lines such as "Twice before he said it, he said, it was twice" and "If you catch them, don't waste it." Here, instead of the title "Still Walking" conjuring a spiritual journey, it suggests through Tutti's disinterest in the sleazy pickup lines that she herself is the one still walking, presumably away from Christopherson. Cutting up the milieu a step further is the repetition and reverberation of the spoken text, an effect of live sampling, processing, and playback (often shifted in pitch and speed), thus producing moments not of two speakers coinciding but three: a literal specter of the third mind.

Why read so much into these recordings? Because the fact that the *Heathen Earth* track purports to be the same song as the jittering noise on *20 Jazz Funk Greats* points to the conclusion that the defining characteristic of "Still Walking," at least as far as Throbbing Gristle is concerned, isn't a strictly musical one at all. The piece is less an arrangement of sound than a highlighting of the cut-up as process.

Composer and archivist of experimental music Michael Nyman writes, "Identity takes on a very different significance for the more open experimental work, where indeterminacy in performance guarantees that two versions of the same piece will have virtually no perceptible musical 'facts' in common."[20] This is wholly in keeping with the notion of the cut-up: the cutter doesn't seek to mold materials into a preconceived final work of art but instead merely enacts the process and allows the randomness of its effects to dictate the ends. As such, if we view "Still Walking" as a process of textual and performative cut-up instead of a prescriptive set of sounds, then it's no surprise these two versions should differ so much to the ear; how indeed could they not?

Throbbing Gristle is a consistently good band for illustrating the importance of process. Beyond the argument by comparison available to us with "Still Walking," we can turn to 1975's "Final Muzak" to get another angle on the issue. The song is an instrumental loop with tuneless drones and a mechanically repeating percussive rhythm. A close listening reveals nonrepeating diffusions of beat emphasis, phasing, and rhythmic displacement in the percussion loop, but more significantly, over the course of the piece's five and a half minutes, the main droning instrument moves very gradually up in pitch by the interval of a minor third. This process is too slow to hear as it happens, but it functions as a large-scale gesture within the illusion of stasis. By virtue of this pitch shift being the only directional change in the music, "Final Muzak" is *de facto* about that shift, which in real time is functionally content-free, both perceptually inaudible and performatively impossible for humans. Owing heavily to Chris Carter's electronic and tape techniques, the work takes on the conceptual sheen of foregrounded structure and process.

### 7. Media

One of the difficulties that plague conversations about industrial music is that the genre has come to include (to the chagrin and outright denial of some purists) anything from gentle synthesized droning to metal-inspired riffage. Recognizing that a process can drive industrial music's creation as much as a desired sonic profile can helps us understand this apparent disparity. As both a practical and an ideological tool of industrial music, the cut-up technique doesn't discriminate between dialogue, guitars, synthesizer textures, or ethnomusicological field recordings; nor should it. This helps explain not only how "Still Walking" takes on different masks but how near-whimsical recordings by a band like Nurse With Wound share a kinship with, say, Nine Inch Nails' disorienting and intricate remix of "Gave Up" (courtesy of Coil) on their *Fixed* EP.

The cut-up itself isn't prerequisite to industrial music, but the freedom it imbues to musicians in their treatment of sonic building blocks remains essential to the genre, as does the larger idea of détournement, of which it is one type. This freedom isn't mere license to move beyond the limits of human logic and performability—indeed, even the most basic cut-ups, edits, and hip-hop record scratches can achieve this—but, getting more directly at the worldview adapted from Burroughs, the cut-up as an idea grants license to test the limits of the technology involved. In 1995, the band Coil released an album as ELpH Vs. Coil, called *Worship the Glitch*. As the title suggests, its central themes come from misfires in sound programming, computer crashes, and accidental damage to recording equipment. In fact, ELpH is the name that Coil gave to the "spiritual entity" that seemed, to them, to create unexpected technological errors and bugs in the execution of their music—yet another third mind, this time between the band's members and their machinery. The record's influence is most strongly heard today in the glitch genre of electronic music, beyond what normally passes for modern industrial. But the aesthetics of failure, born of "following [machine's] mistakes," as Coil's John Balance puts it, is as industrial an idea as any.[21] By challenging the capacity of the machine to operate, musicians bypass having to question whether their own reinterpretations and appropriations of technology are merely part of an even larger hidden control mechanism; Burroughs himself wrote in a pre-digital age, "it is especially difficult to know what side anyone is working on, especially yourself."[22] The randomness is now precisely the error of the machine, and not the operation of its potential sleeper agent.

Among the spiritual ancestors of this practice is the *Black Album*, recorded in December 1975 by Boyd Rice, an American artist who would later found the band NON. The record comprises loops of easy listening and pop from the midtwentieth century, warped, sped up, slowed down, mixed, and shredded. Its packaging indicates that it is to be played at any speed, thus denying the turntable final authority over a "correct" hearing of the piece. To this date, the album has never been given an official CD release, out of recognition of and respect for this insistence that the work not be bound by machine-driven conventions. More recent examples of machine failure as an aesthetic in industrial music include the late 1990s work of the Australian band Snog, and "futurepop" act Icon of Coil's 2004 club hit "Shelter," in which the song's hook—the repetition of the line "where I feel safe"—contains a signature glitch effect created in software by repeating a 0.06 second–long vocal snippet seven times in succession, leaving a jagged, discontinuous digital seam flapping in the breeze between beats. This is visibly indicated in the soundwave of Figure 2.2, excerpted from the song.

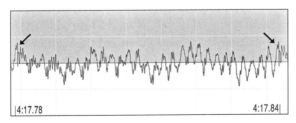

*Figure 2.2: Soundwave of excerpt from "Shelter" by Icon of Coil, showing digital cut-and-paste repetition. Arrows indicate the repeated seam of the cut.*

The point of all this is that the cut-up doesn't need to be dogmatic in order to bear its subversive power. With regard to its strictest form as he and Gysin first developed it, Burroughs acknowledged in 1979 that "one arrives at a point where, cutting a page, you can cut and cut it to infinity; but, as one goes along, the results become less and less convincing."[23] Indeed, Burroughs himself continued to use narrative as a backbone of his writings, recognizing, as beat scholar Oliver Harris puts it, "that to maximize the potency of his texts it was necessary to retain a dialectical relation to the conventional prose that defined the norm against which cut-ups were designed to act."[24] Both Burroughs and P-Orridge, in their respective later works, reveal a more nuanced relationship with the cut-up than one of mere use-and-disuse for effect: having experimented with its randomness for years, having consummated their commitment to the third mind, and having pushed the boundaries of both their own authorhood and their chosen media's capacity to bear it, they involuntarily speak with a transformed artistic voice. Swallowing the cut-up into oneself—and along with it, its jagged denial of consensus—makes for an artistic base state of hyper-association and magical thinking, whatever the technical means of one's creative work. A charitably optimistic view of industrial music might suggest this state of affairs acts as a microcosm of the whole genre's relationship with such overt experimentalism.

## 8. Techno-Ambivalence

In his 1992 collaboration with the band Ministry, Burroughs orders us to "Cut word lines. Cut music lines. Smash the control images. Smash the control machines." This cutting and smashing is by no means a rejection outright of the viral agents of mind control—words, technology, belief—but instead it's a reversal of these agents' powers upon themselves. As both the fragmented recordings to be cut up and as the recording device, machines are necessary to smash the machine, just as vaccination is achieved through viral exposure. It is through this reality that one can't view Burroughs and industrial music as merely technophobic; instead they have a techno-paranoid streak. Industrial music's debt to Futurism's uncomplicated machine idolatry precludes a Luddite, antitechnological response to its perception of media totalitarianism—this isn't folk music we're talking about. So as the music stakes out territory amidst the larger machines it seeks to dismantle and rewire, it's thus appropriately ambivalent. In perusing even the names of industrial bands, albums, and songs, we can see in roughly equal amounts a valorizing and humanizing of technology as well as a reactionary call to destroy it. Examples of technophilic titles include:

"Steelrose" (by Project Pitchfork)
*L'Âme Életrique* (by Die Form)
"Electronic New Self" (by the Fair Sex)
*Futureperfect* (by VNV Nation)
"Passion for the Future" (by Manufacture)
"Utopian Landscapes" (by Cruciform Injection)
"The Gift of Machine" (by Inure)
"Machineries of Joy" (by Die Krupps)
Machines of Loving Grace (band)
"Celestial Circuitry" (by Object)

And examples of techno-paranoid titles include:

"Punish Your Machine" (by Front 242)
"Machine Slave" (by Front Line Assembly)
"Cybernetics and Pavlovian Warfare" (by A Split-Second)
The Pain Machinery (band)
"The Micro-Implant Conspiracy" (by Oneiroid Psychosis)
*Death to Digital* (by Julien-K)
My Psychotic Motor (band)
"Future Dead" (by Tactical Sekt)
"The Agony of the Plasma" (by SPK)
*Dystopian Visions* (compilation album)

This ambivalence remains unresolved throughout industrial music history; individual artists may favor a particular vision for their own deprogramming tactics, but the majority of the genre's ubiquitous conceptual ties to the machine are themselves attitudinally ambivalent, like the band Einstürzende Neubauten's name ("collapsing new buildings"), or "Cyberchrist," a phrase that offers equal parts hope and cynicism, and which was used as a song title by no fewer than seven industrial bands between 1993 and 1995 alone. At the political heart of this ambivalence is the "transforming, liberating potential in new technologies" versus the "fear that the mass media will create passive, onedimensional audiences," cultural historians James Naremore and Patrick Brantlinger famously wrote in 1991, concluding, "Perhaps both [views] are correct. . . ."[25]

The prehistory in this and the preceding chapter has traced specific ideas rather than sounds because these ideas help us understand the baseline condition that makes industrial music possible. Not only is there plentiful documentary evidence of the music's debt to Futurism and Burroughs, but the lenses of their worldviews effortlessly assimilate, interpret, and account for the musical and lyrical themes of the genre.✱ A blunt version of this argument is that industrial music's fascination with technology, experimentation, violence, ugliness, and destruction is Futurism's legacy, while the antiestablishment paranoia, the free polymorphism of authority signifiers, and the haphazard retooling of contexts are the echoes of Burroughs. On the other hand, a more detailed understanding plays into what scholar Bret Wood calls "the ambiguous nature of industrial itself,"[26] where, just as the machine is a stand-in for a number of power structures, the duality of interpretations of the machine can bespeak and account for industrial music's sometimes frustratingly unclear politics. Exemplifying the interactions of these contradictory ideas in practice, when Einstürzende Neubauten performed a sweaty, ear-splitting spectacle of a concert in London in August 1983, Barney Hoskyns wrote in the *New Musical Express*, "They reverse [F]uturism."[27]

✱ Karen Collins, through listener-response surveys, exhaustively identifies these themes: ecology, war, violence, society, sci-fi, Futurism, sociology, philosophy, discontent with society, technological dystopia, oppression, conspiracy, the apocalyptic future, technology, government, religion, censorship, urban decay, dehumanization, alienation, societal chaos, global technocracy, and mechanical fetishism.[28]

# Industrial Music and Art Music

## 1. Imagined Ancestries

Although industrial culture traces an unambiguous paper trail and philosophical heritage back to Futurism and Burroughs, less clear is its connection to previous musical styles that sought to liberate noise under a modernist mandate of innovation. The sonic precursors to industrial music are generally too numerous and too indirect to warrant much specific exploration in this book, but it's worth digressing for a few pages to address the enticing grip that twentieth-century art music (or less precisely, "classical" music) has long held on industrial culture. There's a vague but deep gut feeling that the two musics share a fundamental bond—that a hidden truth about industrial music lurks in the oeuvres of Arnold Schoenberg, Iannis Xenakis, and Philip Glass, encoded in the histories of *musique concrète* and improvisation.

Gracing the pages of *Industrial Nation* and other magazines every now and then, readers find broad, tentative articles surveying the development of the theremin or the rise of the Darmstadt School of composers. Bands and journalists perpetuate this supposed kinship without specifying it when they haphazardly drop names: "comparisons could be made to Front Line Assembly, Numb, Stockhausen, and Skinny Puppy," declares *Phosphor* magazine in a 1993 review of the gritty UK dance act New Mind, offering little follow-through on Karlheinz Stockhausen.[1] Industrial trio Covenant conclude their 2000 album *United States of Mind* with four minutes and thirty-three soundless seconds (on a track called "You Can Make Your Own Music"), nodding slyly to composer John Cage, whose silent *4'33"* of 1952 may be the ultimate open question of what constitutes music; but the other ten songs on Covenant's album are more or less all pop tunes with scarcely a trace of Cage's vital indeterminacy.✿ And in the rare academic overview of industrial music, connections are only a little clearer, usually by way of an obligatory paragraph in which French composer Edgard Varèse's

---

✿ Cage's interest in the unpredictable, "aleatoric" element of performance led Burroughs himself to admit, "John Cage and Earl Brown have carried the cut-up method much further in music than I have in writing."[2]

name is sure to appear alongside mention of his allegedly proto-industrial works *Ionisation* and *Poème Électronique*.

Thankfully, we can largely sweep away this hazy uncertainty if we bear in mind a few guiding parameters as we trace industrial music's connections with art music. First, art music in the twentieth century is exceedingly varied in its attitudes, techniques, and sounds, so when the time comes, we'll need to specify just what music we're talking about. Next, different aspects of art music feed into industrial music with greater or lesser influence, so we need to ask what parts of this music matter to industrial audiences. Is it the timbral sounds, the approaches to harmony or rhythm, a sense of long-range formal development, the attitude of the iconoclastic, the mixing of highbrow and lowbrow, the compositional techniques of synthesis or phasing, the radically new philosophies of chance and silence, the materiality of the music, or just the cultural fact of twentieth-century art music's reputation? Finally, it's useful to ask specifically how these musical elements are inspirational or ancestral to industrial music; they might be objects to imitate or to tear down, or they could be sonic starting points, rarified holy texts, theorizations, or perhaps they are texts to cut up, processes on which to meditate, or a canvas on which to piss.

In light of all the indirect ways that these musics might connect, it's neither an accurate history nor a useful model to categorize western composers or works into mutually exclusive schools and make simple declarations of causality. Try considering it this way instead: a lot of western art music in the twentieth century can be broadly plotted as combinations of three general artistic tendencies that arose more or less in order and came eventually to coexist, to be reasserted, and to respond to one another. These different visions were as much ideological as sonic, because each one implicitly makes assertions about how art should ideally be experienced, and by whom.

We might describe the first common tendency as having sought musical progress by blazing forward down a long-inherited trajectory of classical music's alleged evolution, racing to lead the compositional pack at the foremost extremity of harmonic tension and formal organization. We can think of this tendency as *traditionalist*, because although the sounds of the previous century were themselves passé during the 1900s, they acted as guideposts to the future. The second tendency envisioned a way forward not by continuing classical traditions but by tearing them down along with their supposed modern inheritors. This mind-set was *reactionary* in replacing composition's traditionalist practice of directed harmonic research with a focus on radical new timbres, un-"classical" instruments, and eclectic stylistic palettes. The third tendency arose from the view that attacking tradition meant recognizing—and thus validating—its grip on the present, and that furthermore, those who most

ASSIMILATE

specifically counteracted tradition managed in the process to identify themselves as targets for assimilation into its preservational, academic, and cultural institutions as safely "controversial" new voices. Instead then, this third tendency sought out ways to make music unconcerned with moving unilaterally "forward"—even unconcerned with being "music" at all. We might characterize this artistic tendency as *anarchic* because it purports to reject heritages, hierarchies, binaries, and other deep preconceptions.✿

Each in its own way, these three tendencies perpetuated the modernist obsession with originality that dominated western art throughout the whole century. Whether taken as exclusive dogmas (which was rare) or as combinable strategies (far more common), these three tendencies all sculpted music that expanded the art form to new extremes, pushing into unexplored, often ugly territory. This is rightly part of why so many industrial artists and fans recognize twentieth-century art music's relevance; industrial music is necessarily invested in extremes.✿✿

---

✿ "Anarchic" here is used to characterize a multiangled resistance to hierarchies of various kinds. No connection is intended to anarchy as a political state of (non) governance, nor to anarchism as an intellectual tradition.

✿✿ As a literal reference to the front lines of a struggle, and by extension, to an extreme cutting edge within art, the term *avant-garde* crops up a lot in discussions of both industrial music and twentieth-century art music. Indeed, authors have at various times used "avant-garde" to describe all three of the compositional tendencies outlined here, which indicates that even though it may be potentially useful as a category, it is slippery. Part of the ambiguity comes from the conflict over whether we can use "avant-garde" to describe artistic endeavors both in their contemporary moment and in retrospect. Art historian Hubert F. van den Berg gives an example: "In the 1960s and 1970s there was indeed an avant-garde that understood itself as avant-garde, to a much stronger degree than that configuration of isms in the first half of the twentieth century, which was only *a posteriori* labeled avant-garde."[3] The western musicians he's referring to in this passage broadly include people like La Monte Young, John Cage, Cornelius Cardew, and Robert Ashley, all of whom embraced the second and (especially) the third of the twentieth-century compositional tendencies listed above. By labeling these new approaches of the 1960s and 1970s as avant-garde, van den Berg here knowingly challenges the view of historians such as Peter Bürger, who argue that whatever the literal meaning of avant-garde may be, it should refer strictly to a particular historical moment of surrealism, constructivism, and Dada in the first decades of the twentieth century. (Bürger specifically asserts that the historical avant-garde was a failed attempt to integrate art into the praxis of life.) Musicians Brian Eno and Michael Nyman belonged to the avant-garde cadre that van den Berg writes about, but in yet a third inflection of the term they themselves had used "avant-garde" as a dirty word to classify such rigidly formalistic composers as Stockhausen, Xenakis, and Pierre Boulez, whose hierarchical approaches they wanted to bypass. So amidst all these conflicting uses of the phrase, there isn't much consensus as to what it historically specifies. As time batters confrontational new ideas into acceptable old ideas, the front line by definition becomes an ever-moving target, and so the label of avant-garde on any music is either doomed to inevitable obsolescence or unnaturally freezes in history the very notion of a vanguard, both denying future artists access to a potentially useful descriptor and

## 2. Traditionalist and Reactionist Tendencies

For a few reasons, the traditionalist first tendency offers industrial music relatively little as either a philosophical orientation or a repertoire. Immediately problematic is its reverence to the past (even as it looks to the future). Indeed, it's rare for industrial musicians to boast any "classical training" because not only are such declarations the meaningless stuff of amateur press releases but they are nearly always attempts to legitimize the genre with reference to a regressive conservatism. Granted, in its taste for the epic, industrial music occasionally wolfs down the leftovers of goth's indiscriminant feast upon western culture circa 1000–1900 AD, giving rise to pseudoclassical oddities like the bands E Nomine and Will, and more dubiously, tributes to Johann Sebastian Bach by Die Form and Laibach (both released in 2008).✽ But it's more often the case that in their quest for immediacy and the rejection of tradition, industrial musicians begin their careers with no formal knowledge of music. This is connected to a second reason why high modernists such as Arnold Schoenberg and Milton Babbitt are not really part of the genre's inheritance: their music is driven by (and indeed it usually *sounds* driven by) harmonic and organizational details that few in the industrial community have seriously ever studied, fewer have mimicked, and even fewer still want to listen or dance to. Especially since the mid-1980s, the overwhelming majority of industrial music is, by the standards of traditionalist art music, both tonally and rhythmically conservative, sticking to stable keys and regular groupings of steady beats. Bands such as Zia and Vampire Rodents gesture to more adventurous tonal realms with their occasional digression into alternative tuning systems, but as Zia's Elaine Walker indicates on her website, "I compose microtonal music strictly by ear and leave it to others to analyze, so you won't find ratios or mathematics here."✽✽ Her statement also reveals a third disconnect between traditionalist twentieth-century composition and industrial music: by rejecting the old mind-body di-

---

implicitly dismissing any development beyond that fixed moment. Given this choice, we can cautiously acknowledge that when contextualized properly in a time and place, the term *avant-garde* is broadly useful for describing art that, in a pugnacious and directional march, expands into previously uncharted, generally hostile cultural territory. In specifying this use, we're able to recognize momentary innovations while still embracing the perpetuity of flux at the many edges of expressive possibility.

✽ Some neofolk industrial bands do valorize the past, but with a decidedly mournful antimodernism, as Chapter 13 discusses.

✽✽ It's also worth noting that this sort of experimentation has been well within synth owners' grasp since at least 1989, when the E-MU Proteus 1 came packaged with a nineteen-tone scale option—the very tuning that Zia uses in such songs as 1992's "Pagan Goddess."

vide of Descartes and embracing physicality, industrial music seems morally opposed to traditionalist attitudes such as Milton Babbitt's famous 1958 suggestion that not only were audiences not worth wasting complex music on, but performance (and possibly even hearing) itself got in the way of this music's proper systemic presentation. The fact that many have referred to this strain of composition as "eye music" stands in clear contrast to EBM's "body music."

Traditionalist approaches to composition at best buttress industrial music's broadly modernist revolutionary spirit, but the second aforementioned tendency's reactionary approaches bear much closer inspection. Specifically, reactionary art music of the twentieth century has in some ways provided the genre with actual sounds. This approach to art music often privileges rhythmic or sonic detail, manifesting in works by Henry Cowell, tape music pioneer Pierre Schaeffer, and Varèse and Stockhausen. The scope that these composers encompass is very broad in its time span, in its set of specific compositional techniques, and in its specific ideologies within an overall reaction against tradition. But for our purposes, this breadth matters relatively little because to most industrialists who confronted this music (and arguably to most nonspecialist audiences), its compositional concerns about large-scale shape and process may seem less revolutionary than its immediate surface-level incorporation of noise, percussion, and the timbres of synthesis and tape. It's telling that in 1995, after Stockhausen himself was asked by a journalist to listen (for the first time) to electronica by popular artists who cited him as an influence (such as Aphex Twin), he roiled, "I wish those musicians would not allow themselves any repetitions, and would go faster in developing their ideas or their findings, because I don't appreciate at all this permanent repetitive language," betraying a resolutely classicist take on the large-scale treatment of small-scale noises.[4] In light of industrial music's attitudes toward tradition, hierarchy, and the body, Stockhausen's opinions seem positively relical when he continues, "Music is the product of the highest human intelligence, and of the best senses, the listening senses and of imagination and intuition. And as soon as it becomes just a means for ambiance, as we say, environment, or for being used for certain purposes, then music becomes a whore."[5] The infamous *Prostitution* exhibit of Throbbing Gristle's precursor troupe COUM Transmissions leaps to mind here as an appropriately contrasting view of whoredom itself.

It's not a surprise, then, that the way industrial musicians directly deal with this second tendency in twentieth-century art music—in which Stockhausen's name appears to carry special weight—consistently illustrates just how little they really absorb its values. Across the wide industrial spectrum, perhaps the only compositional element reliably shared from Cabaret Voltaire to Combichrist and from Die Krupps to Doubting Thomas is the sonic use of noise, and so regarding the superficially noisy art music of the reactionary strain, industrial music operates like a cargo cult: Cowell's detailed writings on polyrhythm and an academic understanding of acoustic Fourier transformations have nothing to do with a performer's thrill in overpowering an audience with a distortion pedal.

Here are some examples of the shallowness with which this stuff carries over into the genre. Laibach's "Die Liebe" and Severed Heads' "Acme Instant Dehydrated Boulder Kit" (both from 1985) sample works by Stockhausen, but both lock the sampled formal complexity onto a simple 4/4 rhythmic grid. Steve Law of the band Zen Paradox gives away the game of reducing this music to timbre when he says in a 1995 interview with industrial zine *Music from the Empty Quarter*, "I listen to a lot of avant garde and classical music like Ligeti, Stockhausen, Xenakis, and John Cage, which I can also use for sampling purposes, some of the sounds they create are absolutely incredible."[6] Similarly, the members of Zoviet France, according to founder Ben Ponton, are fans of "Stockhausen, and Pierre Boulez, and Luciano Berio," but like Steve Law, Ponton seems to focus exclusively on the sound itself, continuing, "We're just as much into Motorhead as we are into Stockhausen. I think the common factor in all of it is an element of noise really. Noise is a non-musical sound format, which you find in Motorhead just as much as you do in Stockhausen."[7] Focusing like this on the surface of art music downplays its contextual order and relations—which Stockhausen maintains are central.

To a handful within the industrial scene, this is old news. A 1982 issue of the zine *Flowmotion* affectionately calls Throbbing Gristle, Cabaret Voltaire, and 23 Skidoo "garage Stockhausen dilletantes"[8] [sic], and Genesis P-Orridge in 1981 maintains that the likes of Throbbing Gristle, Nurse With Wound, and NON just "play music that is amplified. I don't think it's electronic music. That implies some kinda Stockhausen."[9] Similarly, in a 1980 interview, Stephen Mallinder of Cabaret Voltaire confirms, "Any avant-garde music we've picked up on is a secondary thing, and we realised the parallels between them and us, but it hasn't been a conscious decision where our music is supposed to parallel that. We've only realised it in retrospect,"[10] later adding, "I'm sure people think we grew up with Stockhausen."[11]

We shouldn't let the superficiality of industrial music's connection to reactionary art music cast a negative light on the genre. In fact, far from a point of criticism, this tenuity is evidence of a vital political difference: it's often asserted that composers such as Schaeffer and Cage believed part of their mission was to musicalize noises, but in contrast, industrial music retains part of its confrontational power by unapologetically treating noise as music's dangerous outland. Although the genre may not fully accomplish the mission to "exterminate all rational thought" (as issued in David Cronenberg's film of *The Naked Lunch*), it's nonetheless a step in the right direction when Test Dept. rehashes the sonic texture of John Cage's 1939 *First Construction (In Metal)* while unharnessing it from the meticulous structural considerations that aspire to make it "more" than angry clatter.✿ To the industrial mind-set, angry clatter is *good*; visceral chaos trumps ordered rationality—at least in nonironic settings. This is evident in the improvisatory phrase lengths shown earlier in à;GRUMH…'s "Ayatollah Jackson," and it is taken to extremes in a piece such as Einstürzende Neubauten's "Seele Brennt," where the timing of the work isn't governed by a metronome but by lead singer Blixa Bargeld's pulse, irrational and carnal. Naut Humon, a member of first-wave industrial act Rhythm & Noise, articulates this pre-intellectual approach when he says, "I saw a bridge between Hendrix and Stockhausen. The challenge was to understand noise in an emotional manner."[12] To industrial music, the most appealing components of art music are noise, ugliness, and the force of the moment, and so in turn these are the features most consistently adapted from the reactionary second tendency.✿✿ This is why it's easier to draw musical connections to Lou Reed's *Metal Machine Music* or to the *Intonarumori* that gave Russolo childlike glee than to Schaeffer or Varèse.

## 3. Anarchic Tendencies

By rejecting high-minded fixed structures and old belief systems in lieu of immediacy, industrial music—as "serious" composition pertains to it—is most productively informed by music of the twentieth century's anarchic third tendency. These musics share a number of attitudes in common—such as the belief that challenging and provoking an audience can be a productive goal rather than a failure of communication—but beyond ideological similarities, there's a comparatively significant mass of evidence that suggests real historical connections. To begin, let's look very briefly at two American works from the early 1960s that exemplify the anarchic tendency.

---

✿ The underlying structure of this noisy early work by Cage is among his more rigid and conservative. Cage would later prove central in developing twentieth-century art music's anarchic third tendency.

✿✿ Because industrial music applies its own (il)logic to these ingredients, an interesting turn of events in recent years is that the contemporary classical scene has begun to appreciate, borrow from, and collaborate with industrial musicians. The Kronos Quartet, for example, arguably the most famous modern classical ensemble in the world, added Einstürzende Neubauten's "Armenia" to their repertory in 2006.

La Monte Young's 1960 "Arabic Numeral (Any Integer) to H. F." is scored for a massive cluster of noise to be repeated loudly and precisely, sounding every one to two seconds for a predetermined but variable number of iterations.✿ Performers most often play it in fortissimo arm-length blows to a piano. The effect is invariably jarring, and by most listeners' standards oppressively unpleasant. Critics' interpretation of "Arabic Numeral (Any Integer) to H. F." has been consistent over time: focusing less on the noisiness and more on the demands of precise repetition, Marjorie Perloff emphasizes that the piece shows, "as Gertrude Stein had already taught us, that there is no such thing as true repetition."[13] To John Cage, it revealed that "the same thing is not the same thing at all, but full of variety."[14] Composer Cornelius Cardew takes the idea a step further when he writes, "What the listener can hear and appreciate are the *errors* in the interpretation. If the piece were performed by a machine this interest would disappear and with it the composition."[15]

But this musing rings false to those of us who are inured to latter-day industrial music's mechanically exact repetition. There can be musical value in tyrannically overwhelming and silencing listeners—perhaps just as much as one finds by empowering listeners to seek out humanity within noise. And this other way of hearing the piece not only represents the industrial take on Young's work, but there's a good argument that it represents Young's own view as well. In 1960, composers such as Erik Satie and John Cage had already raised musical questions about repetition and performance using much less confrontational methods, so it's clear that the piece's aggression isn't merely incidental to the goals that Perloff, Cage, and Cardew identify. Rather, the work's darkness is a necessary part of its appeal. When Young himself performed the piece in 1961 as "1698," his 1,698 repetitions surely became more an exercise in surrendering the body and mind to musical structure such that the varying precision of those repetitions may well have come to matter less than their inevitability, amounting to a decidedly industrial effect. Vitally, Young himself empowers this reading when he specifically articulates that the creation and enjoyment of "good" art—perhaps along with morality itself—is a control machine to dismantle, even as it operates from within each of us. In "Lecture 1960," a prose performance containing the one-word paragraph "Anarchy," the composer famously writes:

> Often I hear somebody say that the most important thing about a work of art is not that it be new but that it be good. But if we define good as

✿ This piece is frequently referred to as "X for Henry Flynt."

what we like, which is the only definition of good I find useful when discussing art, and then say that we are interested in what is good, it seems to me that we will always be interested in the same things (that is, the same things that we already like). I am not interested in good; I am interested in new—even if this includes the possibility of its being evil.[16]

Importantly, the "new" that he talks about here is a nondirectional, nonteleological one, thus differing from the traditionalist and reactionary preconceptions of "progress," which were synonymous with "good." Witnessing the power of the nongood and the primally regressive, Young directly foreshadows some vital ideas underlying the industrial genre's cruelest musical manifestations and its gloomiest theatrics.

Another relevant example of anarchic musical cruelty is 1964's "The Wolfman" by Robert Ashley. A work for voice and tape, the score indicates that the performer be a "sinister lounge singer," but the real source of menace lies in the extreme volume boost on the microphone that makes every point-blank whisper and lip smack a searing torrent of overmodulation and clinging feedback. Listeners who can endure the performance are treated to fifteen minutes of Ashley's own intimate human noises made grotesque, all-enveloping, and machinelike through amplification. The sleeve photo on the accompanying album is fittingly an extreme close-up of Ashley touching the microphone to his mouth, wearing ultra-hip black shades. More than Young's piece, "The Wolfman" resists coolheaded philosophizing; its discourse is unambiguously monstrous, right down to its title.

The drive to create a viscerally powerful, unpredictable experience grants tactical validity to shock and disgust—and indeed as Young says, even to evil. Whereas these experiences had been by-products or simply aesthetic décor in previous music, here horror and oppression take on a functional, structural power. As part of the repertoire of anarchic thought, darkness was explored alongside humor and boredom, which helps explain why most of what Ashley and Young wrote wasn't as confrontationally grim as these pieces, but regardless of mood, their overall output is nonetheless consistent in its industrial-friendly concern with immediacy. Ashley's use of electronics was enlivening, often based on real-time performance through processing and amplification (in contrast to the frozen, premeditated laboratory assemblages by the likes of Stockhausen), and Young helped solidify his legacy by compiling 1963's *Anthology of Chance Operations*, a collection of works that bypassed traditional musical scores, largely obsolesced performers' rehearsing and training, empowered and alienated cultured and unschooled audiences alike with democratic evenhandedness, and broke down walls between music, theater, poetry, and art. The musical aesthetic that would become central to industrial music was thus in place by the early 1960s within art music, but it was not yet singled out, existing instead as one of many ways to throw away old preconceptions. It surfaced in the nastier, confrontational moments to which many new composers were prone but in which few if any expressly wallowed.

There are a handful of direct and careful borrowings from this music on early industrial records: after witnessing a revelatory 1979 concert of Steve Reich's music, Jim G. Thirlwell of the Australian act Foetus began using Reich's phasing practices on his early albums, and Nurse With Wound lifts a beatless ninety-second sample of John Cage's "Credo in Us" on 1980's "Ostranenie."[17] In particular, the focus on repetition in works by Reich, Young, and Glass is shared by many industrial artists, as pervasively illustrated throughout this book, but even though mimicking the noisy timbres of reactionary art music largely misunderstands that music, repetition here is an act, and not a sound. Specifically, repetition is an act best understood through mimicry—for what else is it besides self-copying? Thus, industrial music's imitation of anarchic and quasi-minimalist art music doesn't encounter the same structural misunderstanding to which its aping of Stockhausen was prone.

But beyond all this, the most important connections between anarchic twentieth-century composition and industrial music aren't so imitative; indeed, the *fact* of art music generally has more of an impact on industrial music than its *content*. Rather, the most vital connections are often indirect, spawned from the primordial fertility of the 1960s' and 1970s' artistic zeitgeist that anarchically broke down barriers between high and low culture, between artistic media, and between personal and political expression. There are lots of ways to illustrate this, but three serve particularly well in getting the point across.

Historically important to industrial music is its connection to Fluxus, an international democratizing art movement that didn't define itself through any one aesthetic but instead sought the eternally new cutting edge of art, whatever that was in any time and place. Through this approach, Fluxus viewed itself as ever-changing and incapable of becoming passé; it sought to integrate art and its effects into daily life. Chapter 7 discusses Fluxus in greater depth, but for our purposes here, it suffices to say that the movement's radical assertion of an ever-progressing avant-garde resonated with both Genesis P-Orridge and La Monte Young, who was for a short time quite central in the movement. It's safe to assume that through the wide networks of Fluxus, people like Boyd Rice of NON heard the music and meaningfully encountered the ideas of Terry Riley, Steve Reich, and Charlemagne Palestine. Fluxus was widespread, eclectic, and certainly unfocused, but it serves as an unambiguous historical meeting ground between pioneers in both art music and industrial music.

A second connection comes to us through the Velvet Underground, whose 1967 album with the German chanteuse Nico is a central reference point for nearly all innovations in rock music since. Industrial music's pervasive obsession with repetition and noise and its hero worship of the Lou Reed coolness that David Bowie would later seize upon are just two easy connections to draw. It's also worth acknowledging Clock DVA's cover of the Velvet Underground's "The Black Angel's Death Song" and the full-album remake of Nico's entire *Desertshore* that former Throbbing Gristle members released in 2012. The Velvet Underground's link with anarchic art musics comes through its member John Cale, who performed, composed, and recorded alongside Cage and Riley in the early 1960s prior to the band's formation. With Young, he helped organize the Theatre of Eternal Music in the mid-1960s, which experimented with drone music. Cale himself had even played "Arabic Numeral (Any Integer) to H. F." during solo concerts in 1963, banging on a piano with his elbows while kneeling before it, as if worshipping ugliness itself. Without directly carrying over these experiences to industrial music's language, Cale was as responsible as any musician for exposing pop at large to the techniques, sounds, and personalities of twentieth-century art music.

A third clear line that we can draw between art music's anarchic tendency and industrial music is visible in what record collectors call the "Nurse With Wound List," which was published in the liner notes of Nurse With Wound's first two albums, 1979's *Chance Meeting on a Dissecting Table of a Sewing Machine and an Umbrella* and 1980's *To the Quiet Men from a Tiny Girl*. The list features the names of 291 musicians or groups whom Nurse With Wound's members at the time—Steven Stapleton, John Fothergill, and Heman Pathak—considered especially important or influential. Most were (and still are) outlandishly obscure. As important early figures in what came to be called industrial music, Nurse With Wound effectively issued with the list a declaration, a challenge, and an assignment to the hungry obsessives who constituted nearly the entire industrial fanbase of 1979. Fothergill explains that the list wasn't arbitrary or showy: "Steve or I had at one time or another almost every record that [all those artists] released."[18] In so carefully presenting their music as the sum of the list's influences, Nurse With Wound effectively proclaimed a kinship between their nominally industrial work and that of the musicians on their list. Its inclusions range from noise bands to jazz improvisers to psychedelic freakout acts, but there is a clearly identifiable lineage of composers on the list too: Cage, Ashley, Alvin Lucier (who was Ashley's collaborator in the Sonic Arts Union), Cardew,

Reich, Riley, and Young.✿ These names amidst the list's variety affirm that even though industrial music is no simple inheritor to classical music's radical blood-lines, its claims of muddy bastardy are tough to deny.

The anarchic avant-garde of the 1960s and 1970s is thus the closest indus-trial antecedent within art music by virtue of its compulsion for immediacy (the root of its occasional shock imagery) and its traceable connections to the likes of Throbbing Gristle and Nurse With Wound. The messy indirectness of these connections both contributes to and possibly stems from a sense that noise, confrontation, immediacy, and repetition were very much "in the air" at the time of industrial music's inception. This leads us to one last observation.

## 4. The Revolutionary Class

Consider how the desire to tear down inherited preconceptions is shared by industrial music's forebears: radical art music unseats a preoccupation with hi-erarchical form, Debord and the 1968 rioters sought to unmask the spectacle, the Futurists wanted to sever all ties to the past, and Burroughs tried to reveal that the human condition itself was conspiracy. When Eno writes that art music of this third tendency was "so explicitly anti-academic that it often even claimed to have been written for *non-musicians*," he implies that once music gets too structurally fixed—or learning gets too academic—then it loses its liberating power.[19] If we recall from a few pages ago the idea that artistic strategies make assertions about how art should be experienced and by whom, then we can see that Eno, as if speaking on behalf of all of industrial music's revolutionary an-cestry, inscribes a community of people who are anti-elitist, who do not divorce the body from the mind, who value immediacy, and who distrust authoritative institutions and their rationalizing verbiage of misdirection. Eno, and with him the industrial genre, thus privileges a class that is intellectually and politically engaged, but not academic—one that believes in the aesthetics of political change as much as any detail of its implementation.

The role that noise and revolution as ideas played in the fecund cross-polli-nation of the late twentieth-century zeitgeist can carry this idea further: the anarchic attitudes that spread in the 1960s, 1970s, and 1980s throughout per-formance art, racial protest music, novelty pop, No Wave, experimental jazz, drug-inspired psychedelic jamming, early hip-hop, and dub reggae all help us

---

✿ The list also includes Stockhausen, Xenakis, Pierre Henry, and Luc Ferrari, much of whose work can most easily be plotted with reference to the reactionist second tendency of twentieth-century art music.

see the industrial community as part of a larger whole. Cultural critic Greil Marcus gestures toward some of these moments alongside Situationism and Dada in what he calls a "secret history of the twentieth century," capping his narrative with punk rock, but for our purposes, we might give here a slightly new inflection of meaning to what Marx and Engels call the "revolutionary class."[20] It's useful to know the roots of industrial music, but when we see how they extend in parallel to distantly related contemporary branches we can understand the genre as belonging to a family marked by questioning, immediacy, and the demand for change. This is an important idea that we'll return to much later in this book.

The industrial community sometimes wishes to hear in the noise and dissonance of high modernist music an ancestry more direct than history, analysis, or ideology bears out. Conjuring connections to twentieth-century art music without understanding its historically competing values makes for haphazard revisionism, and even though some important links do exist, understanding how and why they exist is crucial. This is because justifying industrial music vis-à-vis "classical" not only misses the point of both musics, but it risks symbolically yoking whole communities and classes of people to the hierarchies of tradition and control they seek to topple. Recognizing the nature of musical and philosophical kinships, then, is vital to this music's past, present, and future alike.

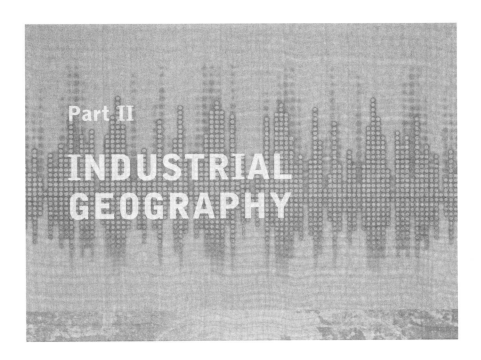

Part II

# INDUSTRIAL GEOGRAPHY

DESPITE ITS TECHNO-OBSESSIVE RHETORIC, INDUSTRIAL MUSIC IS MADE BY PEO-ple, which means it has some kind of motivation behind it. The sounds that are satisfying for a musician to create are neither autonomous nor merely the sum of the artist's record collection or training; instead we can think about the music someone makes as an expression and a marker of who she or he is—or wants to be—at that moment. By definition, this identity stands in relief against and in response to the surrounding world, so in understanding a music in its moment of creation—as the next few chapters on the first wave of industrial music seek to do—three questions in particular arise.

First, *what are these musicians responding to?* Answering this will help us situate industrial music in time and space, and it will probably tell us as much about its makers' worldview as it will about their world. Second, *how are these musicians responding to that stimulus?* The "how" in this question refers to musical, political, and medial methods. Also, in a nonlinear way, this all can help us answer the first question, because an artistic response, when read carefully, can point back at the conditions that originally demanded it. Third, *what assumptions underlie and make possible these responses?* In the case of industrial music, the basic assumption is technological modernity, the notion that technology is a site of both hope and paranoia, at once able to ease our labor and to render us obsolete. Part I of this book addressed the third question: Burroughs and the Futurists together not only constellate a broad model of this assumed technological modernity but do so in a way that industrial music itself has privileged, reinforced, and explicitly referenced throughout its history.

Focusing then on these first two questions, the following few chapters look at some of the most important figures in the genre's geographical hotbeds during its formative years of the 1970s and early 1980s. We'll ask what qualities in the urban geography and cultural history of northern England, Berlin (with a brief excursion into West Germany), and San Francisco allowed industrial music to arise from these three spaces. Each contributed its own voice to the genre's cacophony, and prior to 1983 effectively no industrial band achieved lasting importance without first passing through either these scenes or the global cassette trading scene (more about that in a moment). Understanding industrial music in this way can serve as a more insightful tool for tracing its motivations, character, and nuances than the boilerplate question of who "influenced" whom—surely the most tired of rock journalism clichés.

With a nod to the late Adam Krims, author of the exceptional book *Music and Urban Geography*, by looking at these spaces and the foundational industrial scenes that passed through them, we can see how early industrialists charted "a range of urban representations" that by extension can tell us a lot about industrial music's literal "outlook" on the world.[1]

Finally, as mentioned, in addition to the musical geography of the era, in the last chapter of Part II we'll look at how a vast network of musicians outside these cities managed to use technology to lessen the distance between them in building a global, egalitarian music scene with cassette tapes and zines. We'll also highlight how this technology of placeless virtuality eventually left as strong an imprint on industrial music's sound and popularization as any cityscape.

# 4.
# Northern England

## 1. Progress in Hell

Northern England was both the center of the European industrial revolution and the birthplace of industrial music. From the early nineteenth century, coal and steel works fueled the economies of cities like Manchester and Sheffield and shaped their culture and urban aesthetics. By 1970, the region's continuous mandate of progress had paved roads and erected buildings that told 150 years of industrial history in their ugly, collisive urban planning—ever new growth amidst the expanding junkyard of old progress. In the BBC documentary *Synth Britannia*, the narrator declares that "Victorian slums had been torn down and replaced by ultramodern concrete highrises," but the images on the screen show more brick ruins than clean futurescapes, ceaselessly flashing dystopian skylines of colorless smoke.[1] Chris Watson of the Sheffield band Cabaret Voltaire recalls in the late 1960s "being taken on school trips round the steelworks . . . just seeing it as a vision of hell, you know, never ever wanting to do that."[2] This outdated hell smoldered in spite of the city's supposed growth and improvement; after all, Sheffield had significantly enlarged its administrative territory in 1967, and a year later the M1 motorway opened easy passage to London 170 miles south, and wasn't that progress?

Institutional modernization neither erased northern England's nineteenth-century combination of working-class pride and disenfranchisement nor offered many genuinely new possibilities within culture and labor, the Open University notwithstanding. In literature and the arts, it was a long-acknowledged truism that any municipal attempt at utopia would result in totalitarianism. The theme dates back to Yevgeny Zamyatin's 1924 post–October Revolution novel *We*, Fritz Lang's 1927 film *Metropolis*, George Orwell's postfascist *Nineteen Eighty-Four* of 1949, and the art of George Tooker, whose 1950 *The Subway* illustrated urban technology's underbelly of sadness, paranoia, and disconnect. During industrial music's first years, the wider trope would hit fever pitch with J. G. Ballard's 1975 novel *High Rise*, David Cronenberg's film of the same year *Shivers* (also titled *They Came from Within*), and George Romero's 1978 zombies-in-the-mall think piece *Dawn of the Dead*.

In intellectual and artistic circles of the late 1970s, it was almost universally understood that industrialization was artistically and personally limiting. In 1977, French economist Jacques Attali wrote a book called *Noise: The Political Economy of Music*, which is arguably the most influential piece of Marxist musicology of the last fifty years; in it, he argues convincingly that even though industrialization and capitalism originally gave rise to the middle classes who enabled musicians to support themselves, the musicians ultimately became commoditized, and through repetition—both structurally in their music and in the mass industrial reproduction of their recordings—their art lost its meaning and instead began to reinscribe corporate power.

Young artists in 1970s northern England didn't need science fiction or academic theory to feel the weight of institutional power and cyclicity. Musician Martyn Ware of the Human League and Heaven 17 frames it in terms that are both industrial and spatial: "It really forced you into a choice whether you were gonna accept being a small cog in a relatively small wheel or whether you were gonna try and burst out of there."[3] It's worth asking here not just how Ware and other musicians burst out but how they even recognized that doing so was a possibility.

Writing of industrial music, noise scholar Paul Hegarty asserts, "Modern, technologized industrial society controls our minds, acting as a limiter on expression and attainment of potential."[4] The trouble with mind control, of course, is that the controlled are unaware of it. One function of industrial music is that it seeks through caricature and cut-up to correct this by exposing the face and the methods of this institutional control. Taking a cue from Burroughs, some think this reframing is a metaphysical act; Genesis P-Orridge writes, "No matter how short, or apparently unrecognizable a 'sample' might be in linear time perception, I believe it must, inevitably, contain within it (and [make] accessible through it), the sum total of absolutely everything its original context represented, communicated, or touched in any way."[5] Similarly, the Hafler Trio writes, "A well-made sound recording of a place (or a person or a thing), nevertheless, contains a fragment of the 'soul' of that place (person or thing)."[6] This approach suggests that when an artifact of social control is cut up, its source is magically disrupted. A less supernatural explanation, however, is that in sampling and cutting up, the disruption of time brings the voice of control to the fore while shedding its content. In this way, it can serve as an all-points bulletin to alert listeners to the insidiousness of its source.

If the likes of Cabaret Voltaire and Throbbing Gristle experienced the surrounding signs of northern England's industrialization as limiting, then we shouldn't merely hear their music's burnt-out soundscape as just a vague reflection of the city, assuming that somehow geography "shapes" music. Instead, we can understand the industrialness of their music as a specific reaction against the perceived control, as an attempt to disarm it by postering its sonic mugshot onto freely traded cassette tapes and through club PA systems. That these bands came from industrial cities also makes sense, as they were closest to the real signs of industrialization, authoritarian control, and their negative effects. Not only were the old steel mills hellish and the new highrises faceless, but together they contributed to a lurking cultural and financial depression—one that the government attempted to answer with ubiquitous offices that arose to employ a generation of laid-off workers and despondent students. The government's presence on every street was the up-close reality to which English industrial music responded.

## 2. The Original Sound of Sheffield

In considering industrial music within industrial geography, let's forgo the conventional wisdom of beginning the narrative with Throbbing Gristle—for whom Hull and London were as much a base as Manchester—and instead look to the city of Sheffield and its progeny Cabaret Voltaire and Clock DVA.

Cabaret Voltaire—and indeed Sheffield's modern pop legacy—starts with Chris Watson, born 1948. Introverted and gifted in all matters technical, Watson had come to idolize Brian Eno, a philosopher king of tech geekery and the keyboardist for Roxy Music, whose concerts Watson had twice attended as a student. Watson experimented for two years with tape decks in a loft at his parents' house in the suburb of Totley with the goal of "making music without musical instruments," and by the time he met fellow Eno devotee Richard Kirk in 1973, he had already begun building oscillators from mail-order kits.[7] Watson's work as a telephone engineer helped pay for this do-it-yourself electronics habit. Watson and Kirk together began dedicatedly creating and mixing weird noises, initially just exploring technology and sound aesthetically, but eventually they confirmed a mutual desire to create something more out of the clatter. Kirk recalls, "Any kind of noise looped up would do the job more or less. And then we'd perhaps record some percussion, slow it down or speed it up to make it sound a bit disturbing or whatever, a bit different," to which Watson adds, "The loops would become songs. We would produce these tape collages, oscillator sounds, found sounds."[8] Kirk played a cheap clarinet and eventually took up guitar "because we didn't want to be completely arty and obscure."[9] In late 1973, they recruited singer and sometime bassist Stephen Mallinder, a buddy from Kirk's days as a troublemaking fourteen-year-old skinhead in the late 1960s.

Cabaret Voltaire, who took their name and much of their inspiration from Dada and surrealism, presented themselves as aloof and foreign, so much that *NME* journalist Andy Gill wrote in 1978 that "Cabaret Voltaire could have been spawned in any city, and quite probably in a non-urban area, too. The geographical locus counts for little in the nexus of possibilities which brought about Cabaret Voltaire."[10] But even though experimental sound art is itself not an exclusively Sheffieldian notion, Gill mistakes the high-concept Dada behind Cabaret Voltaire's name for the preconditions of their music. It's telling that Mallinder was recruited because, according to Kirk, "Mal was the only person we knew who didn't have a Yorkshire accent and we thought, 'Oh we might as well get him to do some of the vocal stuff.'"[11] Similarly, faced with the lack of recording studios and electronic equipment commercially available in Sheffield, they stepped outside the typical channels of rock self-development and formed an uneasy alliance with Sheffield University's music department. The faculty couldn't tell if the youngsters were academics in training or just punks, but they nevertheless allowed the trio to use its small electronic studio, which included an EMS VCS3 synthesizer. These moves weren't taken with indifference to Sheffield, but *in spite of* Sheffield. Just as Burroughs tells the story of shutting down an unfriendly restaurant by going into the building and playing back a previously taped recording of its spatial ambience, Cabaret Voltaire's early sampling and playback is an urban tour of provocation. Watson explains, "We'd go round to people's houses on Friday and Saturday evenings with a couple of portable tape recorders and listen to the tape loops. Sometimes we'd set up in pubs or in doorways, even public toilets. We'd go to places like the Buccaneer, Wapentake and pubs on West Street."[12] Sheffield music historian Martin Lilleker reports that the band drove around town blasting Sheffield's own sounds from speakers mounted on top of a friend's van. They would jump out of cars to play high-volume tape loops at the city's unsuspecting pedestrians, interested not just in the sounds but also "in seeing what kind of reaction we'd get. It attracted attention," says Watson.[13] The disruption at the core of Cabaret Voltaire's musical prankishness relied on the assumption that Sheffield needed a shakeup.

Even if Cabaret Voltaire could have come from somewhere else, Sheffield could not have become an electronic music Mecca without them. By 1982, Sheffield bands accounted for 5 percent of the market share of UK singles, though the city's population made up only 1 percent of the nation.[14] Considering this disproportionate chart representation alongside the admiration, affection, and wonder that the city's younger electronic acts felt toward Cabaret Voltaire, one understands that the title of their 2002 best-of, *The Original Sound of Sheffield*

'78/'82, is no exaggeration. Instead, it hints at a double meaning: Was Cabaret Voltaire's music merely the original instance of a style that came to be synonymous with Sheffield, or did they tap into and amplify an essential sonic specter of the city—its *original sound*?

Their practical influence on the other musicians of the city is clear in the performing and recording opportunities they offered. In 1977, using Watson's money, Cabaret Voltaire set up their own recording studio on Portobello Street on the second floor of a development called the Western Works, which had over time served as a cutlery plant, a World War II air raid shelter, and the meeting space for the Sheffield Federation of Young Socialists. In this repurposed old building, they oversaw some of the earliest recordings by Clock DVA, the Human League, 2.3, Hula, and New Order. Kirk told one urban historian, "Western Works [was] like Andy Warhol's Factory on a fifty pence budget."[15] Indeed it was a social space, but as Simon Reynolds writes of it, "You could record-it-yourself and spend as much time fine-tuning as you liked."[16]

This idea is absolutely essential to the sound of Cabaret Voltaire. Their days of rehearsing in the Watson family's attic and their early anarchic borrowing of the University of Sheffield's electronic lab had guided the band to a belief in the importance of sonic detail. Watson recalls the fine-tuning allowed by owning a studio made their work "more like composition than songs," adding, "We were interested in the sounds themselves."[17] In this respect, Cabaret Voltaire established a blueprint for industrial music: throughout all eras of the genre, the home studio is the experimental compositional space. In a city more affluent than Sheffield, owning a studio would have been not only unaffordable for the band but effectively redundant, given the availability of rental establishments elsewhere.

On first glance, it can seem a little tough to reconcile the trio's high-minded, almost scientific approach to sound experimentation with their punkish public antics and raucous live performances; for example, their first concert in May 1975 ended in a fistfight with the audience that sent Mallinder to the hospital. But the honing they did in the studio served as the groundwork for the sounds that, to Cabaret Voltaire's ears, managed to bypass the tired cultural pathways of music's recent past—something that not even punk could do in its amped-up reboot of the 1950s teddy boy scene. This meant that a lot of audiences heard the band's sounds devoid of associative baggage, and thus with a certain visceral immediacy. Mallinder explains, "We try to be very spontaneous, because that's the way people listen to music. We try to be as immediate as possible, and not just try out some all engrossing philosophy and concept."[18] This possibility appealed especially to young Sheffielders wanting to shake free of not just the enveloping specter of nineteenth-century industrialism but their parents' belief—hardened by World War II—that England should be grateful for its institutions of labor, finance, and patriotism, even as they crumbled in plain view.

And so Cabaret Voltaire's first major success was the bratty June 1979 single "Nag Nag Nag," of which biographer Mick Fish writes, "A perfect post-punk ball of fuzz, it summed up a kind of nihilistic desperation. After all who hadn't turned round to their boss, their teacher, their mother at some time or another and thought, 'nag, nag, nag.'"[19] It wasn't the band's first release; they'd made some tapes that Kirk had circulated in mail art communities, and Throbbing Gristle had wanted to sign them to Industrial Records but couldn't afford to as they'd just released their own *The Second Annual Report* in 1977. Instead, on Throbbing Gristle's recommendation, Cabaret Voltaire signed with Rough Trade in early 1978. There'd been an offer from Manchester-based Factory Records too, but Rough Trade bought the trio a four-track Revox tape machine (in lieu of an advance), which was enough to win them over. They released *Extended Play*, a four-song set featuring live favorite "Do the Mussolini (Headkick!)"—not to be confused with the later, greater "Der Mussolini" by Deutsch-Amerikanische Freundschaft—but that debut release essentially served to feed the fans already made hungry by Cabaret Voltaire's reputation as an audacious live act. "Nag Nag Nag" changed the game despite its poor reviews and earned the band new devotees by selling ten thousand copies, including plenty in France and Belgium. Says Mallinder, "People wanted us to do a disco version. People called for it live. Maybe it was quite a significant record for other people; maybe we just hit a nerve, but for us it was just another track."[20]

Part of the single's nagging appeal was the constant 1300-Hz sizzle in its electronic timbres that sounds more like a dental suction tool than a synth or guitar. It plays an intimate, plasticky horror atop the Selmer drum machine's hokey wooden beat. Mallinder's voice is run through heavy distortion, which decentralizes his humanness both through its mechanized timbre and its near-total negation of verbal comprehensibility; he is no longer a singer in a band, not merely an implicitly radical megaphone barker, but part of an aggravation machine, turned equally on its audience and itself.

A few months later, the band's full-length debut *Mix-Up* came out on Rough Trade, reaching number twelve on the UK indie charts. The same grating sound palette pervaded songs such as "No Escape" and "On Every Other Street," but the band was clearly moving toward something moodier and more serious than the petulance of "Nag Nag Nag." Invoking the I-word, *Sounds* magazine called it "muddy, grey, industrial swamp music."[21]

Outfitting their Western Works studio more elaborately with each paycheck from Rough Trade, Cabaret Voltaire's members were dedicated and efficient tinkerers. Their next releases attracted progressively wider listenership: 1980's *The Voice of America* reached number three on the indie charts, even as its title track samples a 1966 recording of a Memphis law enforcement deputy instructing his troops before a Beatles concert, "We will not allow any dancing, running up and down the aisle. Is that clear with everybody?" The tactics they'd applied to Sheffield's local banality—identifying and ridiculing the inscribed social order with its own sonic output played back—were starting to go global, inspired by their November 1979 tour of America. One last full-length with Rough Trade in 1981, *Red Mecca*, took on the escalating conflict between Islam and the west, sleekly smearing washes of noise over funky rhythms. Recorded again at Western Works, the album was an indie number one, and despite a grand conceptual stage it still sounds relentlessly rooted in a sense of locality. The songs "Sly Doubt" and "Landslide" treat drum tracks with an ultrafast echo effect that sonically places them in cramped, hard-walled spaces: a city. "Spread the Virus" cuts in the sound of screeching car tires amid Kirk's jazzy woodwind bleats. The delirious expansion and compression of sonic space and the juxtaposition of the city's quotidian bustle with Islam's ancient transcendent otherness constituted "the most complete and chilling musical representation of Eighties' Britain yet produced," according to Andy Gill in the *NME*.[22]

Within months of the album's release, Watson—the most technical and conceptually experimental of the group—left the band to focus on a career in sound recording for media. Stevo Pearce (more about him in a few chapters) signed the remaining duo to his Some Bizzare label and leveraged a licensing deal with Virgin. The £50,000 advance that Kirk and Mallinder landed for their album *The Crackdown* would eventually help them upgrade their own studio, but the deal was in exchange for recording the LP in London and, as Kirk recalls, "maybe put[ting] the vocals a little higher in the mix and not processed so you can hear them."[23] The band's albums on Some Bizzare would be their best sellers, but many have commented that even as Cabaret Voltaire's star rose, the man-machine dynamic so vital to their sound and so prototypical to later industrial music faded from their records. Listening to the single version of "Just Fascination"—remixed by KC and the Sunshine Band's producer John Luongo—one hears the group amid new surroundings. Mallinder now lived permanently in London (though he still kept a residence up north), and the nightclub as a physical space increasingly reverberated in the band's ethos. As the industrial specter of the urban receded in the duo's output, it became clear that any Sheffield their music responded to was a different city.

## 3. Meatwhistle and Clock DVA

A belief that industrial music widely shares with several radical twentieth-century practices of art, spirituality, and academic theory is that reality itself is no more than a tacit, perceptual consensus, and as such it can duly be shaped by perception, making art a two-way street: it changes the world by reflecting alternative perceptions of it. This tenet of perceptual reality is most famously articulated in the maxim "Nothing Is True; Everything Is Permitted," attributed by Burroughs to the eleventh-century cult leader Hassan-I Sabbah. Accordingly, Cabaret Voltaire's early music not only perceived and responded to Sheffield's reality but clearly shaped it too. In light of this, let's back up a few years again to see some other important musical reactions both to the industrial condition of Sheffield and to its first electronic sons, Cabaret Voltaire.

As early as 1975, Sheffield's plugged-in young musicians saw Cabaret Voltaire as a formidable artistic and social part of their own surroundings; to the brooding, raincoat-clad teenagers at haunts like the Beehive, Watson in particular was understood to be an eccentric genius of sorts. Never aloof among the city's nonconformists, the band readily gave out favors, eventually recording and mentoring younger acts. As Martyn Ware recalls, "Cabaret Voltaire were very generous people in terms of their time and their encouragement for other people around. They were almost like the godfathers of that scene at that time. In fact they were. They encouraged creativity in everybody around them."[24] Kirk is brasher about the situation: "Basically, we were the fucking coolest people in Sheffield."[25]

Despite its proximity to Leeds and Manchester, Sheffield was in many ways an isolated city, a fact that both situationally highlighted Cabaret Voltaire's coolness and more or less necessitated their generosity. From a musical standpoint, two municipal factors had set the city on a unique course. First, as Andy Gill explained in 1979, "Unlike any other city of comparable size Sheffield lacks the basic machinery for indigenous musical growth."[26] For much of the 1970s, there were no high-tech studios, and the only real gig in town was playing northern soul at working men's clubs. This condition effectively isolated the city's musicians—hence the need for establishing Western Works and offering friendly access to it.

Second, as a municipal study in *Geoforum* states, the Sheffield City Council was beginning "to look to cultural and media industries as a new growth sector," hoping to attract investors in the wake of industrial business going south.[27] In their openness to new creative endeavors, they'd made a strange and fortuitous move in February 1973 by approving a proposal by actor Chris Wilkinson and his wife Veronica to create Meatwhistle, a theater and arts space for the city's youth. The anarchic, post-hippy project attracted a regular crowd of about forty offbeat teenagers, who between 1973 and 1977 improvised with art, promiscuously formed and dissolved impromptu bands, abused cameras (purchased by the city), enjoyed activities with titles like "Spray-On Theatre" and "Twinkie Hour," and occasionally put on actual plays. Meatwhistle was a creative breeding ground and an adolescent reprieve from adult supervision; as such, its artistic output skewed toward gross-out aesthetics and us-versus-the-world conspiracy theories.

Taken together, the city's artistic isolation and these teenagers' cross-breeding and mutation seems a recipe for evolution. Indeed, Meatwhistle churned out bands that eventually became the Human League, ABC, and most importantly for this book Clock DVA, all of whom made music in awe of and under the tutelage of Cabaret Voltaire. One could argue that without Meatwhistle and the scene it fermented, Cabaret Voltaire may well have lacked the local support and momentum to succeed (though the University of Sheffield's punkish student group the Now Society also boosted the band).

Among the Meatwhistle ensembles that managed to last longer than a single rehearsal, a few gathered a local following and a legacy. Musical Vomit, for example, is cited by a handful of writers as having prefigured punk's flaunting of ineptitude and crassness; Poly Styrene of X-Ray Spex saw them play in 1974 and later called them "the very first punk group in Britain."[28] More important was the boldly named band the Future, whose lead singer, Adi Newton, would go on to found Clock DVA. Primarily active in 1977, the Future was an experimental electronic act whose presentation and concept was better defined than its music, which was mostly an echoey field of analogue zips and thumps (courtesy of Ian Marsh and Martyn Ware), occasionally punctuated by Newton's sneering vocal commentary. A song such as "Pulse Lovers" compels with its mantralike repetition, and this earned the band some real interest from record companies: on two-day trip to London in 1977, the Future met with nine labels, and both Island and Virgin showed some interest, but ultimately the verdict was that more real songs were needed. Not long after that, the band kicked Newton out over money, musical taste (he wanted a broader sonic palette, but without pop influence), and Ware's perception that Newton was mercurial and paranoid; a press release later declared Newton was "deleted due to malfunction."[29] Ware and Marsh then teamed up with Meatwhistler Philip Oakey to create the Human League, who flirted distantly with industrial aesthetics on such early recordings as "Almost Medieval," "Being Boiled," and "The Black Hit of Space" before becoming pop stars a few years later with the mega-hit "Don't You Want Me."

Newton was born Gary Coates but had been dubbed Adi—short for Adolph—by his friend Glenn Gregory (who himself later became the singer of synthpop act Heaven 17). Like Cabaret Voltaire's Kirk and Mallinder, Newton had been a very young skinhead in the early 1970s before that identity assumed racist connotations. Naturally attracted to the esoteric, Newton's worldview and aesthetics blended vintage European surrealism with a tough-guy aesthetic derived from his fondness for the Marlon Brando motorcycle gang movie *The Wild One*. He and most members of the Sheffield scene had initially latched onto electronic music with the Moog-driven score to *A Clockwork Orange* by Wendy (then Walter) Carlos. Beyond its striking new sound, the electronic score was cinematically combined with a cityscape where the ultramodern barely hid a postindustrial decay. To a young English audience, the film—set in England—all but declares in its totalitarian voice that this will be the music of the future.

An art student, Newton explored deeper, though: "My interests came from people like İlhan Mimaroğlu, John Cage, and so on"—records that he was able to acquire from Rare and Racy, a local oddball store.[30] But beyond the academic work of early electronic music and beyond punk's aggressive yet ultimately conservative musical language, Newton "wanted something more intense, paranoid and totally out of control. Something that couldn't be marketed but could still exist. A sort of totalitarian underground music."[31] When he and his friend Stephen James "Judd" Turner launched Clock DVA, it was "just so screwed up—junk and violence and tape recorders, big kicks. Sex and magic in an industrial setting, the whole incongruity was brilliant."[32] Joining Newton and Turner was a semirotating cast of musicians on guitar, saxophone, and drums; over the years, at least seventeen members have passed through the band, many of whom have been revisionistically excised from the official history.

Early on, Clock DVA recorded and locally distributed a series of homemade tapes, which were often based around long hisses of white noise, distorted bass guitar, and a barely audible rhythm loop. Newton and Judd were insistent that they were on to something, but some of their bandmates grew frustrated with the inability to tell one "song" from another—their first recordings from early 1978 were indeed somewhat anonymous, collectively referred to as "six therapeutic tape loops."[33] The band's first live concert in July 1978, opening for the Human League, was reviled in the local press and by all accounts was made up of little more than the band's wandering improvisations and some arbitrarily constructed tape loops almost completely drowned out by Newton's vocals, which had been run through a delay unit that bounced his words back in endless repetition until the noise was incomprehensible gibberish.

Shortly after, however, their studio work began taking on a distinctly jazz-inflected atmosphere, with tracks such as 1978's "Alien Tapes" using the pitch bending of a variable speed tape machine to sound something like trumpet falls, while Turner's overmodulated bass verges on the funky, even in the absence of a drum track. A sample reminiscent of a foghorn suggests a low, industrial meditation on John Coltrane. Through a series of concerts in 1978 and into 1979, they turned down the reverb and upped the anger: "DVA believe that the audience have played the role of the passive observer for too long and so we are attempting to change that situation both musically and visually. Sometimes I attack the audience. And I usually swear at them," Newton boasted at the time.[34] The musical channeling of this energy was earning them a reputation for "hardly enjoyable music, but . . . strict, disciplined, haunting, compelling stuff, of the Dadaist vision," as Chris Westwood wrote in *ZigZag* magazine's November 1978 issue.[35] Their gear-smashing tendencies seemed at odds with the strangely static nature of the sound—there was no drummer in the band until the summer of 1979—and the music bore little resemblance to punk, which never had much of a foothold in Sheffield to begin with.

Some of their antics were directly in response to their physical surroundings: an August 1978 gig at the Penthouse had a particularly uninterested audience and an uncooperative soundman and bouncers, so the band smashed the fluorescent lights of the club into shards—the audience loved it. Newton explains:

> We wanted to try to open things up because there were a lot of restrictions at that time. The club owners, the promoters were very cautious about what they promote or they were concerned about new music or groups or how they could exploit it in a way, so in many ways we had to take control ourselves.[36]

Rather than respect the system of Sheffield's conservative and isolated club scene, they confronted it.

> There was a kind of independence of operation, a kind of outsiderness almost, in that we would do things ourselves. We would try and do everything ourselves. We'd try and organize concerts, we'd do the posters, we'd do the films. . . . It was very difficult for us to find places to play live.[37]

Clock DVA's habit of looking in vain for gigs and then attempting to incite a riot once finally given a show seems paradoxical, but it mirrors their simultaneous entrapment within and rage against Sheffield. It also may have reflected the personalities involved, agitated by other urban realities including heavy drug use. There are stories about Turner in particular stealing from druggists, lying about his name to landlords and police to avoid arrest, and overdosing repeatedly in the spring of 1979. Newton recalls, "The way we were living seems an idiotic, fucked-up existence. But at the time it made sense. It was the only sense. But without those foundations DVA wouldn't mean anything."[38]

Interestingly, as their music became more beat-driven (due to the addition of drummer Roger Quail in July 1979), Clock DVA's shows grew less violent and more traditionally musical and arty. Newton began dressing like a priest onstage, and those early hints of jazz were more fully realized with the addition of saxophonist Charlie Collins, whose echo-soaked squeals suggest a nighttime city sadness on songs such as "Non," summoning New York through English smog. On 1979's "Brigade," recorded for a compilation of local Sheffield acts, the band sounds practically like a polished pop group, mixing dancepunk and psychedelic guitar solos. Clock DVA's focus edged away from the electronic roots of the Future and indeed away from what the term *industrial* conjures today, but even as this happened, their critical and popular star was rising. Sheffield zine *NMX* wrote:

> They've changed from being one of the more unfashionable and even despised bands around to being the darlings of everyone who claims any connection with Sheffield music, sold out gigs at the Blitz and everyone suddenly saying they've always been into the Clocks. Their sound has gone through a complete transformation, from League-ish simplicity through dark, barely rhythmic cacophony to the present blend of noise and melody, an overpowering mix of guitar and sax over a pounding beat. . . .[39]

Newton and Turner were branching out in other ways too. They played London in the summer of 1979 and had made contact with Throbbing Gristle, whose Industrial Records was starting to release tapes by acts they deemed worthy. "I wrote to [Genesis P-Orridge] because I liked what they were doing . . . this idea of the industrial and the magic all these ideas. I wanted to try to get into one piece and I devised a long track called, 'Genitals & Genosis' which was about all those kind of elements."[40] While the "Genitals & Genosis" recordings wouldn't see daylight until 2012, Industrial Records did release the first full-length tape for Clock DVA, *White Souls in Black Suits*, in December 1980. They had improvised for fifteen hours into a mobile recorder and then mixed and compiled the best cuts at Cabaret Voltaire's Western Works, with Chris Watson even contributing to one track.

Before that album even came out, Clock DVA's connection to Throbbing Gristle had already led to a higher-budget deal with Rod Pearce, whose Fetish Records was pressing and distributing vinyl for Industrial Records and whose roster would soon include other early industrial acts like 23 Skidoo and Z'EV.

In September 1980, Clock DVA used their advance from Pearce to go to Jacobs Farm, a twenty-four-track studio in Surrey, where they recorded a batch of songs they'd been honing live. Co-produced by Ken Thomas and much less improvised than *White Souls in Black Suits*, the resultant album *Thirst* was spacious and clattering, rather than claustrophobically squeezed onto two-track tape. Newton's voice is at times even melodic, following Collins's saxophone over riffs on tracks such as the distinctively Sheffieldian "North Loop."

*Thirst*'s original liner notes feature a short piece by Genesis P-Orridge called "The Lion in a Cage," a title that evokes Clock DVA's combination of urban rage and imprisonment. The essay frames this sort of music as speaking a hidden, private truth from within a surrounding, public oppression, offering "rituals collective yet private, performed in public but invisible. White souls stripped bare to reveal bleeding yet hopeful sadness. The rites of youth. Our alchemical human heritage, encased like a cadaver in a black suit."[41] Here the public sphere precludes truth, expression, and yes, the soul: consider that in Newton's own liner notes to *White Souls in Black Suits*, he writes, "We have adopted chance, the voice of the unconscious—the soul, if you like—as a protest against the rigidity of straight line thinking."[42] The music responds not only to the particulars of Sheffield but to the enforced border between private and public that cultural hegemonies, codes of behavior, and authority bodies depend on. It is a music of place.

Released in early 1981, *Thirst* sold a hundred thousand copies, a number that amazed all involved.[43] For a moment, Newton was bigger than Cabaret Voltaire, bigger than the Human League—acts who'd both mentored and mocked him alike. *Sounds* magazine gushed:

> *Thirst* is the best album I have heard since [the Fall's] *Dragnet* or [Joy Division's] *Unknown Pleasures*. . . . [It] shares with those albums a provincial, coming from nowhere, arrogance. Clock DVA come from Sheffield. This is a lucky break!!! If they'd have come from London they would be on CBS or 4AD and *Thirst* would have sounded like fourth division [Talking Heads'] *Fear of Music*.[44]

But Clock DVA didn't come from London, and probably couldn't have. This music was necessarily shaped by the Hells Angels that Newton buddied up with, the frustration with venues and audiences that led to his violence against them, the invaluable tutelage of Cabaret Voltaire, and—going back to the beginning—the municipal Meatwhistle project whose openness birthed the Future and a creative, questioning youth culture. And finally, the city's drug culture had one more adjustment to make to the group. On May 11, 1981, Newton and Turner fired their bandmates, with replacements already waiting in the wings, but a few months after that, Newton fired Turner, too. Depressed, Judd Turner died of a heroin overdose in August. Sheffield musician Martin Fry (of ABC) recalls, "It was terrible, crap drugs and no money. When I saw the film *Trainspotting* I thought this is Judd. It very much reminded me of the late Seventies in Sheffield. It taught me a fundamental lesson. He was only 22 or whatever when he died."[45]

Clock DVA went on to sign with Polydor in 1982 after six months of negotiations. The next year they released *Advantage*, whose crisp production left critics cold and whose sales—far below *Thirst*'s numbers—left the new record label underwhelmed. Adi Newton quit his own band while on tour in France in 1983, effectively ending the project.

Cabaret Voltaire and Clock DVA both had careers beyond this point; Newton rebooted his band with a decidedly updated "industrial" sound in the late 1980s. Similarly, there were other bands in Sheffield who made a name in the industrial scene: In the Nursery would release records through WaxTrax! a few years down the road, Hula used percussion and live films to simulate sensory overload, Prior To Intercourse was a BDSM-themed performance group, the Anti-Group was a lower-profile but higher-concept project of Adi Newton's, and Chris Watson later helped create the Hafler Trio. In the dialogue between geography and art, however, the particular time and place of Sheffield in the 1970s and early 1980s produced an urban experience that crucially imprinted and solidified a conceptual, practical, and musical set of values onto its creative citizens—a set of values that industrial music unmistakably assimilated into its story.

## 4. Throbbing Gristle

First, some basics.

Throbbing Gristle is by essentially every account the first industrial band, their roots predating even Cabaret Voltaire's early tape experiments. Over the summer of 1975, the group's future members began improvising informally with traditional rock instruments, electronic gear, and tape, recording long jams of mostly beatless sounds and wordless textures, which they would later edit and treat as source material for yet further recordings. All this was happening in a basement studio called the Death Factory on Martello Street near central London, a fact geographically incongruous within a chapter on northern England—though this detail will be addressed soon enough. (A titillating *aper-*

*itif*: members Cosey Fanni Tutti and Genesis P-Orridge fled northern England for London in 1973 for fear of being arrested in gang-related roundups.)

Tutti and P-Orridge, along with members Chris Carter and Peter "Sleazy" Christopherson, declared Throbbing Gristle's official inception on September 3, 1975. It's a peculiar and stilted thing to formalize the launch of a rock band, especially one with months of jamming already on tape. But Throbbing Gristle's inorganicism and self-importance were among its strongest assets. Their talent for high-concept thinking gave rise to a calculated, articulated, and well-documented ideology. They designed and carried out a formidable and unified public presentation. Through hard-earned connections in governmental arts councils, the entertainment business, and post-hippie subculture, Throbbing Gristle's members organized a financial support system that allowed them shortly after their official formation to launch the label Industrial Records. Initially a tape-only endeavor, Industrial Records eventually grew into a prestigious vanity imprint that gave releases to like-minded industrialists such as SPK, Clock DVA, Cabaret Voltaire, Monte Cazazza, and Burroughs himself.

In spite of the foursome's collective intelligence and savvy, they purposefully selected instruments and musical constraints that would highlight their individual ineptitude. When punk and other genres flaunt performers' incompetence, the intent is usually to convey an underclass cultural authenticity. For Throbbing Gristle, however, incompetence wasn't just a way to resist the constraints of supposed correctness; it was a means of achieving an unpremeditated encounter between performer and music—an immediacy that the band imbued with psychic qualities unrelated to an external audience.

Throbbing Gristle's work is conceptual and process-oriented, just as Chapter 2 suggested with its analyses of "Still Walking" and "Final Muzak." For this reason, the band is less often evaluated on the strength of its recordings than on the music's conceptual groundwork and execution. Throbbing Gristle's sound ranges from gray droning on 1977's *The Second Annual Report* to eerily tongue-in-cheek mutant disco on 1979's *20 Jazz Funk Greats*, but to the untrained ear it's all intensely difficult listening. A given Throbbing Gristle record does little to prepare listeners for the next, as the band reveled in confounding expectations. The 1978 single "United" is an engaging, ABBA-influenced synthpop excursion—an attempt at a soccer anthem, in fact—but as a promotional teaser for the arrhythmic, overmodulated panic of *The Second Annual Report* and its tracks such as "Maggot Death" (given wider release that same year on Fetish Records), "United" is just plain false advertising.

Meaningful understanding of industrial music history means grasping Throbbing Gristle as more than their music, more than compositional process and artistic antagonism. Other acts, even some before Throbbing Gristle, had those attributes. Instead, the band's significance and impact is better understood in light of its members' backstories, both in the years immediately prior to 1975 (which we'll discuss presently) and in a broader, more personally formative sense (which we'll address after that).

At the quartet's formation, each member was already an adept veteran of the arts. Carter had played bass in a rock band in the late 1960s, but his real expertise lay in electronics: as a teenager, he started a rock show lighting business where, by designing, controlling, and automating light rigs, he furthered his tech enthusiasm. In the early 1970s, he was touring England with various bands as an engineer and a musician; he built and played his own synthesizers. He additionally had a background in photography and graphics. Christopherson was also gifted with graphic design and electronic know-how. The son of a Cambridge professor, he'd begun to work in 1974 as a designer and photographer with the Hipgnosis art group, of Pink Floyd album sleeve fame. Genesis P-Orridge (born Neil Andrew Megson) had drummed in psychedelic rock bands since the mid-1960s and by the decade's end was immersing himself in poetry and the art worlds of zine printing, Fluxus, and the mail art scene. After dropping out of Hull University in June 1969, P-Orridge joined an Islingston-based kinetic arts group called Transmedia Exploration, who combined improvisatory theater, anarchic reimaginings of circus arts, and the event-based works of the Vienna Aktionists but didn't stay long. Returning back north to Hull and wanting to launch a more ambitious and otherworldly endeavor, P-Orridge and his friend John Shapeero conceptualized a new project in the autumn of 1969 under the mysterious title COUM Transmissions, a phrase that had spontaneously come to P-Orridge in a spiritual revelation of the sort to which his psychic medium grandmother had taught him to be open. In the final weeks of that year, P-Orridge met the quick-witted Christine Carol Newby, an eighteen-year-old anarchist hippie and Hull native, whom he dubbed Cosmosis. A natural social leader and a quick learner in art and music, she nearly immediately involved herself with both P-Orridge and, after first helping with some behind-the-scenes work, eventually joined COUM. With help from artist Robin Klassnik (who would also secure the Death Factory home base for Throbbing Gristle), Cosmosis took on the name Cosey Fanni Tutti. Though Carter is often cast as the technical brain behind Throbbing Gristle and Christopherson as the emotional (if pervy) heart, Tutti and P-Orridge were essentially the face and the voice of both COUM Transmissions and Throbbing Gristle.

In its first years, COUM developed from a chiefly musical and theatrical ensemble to one concerned with public "happenings" and clownish surrealism. They performed on college campuses, in nightclubs, and in public parks, unlicensed and sometimes unannounced. However, the group became progressively better networked within, and more aware of, the national arts scene and beyond, building up a fan base to boot. This growth was such that right as the collective was starting to land shows in galleries and receive both consistent arts council funding and broader media exposure, P-Orridge and Tutti, along with members with names like Foxtrot Echo and Fizzy Paet, became increasingly convinced that improvised dance and harmless rehashings of absurdism were ineffective, unoriginal, and unchallenging.

An important factor in this sense of revolutionary desperation was that by 1973 the hippie movement had fizzled, failing to deliver on its promise of radical change. In bitter fury both at the hippies and at their shared corporatist, traditionalist enemies, young idealists all over the west looked increasingly to extreme measures. For their part, COUM moved beyond the art world's politeness. They studied propaganda and began sloganeering with radical, pornographic postcards and manifestolike advertisements—a testing ground that later helped Throbbing Gristle hone a heartstopping pseudo-fascist visual vocabulary. Later in 1973, COUM angered police when they embarked on vandalism-themed projects, assisted by some friends in the Hells Angels (this is why P-Orridge and Tutti skipped town for London). Nudity and garbage soon became staples of live actions, and P-Orridge's mail art turned nasty as he began sending rotted meat through the post (in what he calls an undeclared gross-out contest with Monte Cazazza). Tutti began posing for pornographic magazines in late 1973. Despite, or more likely, because of the group's increasingly confrontational and audacious moves, they garnered ever more praise and attention, traveling and performing in Germany, France, and eventually the United States.

COUM's biggest moment came well after the launch of Throbbing Gristle. The October 1976 *Prostitution* exhibition at London's Institute for Contemporary Arts was intended as a critique of the body, capitalism, and pornography. The ensemble's new obsession with the body was unambiguously influenced by Christopherson—it's part of why he was called "Sleazy"—but *Prostitution* was most visibly Tutti's project, and her pornographic portraits in high-art frames were centrally featured (though kept in wooden boxes by law—viewers had to sign a waiver to see them). The showcase included other artists' work too, including four sculptures ("Tampax Romana") that P-Orridge made using bloody tampons. In person at the ICA, the exhibition was acknowledged as boundary-pushing, but the British press, whose central audience was decidedly not the ICA crowd, fixated on the shock of the exhibition, with more than one hundred published articles excoriating the alleged moral decrepitude of COUM Transmissions and the travesty that British taxpayers were supporting smut. Most famously, Tory MP Nicholas Fairbairn shrieked, "These people are the wreckers of civilisation."[46]

Taken as a directional step toward sexual critique and personal deprogramming, *Prostitution* served as preparation for the even more extreme performances that COUM brought to America a month later. Although band biographer Simon Ford parenthetically wonders at the truth of P-Orridge's account of their Los Angeles performance, the published script is, even in highly excerpted form, a radical exercise in revulsion:

> 6). Genesis takes another syringe of blood from his testicles and injects it back into his forearm. He does this repeatedly, also injecting a total of seven black eggs with his own blood. He is stood on a square of sharp black nails and ice.
> 7). Cosey opens thee lips of her cunt wide and pushes in her fingers, masturbating.
> 8). Genesis fills a spinal syringe with milk, another with blood. He takes each in turn and injects all their contents in turn up his anus. He pisses into a large glass. As he squeezes out thee last drop he farts and blood mingled with milk shoots out of his arse.
> 9). Cosey slithers through all thee liquid towards him, lapping it up, rubbing it into hereunto.
> 10). Genesis vomits trying to swallow a 10 inch steel nail.[47]

Give all that a moment to sink in, and in the meantime consider how this kind of extreme action functions politically. Shock here is the fallout of a metaphorical dérive: COUM wanders the territory of instinctual prurience, hoping to stumble upon some limit, to locate the unwritten, authoritarian laws of taste, decency, order, and humanity *by exceeding them*. Therefore, in searching for total freedom, they employ every excess, because they must identify and dismantle every law. Once laws are known, COUM and Throbbing Gristle détourn them, flipping them on their head, reducing a text's content to a cut-up's alleged representation of pure structure through nonsense. Some easy examples of this include Throbbing Gristle's military costumes in 1977 and their overwhelming attack on the audience in their song "Discipline."

Returning now to the graphic 1976 Los Angeles performance, consider how Cosey Fanni Tutti cites the importance of *honesty* in her work: "If I give off the genuine feeling . . . maybe people will receive that, assimilate and understand it and give meaning to the work in their own way. Then I'm happy, because I've given them something that is honest, my work is based on total honesty, people can run with that."[48] Although Tutti remains convinced of the baseline politi-

ASSIMILATE

cal program that Throbbing Gristle and industrial music developed, in the end she recognizes and values that her instinctual navigation of sonic and social territory ultimately says as much about her as it does about the territory. If the music provides no catharsis, then she's simply not interested. Tutti's performance seems extreme because it presumes that only outside of the hegemonically controlled territory of behavior can one find honesty—that mythical, uncontaminated condition beyond cultural mediation and separate from class-based "authenticity."

P-Orridge is much the same way, explaining in 1978 that performances like the one in Los Angeles are "a means of deconditioning myself psychologically. I believe all bodily and all erotic functions of the human being, both male and female, are both natural and interesting. I hate shame."[49] He clarifies, "I get NO masochistic pleasure from my risks, but I do get the satisfaction of facing up to my fears and relinquishing inherited, and to me false, taboos and neuroses in a way that offers a system of revelation and education to a percentage of bystanders."[50] By admitting that only "a percentage of bystanders" would grab hold of this music, P-Orridge implicitly delimits the band's public efforts. In a 1979 letter, he explains,

if TG is trying to do anything specific, it's trying to de-condition people's er responses, demystify creative, musical activity and life too, and most of all it's er trying to make people think for themselves, decide for themselves and direct their own lives by their own values and experiences, by experience learned BY THEM from life and not second hand, unproven experiences handed down by education and religion and dogma politics.[51]

The people to whom P-Orridge refers, however, were nearly always in reality already a few steps down the path of like-mindedness, having discovered the band through galleries and the tape scene, and usually not at rock clubs. Dismissing as futile the notion of offering revelation and education to a wider public, Throbbing Gristle was strictly a take-it-or-leave-it affair; if they couldn't do the service of awakening England en masse, then they at least served the revolutionary purpose of dividing those who were in from those who were out. Over time, this earned them a reputation as *the* ur-industrial, ur-noise act. Commonly perceived as a musical extreme beyond which no artist or audience could venture, they've thus sold hundreds of thousands of records.

Looking closely at the individual histories and experiences of Throbbing Gristle's members helps us see them as more than noise technicians, algorithmic composers, or pranksters. Over time, Tutti and P-Orridge in particular came to believe in the need to cast off false inheritances that were politically the agents of control structures and personal impediments to honest self-knowledge. The political and the personal are joined here. P-Orridge, in renaming himself and staging self-destruction, lays his inborn identity at the altar of freedom, because identity itself is necessarily a known plot—something *finite*, *defined*, and thus externally governed in the most literal sense. Likewise, Tutti seeks through performance to explore "that intangible space between your internal feelings and the world around you."[52] This is the border between the self and everything else, usually hidden, but like all borders it is revealed in transgression. Both she and P-Orridge are concerned with bypassing, even destroying the ego, the last defense of internalized control machines. Attempting this kind of sublimation reveals a commitment to the politics of deprogramming—in this case, practically wiping the metaphorical hard disk clean—but it also reveals in reverse that these musicians knew the totalizing role that their environment had played in shaping who they were. To this end, let's come back to musical geography and again look at northern England, this time through Throbbing Gristle's eyes.

## 5. Manchester in the Shadow of War

"It was just an ordinary day in Manchester," begins "Very Friendly," the first Throbbing Gristle song to which Genesis P-Orridge put lyrics.✤ On this ordinary Mancunian day that he narrates—October 6, 1965—Ian Brady and Myra Hindley killed seventeen-year-old Edward Smith with an axe to the head. It was the last chapter in a killing spree that was dubbed the Moors Murders, on account of Brady and Hindley's burying their adolescent victims in nearby Saddleworth Moor. Throughout the young couple's ensuing trial, British tabloids electrified the public's prurience, dramatizing Brady and Hindley's taste for orgies, pedophilia, sadomasochism, and Nazi iconography—not entirely

---

✤ Lyrical attribution in Throbbing Gristle's work is thorny. Tutti recalls, "The lyrics were, more often than not, a group effort regarding topics, particularly some 'wording' and 'phrases,'" though she grants that P-Orridge ad-libbed a fair bit both in concert and on record.[53] The most famous example of this process is the song "Discipline," whose titular theme was suggested by Christopherson shortly before its improvised live debut at SO36 in Berlin over a beat of Carter's. In contrast to this account—and perhaps in tension with the live version of "Still Walking" discussed earlier—P-Orridge today claims "Throbbing Gristle did NOT write any lyrics. I wrote the lyrics to every single TG song. Once in a while I would ask, what shall I sing about."[54] P-Orridge also adds, "One or two times Cosey would edit down lyrics I'd written. She did this on 'Almost A Kiss.'"[55] Tutti responds to P-Orridge's claimed authorship of the band's lyrics, declaring it "counter to the known and recorded history."[56] Disagreements over Throbbing Gristle's lyrics—specifically their ideological function in the music—contributed to the foursome's second dissolution in late 2010.

unlike the newspapers' posed outrage over the *Prostitution* exhibition. Within months of the couple's arrest, author John Deane Potter had breathlessly written and published a whole book on the killers—complete with photos—hotly capitalizing on the brand new True Crime genre that Truman Capote's *In Cold Blood* had birthed just a year earlier. Gleeful with indignation and woe, journalists ensured that in English popular culture the infamy of Brady and Hindley would rank second only to Jack the Ripper.

Tabloid sensationalism emphasizes to readers the strangeness and monstrosity of criminals, painting them as unrelatable. By conflating strangeness with evil, this coverage by extension reassures readers that if they are normal people, then they are morally good people. Propagating this *normative-is-desirable* idea is smart business for the media: the public gets to read about thrilling perversity in the name of strengthening civic and moral conformity, while the press rakes in money selling papers. Everybody wins.

Written ten years after the trial's public frenzy, "Very Friendly" does little to sensationalize the crime narrative. Nazism, for example, makes no lyrical appearance (although "German wine" makes four). Instead, when P-Orridge repeats that Ian Brady and Myra Hindley were "very friendly," his biting, inverted suggestion isn't just that killers can be perfectly normal but that normativity—a desirable trait, as media sensationalism tells us—may just as well be a path to evil and monstrosity. This comes through especially in the contrast between the relative deadpan in which P-Orridge intones the story's more brutal details and the increasing hysteria with which he whoops that blandest of compliments, "very friendly." Never mind suspecting that the nice, quiet neighbor might be a psychopath; you should take a close look at yourself.

Throbbing Gristle acts out this critique musically and lyrically. P-Orridge focuses on little banalities, like the couple's dog. Such flat recollection of details would be funny if it weren't so chilling—"Bits of bone and white brain landed onto the hearth, just near the brass brush that they used to sweep the chimney"—and indeed, a wry humor accompanies dread in a vast amount of the band's work. Tellingly, P-Orridge notes that throughout the axe murder, Hindley's TV is tuned to "This Is Your Life," a clever warning that there's a little Myra Hindley in all of us. Twice in the opus, P-Orridge focuses by name on the suburb of Hyde, both painting the ordinary Manchester day with local color and dropping a subliminal reminder of a certain Dr. Jekyll, who in all his upstanding decorum nonetheless nurtured a monster within. Sonically, the song is typical of early Throbbing Gristle, which is to say that it's a chunky, jittering mess of distorted bass and echoing drones. As a function of the track's eighteen-minute duration, though, the noise becomes absolutely normative; it is the state of things. Remarkably, beneath P-Orridge's narrative, this noisy state gets perceptually relegated to the background over time; the listener becomes entirely inured to its ugliness.

We can tell that this is an important part of how the song works, because in the final three minutes, the sound gives way to a repetitive texture in D-flat major (courtesy of Peter Christopherson) that is arresting, even lovely. This arrival upon pitched musical material is striking chiefly because it defies expectations: the listener by this point has come to assume noise as the baseline state. The moment verges on beauty despite P-Orridge's seemingly endless repetition of a panicked phone call to the police in which he stutters, "There's been a m-m-m-murder." Throbbing Gristle obtain this strange splendor by again cloaking the song's horror in banality: by the end of "Very Friendly," somehow, just as a major key has become stranger than noise, a speech impediment is more sensational than killing a boy tied to a chair. In Throbbing Gristle's output, works like this are not evil glorifications of aggression. Nor are they holy lamentations, as some have supposed, of an alleged cultural desensitization to noise and violence via reenactment. Instead, "Very Friendly," like many other works by Throbbing Gristle, offers a wide-angled critique of the assumption that being "normal" is desirable, and by extension, the music condemns the public attitudes and institutions that reinforce the idea.

Beyond the factual geography of the Moors murders, it's worth asking why P-Orridge maps this exceedingly broad critique of normativity so specifically to Manchester, especially when it was the northeast city of Hull that shaped Throbbing Gristle in so many other clear ways (the band's name and the song title "Five Knuckle Shuffle" are both local slang, for instance). To begin with, Manchester is where P-Orridge was born in 1950. He spent his early years there, "in the shadow of war, without the light of peace," as he sings in a 2001 autobiographical piece called "Manchester." Though the city is culturally luminous today, this shadow of war still looms in P-Orridge's recollection.

> Manchester was blitzed, like London, by the Germans. Around where we were, in Victoria Park in Manchester, were all these holes from bombs, collapsed buildings—the war zone. It definitely had an impact on me. Being a precocious little so-and-so, [I] can remember thinking, what the fuck did people do this for? At the end of the street were prefabs—lots of those little chunky houses that they built to house people whose homes were blown up. That's my memory of Manchester, the decay and destruction.[57]

There are a few ways that Mancunians in the 1950s and 1960s reconciled the cognitive dissonance between the normal-is-desirable assumption and the city's

　　　　　　　　　　　　　　　　　　　　**A S S I M I L A T E**

new state of dilapidation. Many who'd known Manchester before the 1940s saw the war's ugly damage as cause for mourning, the disgracing of a metropolis once austere, if not classically beautiful. This older set's understanding of their new surroundings was rooted in the past: postwar Manchester, in its tragic damage, simply could not be normal. Others were thankful just to have come out of the war alive, and they took a proletarian pride in putting the past behind them and getting back to work. To these future-minded opportunists, Manchester meant work, family, and stability; it was definitionally normal, and thus desirable. However, perceiving Manchester like this required people to sustain willful blindness to the city's undeniably ugly scars—that is, until they'd saved enough to move into a new development outside town.

Young Genesis P-Orridge—back when he was Neil Megson—took neither of these approaches, perceiving that Manchester's ruination at the time was both undeniably its normative state of affairs and certainly undesirable. It was ugly. The logical conclusion was to reject the premise of normal-as-desirable.

The assertion here is not that Manchester itself forced on Genesis P-Orridge some revelation of nonconformity or negative aesthetics when he was still a child; indeed, if one believes P-Orridge's well-rehearsed and charming conversational yarns, he emerged from the womb a druid and a dandy. Rather, the point is that P-Orridge's boyhood understanding of his urban surroundings testifies that he was never clouded by reverence for conformity and normality—an attitude that in stereotype and reality alike both fed into and derived from the British class system.

His father's work as a traveling salesman took the family from Manchester, but the city's shadow loomed again in the mid-1960s, when P-Orridge was attending Solihull Public School. In his four years there, as band biographer Simon Ford writes, "nobody spoke to him because of his Northern accent."[58] Years after leaving Manchester, he spoke its language, marking himself with his thin voice. In P-Orridge's words, Solihull "crystallised my hatred of authority, the British class system, the Royal family, privilege, hypocrisy, cruelty—the entire bag of tricks."[59]

It was thus at a moment of raging against authority and class, of facing daily ostracism on account of his Mancunian roots, and likely by extension of foregrounding his antinormative, anti-aesthetic Manchester memories that a precocious Megson read about Ian Brady and Myra Hindley killing Edward Smith and at least three other kids, and burying them by the A635 road east of town. To this budding, nonviolent hippie with a kinky streak and clandestine literary tastes, the notion that Brady's bisexuality and taste in books were to blame for axe murder and sexual assault simply didn't compute. Hidden in plain view were far more likely causes: the 1940 Christmas blitz and a host of lesser blows still haunted the old streets and the new buildings of Manchester, and every citizen who ignored them or denied hearing their ghostly wail only incited them to shriek louder. An unwritten code of normativity still hung over England, silencing sexuality and declaring all things German as beyond the pale. These realities don't downplay the evil that Brady and Hindley committed; nor do they excuse murder, sexual assault, or Nazism. But viewed systemically, might not the pressure within such a consensus of denial cause the occasional overheating?

Again, the political and personal converge: for P-Orridge, the public articulation of nonconformity as evil would have hit close to home. While he was figuring out his disdain for authority, he found that on a colossal scale, authority now fixed its crosshairs on him for simply being who he was, for liking what he liked, and indeed, for seeing something undesirable and ugly in the geographic and cultural terrain of England. The secret terror of being hunted by the widest, most diffuse sort of authority is a life-changing one; it fueled the entire career of William S. Burroughs, for example. It also arouses the nagging suspicion that normality's justification is wholly circular—that it exists simply to squash and assimilate any abnormal behavior. Given the first chapters' discussion of hegemony, it's easy to connect this idea back to Marx, Debord, and Burroughs.

P-Orridge poignantly illustrates this assimilation with his familial memory of this murderous, ordinary day in Manchester.

When the story started to break that there were some serial killers in the Manchester area, my parents would tell me, "You can't go out anymore, not after six." Our whole lives changed overnight into being really controlled and intimidated with severe paranoia and fear. "If you don't do as you're told, you're going to get killed!" Our parents got all weird on us and we couldn't do what we wanted anymore.

There's something suggestive in Brady and Hindley, to me, about the end of childhood. It doesn't just come from growing up, but it happens because people who have power over you say, "Now it stops. You can't play in the fields where the derelict building is anymore. You can't play football there anymore. You can't have bonfires. You can't have treehouses. That's all over. If you don't agree, we'll take your bike away."

It's a hell of a thing to happen overnight, all because of something someone else has done. It seemed very abstract. So my first ever song was about the interplay between the media and society, parental control, and childhood, and the way all those things are arbitrary. Childhood is given by someone else, and can also be taken away, in every sense.[60]

ASSIMILATE

Here, by demanding even with the best intentions that children behave within a code of normative propriety, adults privilege safety over self-discovery, ridding their children of childhood, and rendering them no longer children but assimilated adults.

This sort of insight and commentary is available to Throbbing Gristle because unlike, say, John Cage, their sonic mission was not one of revealing hidden beauty in the unbeautiful. Instead, by emphasizing the categorically undesirable, the closest they can hope to achieve is the destigmatizing of ugliness-as-ugliness, just as "Very Friendly" strives for. Ugliness is equated with the irrational and the indefensible, both in the teeth-clenching experience of listening-as-endurance and in the suffocating banality of unchanging textures.

"Beauty is the enemy," intones P-Orridge on cEvin Key's 1998 song of that title. He continues, "Acceptance of ugliness is the redemption of sanity," empowering ugliness as both a musical directive and a reframing of all it touches. The sanity that Throbbing Gristle seeks to redeem is not one of reason or beauty. The normativity they seek to dismantle is not to be replaced with a new standard, for that would be just as tyrannical. Instead, the ever-shifting absence, the ugly, the noise is that which reveals the dangerous instinct to impose control through beauty, the oppressor, the killer inside.

Throbbing Gristle's ideologies are deep and worthy of more time than this chapter can offer. However, they are also pervasively influential in every era of industrial music, having reverberated as background noise over the decades, occasionally roaring to crescendo, radiating from one geography into others. Their fuller articulation similarly echoes through the rest of this book.

**ICONIC:**

Cabaret Voltaire – "Nag Nag Nag" (1979)

Cabaret Voltaire – "Yashar (John Robie remix)" (1982)

Clock DVA – "4 Hours" (1981)

Throbbing Gristle – "Hamburger Lady" (1978)

Throbbing Gristle – "Discipline" (1980)

**ARCANE:**

Wendy Carlos – "Timesteps" (1971)

COUM Transmissions – "73 Vibrant" (1971)

The Future – "Blank Clocks" (1977)

Hula – "Feeding the Animal" (1982)

Thomas Leer and Robert Rental – "Perpetual" (1979)

# 5.
# Berlin

## 1. An Island out of This Planet

Berlin in the 1970s was cavernous, its empty buildings echoing the voices, politics, and gunfire of a tumultuous twentieth century. In 1919 the Weimar National Assembly effectively replaced the German empire with a parliamentary republic, empowering the capital Berlin with democratic heft; its population doubled in one year to nearly four million. The seat of the Third Reich two decades later, Berlin was the epicenter of both Germany's growth and its military conscription. As such, it was also a desperate battlefield by the close of the war, enduring 363 bombing raids, each blasting away more of the city's nineteenth-century architecture. From a peak of four and a half million inhabitants at the start of 1943, Berlin's population dropped well below three million by the war's end. Many were killed or left homeless; others simply retreated to the safer countryside. Fully half of Berlin's buildings were damaged or destroyed.

The division of Berlin in 1949 into East (under the military occupation of the Soviet Union) and West (occupied by American, French, and English forces) was a traumatic schism: Berlin would be a microcosm of the Cold War that followed, one foot in the communist DDR and the other under the Allied Control Council in alliance with the Bundesrepublik. To stop the illegal escape of East Germans to the west, the DDR cordoned off West Berlin with the Berlin Wall in 1961, effectively silencing any exchange between the city's halves. Immediately felt as a toxic presence, the wall drove businesses and families away from the neighborhoods it cut through, particularly leaving the borough of Kreuzberg a ghost town. On both sides of the wall rose facelessly blocky and functional modern buildings—*neubauten*, as they were called. But rather than replace dilapidated structures, they mostly stood amidst the ruins of both grand old buildings and hastily erected edifices from the Nazi boom, rising above the smattering of foreign military encampments.

By the late 1960s, students in West Berlin—children of the war generation—had become increasingly radical in their leftist politics as they witnessed and participated in the rise of anti-establishment hippie culture, including rock music and drug use. Growing up in a state that mandated a social remorse for the war and the Holocaust induced both shame for the previous generation's complicit cowardice and more generally suspicion toward traditional values and aesthetics. Housing was cheap because old buildings were plentiful—this was a city of three million built for five million—so it was easy for young people to gather en masse, incubating and reinforcing their sentiments into real political stances. An economic recession, the Vietnam War, insufficient support for students, and eventually the attempted assassination of Rudi Dutschke, a young leftist leader critical of government hypocrisy, led to an organized youth uprising and riots in April 1968. These actions were taken in solidarity with similar movements in the United States, England, the Netherlands, and especially France, and they left the city tense, divided now by generation as well as geography. Militant leftist organizations such as Andreas Baader and Ulrike Meinhof's Red Army Faction became infamous forces of political change.

When a new cast of students came to the graffiti-covered West Berlin in the 1970s, it had tempered only slightly from the Situationist-inspired riots of 1968, but now the reputation of its reappropriated landscape and idealist politics ensured the blossoming of artistic scenes, new fire amidst the old rubble. In a mismanaged attempted at rubbing the DDR's nose in the artistic opulence of a free society, the Bundesrepublik enticed these creative youths to come to the city, promising financial assistance and—perhaps most important—exemption from military service. As teens and twentysomethings gathered, they turned welfare distribution centers and student administration offices into subcultural hangouts.

Beyond that, as if wandering a dérive of Berlin's ruins emptied by the war, these students declared squatting the natural response to a city on the edge of nowhere, and they formally organized the first squatting communes in late 1971, beginning on Mariannenplatz in Kreuzberg. Hartwig Schierbaum, who would later front the synthpop band Alphaville, came to Berlin in 1976. He says, "It was like an island out of this planet. It was a terrible thing, this monster, but at that time it was where you just could escape reality."[1] For those teens and twentysomethings, the economic reality of the city helped to ferment both heavy drug use and ideological experimentation. Schierbaum continues:

> It was inexpensive. It was free. You actually didn't have to care too much for a living, because there were so many subventions, so much money being putting in. It was the spearhead of western ideology in the heart of the communist empire. So actually nobody in Berlin at that time

really worked very hard. There was no reason. You could just go there and just live there without doing too much for it.[2]

As the 1970s crept on, this experience would become well known through books such as Christiane F.'s wildly popular heroin autobiography *Wir Kinder vom Bahnhof Zoo* and films such as Werner Herzog's ultrableak *Stroszek*. To adventurous musicians and artists, West Berlin was acquiring a reputation. Certainly the fruitful residency of hipster gods David Bowie, Brian Eno, and Iggy Pop in 1977 didn't hurt this perception; Bowie's proto-postpunk *Low* and *Heroes* albums were respectively mixed and recorded at Kreuzberg's Hansa Studio by the Wall.

Musical *community*, as posited by the popular music scholar Will Straw, "presumes a population group whose composition is relatively stable . . . and whose involvement in music takes the form of an ongoing exploration of one or more musical idioms said to be rooted within a geographically specific historical heritage," whereas a *scene*, "in contrast, is that cultural space in which a range of musical practices coexist, interacting with each other . . . work[ing] to disrupt [historical] continuities, to cosmopolitanize and relativize them."[3] More than any other industrial crèche, Berlin in the 1970s had a vibrant experimental scene that was greater than the sum of its inhabitants' creative and social output. This makes a bit more sense when we look at how ever-shifting casts of young artists lived and created at the time.

At any moment in the late 1970s, 150 unlawfully occupied squats operated in West Berlin, mostly in or near Kreuzberg. Just south of the Spree River and separated by the wall from the East Berlin borough of Friedrichshain, Kreuzberg was an impoverished, ugly part of Berlin. Those who lived there were generally vagrants, students, or Turkish immigrants who had come to Germany for postwar work rebuilding the country. Young anarchists and socialists took over entire streets and parks in the corners of West Berlin. Any given squat would house between eight and fifty people, either living rent-free or paying a low lease, sometimes attending the Berlin State School of Fine Arts or the Technical University, but fundamentally acting on anti-establishment rage. The numbers were too great for the police to control: phone trees powered by hacked communication lines enabled these young people to assemble by the thousand within an hour. The organizational soundness of the culture afforded an artistic scene complete with cafes (the Rote Harfe was a favorite), discos, and makeshift libraries. Berlin's constantly changing cast didn't impede the microcosm's day-to-day life, but instead, change was built into the scene's basic operation. Indeed, a student's political shift or a change of drug habits might mean moving from, say, Albertstrasse 86 to Wienerstrasse 25. Some squats were ideologically dogmatic; others offered nonstop partying.

## 2. Strategies Against Architecture

For Berlin's young artists, rejecting tradition and old values meant that formal training and craft were no longer requisite or even desirable—an idea that also inspired the punk movement in England. Because of this, the experimental nature of the early films by Christoph Döring and Yana Yo, recordings by Einstürzende Neubauten and Die Tödliche Doris, and paintings by Kiddy Citny all testify to these artists' learning by doing. Their work, in all its visceral directness, therefore gives us a relatively unfiltered view of its makers' remarkably consistent desires.

Consider the trope of destruction as a means of escape within the West Berlin art scene. *3302 Taxi* is a 1979 short film by Döring that puts viewers in the driver's seat of a car that repeatedly accelerates head-on toward sections of the Berlin Wall. The presumed collisions are themselves unseen, and although the most banal explanation is that actually driving into the wall would have been logistically prohibitive, a more artful interpretation is that whether the wall breaks down or the driver is killed doesn't actually matter: both are alternatives to a life confined.

Other Berlin short films reinforce the destruction-as-escape theme. In Horst Markgraf and Rolf S. Wolkenstein's 1983 *Craex Apart*, an intense, wordless actor ("Ogar"—no relation to the Skinny Puppy singer) simply pounds huge logs, pipes, and sledgehammers on the interior of an abandoned room. Yana Yo's 1982 *Sax* reverently follows a procession of three young saxophonists (members of the punk act Nachdenkliche Wehrpflichtige) through the disused innards of a Berlin factory to its rooftop, from which they then faithfully leap. The destruction either of the self or the other disrupts the static binary: Berliner and Berlin, new and old, man and machine. It's a pessimistic twist on the Futurist fascination with the crash explored in Chapter 1.

And so when we turn to the early work of Einstürzende Neubauten, the most radical and enduring of the early German industrial acts, it's easy in this context to understand their place within a Berlin scene hell-bent on literally clashing with the surrounding cityscape. In the squatters' street battles against local authorities, "People started to build barricades and they drummed for hours on the metal fences and barricades," lead singer Blixa Bargeld (born Hans Christian Emmerich) explains, "and [ours] was fundamentally the same music."[4] For example, the "Stahlversion" B-side of the 1980 single "Für den Untergang" was recorded in the empty steel interior of a highway overpass: literally enclosed by the functional architecture of the city, percussionist N. U. Unruh (born Andrew Chudy) banged out rhythms with concrete blocks on the metal floor. Similarly, their later music video for "Der Tod ist ein Dandy" concludes with the image of a sledgehammer beating a hole through a wall (*the* wall?), revealing ever more inescapable city beyond the city.

The pounding and banging that Einstürzende Neubauten is known for wasn't just the behavior of a band stuck in Berlin, but the presence of Berlin in their blood, inasmuch as the city's understaffed police, secret slums, and slacker population readily encouraged drug use. Band member FM Einheit recalls, "Taking speed was a way of life. This of course influenced our recordings. Being as crazy as one is on speed can only be achieved by actually taking speed."[5] Speed is an antisocial, antisensual drug that builds up mental and muscular tension and demands that its user release that tension immediately and aggressively. The constant themes of extreme physical exertion and obliteration in West Berlin's film and records likely both fueled and were fueled by amphetamine usage. There is arguably also a political dimension to the city's speed trade: it's true that Nazi soldiers were given amphetamines as performance enhancers, but more significantly, the amount of drug use among youth in the city in a similarly circular manner both reflected and contributed to West Berlin's aggregate psychological condition—a disillusionment no doubt framed as normative by its isolation from the rest of West Germany. [6] As Schierbaum recalls, "There was lots, especially the heavy drugs like heroin and that kind of shit."[7] He continues, anecdotally connecting this with an urban politics of negation, "When you're in the drug scene you're really confronted with the more direct possibilities of human behavior. This just led to my having a very deep disbelief in political movements."[8]

### 3. German-ness

Einstürzende Neubauten's relationship to their surroundings is highlighted by their choice to sing in German—a decision that their West Berlin scene contemporaries shared. By and large, German, Belgian, and Dutch popular culture had been infatuated with singing in English since the 1960s, and when Anglophone punk music and journalism reached continental Europe, the cachet it carried meant that singing in German could actively brand a young act *anticool* by continental standards.✿ But Einstürzende Neubauten and their scenemates effectively rejected geographically external standards, and in doing so they managed to address directly the condition of *being where they were*. Crucially, singing in German meant rediscovering and reclaiming German-ness.

✿ As Jennifer Shryane points out, this trend had begun with German folk protest singers in the 1960s.[9]

To the parents of this young generation, Anglophone music had offered a way to silence the uncomfortable questions of German identity after their own unforgivable complicity under Hitler. Making German music here and now in Hitler's capital thus did the vital work of breaking that silence and fulfilling every rebel's longing to cut loose once and for all from parents, teachers, and bosses, to burst free from the past's quietly tightening stranglehold on the present. It's a kind of détournement that industrial music invokes again and again: by embracing the forbidden, one rejects the original behavior that inspired the fear of taboo.

There's something about the German language itself that was important, too—the way its rhythmic mechanics shape a song's delivery. German's predominance of strong-weak vowel patterns (*trochees*) means that lyrical phrases often start on musical downbeats, and its decidedly un-English, raspy, fricative consonants make for a certain level of mouth noise in singing. In German, a song like Einstürzende Neubauten's "Ich Bin's" (which means "It's Me") repeatedly hits the word "ich" on a musical downbeat, scraping the Teutonic "ch" suddenly against a pounding ictus, then delivering the weaker, staccato "bins" an eighth-note later, the afterthought of a collision in time.

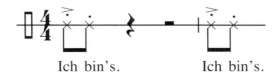

Ich bin's.          Ich bin's.

*Figure 5.1*

Singing the title lyric "it's me" in English would mean aligning the melodiously smooth "me" with the downbeat, ambiguously trailing off, with "it's" having come before the downbeat. This not only ruins the rhythmic surprise of the lyric's arrival but turns the song from a march into a gallop.

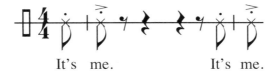

It's  me.          It's  me.

*Figure 5.2*

All this helps to explain the common belief among industrial musicians and fans that Germany as a technological, political presence in history and that German as a spoken language together resonate uniquely with industrial music's penchant for technological and tragic themes and its rhythmic, timbral aggression. This belief extends well beyond Berlin, and even beyond Germany's borders: America's Stromkern, Italy's Pankow, Slovenia's Laibach, and France's Die Form, in addition to taking Germanic names, have all chosen on occasion to sing in German. Similarly, the name of DRP, Japan's first EBM band (formed in 1983), stood for Deutsche Reiche Patent. As SPK's Graham Revell once said "I'm shouting quite a lot in German because I like the language—it's a little fetish of mine."[10] The idea of nation runs through industrial identity, and in this regard Germany holds a privileged role.✿

## 4. Ingenious Dilettantes

Einstürzende Neubauten was only one permutation of artists within the city's scene. They regularly shared club gigs with new wave, electronic, and punk acts such as Mania D., Frieder Butzmann, Din A Testbild, Sprung aus den Wolken, Sentimentale Jugend, and the ferocious Nina Hagen, a rare East German emigrée in West Berlin. But beyond that, all these acts shared band members with near-promiscuous turnover, collaborated across media, and released recordings on one another's makeshift tape labels—for example, Kiddy Citny, a Berlin Wall muralist and member of Sprung aus den Wolken, ran the influential small-run imprint Das Cassetten Combinat from 1980 to 1983, the year the squats were finally evicted. This social fluidity in the scene may have been as responsible for the aesthetic overlap between its participants as any preconceived ideology; like no other city, Berlin and its postpunk zeitgeist were a feedback loop of cause and effect.

Part of Will Straw's definition of musical scenes stipulates their artistic cross-pollination and its dismantling of traditions and historical narratives. Though the interactions of artists in the city didn't exactly give rise to a willful third mind in the Burroughs-Gysin sense, the variety of artistic media and politics that interacted calcified the need for young artists to tear down everything old. Whether witnessed in the 1983 film by Notorische Reflexe that projects footage of car burning and rioting in West Berlin onto a pulsing kick drum head or in Bargeld's declaration that "all traces of the past are abandoned: only out of destruction can something really new be created," the calamitous man-

---

✿ During the Cold War, the Soviet Union was similarly a point of fascination. In a 1982 interview, Esplendor Geométrico declare, "We are Spanish, but we would like to be Russian."[11] More confusing is U.S.-based Michael Gutierrez's adoption of the Germanic Hans Schiller as a pseudonym and his subsequent creation of the band Kozmonaut, whose name is ostensibly Russian.

date for innovation was not merely an intellectual dalliance with modernism, but a vital social response to real desperation. [12] And of course poor students in West Berlin had little to lose by destroying so much: one impetus behind Einstürzende Neubauten's banging on metal for percussion was Unruh's having sold his drums to pay rent in December 1980. Poverty was desperate; a photo of Bargeld's apartment at the time again shows conflict with his surroundings. "Half evicted" from it, in his words, there is a collection of trash, noisemaking junk, and secondhand clothes strewn about. The word DILDO is spraypainted on a concrete wall, underlined. [13]

Central to but not synonymous with the West Berlin scene of the era was the loose collective of fifty or so people that ringleader artist Wolfgang Müller and Blixa Bargeld called Die Geniale Dilletanten [sic]—the ingenious dilettantes. The idea evolved from projects including a used clothing store (Eisengrau, created in 1979 by Gudrun Gut and Bettina Köster, who designed fashion and who later handed its management over to Bargeld), Müller's fanzine, and ultimately a massive antirealist festival on September 4, 1981, with fourteen hundred attendees at the Berlin Tempodrom. Müller proclaimed a kinship with Dada and its trickster tactics, evident in the oddly placed near-humor of his band Die Tödliche Doris and in his 1982 book on the Dilletanten, which proclaims, "to find the unknown, one must take joy in playing the lustful game that goes with extreme pain." [14] This mix of joy and pain extended throughout the Dilletanten: artist Dimitri Hegemann went on to organize both the industrial 1982 Berlin Atonal festival and later the legendary techno-driven annual Love Parade in Berlin. In its sense of nothing to lose, Berlin in the 1970s and early 1980s routinely draws comparison with the flapper free-for-all of Germany's Weimar era.

But with only the dimmest, most obsessive hint of glee, it was Einstürzende Neubauten's frantic desperation and ritualized demolition that ultimately instilled actual fear and shock in audiences, earning the band a more immediate and lasting reputation with listeners than other members of the Berlin scene. With less of a division between popular styles and subcultural crowds than other western cities, West Berlin's audiences and record stores—Zensor on Belgizer Strasse was the best one—conflated punk, noise, disco, and industrial musics into one scene, and so it was rare in playing to the city's well-versed crowds that any band managed to do more than preach to the converted. But by 1981, when their lineup and instrumentation took a decidedly unmusical turn, Einstürzende Neubauten bore a darkness: their jackhammers, fires, hatchets, and broken glass were religious signifiers in their apocalyptic imagery. Indeed, their motto in 1980 had been "two years to the apocalypse." At the Geniale Dilletanten festival, Bargeld declared, "it is now time of the decline, the end of time, definitely. It goes on for 3 or 4 years and then it is over. . . . I'm dancing for the decline, I'm not against it. I'd like it as soon as possible."[15] Demand for the band's performances elsewhere in Germany began to set them apart from the Dilletanten and the rest of the Berlin scene, but their roots in the bleak architecture and pan-disciplinary makeup of the city were clear: on October 27, 1981, they embarked on a set of fifteen concerts around West Germany with Sprung aus den Wolken and the gothic new wave act MDK that they billed as the Berliner Krankheit—the Berlin sickness tour.

Einstürzende Neubauten's story and music extend well past this short era. As Mark Chung recalls, by 1984 "we began thinking of ourselves as musicians primarily," and indeed that was when the group's members were able to go "full-time" in their work.[16] In particular, their Concerto for Voice and Machinery performance at London's Institute of Contemporary Arts on January 3, 1984, was a legendary bit of venue destruction, and their excursions into theater, video, and dance could constitute a legacy of their own were they not over-shadowed by a long line of excellent albums in the 1980s, 1990s, and beyond. However, as far as industrial music at large is concerned, the focus given to Berlin in this chapter can help us understand more specifically the ground-level situation and some of the motivations from which people created this thing we call industrial music.

West Berlin was claimed by the government in Bonn, but given no voting representation; it was where companies claimed to relocate so they could grab government subventions, but they only opened shill offices; it was where students enrolled in universities but never attended; it was where new buildings arose while bombed ruins were never swept away. All in all, centralized administration, depressed commerce, and Germany's own history played the role of absentee landlord to the youth of West Berlin, a city that was itself squatting in a neglected pocket of Europe. Authority, whether the government, the police, the universities, or the gun-wielding phantom limb of East Germany, could not be trusted. Even the '68ers who had taught this generation how to riot were branded as out-of-touch hippies, all this to say nothing of the French, English, and American troops who patrolled the city, interchangeable and anonymous, ostensibly the good guys. Control was thus everywhere and nowhere at once. The trace of Burroughs's paranoia in this conflation of power serves to emphasize the cut-up city skyline; as Tobias Rapp writes of Berlin's youth culture, "the misappropriation of old buildings had been one of the most visible features," whether real in the squats or fantasized in the willed collapse of new buildings.[17] West Berlin offered a drug-fed dystopian pastiche that gave real urban echoes to a techno-ambivalent spirit of the age.

Reunified today, Berlin is increasingly gentrified, all the way to the slums east of the divide. When the wall was torn down in 1989, its most opulent graffiti-

covered slabs, painted by Thierry Noir and Kiddy Citny of Die Geniale Dilletanten, were carted away and auctioned off in Monaco without the artists' consent. Even as the traces of early industrial music's Berlin disappear into a
moderate twenty-first century, its recordings replay a rare memory of a unique
urban moment.

## 5. West Germany Beyond Berlin

It's worth mentioning at this point that there were important developments in
early industrial music elsewhere in West Germany (even if their relationship to
a specific urban geography may not be as clear as Berlin's contributions). Some
acts, such as Frankfurt's abstract noise group P16.D4, were isolated, almost
anomalous. However, most of Germany's industrially tinged music beyond
Berlin was happening in Hamburg and Düsseldorf.

Alfred Hilsberg, a journalist for *Sounds* magazine, launched the shoestring
label ZickZack in Hamburg in 1979, releasing records mostly by German electronic and punk acts—styles that, as mentioned, were functionally less divided
in Germany than elsewhere at the time. Hilsberg, as singer Mona Mur recalls,
"was this kind of weird drunken historian, living with his parents in a flat, releasing music from people from pretty much all over Germany."[18] ZickZack's first
release was the "Computerstaat" single by Abwärts, from whom Einstürzende
Neubauten shortly afterward poached members Mark Chung and FM Einheit. ZickZack would also release music by postpunkers Palais Schaumburg,
Hamburg-based proto-goths X-Mal Deutschland, and Düsseldorf's seminal
industrial band Die Krupps, formed by ex-members of the band Male ("Germany's first proper punk band," according to a Die Krupps album sleeve).[19]

In December 1980, Die Krupps recorded the basis of their *Stahlwerksymphonie*, and then refined the work in late March 1981 at the studios of krautrock
legends Can. Under the direction of local punker Peter Hein (lead singer of
Fehlfarben) the band created two fourteen-minute pieces, each built on the
same lumbering dance groove of bass and drums, but layered throughout with
clattering on what frontman Jürgen Engler called "environmental instruments,"
being whatever scraps of metal and plastic they could assemble on site.[20] The
heaviness and reverberation of the drums resemble dub reggae in no small
amount, and amidst the recordings' tuneless guitar squawks Eva Gössling's
saxophone reminds us, like Clock DVA's first albums, of free jazz pioneer Ornette Coleman's place in the family tree of experimental pop at the turn of the
decade. Later in 1981, ZickZack put out Die Krupps' unabashedly Marxist
single "Wahre Arbeit—Wahrer Lohn" ("True Work—True Wage"), which recast

their metal banging within a synth-driven pop frenzy. As with so much indus-trial music, the song emphasizes the connection between body and machine. Its lyrics (in the band's own translation) are:

All my muscles work machine-like
Steely tendons, sweat like oil
Dirt and filth are real labour
Pain and blame reward the toil
Pay—Labour

Given the song's lyrics, it's prophetic that the band was not properly paid for the record, despite it becoming an outright hit at Düsseldorf's hippest clubs such as Der Ratinger Hof and Match Moore, and eventually across Germany's youth culture. Mona Mur says of Hilsberg, "He wouldn't pay the printing factory, he wouldn't pay anyone."[21] To this day, there is a "rumour that ZickZack invested Die Krupps' hefty 'Wahre Arbeit' royalties into its new stars, Einstürzende Neu-bauten's first record."[22]

With "Wahre Arbeit—Wahrer Lohn," Die Krupps joined an increasing num-ber of midbudget acts who used eight- or sixteen-step sequencers to create rigidly timed ("quantized") pulsing synth-based loops. The basic approach of creating a two-measure bassline and playing it over a fast beat (with either real percussion or a drum machine) offered a lot of reward for its limited effort. With vocals sung none-too-melodically through an echobox, this was more or less the musical template for what would become Electronic Body Music.

Fellow Düsseldorf act Der Plan had a striking influence on Die Krupps, and eventually on electronic pop worldwide, although in their productive early days from 1978 to 1980 only a few appreciated their pioneering oddball synth-pop. The band's friend and eventual member Kurt Dahlke set up Ata Tak rec-ords to release their work (and that of his own post-disco project Pyrolator), but much of the original lineup found greater success elsewhere. Der Plan's Chrislo Haas had a big hit in this step-sequenced style with his act Liaisons Dangereuses and their 1981 single "Los Niños del Parque," and along with Der Plan band-mate Robert Görl he founded Deutsche-Amerikanische Freundschaft.

Deutsche-Amerikanische Freundschaft is perhaps the band most closely associated with this sequenced sound, despite initially focusing on improvisa-tional noise music (again with saxophone). Despite the band's name, no Ameri-cans were involved: the name is taken ironically "from local posters depicting rosy German-US relations."[23] Deutsche-Amerikanische Freundschaft's first flir-tations with sequenced dance music came on their minor hits from 1980, "Co Co Pino" and the superb "Kebab-Träume," but much of their full-length album from that year, *Die Kleine und die Böse*, retained the experimentation and expansive, slow-moving textures of their more ponderous debut (also on Ata Tak). They temporarily moved to London, and after a few months of extreme poverty and tough luck in the squats the band was reduced to singer Gabriel "Gabi" Delgado-López and drummer/synth programmer Robert Görl. This duo, inspired by the UK's burgeoning synthpop trend, would become Deutsche-Amerikanische Freundschaft's most famous incarnation, beginning with 1981's *Alles Ist Gut*. The album was produced by Conny Plank, who'd helmed records by Kraftwerk, Can, Neu! and Ultravox, and it featured effectively nothing more than repeating patterns on an ARP Avatar synthesizer, Görl's unchangingly fortissimo live drums, and Delgado-López's tensely stilted voice, singing low in oddly accented German—he came from Cordoba, Spain, and at the time was barely conversant in German. Deutsche-Amerikanische Freundschaft had a lot of emptiness to fill both sonically and spatially onstage. The duo achieved this through a sheer kinetic aggression that might have come across as archetypically punk if the band's image had not been so buzz-cut, muscle-bound, and hairy-chested—attributes they were happy to show off on album covers. The band thus appealed simultaneously to a European gay market ready to move beyond the disco of the 1970s and to straight-up punks who heard in them a similarity to the French aggro pioneers Metal Urbain—all while retaining the avant-garde contingent who had followed their early, arrhythmic sound collages. A common appeal for these audiences in Deutsche-Amerikanische Freundschaft was their irreverence: the biggest hit on *Alles Ist Gut* was "Der Mussolini," which barked orders to shake your hips, move your ass, dance the "Mussolini," the "Adolf Hitler," and the "Jesus Christ." The album went on to receive the Deutsche Phono-Akademie's Schallplattenpreis.

Like Throbbing Gristle's *20 Jazz Funk Greats* album, the shift of both Die Krupps and Deutsche-Amerikanische Freundschaft to synthetic dance styles marks an important connection between noise-based, heady, "pure" industrial and the electronic, rhythmic music that has predominated public understanding of the term.

The popularity of Deutsche-Amerikanische Freundschaft and the electronic dance sound they were starting to share with Die Krupps extended beyond any ancestral industrial scene. The independent hits from Germany's synth-driven underground were making money and receiving attention abroad, especially in the UK, where in 1980 alone the *New Musical Express* named German songs "Single of the Week" three times.[24] For a brief moment in the underground scenes of Germany, fans, musicians, and independent distributors felt a yearning optimism that the day's constellation of new musical styles—the Neue Deutsche Welle or New German Wave—would bring wider audiences to innovative music. Singles like No More's "Suicide Commando" balanced attractively between the Berlin scene's darkness and the blasé silliness of Der Plan. Ultimately, though, wide commercial popularity remained beyond the reach of artists who had shaped West Germany's experimental and industrial awaking between 1978 and 1981, Deutsche-Amerikanische Freundschaft's record deal with Virgin notwithstanding. Mona Mur worked at the independent music distributor Rip Off at the time. As she tells the story:

> Everyone worked there—Mufti [FM Einheit] from Neubauten, Mark Chung. We would take the records, put them in huge packages, and carry them to the other stores. And it went well until 1981 when someone from EMI knocked on the door, saying, "Oh who are you? I just want to have a look at what track you are on." We mistook him for some vacuum cleaner salesman and said we don't need any. Bye bye. Half a year later the whole thing was bankrupt. The industry took over this energy, this [Neue Deutsche Welle]. They took the brand. Nena was number one on the US charts [with "99 Luftballons"]. That was a really bitter pill, let me tell you. . . . There was a small amount of time when we thought we could change the world and change the record industry.

### ICONIC:

Deutsche-Amerikanische Freundschaft – "Kebab-Träume" (1980)

Die Krupps – "Wahre Arbeit—Wahrer Lohn" (1981)

Einstürzende Neubauten – "Armenia" (1983)

Einstürzende Neubauten – "Kollaps" (1981)

Liaisons Dangereuses – "Los Niños Del Parque" (1981)

### ARCANE:

Borsig – "Hiroshima" (1982)

Die Tödliche Doris – "Tanz Im Quadrat" (1981)

Din A Testbild – "No Repeat" (1980)

Mona Mur – "My Lie" (1982)

No More – "Suicide Commando" (1981)

6.

# San Francisco

## 1. Embracing Memory: Chrome and the 1960s

"There were seven hills of Rome, and seven hills in Athens. Well, San Francisco has seven hills too. Topography affects your mentality; it gets reflected in a mental topography. Living here makes you think big," says V. Vale, subcultural archivist and founder of RE/Search Publications.[1] The left coast city's big thinking extends from the high-tech empire of Silicon Valley at the south end of San Francisco Bay to the hotbed of liberal politics in Berkeley, fifty miles north. Vivid and loud, arts in the Bay Area have buzzed perpetually for a century with the work of poets, publishers, artists, and performers whose collective ingenuity paints San Francisco's history as daring, even reckless. At the height of flower power, it was a world capital of psychedelic rock and LSD manufacturing, and as Hunter S. Thompson put it, "There was madness in any direction, at any hour. If not across the Bay, then up the Golden Gate or down 101 to Los Altos or La Honda. . . . You could strike sparks anywhere."[2]

Because of its tradition of experimentation, San Francisco gave rise to industrial music that broadcasts a dialogue between present and past, between the angry 1970s and the decades that came before. In stark contrast to West Berlin's year zero and northern England's response to working-class banality, California-based musicians, artists, and publishers such as Chrome, Monte Cazazza, Z'EV, Survival Research Laboratories, Factrix, and RE/Search Publications collectively engage with the memory of time and place.

The transition out of the 1960s and into the industrial is heard with the simplest continuity in the music of Chrome. Founder and drummer Damon Edge (born Thomas Wisse) was old enough to have been a hippie himself, and as he explained in 1980, "I'm not into projecting negative crap. We're into positives. We're not Devo. Dig?"[3] In 1976, Edge and three bandmates had recorded *The Visitation*, a trippy if unremarkable self-funded record of 1969-ish garage rock. When singer-guitarist Helios Creed (born Barry Johnson) moved to San Francisco from Oahu and joined the band for their next album a year later, he was determined not just to create new sounds with his suitcase full of effects pedals but also to tap into the energy that was starting to reemerge in San Francisco's post-hippie daze: "Punk came into view. We sorta' wanted to be a punk band, but it was too late . . . there were already a bunch of punk bands in the city."[4] Half krautrock timbre twiddling and half psychedelic throwback, the band was too old and heady for the punk scene, not bluesy enough to mesh with post-hippie rock, and lacking the sense of terror that characterized the city's industrial crowd, as we'll see; Chrome's uneasy fit within San Francisco's music scene wasn't helped by the fact that they almost never played live. Instead, Damon Edge, Helios Creed, and their bandmates spent time dropping acid ("LSD was very square") and fiddling with recording technology—a decidedly unpunk thing to do at this early point.[5]

Specifically, they stumbled onto noise collage and effects processing, taking them to sonically disfiguring extremes. Creed recalls:

> Damon played me these weird tapes he'd made, I go, "Man, I like that better than our [rock] set, why don't we do something like that." Then we talked about it for hours, all of a sudden we cut up our set with this weird shit next thing you know we made *Alien Soundtracks*.

This was the band's second album.[6] The record came packaged with photocollages of facially rearranged children and a portrait of Dwight Eisenhower. Its lyrics were laced with Fritz Lang–inspired science fiction, and its blend of tape drones and punk songs played through flangers sounded like little else at the time. "TV As Eyes" is a good all-in-one example of their sound: ninety seconds of an overmodulated backbeat and glammy singing followed by forty-five seconds of rhythmless cut-up television dialogue, distorted, flanged, and underlaid with a doomy electronic bassline.

The closest of any early quasi-industrial act to actual rock and roll, Chrome occupies an important space in the long history of the guitar within industrial music. While Throbbing Gristle carefully avoided the trappings of traditional chord-based musicality, Chrome was less compelled by the pan-revolutionary than by the promise of a good psychedelic freakout. More specifically, amid thin, uncompressed real drums and an occasional use of verse-chorus structures, one hears in Chrome's music a washy phasing effect on Creed's guitar. KMFDM's En Esch warns that in industrial music, if you "were over the hippie thing, [you] didn't use the phaser anymore," and indeed these features in Chrome's music have led critics and fans alike to suppose that the band was decidedly not "over the hippie thing," imbuing them with a certain passé groovyness.[7] Something of a missing link, Chrome helps to clarify an industrial musical heritage of circa-1970 space rock, including Hawkwind (cited by P-Orridge as an oft-overlooked influence), Brian Eno (idolized by Cabaret Voltaire), Arthur Brown (who later collaborated with Die Krupps), and the pantheon of German experimental outfits: Kraftwerk, Can, Neu!, Amon Düül, Faust, Cluster, Popol Vuh, and Tangerine Dream.

Chrome's role in industrial music is transitional, though their professed inheritors include the likes of Skinny Puppy. The band occupies an optimistic convergence of San Francisco old and new, where the city's other noisemakers, as we'll see, take a more vexed position. Chrome embraced the past while tripping into the future, but in doing so they help us see, by contrast, the anti-hippie streak that pervades so much industrial music otherwise, one that reveals an Oedipal rage: a simultaneous rejection of and longing for the optimistic womb of 1960s idealism.

## 2. Rejecting Memory

An historical and ideological tension specifically took hold in San Francisco because of the role of radical art and politics in shaping the city's tolerance for the strange. An edgy streak thoroughly pervaded the local culture, even to the point where it may have risked undermining an actual sense of rebellion. Universities, corporations, nonprofits, and municipal government have long invested in San Francisco's freethinking politics and the arts, greasing the wheels for many to live off their creativity. As far as industrial music is concerned, examples of this go back at least to 1947, when Kenneth Rexroth and Richard Moore, libertarian poets and activists, founded KPFA (with the help of pacifist Lewis Hill); it became the first expressly progressive radio station in the United States, later serving as a mouthpiece for the city's forward-looking artistic, social, and political communities. A later instance is the Tape Music Center, established in 1961 when students Pauline Oliveros, Morton Subotnick, and Ramon Sender assembled a makeshift electronic studio in a San Francisco Conservatory attic. After functioning autonomously for several noisy years, the group received a $15,000 grant that led to their being wholly assimilated into Mills College's Center for Contemporary Music. And it wasn't just that offbeat ideas easily landed organizational funding; San Francisco citizens were often game for avant-garde happenings en masse. In 1969, artist Paul Crowley teamed up with composer Robert Moran and musician Margaret Fabrizio to conduct the free-for-all event "39 Minutes for 39 Autos," a coordinated dance of timed headlights and car horns, the score of which had been printed in that morning's

*San Francisco Chronicle.* According to *Baker's Biographical Dictionary,* a hundred thousand San Franciscans joined in.

The success of radical arts in the city meant that in the 1970s, some composers, poets, publishers, dancers, and sculptors who might have been *enfants terribles* a few years earlier or a hundred miles away were instead institutionally celebrated and publicly accepted as elders. Examples abound, such as the veneration of publishers like City Lights Books, the postmortem apotheosis of Jack Kerouac and Janis Joplin, and the hipster intelligentsia's acceptance of Terry Riley, La Monte Young, and Steve Reich as new faces of twentieth-century composition. A cynical eye in the 1970s might already have begun to see the city's role in trickling up the PBS-cool yuppie highbrow of the future.

Popular retrospectives of the late 1960s sometimes cast the hippie movement and its outgrowths as idealistic voices for positive change, waging peace against a backward culture and oppressive, warmaking governments. In the mid-1970s, though, the triumphs and failures of the hippies were unromantically fresh and bitter in the minds of their younger siblings, who now as twenty-year-olds were hanging out at Cafe Flore in the Castro and going to shows at the Art Institute. In the tired aftermath of the 1960s, this group redrew an alternative map of the decade into one that allowed a way forward, one whose lines of flight had not already been trampled by a failed movement. For these brooders, a secret history of the 1960s might focus on the exploitative Italian Mondo films that in the tradition of circus freakshows displayed animal cruelty and third-world mystic rituals, complete with naked tribespeople. Or the syndicated gothic soap operas *Dark Shadows* and *Strange Paradise.* Or right there on the streets of San Francisco, one could focus on Anton LaVey's 1966 founding of the Church of Satan. Or the cult murders in the spring and summer of 1969 by sometime Bay Area resident Charles Manson and his followers. Or the local filmmaker Kenneth Anger, who in 1964 imbued his film *Scorpio Rising* with concentration camp imagery and a homoerotic Christ narrative, and whose 1969 *Invocation of My Demon Brother* portrayed an obscure occultic ritual that prefigured the *giallo* horror of Dario Argento.

### 3. Disinforming Memory: Monte Cazazza

This had been the 1960s for Monte Cazazza, who was among the first would-be industrialists to start making noise. Cazazza's early art and collaboration cast him as an astute torchbearer of Dada, participating in Ray Johnson's 1970 *New York Correspondence School* exhibit and joining the Bay Area Dadaists. But toward the mid-1970s, he began showing off a pre-punk verve: his 1973 zine

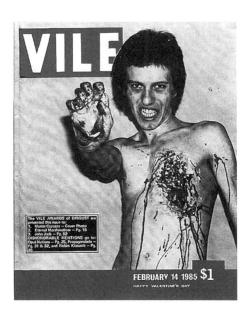

*Figure 6.1: Cazazza on the cover of* Vile *exemplifies an emerging strain of misanthropy in mail art. Photograph by Monte Cazazza.*

*Nitrous Oxide* contained spray-painted pages and a savagely tasteless romance column, and his visual art also appeared in issue two of *The West Bay Dadaist*, a thin 1973 volume emblazoned with the slogan "Do It Yourself!" (In this home-made publication, incidentally, art by Genesis P-Orridge appeared alongside Cazazza's; they would meet in 1976 and collaborate for years after.) In 1974, he modeled on the cover of *Vile*, a zine drafted to mock the Canadian anti-mail art publication *File* (itself a parody of *Life*). Growing tired of mail art's tame fun, in the picture, Cazazza appears to have ripped his heart out of his own chest. He sneers salaciously as he holds the organ up to the camera.

Cazazza sought to portray himself as uncouth, craven, and genuinely dangerous. Ultimately these leanings developed into a compendium of anecdotes about his artmaking. For his first sculpture assignment at the Oakland College of Arts and Crafts, he supposedly poured a "waterfall" of cement over the school's main entrance—a prank for which, rumor has it, he was expelled. *Slash* vol. 2 no. 3 regales that at an arts retreat Cazazza "arrived with an armed bodyguard and sprinkled arsenic into all the food. At lunch he dropped bricks with the word 'dada' painted on them on artistic feet. At dinner he burned a partially decomposed, maggot-infested cat at the table."[8]

Given Cazazza's proclaimed affinity for James Patrick Chaplin's book *Rumour, Fear, and the Madness of Crowds*[9] and his own musings on the importance of "Misdirection: making something that isn't seem to be what it is,"[10] one might see through this lens that perhaps Cazazza's physical and sonic artifacts are less the site of his artistic achievement than their memory and the reputation to which they contribute. Cazazza's art blends cultural realities with his own disinformation. He did this initially through photocopied collage, later through sampling (his excellent 1982 song "Sex Is No Emergency" lifts its rhythm track entirely from Trio's hit of the same year "Da Da Da"), and eventually in his 1987 mondo-esque shockumentary *True Gore*, where fake interviews with serial killers and bloody special effects flank real news footage. In 1977, he staged photographs with the members of Throbbing Gristle to resemble the execution of murderer Gary Gilmore, one of which was convincing enough when mailed as a postcard that it allegedly made the cover of the *Hong Kong Daily News*. His compilation album *The Worst of Monte Cazazza* begins with a fictional "Dr Alberti" delivering his "Psychiatric Review" of Cazazza: "We're dealing with a primitive filthy-minded vulgar embarrassing twisted mind. . . . Basically, this is a worthless racket. The man is mentally incompetent."

Cazazza, by integrating fact with his own invention so consistently, balances on the border of urban legend believability, retaining his image as a rabid man-child art terrorist (whether or not, in his erudition, he actually lives up to it). As a connecting personality between the U.S. and UK industrial scenes, he's repeatedly cited by industrial archivists V. Vale, Karen Collins, and Brian Duguid as a leader in the genre's history, but his musical output is nearly nonexistent: as a solo artist in the 1970s and 1980s, he released two singles, a four-song EP, and a small handful of compilation tracks—barely a half-hour of music, all told. Cazazza's work is marked by scarcity. His personal narrative is similarly marked by outlandish irreproducibility—for example, when asked about allegedly killing an assailant in self-defense, he replies, "Of course I can't confirm a story like that."[11] This combination of attributes calls to mind the early media theorist Walter Benjamin, who asserted that not only are original, nonreproduced artworks ritual in their nature (as is literally the case with so much of Cazazza's performance art) but "what matter[s] is their existence, not their being on view."[12] Taken into account with the democratizing reproducibility of mail art and zines—media in which Cazazza was also active—his oeuvre makes for a multilayered study in access to information. It wasn't until Cazazza's reputation was more fixed that any amount of his recordings (the aforementioned *Worst of* compilation from 1991) became readily available at all—and this might have more to do with public interest in industrial music than in Cazazza at that moment. It's true that he coined the Industrial Records slogan "Industrial Music for Industrial People" and might by extension be responsible for the whole genre's name, but when we consider Monte Cazazza and his role both in the San Francisco scene and in industrial music, his contributions are only limitedly as a sonic pioneer; arguably his best music was produced in collaborations. But to be sure, Cazazza is a propagandist—living evidence that reality is nothing more than the perception of reality. The notion of memory on which his significance relies both further connects San Francisco's scene to a dialogue with the past and renders his past provocations ongoing still.

## 4. Theorizing Memory: Z'EV and Survival Research Laboratories

Z'EV (born Stefan Joel Weisser) was another important character in San Francisco's late 1970s industrial scene. Already a veteran of the rock circuit and an armchair ethnomusicologist, after moving to the city in 1975 he quickly fell in with well-read misfits, playing in bands at art spaces and at Mills College. He eventually achieved greater notoriety by touring the East Coast of the United States and heading to Europe. His politics were radically anticorporate, antigovernment, and ecologically prescient. Using recycled, reappropriated, and stolen materials ("thievery . . . has to do with the very big premium I put on *risk* in the production of works"), Z'EV would pound on, drag, and crush his homemade instruments. [13] Trained initially as a drummer, he, like many other well-educated industrialists, attempted to bypass his schooling in favor of something more immediate. Where Cazazza turned toward the bestial, Z'EV sought out the mystical, conceiving of his performances as rituals. An enthusiast of voodoo, Kabbalah, and the writings of Edwardian occultist Aleister Crowley, Z'EV lists among his axioms "DEVOTION THROUGH SACRIFICE the DISCIPLINE (purifying and consecrating the vessel) to translate/transpose this into a/the performance context; DOING not THINKING: invoking/evoking, by analogy, a 'model' on the physical plane of the archetypical process, channeling 'thought-form/energy/action(s)' into manifestation." [14] The quasi-Burroughsian desire to "exterminate all rational thought" is a consistent thread in industrial music: Boyd Rice of NON, who would later collaborate with many in the San Francisco set, explains, "My ideology then was about the instinct. It was about not thinking. My intention in doing music was just to drive the thought out of people's heads." [15] The irony in these musicians' privileging the physical and the psychic over the intellectual is that, as mentioned, they nearly all chose this primitivist path as a reasoned, intellectual response. Industrialists' modernist desire for something genuinely new speaks to the very headiness from which they tried to escape. Rice continues:

I was interested in music, and there were always people in the press who would say, "This is the next big thing. Oh my God, this is going to change everything," and then I'd get the record and it would be the same old stuff that everybody has been doing for years. I mean, Patti Smith— "Oh she's a poet, it's completely different!" and you'd get this album and you'd think, "Big fucking deal. . . ." I want to have music that's *completely different*.[16]

Another artistic and spiritual axiom that Z'EV lists is that "PROCESS is THE Vehicle for the source and protection of experimental information/influx— situations/manifestations as performance (and yes, even entertainment)."[17] As discussed in this book's early chapters, the process and ideology behind early industrial is often a stronger defining feature than the notes, rhythms, and timbres of the music. Indeed, some of Z'EV's early recordings exhibit a clear organizational process, such as the use of phasing on his 1977 speech-based "Book Of Love Being Written As They Touched . . ." while other works of his become undifferentiable washes of plastic and bells, clattering through echo devices until, by processing, rhythm melts into timbre. Witnessed live, this music is immensely physical—something lost on record.

In the same vein, Mark Pauline and his Survival Research Laboratories are an industrial spectacle without peer, but as with both Z'EV and Cazazza, their significance lies beyond the scope of vinyl and tape. Founded in 1978, initially they in fact made no "music" at all. (Matt Heckert introduced a "soundtrack" component to the group in 1981, but departed in the summer of 1988). Pauline, a college-educated recreational vandal and political prankster, teamed up with Heckert and Eric Werner to build large machines that wreaked destruction on one another and their surroundings. Survival Research Laboratories' performances—the first was called "Machine Sex" in early 1979—took up huge spaces and occurred at gas stations, in vacant lots, and beneath bridges. In them, these colossal robots would shatter glass with air pressure, hurl explosives, blow flame, and circle one another with swinging blades. It was an expensive endeavor, but partially enabled by Pauline's free access to a junkyard and his brazen enjoyment of outright theft. Shows were organized around political or mechanical themes—"*an exploration of the mechanics underlying reactionary thought*"—or the animation of dead animals with robotics. With loud soundtracks often provided by the other San Francisco artists discussed here, the shows reveled in an antisocial violence that didn't just reimagine the San Francisco of the 1960s but detested it—"I hated hippies. Hippies were for peace," Pauline says.[18] On many occasions, spectators have been injured. During a 1982 concert, SPK's Graeme Revell set an audience member on fire with Mark

Pauline's flame thrower, and in a 2007 performance in Amsterdam, Survival Research Laboratories crew member Todd Blair was struck in the head by a machine, disabling him permanently.

Survival Research Laboratories offered a cathartic experience in which technology served no purpose other than to destroy itself exhibitionistically. Where Einstürzende Neubauten and the Berlin scene centralize and exhaust the body in breaking free from (and with) technology, humans are absent from Mark Pauline's stage ("If you start having human performers, you're very limited").[19] Here there's no need to tear buildings down: they will do it themselves. This may reflect a key difference between Berlin's history of suffering and San Francisco's sunny art-as-life-as-art. Pauline's blowing apart his right hand with a rocket motor in 1982 probably also reinforced his desire to keep some distance between machines and makers.

The size and spectacle of Survival Research Laboratories' performances made them an exciting and unique part of the San Francisco scene, and they were very much in dialogue with other early industrial musicians. In their social and totemic role, they acted as essential nodes at a time and in a place vital to industrial music's momentum as an art, but Survival Research Laboratories greased the gears rather than made the noises: they had no product to distribute, their machines were dismantled after (or destroyed by) shows, and their performances were infrequent and usually unrecorded. The group is thus legend within industrial communities in the truly folkloric sense that a trail of recordings might even disrupt. In fact, given the broad scarcity of available artifacts from the San Francisco industrial scene in the late 1970s and early 1980s, we might see a resonance in Z'EV's observation: "It is most telling that the songs sung by the Nine Muses are designated as *mnemosyne*: the *memory* of what is, what was, and what will be. True music? No one writes it or plays it so much as you remember—to—hear it."[20]

That view is an historical one, however. In the actual moment of late 1970s San Francisco, the value of art and music was staked on its living politics and not on some envisioned future legacy. The city particularly privileged music's social dimensions over its formal ones; just think of the cult that surrounded the ever-changing performances of hometown heroes the Grateful Dead.

Integral to these social interactions within the Bay Area soundscape was San Francisco's visible gay community, which fostered a racially diverse cast of artists, promoters, and patrons. The synergy they cultivated was evident even in traditionally straight and white subcultures, as Factrix's Bond Bergland remembers: "The gay scene and the punk scene were very fused. The gay thing was instrumental in forming the punk aesthetic and everything about it. It was the most advanced scene artistically. It was the only game in town."[21]

Culturally savvy, San Francisco was therefore immediately plugged into punk once it began in 1976. By 1978, live punk shows were the religion of San Francisco's underground music scene, and the Mabuhay Gardens in North Beach was its church. With concerts serving as a flexible, affordable, and interactive means of musical socializing, San Francisco bands of the day were less likely to put out independent vinyl releases than acts in London or New York, but the nightlife was just as vibrant. "All the people in *The Industrial Culture Handbook* started out with punk rock," says the volume's editor V. Vale.[22] In particular Mark Pauline recalls, "I appreciated a lot of [punk's] ideas and the fact that it was geared . . . toward getting out information that had previously been relegated to the underground art scene of the sixties and seventies."[23]

"Getting out information" served as an important common ground between punk and industrial movements both in exposing the evils of control authorities and in offering alternative worldviews, histories, and entertainment to a hungry counterculture. Monte Cazazza, for example, prided himself on publicly playing obscure rare audio recordings of cult leader Jim Jones, or screening stolen medical testing videos during live performances. Whatever the venue and whatever the crowd, San Francisco's musicians seem to have focused more on the *act* of disseminating subversive ideas than on the particulars or the fixity of the material itself. The most opulently bizarre underground performers in town were the Residents, whose elaborate stage productions featured the band's members wearing tuxedos and, beginning in 1979, giant eyeballs as full headmasks.

Performance extended beyond the concert venue too. No study of information access in the San Francisco scene would be complete without acknowledging the project that Mark Hosler and his friends dubbed Negativland. In 1979, when Hosler was still in high school, he began experimenting with tape collage, inspired significantly by the Residents' work on their 1976 *The Third Reich 'n Roll*, in which they overlaid and manipulated vintage pop to create montage monstrosities. Starting in 1981, Negativland melded recording and live performance by hosting a weekly radio show every Thursday at midnight on the aforementioned KPFA. On this show, called *Over the Edge*, the group would improvise live cut-ups, mashups, and collage in the name of "culture jamming" (Hosler's own term, which has since taken on a life of its own). The focus on improvisation and music making in real time ostensibly safeguards against one's art becoming reproducible and commodified, though Negativland did make records too. Like the Residents, Negativland wasn't ever fully part of any industrial scene (despite their 1987 club hit "Christianity is Stupid"), but their oddball contributions to the experimental soundscape of the Bay Area and to sampling as a political practice both warrant their mention here.

## 6. Haunting Memory: Factrix and RE/Search

In his introduction to RE/Search Publications' 1983 *Industrial Culture Handbook*, the famous punk journalist Jon Savage identifies five ideas central to industrial music practice:

1. Organizational autonomy
2. Access to information
3. The use of synthesizers and antimusic
4. Extramusical elements
5. Shock tactics[24]

This little list has taken on a life of its own in scholarship about industrial music, and even though this book doesn't especially take the list's items as gospel—for they are collapsible, of incomparable orders, and incomplete—Savage's tenets still make for a good checklist of the Bay Area industrial music practices in the late 1970s and early 1980s. To many, in fact, Savage's two-page introduction in which he lays out these tenets is the most memorable part of the *Industrial Culture Handbook*.

A heady band like Factrix has a lot to say about organizational autonomy and shock tactics. They describe themselves, for example, as "the sound of a bad trip. Like you suddenly wake up with no memory of what happened, but the knife is still in your hand."[25] Factrix established an aesthetic template that many acts in the genre would adhere to in the coming years.

Although Z'EV's music was almost solely percussion, Factrix (like local synthpop stars Tuxedomoon) used no drums, instead employing a low-tech drum machine and tapes. When they really needed to bang on something, a battery of metal, plastic, and glass did the job. Factrix could write actual songs—the two-chord "Ballad of the Grim Rider" has a postpunk Ennio Morricone flavor—but obscuring this on most of their studio and live recordings is a never-ending wash of noise, either from member Joseph Jacobs's tape recorder or from modified guitars, processed Throbbing Gristle–style until they groaned dully. At live shows, singers Bond Bergland and Cole Palme would hunch over their instruments, their high mumbles cutting through the shifting reverb that the band applied to every sound. Their music was undanceable, creaking, and often asphyxiatingly dense, but it managed at times to find a proto-goth vibe that verged on enjoyable; check out their *Scheintot* album's sendoff track "Phantom Pain," recorded in 1980.

Like the English industrial bands of the era, Factrix had an interest in new sound textures afforded by technology: their tools guided their music in a way that separates them from Z'EV and Cazazza, whose personalities and artistic intent relegated musical materials to secondary importance. Perhaps more than any other industrial act of the 1970s, Factrix were aesthetically honed in on the emotively eerie. Dressed in black with black-dyed hair, the band proclaimed allegiance to ex-surrealist Antonin Artaud and his Theatre of Cruelty. Factrix were, according to postpunk chronicler Simon Reynolds, not so much "art damaged as Artaud-damaged."[26]

All cleverness aside, the band's specific adherence to the Theatre of Cruelty ought not be taken as simply yet another shade of modernism in the industrial patina. As will be discussed in Chapter 11, Artaud's ideas about performance are insightful lenses for looking at industrial music. But for the purposes of understanding what industrial music gained from Factrix's San Francisco–based work, it's enough at the moment to say that their interest in Artaud compelled them to shock audiences with the grotesque, the dreamlike incomprehensible, and the excruciating interruption of drumless, womblike textures with jarring taped noise. Reciprocally, San Francisco was uniquely equipped to introduce Artaud as a precondition to Factrix: local beatnik Lawrence Ferlinghetti compiled, translated, and published (through City Lights Books) the 1965 *Artaud Anthology*, and the nonprofit arts complex Project Artaud has operated in the Mission District since 1971. Factrix performed there in March 1980 with Mark Pauline, Z'EV, and NON.

Factrix is lesser known today than Cazazza, Survival Research Laboratories, and Z'EV, but this isn't because they were lesser artists; nor is it for a comparative lack of recordings. Instead, it comes back again to the issue of memory— specifically the fact that the aforementioned *Industrial Culture Handbook* of 1983 devoted articles to the likes of Cazazza and Z'EV ("I did him a huge favor by putting him in there," says editor V. Vale) but not to Factrix.[27] In the late 1970s, Vale (born Vale Hamanaka) had been in charge of San Francisco's influential punk zine *Search and Destroy*, which he'd begun as an employee at City Lights. When he and Andrea Juno published *The Industrial Culture Handbook* in 1983, they were compiling and bibliographing what they considered a collective cultural statement whose incendiary articulation was short-lived. In fact, the book's introduction declared industrial "over," though Vale says, "I think Jon Savage was saying that as a provocation."[28] At any rate, Vale and Juno hadn't anticipated the book's steady popularity over thirty years, which not only helped to rebirth and perpetuate an increasingly global scene that some had left for dead but also inadvertently served to calcify it somewhat—note the instructional overtones of the word "handbook." In this regard the memory of the recent past feeds into the reality of the future. *The Industrial Culture Handbook* has gone through seven printings, selling between twenty thousand and thirty thousand copies by Vale's 2012 estimate; its inclusions and omissions have become as much a part of industrial music as any record's noise.[29]

The San Francisco industrial scene changed but never fully wound down. Factrix disbanded after their live 1982 Cazazza collaboration record *California Babylon*, and Z'EV moved out of town. Early in the 1980s, Boyd Rice of NON connected with the city's scene (more about him later), and extremist bands such as the German Shepherds were playing raucous shows. In the mid-1980s, the poppy Until December came out of the city's leather culture (despite singer Adam Sherburne's heterosexuality), and into the next decade the label COP International and acts such as Grotus and Gridlock would emerge.

From San Francisco's original cast, industrial music gained a highly literate if self-rejecting sense of intellectual heritage, a knack for shock (both as Artaudian tactics and self-promoting villainy), and a sonic fondness for guitar-rich swirls that hint almost optimistically at a science fiction horizon beyond the postindustrial. An urban microcosm of twentieth-century revolutionary politics, San Francisco gives a steeply pitched landscape to industrial music's role in the history of artistic radicalism.

### ICONIC:

Monte Cazazza – "To Mom on Mother's Day" (1979)

Chrome – "The Monitors" (1977)

Factrix – "Anemone Housing" (1980)

The Residents – "Constantinople" (1978)

Tuxedomoon – "No Tears" (1978)

### ARCANE:

The German Shepherds – "I Adore You" (1981)

Minimal Man – "Loneliness" (1981)

Negativland – "#12" (1980)

Boyd Rice – *The Black Album* (1975)

Uns – "Aldo's Bar" (1980)

# Mail Art, Tape Technology, and the Network

## 1. Fluxus and UFOs

Beyond the localized industrial music sites discussed here, there were dozens of other important artists and developments early in the genre's history. Patrick Codenys of the Belgian EBM act Front 242 recalls, "You have what I called the 'UFOs'—like Crash Course in Science from Philadelphia . . . Severed Heads from Australia. They came out of the blue like that. . . . They were isolated in the eighties, small units, self producing."[1]

But the isolation in which most of these UFOs operated was merely a geographic one; a vital connection exists between early industrial music and the global network established through the Fluxus art movement, its outgrowth of mail art, and the cassette and small press cultures that arose in the late 1970s. These are the surroundings that we might take to be this network's techno-cultural geography. This global communication system existed years before the online communities afforded by today's internet, but nevertheless was in many ways an international virtual scene—one whose virtuality indelibly shaped the music it produced.

An important origin of this network lies in the democratizing art movement Fluxus. George Maciunas, whose family immigrated to the United States from Lithuania after World War II, studied art and design at some of the finest schools in the country, focusing in particular on the history and interaction of modernist movements. Driven by the belief that art can be more than merely the one-time manipulation of a stable physical medium by a single artist for a discrete audience, Maciunas turned his attention to the questions raised by John Cage's writing and music. With a solid grounding in Dada and the movements connected to it (as well as a correspondence with some of its original progenitors, now much older), Maciunas and a growing cadre of intellectual troublemakers began organizing multimedia Fluxus "happenings" in New York, at the short-lived radical Black Mountain College in North Carolina, and across Europe (Maciunas had a job in the early 1960s at an American Air Force base in West Germany). Out of a desire to bring art to new audiences in non-elitist, mass-produced means, members of this network began to exchange what they called mail art.

Instigated in 1958, chiefly by New York artist Ray Johnson, mail art isn't merely art sent via post to a specified recipient, but it takes the epistolary act as its artistic locus. Mail art might be a handmade collage postcard sent to a friend, or a single-printing fanzine of cryptic phrases passed through the post to a dozen recipients from one to the next, or it might be mass mailings of doll parts to entire streets of strangers meant to bewilder and shock. The act matters as much as the artifact, and an audience's interpretation of the art is almost necessarily diffuse, with each sender, courier, or recipient possessing a partial understanding. By duplicating and forwarding art, adding names to ever-growing mailing lists, and incorporating new details—suggestive stamp arranging or addressing with "Do Not Deliver To"—the line between artist and audience eroded.

As discussed in Chapter 3, a variety of ideas from Fluxus influenced early industrial music, but the particular importance of its mail art wing cannot be overstated. It's worth noting that mail art historically coincided with and was empowered by certain key technological developments. Media scholar Paul Théberge reminds us that "electronic technologies and the industries that supply them are not simply the technical and economic context within which 'music' is made, but rather, they are among the very preconditions for contemporary musical culture."[2] In the case of Fluxus, mail art, and industrial music, the preconditional new technologies include the photocopier and the cassette tape, which were developed in 1959 and 1962, respectively.✿ (Significantly, this is also a period during which popular music—especially hard bop and rock 'n' roll—attained more power than ever before to congregate youth subculture.) These reproduction technologies enabled the consumer-level mass distribution of images, written ideas, and recorded sound. Artists could create postcards, collages, and homemade pamphlets with visual panache using photocopiers and also new instant cameras—the folding Polaroid 100 series was introduced in 1963. By 1966, the confluence of rock music and all this technology allowed the self-produced newsletter to break out of the underground nerd network and into the public "cool" with the rags *Crawdaddy* and *Mojo Navigator*. Most of the early readers of these zines were obsessive fans in science fiction and garage rock communities, largely unaware of Fluxus, but artistic and radical leftist gangs had their own publications too. Independently printed specialized publications in art and politics date back more than a hundred years, but copy

---

✿ The first mass-market cassette recorders didn't hit shelves until 1964. The medium began to be used regularly for music only around 1970.

shops allowed faster, more anonymous, more parodic, and more radical zines and lit mags. In fact, the movement's name is taken from Maciunas's own *Fluxus* artist book, which made extensive use of Xerox techniques.

## 2. A History of Tape Trading

More directly relevant to industrial music is the huge network of cassette-based musicians and record labels that developed in the late 1970s and early 1980s all around the world. Nearly every active industrial musician in the world from 1975 to 1983 participated in this network. Although Northern England, Berlin, and San Francisco were geographical centers of the style, industrial music boasted a sparse, covert ubiquity nearly from the start. Its makers contributed to and were inspired by this underground cassette scene, itself the crossroads of cassette tape technology with the mail art submovement within Fluxus.

It's important to understand how this network came into being, because it's not merely a question of mail artists making music. Fluxus questions the fixity of art objects by allowing events and acts to be living, social art, but the rise of tape exchange networks began independent of Fluxus, like the rock and sci-fi zines mentioned above. The actual medium of the cassette inspires politicized networking. The core idea of this—that an artistic medium exists to be questioned, to be manipulated, and, as the site of communication, to be shared— resonated strongly with the work of Maciunas and Fluxus, and the movement's cross-pollination with tape technology is a seminal moment in industrial music history.

Reel-to-reel magnetic tape recording as we know it was invented in 1933, but as previously mentioned, the portable and convenient cassette wasn't developed until thirty years later. When that happened, hi-fi enthusiasts quickly learned how to copy music to tape from the radio, LPs, and other cassettes. Secretly taping concerts was now an enticing possibility to many fans. Overlapping significantly with the rock fanzine crowd, the bootleg circuit was coming alive. Into the 1970s, many bootleggers paid to have recordings cheaply pressed to vinyl by small manufacturing plants, in some cases packaging them to look official so as to fool completist fans into buying them. But in the networks of tape traders—Grateful Dead fans serving as the most famous example—there was no subterfuge as to what was going on: as soon as London's Camden Market opened in 1975, tapes with hand-scrawled labels were sold alongside new major-label releases. America had done its part too, with a 1971 congressional ruling that amended copyright law to allow home taping, which meant a boom for the blank cassette industry. The entry of the Japanese brand Maxell into the tape market in the early 1970s was also a major turning point, as they offered higher-quality media, raising the bar for sound quality.

Not all tape mailing was musical: many people in the 1970s first received or mailed tapes during the Vietnam War, when some soldiers found cassettes an immediate, durable, and personal way to communicate with their families. The cassette letter became a phenomenon widespread enough that in the Netherlands post offices sold tape-and-envelope kits for the equivalent of $1.50.[3] In other parts of the world such as India, the Middle East, and Eastern Europe, translocal and sometimes clandestine networks exchanged tapes of poetry, political speeches, and religious instruction. In the 1978 Iranian revolution, for example, this was instrumental in spreading the words of Ayatollah Khomeini to largely illiterate populations.

The cassette's most immediate appeal was personal empowerment: it could immortalize a user's experience and preserve the sounds and ideas of people's lives. As with audio letters, early cassette music bore intimate personality. Tape scene veterans Rich Jensen and Robin James write that the cassette invites people to "record things that have never been recorded before," and in doing so to forge a "new form of literature, beyond the illusion of theater and into reality."[4]

Among the first self-distributing cassette-based musicians was Nashville native R. Stevie Moore, who as the son of Bob Moore, bassist for Elvis Presley and Roy Orbison, had grown up with access to recording technology. Moore had begun distributing his homemade cassettes to friends and family as early as 1968. In 1971, he left school to focus his efforts expressly on tape music making and distribution.

Another turning point in cassette recording came in 1973, when Virgin records (still very much Richard Branson's maverick brainchild at the time) pulled the stunt of marketing German act Faust's LP *The Faust Tapes* for only 49 pence. The record, which contained two long untitled tracks of spliced noisiness, declares on its sleeve, "These tapes been left exactly as they were recorded—frequently live—and no post-production work has been imposed on them."[5] Thanks to its ultra-low price, the album sold fifty thousand copies in the UK, giving a boost to the idea that music could be cheaply made, poorly recorded, and freely distributed to a nonetheless hungry audience.

1973 was also the year TEAC began manufacturing the consumer-level 2340 multitrack reel-to-reel recorder, which was still more expensive and complicated than most musicians were ready for, but some splurged for it. Others were simply recording their music live to stereo cassette tape. In these pre-1975 years, a few musicians such as English synthesist Paul Kelday and saxophonist Barry E. Pilcher began offering their tapes for purchase in small music magazines. Over the next few years, home recording began to expand as a hobby both for bookish experimenters and as a rehearsal for motivated pop hopefuls. In April 1977, the first Multi-Track Expo was held in Los Angeles and drew forty-five hundred participants.[6]

### 3. Taping as a Political Act

It was the public availability of the Tascam and Fostex four-track cassette re-corders in 1979 that opened the floodgates of independent tape artists. Al-though reel-to-reel recording was intensive and expensive, these machines (at a steep but not prohibitive $1,000) used and reused simple cassettes and were more or less portable.

The cassette tape allowed curious intimacies and budding ambitions to cross boundaries, playing a role in "the plastic arts because it plays with space, and non-space," as counterculture poet-publisher William Levy writes.[7] This ability to transport environments was in fact the guiding impetus behind the first-ever tape trading network, a reel-to-reel penpal circle established in 1953 by media scholar Philip C. Geraci as "a nationwide club of tape enthusiasts who would record events indigenous to their localities and exchange the tapes by mail."[8] Ethnomusicologist Peter Manuel, who has studied cassette usage and trading networks in India, argues that the medium influences the music it contains, and that—as networks like Geraci's and the later mail art-inspired underground illustrate—it can create significant new economies, virtual spaces, and "scenes":

> Cassette technology . . . constitutes a particular mode of production which is itself conducive to particular forms of control, and which has had profound effects on the production, distribution, consumption, and content of popular music. . . . It is most fruitful, then, to recognize cas-sette technology as constituting and engendering a set of modes of pro-duction, which themselves not only influence but constitute cultural phenomena, from the social relations of musical production and con-sumption to musical style itself.[9]

The cassette as a medium impels its users to create, to cut up. William S. Bur-roughs used a Philips recorder (and later a Sony TC) that, by virtue of its stan-dard play/record, rewind, fast-forward, and pause/stop buttons, enabled the immediate reshuffling of time—a selective, fungible chronology. Of course academic experiments with tape splicing and collage predated all this, but the access that was due to the affordability, expertise-free physicality, and social translocation that these tools enabled was a revelation. In fact, one might argue that a key generative difference between proto-industrial pop and the musique concrète of Pierre Schaeffer and his cohort is precisely this consumerist, social dimension.

All of this contributes to what scholar John Corbett calls the "increased possibility for subversion provided by the ever-cheapening technology of cassette tape."[10] The cassette's techno-history also boosts its antiauthoritarian power to steal entertainment and information through copying, as well as its ability to watch the watchmen, empowering users with evidence both of and against their surroundings; recall the damning tapes that unseated President Richard Nixon in 1974. So even to a singer who records linear songs in real time to two-track, these anarchic qualities could impart a sense of the experimental, a connotation of the proletarian underground. Unsurprisingly, though, most of the musicians in these networks weren't simply singers and songwriters. As recordist and zine journalist Carl Howard writes of the tape scene, "As I look at the work of my most stalwart networking friends, their music has all graduated from the industrial model."[11] Not only is the rise of "cassette culture" and its attendant politics no mystery at all when one considers the cassette's implied social bond taken in light of its medial manipulability, but the industrial music that thrived on these tapes is similarly consonant with these ideas. Burroughs in *The Ticket That Exploded* and cyberpunk author William Gibson in "Fragments of a Hologram Rose" both ally the physical acts of recording to and playing from tape with a dizzying, irrational future. In the 1980 song "All Stood Still," UK synthpop act Ultravox situates the tape medium as dystopian: "Please remember to mention me in tapes you leave behind." David Cronenberg's industrial 1983 movie *Videodrome* is certainly the most famous extension of this idea to videotape.✿ Though the cassette tape is not deterministic of the content it holds, it was nevertheless understood as a strong wind through the period's political, subcultural, and artistic climates, contributing to industrial music's perfect storm.

## 4. The Eternal Network

Part of the encounter between the tape scene in the early days and Fluxus had to do with mail art's mid-1970s proliferation, which owed in its own right to the

---

✿ In a funny instance of media and message intertwining, *Videodrome* is, according to Peter Cigéhn's "The Top 1319 Sample Sources," one of the most sampled sources in all of industrial music, with Apoptygma Berzerk, Coptic Rain, Cyberaktif, Emergency Broadcast Network, Front 242, Haujobb, Hyperdex-1 Sect, Implant, Index, Klinik, Meat Beat Manifesto, Psychic TV, Revolting Cocks, and Snog all reappropriating it.[12]

ease of participation. Most of those in its network had an introductory moment similar to that of Boyd Rice of NON:

> I was really interested in European art movements of the early twentieth century, particularly Dadaism. So somebody said to me one day, "Have you seen this ad in the local reader? Some guy wants to put out a magazine about Dadaism." And I went out and I contacted this guy, Steve Hitchcock, and he knew all about the mail art scene. He was already in touch with all these people. He said, "Oh you should give me something to put in this," and I gave him a clipping of the newspaper article about when I tried to give Betty Ford a skinned sheep's head, and all of a sudden I got on all of these lists and I started getting these weird postcards from all over the world. I started getting invitations to send art to art galleries in Prague and you name it. So as a teenager, that's pretty exciting, getting mail from all over the world with these foreign stamps.[13]

Because mail art was geographically diffuse and based as much on the receipt of a parcel as a gallery opening, it seemed a post-industrial egalitarian form *par excellence*: though quality certainly mattered, the quantity of art in circulation helped to subvert the bourgeois value of scarcity. The nature of mail art makes it hard to estimate how many participants there were, but Oberlin College's collection alone contains the work of thirteen hundred artists, which one may presume constituted only a small fraction of the total. The expansion of the mailing lists was always a goal, to the point where insiders started calling the scene "the eternal network." As a result, it was inevitable that mail artists and tapers started overlapping more and more. A lot of Fluxus artists had an interest in experimental music, but owing to technological limitations or to the ephemeral, living nature of performance art, they'd seldom previously recorded or distributed their music. [14] Such was the case with Genesis P-Orridge and Cosey Fanni Tutti, who were involved with mail art even in 1971, well before they specifically committed to music.[15] The same goes for Monte Cazazza.

By the end of 1976, though, punk was becoming common ground between art and music scenes; New York City's hipsters had hinted at this years earlier when Andy Warhol teamed up with the Velvet Underground. With the emergence of punk music came zines such as *Sniffin' Glue*, *Punk*, and V. Vale's *Search and Destroy*. These publications were especially important to fans outside of urban areas, as they offered mail-order addresses and information about music that was otherwise inaccessible, sometimes oceans away. Mail art communities quickly tapped into these zines' back pages, and curious tape scenesters connected that way. Included among these earliest isolated UFOs were French photographer Philippe Fichot, who launched his record label Bain Total and the seminal industrial band Die Form in 1977, and Vittore Baroni, an Italian artist who founded the cassette label Trax and would release music by Laibach and Lustmord.

Throbbing Gristle had sent their earliest tapes to "mail art friends," and as Genesis P-Orridge recalls, they carried over the ideas of Fluxus to music.

> When we decided to do TG we applied all those strategies to the band. We still use those strategies. So we, for example, in an album put a questionnaire.✿ No one was doing that at the time. We pretty much got them back one for one: we sold an album, we got back a questionnaire. We were getting all these back, and we thought, well, what do we do? Now people are thinking and reacting and writing. That's a hell of a step, to get people that involved that they'll take the effort. These are the people who really want to be involved. So what can we do to speak to them? Let's do a newsletter like the Beatles used to do, take a tried and tested technique and warp it to your own particular end. . . . Then they started sending in these fucking cassettes, dozens and dozens and dozens.[16]

The glut of tapes came from fans looking for validation from Throbbing Gristle or musicians looking for a deal with Industrial Records. Chris Carter continues, stating that the unsolicited tapes were "far too many to listen to, or even reply to."[18] However, "we did 'connect' bands we knew and friends, but that's just what you do with friends," Carter adds. "When it came to fans what we did was to publish small lists of selected names and addresses in our IR Newsletters. They could then hook up with one another if they desired."[19]

P-Orridge remembers, "That definitely had a huge impact we found out later. . . . There's definitely a very good argument to say TG newsletters and the cassette network exchange really had a big influence and maybe even began the whole cassette label thing."[20]

It's not at all unreasonable to argue that Throbbing Gristle not only continued the introduction of cassette trading and mail art to one another but specifically brought their industrial fans and imitators into the conversation. We can consider this a crucial moment in the genre's history.

---

✿ P-Orridge here is referring to the questionnaire the band included in their photocopied June 1978 newsletter, the first issue of *Industrial News,* and the insert into the December 1978 repressing of their debut album for Fetish Records.[17]

This merging left the tape scene with more of a scent of Fluxus than the other way around: 1980s tape zines such as *ND*, *U-Bahn*, and *Electronic Cottage* readily covered nonmusicians like the extreme film collective Coup De Grace, while mail art continued (and continues) to exist largely irrespective of the tape scene—acknowledging it as part of the family, but leaving it to those who care most. This is probably the case because, first, the tape scene prior to the advent of the four-track cassette recorder was simply much smaller than the mail art scene, and second, it was at that point centered more around a technology than a credo.

The tape scene didn't come into full swing until 1979, when *Op* magazine began publication, and starting in its fifth issue it launched the "Castanets" column, which reviewed all the tapes submitted to the magazine—something no other major publication dared. Most musicians who participated in the tape network as it's remembered today got involved after an encounter with mail art, but they quickly adapted the ethics and aesthetics of the style, usually to highlight the materiality of the music or the ever-shifting roles of artist and consumer. Some gestures to this effect were subtle: Belgian noise act Etat Brut's 1980 debut cassette *EB001* states that the group "doesn't have to [sic] the desire to communicate with anyone" just inches above their clearly printed address, as if issuing a dare.[21] Other acts were more antagonistic: ambient industrial group Zoviet France packaged their tapes in sandpaper, tar, and porcelain, and Scott Marshall's label Panic Records and Tapes (founded in 1984) "package[d] all its catalogue cassette sales in melted and wrapped junk LP records" so that each parcel "requires a small level of violence to break into."[22]

This small violence, however, bespeaks an undercurrent of the industrial scene. The difficult aesthetics of many industrial musicians bore a nasty streak that ultimately led to tension both with mail art networks and with the law. In 1976, P-Orridge was put on trial for violating the 1953 Post Office Act by sending a collage postcard featuring pornography alongside a portrait of the Queen. His defense rested on the validity of mail art as an artform—an argument that the magistrate deemed "irrelevant" when she found him guilty and fined him £100. P-Orridge recalls:

> I started getting fiberglass resin and making big parcels with mutant animals made out of bits of rabbits and chickens and I'd send them in the mail. And at one point [the recipient] nearly got prosecuted by the post office for receiving maggot-ridden, disgusting, stinking parcels . . . for all their so-called radicalism, they were incredibly conservative and very moral—they used to get really incensed at some of my pornographic collages—especially people in "mail art."[23]

Ultimately, P-Orridge, Cazazza, Rice, and others like them largely abandoned the mail art network, finding it bland and bloated—not a surprise given that the 1963 founding manifesto of Fluxus demanded that art be "grasped by all peoples." Thus, according to Hal McGee, founder of the Cause and Effect cassette label, "Everyone acknowledges the tape scene's roots in mail art," but many of its more confrontational musicians have appreciated their distance from the latter-day mail art scene and the comparatively sunny pockets it incubated with its democratizing imperative.[24]✿

By the early 1980s, the idea of the cassette as a globally available medium that embodied culture cheaply harmonized well with the squat-based militant leftists in Western Europe, the ecologically minded anarchists in California, and even a few adventurous Eastern Bloc artists such as Slovenia-based noise-maker Mario Marzidovšek: the cassette helped to break down barriers between production, distribution, and consumption. It encouraged users to be fans, distributors, musicians, and journalists all at once. For example, Geert-Jan Hobijn founded Staalplaat, initially a cassette-only shop in Amsterdam's NRC squat in 1982. Being plugged into the cassette network, he found it easy within a year to release Laibach's tape *Through the Occupied Netherlands*, thus expanding Staalplaat into a label. After that, he would go on to record and release tapes of his own. He recalls, "If you were in the family, you would be an alien if you weren't doing your own cassettes. You had to, in a way."[25]

The tapes that circulated in the network contained all manner of homemade oddities. Hobijn continues, "Extreme noise was in there, but there were also people who were making synthpop music at home on their equipment."[26] In this burgeoning global community, autonomy and a collective stance against the perceived authority of major labels, government, and tradition mattered more than a unified aesthetic or even a common politic. Some tape acts were on the political right, notably UK-based Con-Dom and Belgian duo Club Moral, but liberal ideologies were more common. For instance, Nigel Ayers, a UK squatter for ten years and a highly active tape scene participant, created his industrial act Nocturnal Emissions from an explicitly antifascist "free festival culture" viewpoint.[27] Many industrial acts, most famously Laibach, negotiate processes of signification that eschew simple distinctions like these—a topic to be addressed in Chapter 13.

---

✿ To be fair, Fluxus-affiliated artists were capable of real transgression, as Chapter 3 noted. Takehisa Kosugi's "Music for a Revolution" instructs the performer, "Scoop out one of your eyes 5 years from now and do the same with the other eye 5 years later," and Nam June Paik's "Danger Music No. 5" tells us to "Creep into the vagina of a living whale."

The industrial scene was almost entirely male. Dejan Knez of Laibach says flatly that "girls are afraid of us."[28] This was also more or less the case in cassette culture as a whole. There were exceptions—Annea Lockwood, Amy Denio, Jarboe, Caroline Kaye Walters (of Nocturnal Emissions), Audio Leter's Sue Ann Harkey, and Diana Rogerson (of Fistfuck and Chrystal Belle Scrodd)—but they were making music amid a network of thousands of men. The prevailing attitude hinted, in fact, that women actively hindered the scene. Hobijn says that his tape shop attracted "pale male types. If there was a woman, she was someone's girlfriend, and they were like, 'Are you ready yet? Is this going to take long?' We considered making a special corner for them in the shop because they cost us because they were complaining."[29]

The sheer amount of music being circulated was staggering—enough that it may well have had large-scale effects on the global music market. In 1979 and 1980, the major-label record industry experienced its worst-ever financial downturn. Although some blamed punk and its anticapitalism, and some disco (an easy target, as many felt it threatened their whiteness and heterosexuality), the industry fixed the crosshairs on the cassette business: young African Americans bought large boomboxes and were visible users of the tape medium—these were also the early days of breakdance and the hip-hop mixtape—and the underground taping network (entirely separate from the rap scene) was growing every day. In the United States, the RIAA attempted unsuccessfully to levy a significant tax on every blank tape sold. It didn't matter whether tape users were copying albums illegally or making their own; as far as the record industry was concerned, they weren't buying major label records, either way. "Home Taping Is Killing Music," declared the RIAA's campaign (in response to which tape zines declared "Home Fucking Is Killing Prostitution"). Though it's hard to say for certain that the campaign backfired and directly inspired more home taping, it's absolutely the case that the network grew in size and solidarity aggressively over the first few years of the 1980s.

The breadth of music and attitudes circulating in this network made for exciting collaboration, and so not only did musicians share space on split releases like Current 93 and Nurse With Wound's 1983 *Mi-Mort* but they would also trade in-progress four-track tapes, each act contributing layers to the total, as was the case with the same year's *Action and Reaction (Critique of Leisure Consumption)* by UK industrialists Attrition and Seattle's erudite act Audio Leter. Germany's P16.D4 helmed the scene's most impressive collaboration album with *Distruct*, for which source material and sounds were submitted via post by Nurse With Wound, Nocturnal Emissions, Die Tödliche Doris, the Haters, and many others. And even though plenty of groups released albums and EPs on cassette, perhaps the network's most emblematic tool was the compilation tape, on which ambient drone music, low-budget postpunk, appliance banging, free jazz, and noisy Throbbing Gristle wannabes all commingled. Most of the bands of this era have faded into total obscurity, but music by some of the compilation tape regulars has endured, largely through reissues and usually owing to the sheer quality or tenacity of the artist. Examples include English expat psychedelic goths the Legendary Pink Dots, New York–based noise act Controlled Bleeding, UK-based Bryn Jones's curiously Palestine-centric act Muslimgauze (who rightfully earn a full study of their own in Ibrahim Khider's scholarship), proto EBM act Portion Control, Factory Records artist Section 25, and Japanoise god Masami Akita's Merzbow project. Other important tape scene acts already mentioned thus far were Zoviet France, Attrition, Lustmord, Test Dept., Whitehouse, and Coil. Still other musicians important to the scene remain less known but certainly deserve a listen, such as Colin Potter, Sleep Chamber, Bene Gesserit, Bourbonese Qualk, Konstruktivists, and 400 Blows.

A few of the compilations featuring bands like these have become classics in their own right, most notably 1982's *Rising From the Red Sand*, which Third Mind founder Gary Levermore assembled as an extension of his zine, and 1983's *The Elephant Table,* compiled by *Sounds* journalist Dave Henderson after writing his gigantic state-of-industrial-music assessment "Hidden Planet," itself inspired by his marveling review of *Rising From the Red Sand*.[30] Most tapes of the day were distributed in runs of twenty-five to two hundred, but these compilations sold thousands.

The compilations were not released just through the mail order cassette scene; they (and plenty of artists' own releases) found their way into shops, and even onto vinyl eventually—for example, *Flexipop* magazine launched in 1980 and included in every issue a seven-inch record of experimental new wave, handpicked from the tape scene. Levermore recalls *Rising From the Red Sand* forcing his transition from zine enthusiast into label owner:

My idea was just to sell them on mail order and to sell some to the Rough Trade shop in London and maybe one or two other shops that might be interested. I think I sent out three promo copies. One of those copies was given a five star review in *Sounds* magazine . . . they published my address, which at the time was my parents' house, and of course I started getting inundated with checks for four pounds fifty. So my lunchtimes were spent in the post office—of course I still had my job at the time—they were spent at the local post office, mailing out all these cassettes that people had ordered from me. But in the wake of the review, I also had a phone call from Rough Trade distribution in London, and they said . . . "Well how many have you got," and I'd sent out some promos to the bands, and I said I had about two hundred. And he said, "Oh you're going to need a bit more than that," and it basically went from there.[31]

As some labels and artists attracted wider recognition and financial success, the otherwise egalitarian tape scene began in small ways to factionalize. In the early 1980s the growing cachet of new wave, industrial, and "downtown" classical music meant that there was demand for live performances (a rarity among tape artists) and higher-quality recordings. It started becoming clear that there was money to be made, though it lay beyond the limits of the cassette as a medium. Andrew Szava-Kovats of industrial bands Data-Bank-A and Dominion concedes in his tape scene documentary *Grindstone Redux*, "Making the leap from cassette to vinyl was important because that opened up a lot of doors that were closed to cassette, for instance the radio scene."[32]✿ Indeed, whereas the tape scene fostered organizational autonomy, in the end every UFO steered its own course through the darkness.

## 5. A Virtual Scene

Recall the definition of a musical scene as having centralized participation but an ever-changing cast. In the case of tape music, this managed to occur in the absence of a single location; the network spread across the west and also included a handful of musicians in Asia, Africa, and South America. Rather than hinder activity, however, the globality and facelessness of the network imbued it with greater cultural variety than an in-person scene, while simultaneously reducing the risk of interpersonal bristling through misunderstanding (to put it gently, social awkwardness frequently accompanied the reclusive collector mentality that encouraged participation in the tape scene). The scene was enduring, politically engaged—someone really ought to anthologize the era's zine manifestos—and set on developing a new transgressive folk discourse, rather than rehashing old ones.[33]

Its audiences, producers, and distributors not only congregated and collaborated but perpetuated and encouraged music. What Phil Dink says about

---

✿ It's worth noting that although tapes could hold up to sixty minutes per side, once a band cut a seven-inch record, they were all but necessarily making songs whose length, if not their content, was radio-friendly. A quick glance at early industrial recordings shows that track lengths were becoming more standardized and poppish by the early 1980s.

his own label, Home Recordings, in fact applies to the entire cassette label phenomenon:

> A large number of local groups were formed which probably would never have existed without the label. . . . Of the groups that would have existed, few would have released anything. . . . Many of the musicians . . . actively participated in several ensembles, with more and more on the way. Entire projects can be shelved for extended periods of time and then resurrected at any later date.[34]

These practices apply to vibrant music scenes, and as we'll see, several scenarios in industrial music history recapitulate them, particularly those involving the WaxTrax! record label.

The point here is that through this virtual scene and its interpersonal, musical, organizational, and technological facets, industrial music not only spread on the wings of airmail but rose up and coalesced in a variety of independent locales by the mere suggestion of artistic and technological possibility. This not only adds a rich new dimension to a mapping of the genre's history but helps us understand—even outside of online communities—how local and global scenes can bear greater resemblance than difference.


## 6. Industrial Geography Revisited

Tracing industrial music's aesthetic, ethical, and social inheritance isn't a simple case of attributing working-class grit to Northern England or nihilistic aggression to Berlin. When ideas come into contact, they don't just stack on top of each other; instead they interrelate in complicated ways. And we can't forget, as this part of the book stated at the outset, that ultimately people are the ones making the records and playing the concerts, and a manifesto doesn't accurately model what really happens in the social and pragmatic trenches of music making.

Returning to the big issue of industrial geography, it's not just that industrial music responded to certain cities; it responded to a particular way of being in (and thus of perceiving) these cities and scenes, as portrayed in the selective histories and environments presented here. Whether with tape, guitars, synthesizers, or flame-spitting robots, industrial music's responses to a modern landscape involve rejecting the politically shameful past, reviving the revolutionary spirit of modernism and socialism, celebrating the human body's modalities, invoking new gods, publicizing the hidden while hiding the public, questioning the very worth of thought itself, and condemning the convergence of capitalism, technology, one-way media, government, and the military. Industrial music's earliest tactics were both earnest and ironic, altruistic and self-aggrandizing, and at times premeditated, spontaneous, and retrofitted. This gray cloud of responses hovers over a very real map of motivations, and as it shifts from the early 1980s to the present, the shapes it assumes are recombinations—cut-ups—of these people's work.

### ICONIC:

Maurizio Bianchi – "Treblinka" (1981)

Iron Curtain – "The Condos" (1984)

Konstruktivists – "Andropov '84" (1983)

Lustmord – "At Thee Mountains of Madness" (1981)

Severed Heads – "Dead Eyes Opened" (1983)

### ARCANE:

Bourbonese Qualk – "Return to Order" (1985)

Data-Bank-A – "Group Six" (1984)

P16.D4 – *Distruct* (1984)

Romans – "Membrum Lucis" (1983)

Smegma – "Can't Look Straight" (1979)

Part III

# INDUSTRIAL MUSICAL STYLE

AESTHETICS EMERGE EVEN WHEN ARTISTS BELIEVE THEIR WORK TO BE A MEANS to an end, rather than an end unto itself. In the first half of the 1980s, while industrial music retained the power to express informational struggles of the urban west (as it still does today), new audiences gave new contexts and meanings to the genre. The music's sound and stylistic features thus became the shared commonality among fans and among makers around the world. As a sonic negotiation of *what industrial music would be*, this era can be understood as the genre's first real engagement with its own aesthetics.

# The Tyranny of the Beat: Dance Music and Identity Crisis

## 1. Those Heady Days of Idealism Are Over

Not long after Sandy Robertson gave Throbbing Gristle's *The Second Annual Report* a five-star review in *Sounds* in November 1977, London's Virgin Records outlet store ordered 200 copies of the LP (the band had pressed just 785 in total). Robertson's review states boldly, "It isn't punk rock, it isn't anything you could name."[1] But as P-Orridge remembers:

> Saturday we went in to look around and see if it was on the shelves yet. We were looking around and it was not under *T*. We figured those fuckers hadn't put it out. We looked under *I* for industrial and there it was, written "industrial" and they spelled it wrong too. The next time we went in, there was Cabaret Voltaire there under *I*. They really swallowed it. They'd gone for it. Industrial music was now a genre. We were all "Wow! We did it! We invented a genre of music!"[2]

It makes for a good story (P-Orridge excels as a storyteller), but this swift appropriation of the I-word was fairly isolated.✿ As discussed earlier, genre is a negotiation among communities of artists, fans, marketers, and cultural commentators, including journalists and academics. As such, it takes time for these parties to agree with one another about just what a given genre is, by which point it might be a few years old, or worse, totally over. For example, a 1986 issue of *Spin* suggests that "Industrial music got its name in Cleveland when the 1978 wave of new rockers began experimenting with factory hisses and mechanical

---

✿ Excerpt from an interview by the author and Meredith Collins with Genesis Breyer P-Orridge (who self-identifies using the plural, in remembrance of Lady Jaye, late spouse and partner in their Pandrogyne project):

GBPO: We've never called ourself a musician in an interview. Ever. Nor have we ever called ourself an artist or a writer in an interview. We never ever use those words. . . .

MC: Would you call yourself a storyteller?

GBPO: Yes, we would.

beats," revealing, regardless of its truth content, that our understanding of the genre's boundaries and history has changed over time.[3] (Incidentally, the acts to whom *Spin* alludes are almost certainly Cleveland's Pere Ubu and Canton's Devo, bands whose political and sonic extremism came packaged in too cartoonish a whimsy and who were too song-oriented to fit into the pantheon of early industrial music in all its abstract, oppressive direness.) But *Spin*'s odd assessment aside, 1985 and 1986 are without doubt the first years in which widely popular western media repeatedly acknowledged the existence of industrial music. These years also mark the beginning of a long period during which industrial music would be financially profitable, socially cool, and, to wide public audiences, musically pleasurable.

This chapter, however, is chiefly concerned with the period from the early 1980s to 1985 or so, during which the aforementioned negotiations of genre took place in a newly self-aware and fast-growing musical milieu generated from the collective contributions of the aforementioned English, German, and California-based scenes as well as the tape networks that gave voice to virtual scenesters the world over. Many musicians of this time were hardly concerned with (or even aware of) "industrial music" as an idea, and so mass culture's retroactive assignment of the genre label to acts such as Foetus, NON, and Nocturnal Emissions has been met—perhaps rightly—with some skepticism and even hostility from those artists. Similarly, some acts who socially operated within what was functionally the industrial fold made music that, heard three decades later, doesn't ring as especially industrial—23 Skidoo, for instance. This is all part of the extended dialogue of the scene during those years.

More directly, Industrial Records folded, and the likes of Jon Savage and V. Vale penned jeremiads that marked the end of the music's first chapter. "1980! 1981! THOSE WERE THE DAYS! Those heady days of idealism are over," wrote Savage.[4] This pessimism was enough to raise the question of whether industrial music, whatever it was, would cease to exist. On one hand, how could it continue, progressing beyond the extremes of confrontation, noise, and high-concept PR embodied in its first wave? And didn't the formalizing of a sound into a "genre" risk turning the music into just the kind of unobtrusive commodity that it railed against? On the other hand, how could it not continue, having hinted only momentarily at so many new ways of doing music? Was it against industrial music's ethics to drop the directive of constant change and instead focus on a particularly engaging sound that the genre happened upon amid all its change? And did it matter? Questions like this, whether knowingly confronted or not, preoccupied musicians and fans during this "lost era" of industrial music.

## 2. Irony

On the sonic level, the biggest change during this time was the increased in-corporation of pop and rock practices, particularly the use of dance beats. The immediate boost they provided to industrial music's listenability marks this era as the beginning of "the good stuff" for some fans, while for others it was an irredeemable misstep. Journalist Bill Meyer writes in *The Wire*:

> The assumption made by the bulk of the second wave Industrial groups . . . was that their music's challenge resided in its rawness of texture, its crushing volume, its favouring of brutal tonality. In reality, it was the lack of a regular beat that made first wave outfits like London based Antipodeans SPK harder to digest. Rock audiences can deal with pretty much anything if there's a big fat drum track on it. The idea that ever more massive clanking backbeats constituted an intense, iconoclastic experience rather than a huge compromise and watering down of the music's power was self-delusional at best, Machiavellian at worst.[5]

But not all drumbeats serve the same purpose. The different ways that musi-cians incorporated pop can tell us a lot about how they were responding to in-dustrial music's potential identity crisis. Musical meaning and motivation vary with every artist, song, and audience, but we can broadly attribute three func-tions to industrial music's pop excursions. These aren't mutually exclusive—they stack—but in most cases a given industrial dance song employs one of these three behaviors dominantly.

First is the explicitly political appropriation of pop, which can include par-ody, but which usually instead of mocking popular music uses and recontex-tualizes it to assert social commentary about that pop and the culture that consumes it. In doing so, it also presents the industrial artist as knowing and empowered: he or she can *do* pop without *being* pop.

One example is the LP version of song "Today I Started Slogging Again" by You've Got Foetus On Your Breath, one of the many "Foetus" band names that Jim G. Thirlwell has used for his mostly solo endeavors. Atop a funky, unquan-tized drum machine, he begins by invoking cheap-sounding synthesizer imi-tations of a supposed backing band: "Are you ready on bass? Organ? Are you ready on guitar? Shut up! Shut up, guitar! *A-hit me now! Ow!*" In rejecting the guitar (which keeps practically silent after its initial masturbatory noodle), there's a twinge of postpunk's real antirock sentiment. More broadly, when cou-pled with the James Brown-isms in the vocal take and the drums, the intro helps the song merge longstanding popisms with its subject matter—the Marquis de Sade—in a way that exposes pop music's hidden prohibition against truly radical sexuality and politics by violating it.

If this interpretation seems farfetched, consider Laibach's 1984 song "Perspektive," one of the band's first recordings to use a metronomic 4/4 drum rhythm. Syncopated accents ornament an otherwise rigid backbeat as a narrator intones:

> Laibach practices a sound force in a form of systematic, psycho-physical terror as social organizational principle, in order to effectively discipline and raise a feeling of total adherent bond of a certain, revolted and alienated audience, which results in a state of collective aphasia, which is the principle of social organization.

In this passage—less a lyric than a manifesto—the band declares their intent to force the compliance of a dissident audience (after all, who else listened to Laibach?). They do this in order to display through imitation the nature of centralized government: "One transmitter and a multitude of receivers . . . with a communication through uncommunication." With this last bit, Laibach asserts that a broadcast monoculture handed down through one-way media such as recorded music silences its recipients, but this silencing is itself a political act of such significance that the one-way nature of the broadcast is more important than its supposed content. The band's mission, then, is to oppose tyranny by revealing it through its own language, acknowledging, "All art is subject to political manipulation, except for that which speaks the language of this same manipulation."[6]

As "Perspektive" marches relentlessly onward, Laibach instructs the silent listener in the dance beat's uses: "Disco rhythm, as a regular repetition, is the purest, the most radical form of the militantly organized rhythmicity of technicist production, and as such the most appropriate means of media manipulation." Relevant to this idea, musicologist Robert Fink comments that repetition "can be interpreted as both the sonic analogue and, at times, a sonorous constituent of a characteristic repetitive experience of self in a mass-media consumer society"—that is to say, the modern world is one in which we repeat ourselves.[7] Staging our subjugation to modernity, Laibach then points out the dance beat's theatrical power to synchronize masses of people into a single physical rhythm, a common machinelike choreography resulting from their shared experience in receiving the music's ultrasteady metering of time: "Laibach is a recognition of time universality," the narrator declares at the start of "Perspektive." The band's obsession with one-way dictation's imperative of conformity is why, incidentally, they delight in recording cover songs; to Laibach, it's an ideological double whammy to force another artist's song to fit their own needs even as they assert that same unifying force on their audience.

Even among industrial acts, Laibach is uncommon in their explicit self-awareness and the complexity of their authorial intent, but in light of works such as "Perspektive" and "Today I Started Slogging Again," and beyond that, in light of industrial music's prankster cousin plunderphonics, it's easy to see that pop appropriation can be a snarky middle finger or a dreadful arraignment of mass culture's crimes. Drew Daniel says of Throbbing Gristle's 1979 song "Hot on the Heels of Love," it "had to be a parody designed to infiltrate the subversive TG message into dance clubs."[8] Indeed, the belief that pop was there to exploit had been in the underground air since the collapse of punk in 1978; just listen to 1979's "Death Disco" by ex-Sex Pistol John Lydon's band Public Image Ltd.

### 3. Technology and Rhythm

The second way that industrial musicians in the early 1980s started using pop music's signifiers recognizes that in the historical moment, these new elements were not as identifiably poppish as we take them to be today. Instead, they might reflect a time when industrial music's exploration of technology aligned itself in parallel with pop's. One reason for this is that readily available consumer-level synthesizer gear encouraged musical possibilities that lay within a certain range of dance music styles. Because musicians from different genres began using these instruments—machines made by Korg, Roland, Oberheim, and perhaps most famously Moog—not only did their sonic profiles as a result converged in resemblance but they nearly all began working with the same musical signifiers of dance, even if these artists had no specific desire to channel disco or rock. This book's previous discussion of cassette technology, along with writings by the likes of Paul Théberge and Mark Katz, should suggest that although a musician's tools might not entirely determine the music produced, they bear a strong influence on it.

David Tibet, singer of pagan neo-folk act Current 93 and early industrial scenester, says of this era, "At this time a lot of people around me were moving into more dance-oriented stuff. That absolutely dumbfounded me. Most of them were people who had shown no interest in dance music whatsoever, but so-called Industrial music became dance music. . . . I never understood why people started dancing."[9] Perhaps Tibet would have understood if, like Die Krupps, he had bought a step sequencer. When attached to a synthesizer, a step sequencer could play an automatic loop of eight or sixteen notes of equal length;

the hardware didn't allow other possibilities. As such, the music these machines made was always in a 4/4 time signature; you can't divide the sequencer's eight beats into a 3/4 waltz. The same thing goes with that most famous of all drum machines, the Roland TR-808. Manufactured from 1980 to 1984, the TR-808 gave users sixteen equal steps of time to fill with the drum sounds it generated. These were represented in four sets of four buttons with LEDs, and each set of four buttons was a different color (red, orange, yellow, and white). This scheme, like the sequencer, enforces through its colors a four-beat pattern, visually dissuading even a syncopated clavé rhythm.

Computer scientist and virtual reality pioneer Jaron Lanier warns that when machines are designed to facilitate one kind of creativity, they often stamp out other kinds. This basic phenomenon is called "lock-in":

> Lock-in, however, removes design options based on what is easiest to program, what is politically feasible, what is fashionable, or what is created by chance.
>
> Lock-in removes ideas that do not fit into the winning digital representation scheme, but it also reduces or narrows the ideas it immortalizes, by cutting away the unfathomable penumbra of meaning that distinguishes a word in natural language from a command in a computer program.[10]

So when bands such as Clock DVA and Cabaret Voltaire threw out their guitars, saxophones, and tape splicing tools and built studios with ever more synth gear, the new sounds they made were exciting, but they existed within a range that in retrospect we perceive to be tied to that particular era, and in their digital precision and instant looping they encouraged repetitive, rigid music.

The gear situation was timbrally limiting, too: guitars sounded good through many kinds of distortion, for example, but most synthesizer tones are too acoustically rich to be musically versatile when run through a fuzz box—especially if played in chords. The limited palette of drum sounds during the early 1980s is duly instructive; there were only a handful of drum machines that were affordable to consumers, and so their sounds became quickly known. As Die Krupps had done, a lot of bands supplemented their sequences with live noise percussion, but at the heart of most early industrial dance music is a thin, familiar ticking.

There were few exceptions. One perpetually underrated act worth noting, however, is Esplendor Geométrico, from Spain, who exhibited real inventiveness in their use of limited technology to create changing, thick, and engagingly syncopated rhythm tracks. Active in the cassette scene, they foreshadow the subgenre of powernoise by well over a decade in songs such as 1982's "Neuridina."

## 4. Futurist Pop

The other thing to remember in considering the impact of technology on industrial music's early dance elements is that the genre wasn't solidified yet. Certainly not all industrial music was synth-based (see Test Dept.'s barrel drumming and Nurse With Wound's staunch adherence to relatively pure tape manipulation), and certainly not all synth-based acts were industrial. In the late 1970s, a handful of musicians had independently scored left-field hits with electronic pop sounds, among them the Normal's manic "Warm Leatherette" and Thomas Leer's dreamy "Private Plane." Many early synth acts were grouped together as a de facto movement because they all regularly appeared on the "Futurist" charts in *Sounds* magazine and *Record Mirror* in 1980 and 1981. Industrial music was very much in dialogue with this particular pop scene at the time, and even today it's a blurry edge of the genre's history: any postmillennial "old school" industrial club night will welcome the Human League's "Being Boiled," but no DJ would dare spin the group's "Love Action" for fear of risking credibility. The early 1980s "Futurist" set had a similarly fickle logic that was due to its charts' being assembled at the whim of seventeen-year-old Stevo Pearce.

> I got a chart because I was DJing. . . . I had a residency in a club in Soho called Billy's and also residency every week in the Kings Road in what's now a McDonald's. It used to be called the Chelsea Drugstore. I did lots of evenings at the Clarendon Hotel, which is no longer there; it's now a part of the Hammersmith train station. But that was a big place and I put DAF and The Normal and Fad Gadget on, and I put loads and loads of artists on there. I had a residency at the Redford Pool House, which is north of Mansfield. From having the chart in *Sounds*, which they then tagged "Futurist"– I had no say in that tag—I suddenly got a job in *Record Mirror*. So now there were two weekly charts, both called the "Futurist" charts. It was my selection. . . . When A&R people would look at the chart, it would be full of demo tapes: Blancmange, The The, or Soft Cell or Depeche Mode or whatever and it was like, "What are all of these unsigned demo tapes getting a national, weekly presence?"[11]

Many acts from this wave achieved commercial success with the same equipment and sounds as the less-song-driven industrial bands of the day: Front 242 may have seen their use of Korg synthesizers as "architecture . . . linked with the technology," but their 1981 "Operating Tracks" has the same sonic profile as Soft Cell's megahit of the same year, "Tainted Love."[12] The biggest difference between the songs is Front 242's barking male vocals and unadorned modal harmony versus Soft Cell's lusty fey swagger, as "Tainted Love" was originally a 1965 Gloria Jones soul single.✿ Rather than separate industrial music from pop, technology draws them closer together.

As Nigel Ayers of Nocturnal Emissions recalls, "Popular music picked up on what we were doing, '83, '84,"[13] which helps explain why records such as Nocturnal Emissions' 1983 *Viral Shedding* sound clubbier today than they did at the time, but the technology of music making locked in a set of aesthetics in those days that shaped pop as a whole more than industrial music itself did. Whether by synthesizer manufacturers' musical design or through engineering limitations (probably both), the more automated a band allowed their music to become, the dancier it was likely to be—a strange rearview of Laibach's proclamations about disco. And even as synths, samplers, and sequencers went digital in the mid-1980s, the analogue hardware ethos of repetition persisted in the software and the music alike.

## 5. Pleasure

The third way that industrial music uses dance and rock tropes is for their sheer musical and bodily pleasure. Simply put, Big Black's 1984 guitar-driven "Racer X" *rocks*. And Cabaret Voltaire's 1982 hit "Yashar" is a brilliant, sexy dance track.

Musical pleasure interfaces in obvious ways with industrial music's technology-driven second mode of pop incorporation: the tools of music were in part designed to optimize musical pleasure, and in exploring these tools a musician instinctively seeks to maximize the pleasure they produce.

Taken in light of the ironic first category of pop tropes in industrial music, though, this issue of pleasure can seem tough to grapple with. From the Marxist viewpoint that inspires Laibach, along with a host of social perspectives like those of Michel Foucault and Theodor Adorno, pop music's most insidious power is one of mass control. The preeminent musicologist Susan McClary comments:

> Social critics have typically been scornful of the pleasurable aspects of the arts, favoring those works that could be shown to have the proper political stance; to dwell on the actual details of the artifice was to be seduced by it into false consciousness, to be drawn away from the central issues of the class struggle.[14]

✿ The swing rhythm in "Tainted Love" is of course also a vital feature, and it may be this very uncharacteristic, even un-idiomatic use of synthesizer technology in service of a retro song that differentiated the song from the typical "Futurist" fare and allowed it to break as a hit.

But the phrase "social critics" here applies just as easily to some staunchly ideological makers and fans of industrial noise music to whom the art is not just political but unwelcoming of any acknowledged social pleasure. A central theme in music by Throbbing Gristle, Factrix, Merzbow, and others is the intentionally ugly and alienating. If the genre is a critique of western culture's assumptions about power, politics, and communication, then surely there is something problematic in simply lying back and happily partaking of the most standard musical signs of that culture.

Think again about what Laibach says in "Perspektive," though. At one point, the lyric declares, "The dualism of Laibach's message, perception, and receiver structure uncovers the social neurosis." The dualism here refers to the band's simultaneous use and critique of totalitarian methods; the social neurosis they reveal in "unit[ing] the biters and antagonistics into an expression of static totalitarism" is that audiences willingly sign up to submit to music, to be silenced by it.

Here we have to ask: Is the point of uncovering the social neurosis to cure it? "It's 1984. . . . It's the death factory society, hypnotic, mechanical grinding, music of hopelessness. Film music to cover the holocaust," warns a 1976 Throbbing Gristle press release.[15] Bodily pain thematically pervades this music as a suggestion that its listeners are anaesthetized, but beyond the near universal cry of "wake up!" there is relatively little industrial music that directly rallies the newly awakened to action.

Instead, a lot of industrial dance music admits and revels in its own pop pleasure. Masochism is therefore the most explicit reconciliation of this self-aware submission—especially in light of the thematics of pain. Whereas in punk contexts masochistic imagery served as a means to shock and revolt (think of Vivienne Westwood's popularizing bondage gear in outfitting the Sex Pistols), with industrial music it takes on the added role of playing out a paradox. Nearly all of Die Form's oeuvre is devoted to bondage and sadomasochism, and Swedish Industrial Records signees the Leather Nun embodied the idea as well. Similarly, a young London-based Irishman named Rod Pearce launched Fetish Records in 1978 (adapting the name from a mail art t-shirt) and, through five years of releasing music by Throbbing Gristle, 23 Skidoo, and Clock DVA under the label's name, quietly connected perversion and Marxist commodity fetishism.[16]

Among the most infamous of industrial excursions into pop was that of SPK, who until 1983 were arguably the genre's most outspoken ideologues and among its noisiest performers. Gary Levermore recalls:

> Graeme Revell [of SPK] was one of the most intelligent men ever to walk the earth. He was not a stupid guy—a very learned guy. He starts

out making pretty combustible hard electronic music, very uncompromising, and then suddenly decides, "This isn't what I want to spend the rest of my life doing. . . ." I still remember taking a delivery of cassettes to the Rough Trade warehouse in Ladbroke Grove in London, so this would have been about April 1983, and as I did in those days, I would buy a bunch of stuff they were distributing, because you could get a cheaper price than you could in record stores. And I picked up the brand new 12" by New Order, which was called "Blue Monday." And I was walking down the street and I bumped into Nigel Ayers from Nocturnal Emissions. And he said, "Oh I was just going to get that myself. I know Graeme is really keen to hear that as well," and of course within a month or two, SPK were working with Mike Johnson, who was the engineer for "Blue Monday," and of course they were in the process of putting together a record deal with Fiction Records. . . . Obviously it's no exaggeration to say that in April of 1983, "Blue Monday" was a way forward.[17]

SPK's ripoff of the massive dancepop hit "Blue Monday" was a single called "Metal Dance," and it marked the beginning of a dizzying change in fortune for the band. SPK played the song live for the first time in late July 1983, and less than two weeks later they were sharing the stage with Howard Devoto and the Smiths—comparatively less dour openers than their previous support acts (of whom the Birthday Party and the Virgin Prunes were the most well known). SPK then played the song for a BBC session with John Peel on August 31, and by the year's end they'd played on the national TV show *The Tube* with Depeche Mode and headlined at the Venue, with Sonic Youth and Danielle Dax opening. "Metal Dance" sold thirty thousand copies and earned the band a seven-album, million-dollar contract with Elektra/Warner Brothers (who dropped them after one record, letting them keep the full advance).[18]✿ The money was a welcome windfall, as Revell had been living in a squat and now had a child.

"Metal Dance" expresses a desire to move forward musically, strongly hinting at the second, technologically driven way in which industrial music veers toward pop, but the alarming melodic and centrally mixed female vocal (sung by Revell's soon-to-be wife Sinan Leong) shows a kind of pop indulgence that the sequencer's ready-made synth patterns can't account for. SPK attempts to have its revolution and dance to it too: despite Leong's centrality in the mix, the

✿ Allegedly, the record company wanted SPK to tour with Metallica, not understanding that "metal" meant entirely different things to these acts and their fans.

lyrics place her firmly in submission (sexual? political?) to the accompanying music in all its techno-newness. Physically exhausted and damaged, she is enslaved to its Marxist, opiate potential.

Can't help moving to the rhythm
Feel so breathless
Can't shake out that breathless voice
Crashing steel
Strange new sounds intoxicate me
Cutting hard

In some ways, this resembles the ambivalence between technophilia and techno-paranoia explored in the Futurism-Burroughs equation. It's doubtful in this case that SPK felt optimistic about their ability to retain critical power over the hypnotizing erotics of pop frameworks while simultaneously enjoying them. Ever self-aware, they conclude the song (after an unsurprising drum-machine-plus-metal-banging breakdown) with a lyrical concession, "One step forward, two steps back."

Of course, there are other ways to think about pleasure in music. If taking pleasure in popular music is, to the likes of Adorno or Laibach, a surrender to the oppressors, it's just as conceptually oppressive to suppose that audiences are unable to adapt their own experience of music to new uses and pleasures, including an exerted resistance to a musical message, an identification with the dictatorial power of the music or its makers (rather than the silence of a supposed audience), or a creative empowerment through open-ended signifiers that invite a kind of playfulness at the interpretive level. We need to grant these possibilities in understanding industrial music. If we don't, then ideologically speaking the entire genre is without capacity for contact or humor, and it effectively derails itself in the early 1980s (an assertion that indeed some hold to be true). Adam Krims warns against musicology privileging and rehabilitating every movement and genre as if it were operating against an unspoken mainstream, but it's beyond debate that industrial music has expressly framed itself as an antiestablishment mouthpiece for decades since its first pop flirtations, and so this is a natural approach to the genre.[19] We also need to grant that there are other possibilities of meaning and use for pop pleasure within industrial music because, despite its often explicit use of Marxist themes, the music engages vitally with other ideas too. During this era, for instance, it developed a polymorphous obsession with the body as a site of both purity (see the early work of Front 242 and Nitzer Ebb) and revulsion (Skinny Puppy).

## 6. Industrial Identity

Reflecting the music's simultaneous roots in urban subculture and isolated home studio experimentation, the audience for industrial music was a social blend. There were makeup-wearing punks who (in the words of Cabaret Voltaire biographer Mick Fish) "looked suspiciously like they had a copy of Jean Paul Sartre's *Nausea* hidden under their coats."[20] There were working-class skinheads and university eggheads. There were clubgoers—gay, straight, and everything between—who'd heard about a more dangerous music. There were hipster DJs like Stevo Pearce who'd sneak in songs by Absolute Body Control between Depeche Mode and Joy Division. On occasion, there were Hells Angels. Beyond the cities was a huge swarm of indistinguishably normal-looking suburban boys—English, American, Belgian, and German—who subscribed to *Sounds* and who hounded their local record stores to special-order albums from distributors like Rough Trade and the Cartel. Bon Harris of English EBM act Nitzer Ebb recalls:

> You'd have the holdovers from goth and postpunk, you'd have rastas, a few hippies, a couple of heavy metal blokes. I'd wonder what are each of these groups here getting out of this. Overall, I think they just got the fact that we were up for it. We would get up there and it was very energetic."[21]

Even as musicians, marketers, and fans slowly came to recognize industrial music as a distinct (if hazily defined) genre, the idea of listening to it exclusively or even primarily didn't yet make much sense. It wouldn't be until the late 1980s that venues expressly launched industrial nights, but clubs such as Blitz in London (famously the cradle of the New Romantic movement) were friendly to the genre. At concerts, audiences would brood, yell, and occasionally dance. On the stage, dozens of bands imitated the military chic of Throbbing Gristle. Others wore futuristic black plastic jumpers, and others still blended in with the postpunk set, dressing in trenchcoats. Some fans went shirtless, modeling themselves after Soviet labor posters, contrasting with the Kraftwerk-inspired image of sweatless android performers. As KMFDM's En Esch remembers, audiences followed performers' leads: "There were people, just like in every era, who looked like the band themselves. Millions of mini-Blixa Bargelds and Mark Chungs."[22]

All these modes of reinforcing an identity reflect fans' and makers' aforementioned variety of meanings and uses for industrial music—whether rooted in an acknowledged political discourse, a search for the technologically new, or a personal angle on pop's sounds themselves. This also comes through in the album art of the period, from the constructivist style of designer Neville Brody (Z'EV, Cabaret Voltaire, 23 Skidoo) to the cyberpunk chic of Portion Control's logo to the Darth Vader-esque gothic record sleeves of German grunters Warning. It is easy to chalk up any given image or sound in the genre to some aspect of the functional symbolism and supposed ideology of the music as outlined in the previous chapters, but it's simply wrongheaded to ignore the fact that aesthetics and pleasure ultimately lie at the heart of most actual participation in any music.

So with an understanding of how and why so much beat-driven, even melodic industrial music began to happen, as well as its place within the still-ongoing development of a genre, it's now worth looking at some important highlights of the era.

**ICONIC:**
> Cabaret Voltaire – "Sensoria" (1984)
> Die Form – "Masochist" (1984)
> Nocturnal Emissions – "No Separation" (1983)
> Einstürzende Neubauten – "Yü Gung" (1985)
> Hunting Lodge – "Tribal Warning Shot" (1985)

**ARCANE**
> Esplendor Geométrico – "Moscú Está Helado" (1980)
> Laibach – "Panorama" (1984)
> Les Vampyrettes – "Biomutanten" (1981)
> Pankow – "God's Deneuve" (1984)
> Warning – "Why Can the Bodies Fly" (1982)

# "After Cease to Exist":
# England 1981–1985

## 1. The Mission Is Terminated

After Throbbing Gristle announced on June 23, 1981, that "The Mission Is Terminated," they initially split into two. Chris Carter and Cosey Fanni Tutti had an offer waiting from Rough Trade to launch their new project Chris & Cosey. Tutti remembers:

> Because TG was all about honesty and truth, I found there was a lot I couldn't be honest about regarding the fact that I'd left Genesis, because it had to be publicly upheld that he was okay still. I found that a real problem, so when TG split, it was great for me because I had that honesty back again, and I wasn't promoting something that was untrue.[1]

In Chris & Cosey's music, a heavy sonic reverberation in the relative absence of high harmonic frequencies conveys a mild claustrophobia, which is impressive, given how sparse their arrangements are—often just one or two synthesizer patterns in minor keys over a two-beat drum pattern. The singing is undeniably melodic, though, and the rhythms are rooted in dance. In an unambiguous recognition of industrial music's tension between the politics of pop and its pleasures, Carter says of the dance excursions that had begun on Throbbing Gristle's *20 Jazz Funk Greats*:

> It was ironic at the beginning. It was more an experiment to see if we could do it, because none of us were trained in any sort of musical way other than a few piano lessons. Then when we did that and it worked, we said okay, this is quite enjoyable doing this. Let's actually do it. That was when we left and did Chris & Cosey.[2]

The band's 1981 album *Heartbeat* embraces a human vulnerability amid its quiet, cavernous mechanized looping. In the song "This Is Me," Carter and Tutti alternate singing "Here I come. I'm gonna get you," seemingly drawing new meaning from the ambiguous line each time. The effect is a little reminiscent of the open-endedness in the lyrics to Throbbing Gristle's "Still Walking." Tutti explains, "It was still ideological for me, but in terms of relationships, after everything we'd been through with TG—it did get ugly. That came into the songs we did as Chris & Cosey. That's why the lyrics had double meanings."[3] This kind of songwriting built on the work of previous incarnations of the genre, opening up an established set of industrial lyrical themes as poetic metaphors for personal experience.

In 1982, Chris & Cosey scored an underground hit with "October (Love Song)," but despite the signifiers of pop, their songs were more atmospheric than catchy. As Mick Fish puts it, to many industrial fans "without P-Orridge's mischievous intent, Chris & Cosey were too tame an outfit to confront, nor were they able to display any pop potential despite becoming friendly with the Eurythmics."[4]

Carter recalls, "We could see the end of TG coming—all of us could—so we were planning what to do post-TG." Shortly before the breakup, Genesis P-Orridge explained in an interview, "I think that the technology has been explored and the roots of blues music and slave music has been explored, and now we've done the Industrial music. We have to go beyond into where man meets space. I don't mean cosmic like Tangerine Dream, I mean inside the head."[5] Here P-Orridge indicates the beginning of his next project, Psychic TV. Its origins date back to 1979, when P-Orridge, Tutti, and Monte Cazazza conceived of "giving a public and media illusion of a large, well organized, disciplined and meticulously accessorized 'anti-cult.'"[6] Indeed, they'd all shared a strong interest in both the paramilitary and the occult.

P-Orridge recruited Alex Fergusson, Scottish guitarist of Alternative TV. P-Orridge had originally played drums with Alternative TV in 1976 and had maintained a friendship with Fergusson throughout Throbbing Gristle's run. Around this time, Fergusson moved in next door to P-Orridge in the semilegally reclaimed artist squats on Beck Road in London's Hackney borough. Their first musical composition together was "Just Drifting," which began as a poem P-Orridge had written for his newborn daughter, Caresse. Visiting P-Orridge's flat, Fergusson noticed the verse on the water heater and within a day had set it to music on his acoustic guitar. A few months later, Christopherson, ever easygoing and diplomatic, agreed to join the project, even as he maintained his friendship with Carter and Tutti.

On the surface, Psychic TV's music was a departure from all things Throbbing Gristle: it was lush, melodic, hippyish, and usually beat-driven. Carter says, "A lot of the feeling in Throbbing Gristle came from the tension between the four members," but Psychic TV was less inwardly focused and more of an open, communal affair.[7] The first album, *Force the Hand of Chance*, featured contributions from Marc Almond of Soft Cell, body piercing guru Alan Oversby ("Mr. Sebastian"), and postminimalist composer Andrew Poppy. These appearances, along with the presence of postpunk über-producer Ken Thomas, were paid for in part by WEA (Warner Brothers), with whom Stevo Pearce, owner of his own label—Some Bizzare—had brokered a record deal for the band. Psychic TV's later endeavors continued the movable feast, involving Throbbing Gristle's soundman Stan Bingo, Z'EV, David Tibet of Current 93, Geoffrey Rushton (later John Balance) of Coil, filmmaker Derek Jarman, gay icon Quentin Crisp, and P-Orridge's first wife Paula (Alaura O'Dell), to whom he was impulsively married on a day trip to Tijuana a month before Throbbing Gristle's split. Over time, members would leave, not always happily. Christopherson and Rushton departed in early 1984 to found the band Coil. Rushton politely explained that they "found things getting too autocratic and one lined."[8] Tutti suggests, however, that the split was due to a bad falling out: "It was worse for Peter than [Carter and Tutti's split with P-Orridge] was for us. We had no idea what had gone on afterwards, but he said, 'Believe me, it's worse for me.'"[9] Fergusson left the band in the late 1980s (to be replaced by American Fred Giannelli), and following the breakup of P-Orridge's first marriage Paula's name was removed from rereleases. She later said, "I think Gen needs to look at his motives for excluding me . . . his own illusion is not only cheating me [and] the public, but also our children."[10]

Psychic TV was conceived of as a fully multimedia project, integrating music (most of the early composition and production was Fergusson's work), video (handled by Christopherson), and a philosophical propaganda wing, Thee Temple ov Psychick Youth (TOPY). TOPY eventually took on a life of its own as a visible religious movement. In its questioning of consensus reality and in its ties to discordianism, chaos magick, and the Ordo Templi Orientis, TOPY surely deserves its own study (*Thee Psychick Bible* is a good primer), but its story increasingly deviates from that of industrial music. It was one thing to buy and enjoy a record; it was another entirely to correspond with an organization that many perceived as a cult (ten thousand members at its peak), conducting rituals concerned with the mysticism of the number twenty-three. P-Orridge's *raison d'être* revealed itself to be an esoteric study in culture jamming (eventually including popularizing body piercing, championing acid house music, and embarking with his second wife Lady Jaye on the gender-erasing surgical art project Pandrogyne). As such, Psychic TV was happy enough to be rid of the "industrial" label. By the time the band released their 1985 out-of-nowhere pop hit "Godstar," it was clear that between P-Orridge and industrial music's fan base, one party had moved on. As for which, that depends on whom you ask.

The most consistently beloved and "industrially" relevant of the ex-Throbbing Gristle excursions was Coil, a mystic project launched by Geoffrey Rushton, who adopted the name John Balance. When he was a teenage zine journalist (writing under the name Scabmental), Balance met Christopherson while interviewing Psychic TV; they became very close and Balance joined the ensemble for a while, during which time he was romantically involved not only with Christopherson but apparently also in a brief, triadic relationship with Genesis P-Orridge and bassist Sharon Beaumont (who used the name Mouse). Coil began chiefly as Balance's solo side project, and a cast of friends contributed early on, including Christopherson, Jim G. Thirlwell, Marc Almond, Gavin Friday (of Irish goth act the Virgin Prunes), and John Gosling (whose Zos Kia project Balance was also involved with, and with whom Coil split their first release, the 1983 *Transparent* tape). But after leaving Psychic TV following a gig at the second Berlin Atonal Festival on December 2, 1983, Balance and Christopherson began working together on Coil more dedicatedly. In mid-1984, they invited Stephen E. Thrower, a penpal friend of Christopherson's since 1979 (via his Throbbing Gristle fandom) to join them in the studio (playing drums, brass, and woodwinds) as they recorded Coil's full-length debut *Scatology*.

The album was quite the big-budget affair for industrial music. As Balance remembers, "On *Scatology*, we hired a Fairlight 2 and we had a mixing desk upstairs in the middle of the room, and we said 'We're going to do an album.' We just went to work every day and we went to finish it in other studios."[11] *Scatology* indeed bears the sound of 1984's not-yet-perfected technology: on tracks like the instrumental opener "Ubu Noir," there's a lo-fi strangeness in the sample of a large orchestral ensemble looped and triggered until it seems small, and the inconsistent echo applied to the song's sounds gives it a strange sense of unreal space; similarly, the gated reverb on the drums of the album's single "Panic" would sound at home on a Phil Collins album. Far from pop, though, *Scatology* uses samplers to create a bombastic, brassy flair. Its tracks are divided between dire, Wagnerian vocal pieces such as "Tenderness of Wolves"—which comes off like a druidic take on Laibach and Foetus—and little excursions into FM synthesis, a new kind of electronic soundmaking popularized by Yamaha's 1983 DX7 synthesizer.

*Scatology* resonated at its release (and still does) because it was at once a step away from the postmodern, the prankish, and the punk. While Chris & Cosey were exploring Carter's fascination with ABBA, and while Psychic TV increasingly became a personal mouthpiece for P-Orridge, Coil proudly politicized their identity as self-declared gay, pagan men, a combination illustrated in the subtitle of their 1984 EP *How To Destroy Angels*: "Ritual music for the accumu-

lation of male sexual energy." Their spiritual practice was exceedingly important in their music: less cultish and chaotic than TOPY, and more grounded in
an Albionic arcane.

It necessarily calls to mind the early-twentieth-century magician Aleister
Crowley. Occult historian Francis King writes, "With the exception of Aleister
Crowley and his followers I know of no western occultists—either 'black' or
'white'—who used homosexual acts as magical methods of gaining power."[12]
Though Crowley's interest in occultism was preceded by his same-sex desires
(and it may well have served as a justification of them), his conflation of the two
is instructive. Like so many points of entry in industrial music, this is reminiscent of Artaud's desire to pull people out of themselves—ek-stasis. As scholar
Hugh Urban explains, "Crowley found in sexual magic the most intense experience of transgression, the overstepping of conventional taboos, as a means to
unleash an ecstatic, liberating power."[13] As with Psychic TV, not all Coil's listeners related immediately to their religious leanings, but amid the outbreak of
AIDS, Coil's sexuality had obvious ramifications that affected their music's creation and reception. Their terrifying ultra-slow cover of "Tainted Love" from
1985 was framed by a mournful video of a man on his deathbed, confronted
by a blasé leather-clad biker—a former lover? Death?—played by Marc Almond,
whose Soft Cell popularized the song. Intercutting these scenes are closeups of
Crowley's maxim "Love is the Law, Love under Will," chiseled in stone. Unlike
nearly every other industrial band of the era, when Coil sings of death (as they
especially do on their 1986 LP Horse Rotorvator), they do so with a real and
fearful, first-person closeness. In John Balance's 2004 obituary (he died after falling from his balcony), The Guardian put it, "In the mid-1980s, gay pop was coming out of the closet, but Coil were the first resolutely queer group; their words
dealt with desire, disease, dirt, death and drugs, and their collages sounded dark,
dank and dangerous."[14]

Coil gets much deeper coverage in David Keenan's book England's Hidden
Reverse. Their legacy, though, is one of ever hinting at a secret world, an unspoken, unspeakable way of being. This perception was unintentionally fueled
by the notorious difficulty of finding their records, which was due to poor distribution and sour dealings between them, Stevo Pearce (whose Some Bizzare
label distributed several of their early albums), and Dimehart Ltd., a publishing
company run by Einstürzende Neubauten's Mark Chung.✿ Coil explored acid

✿ When Some Bizzare reissued Coil's recordings in the 1990s, the band claimed Pearce had no
right to do so, as they believed he still owed them an estimated £30,000 in mechanical and publishing royalties. In 2001, Coil then reissued Scatology and Horse Rotorvator on their own in retaliation, newly titling them Stevø, Pay Us What You Owe Us. Pearce alleges as of 2011 that he has

house music on their album *Love's Secret Domain* and in a set of unreleased recordings made around 1997 for Trent Reznor's Nothing Records; later, they plumbed ambient soundscapes on their exquisite 1999 *Musick to Play in the Dark*, and eventually they achieved a kind of critical respect that few industrial bands maintained beyond the early 1980s. In an illustrative reversal, Karlheinz Stockhausen namechecked them as among his favorites. As is so often the case in pop music when an act's critical respect is so disproportionate to others in its genre, Coil in its later years was frequently treated by some writers as too good to be industrial—again, the old cliché of "transcending the genre." During the mid-1980s, however, not only were they a central lattice in industrial music's widening net, but they were vital in the development of a largely English esoteric underground.

## 2. London

Unlike America or West Germany, England's culture, history, finance, and government are ultimately centered around one city. Northern England had been able to foster a postindustrial "outsider" sensibility on account of its *not* being London, but once the northern scenes and sounds caught the attention of the big city's record labels and music journalists, London quickly became home to a large number of industrial acts in the early and mid-1980s. It's telling that Throbbing Gristle's members moved there from the north before the band even began.

In 1980, both Jim G. Thirlwell of Foetus and Graeme Revell of SPK relocated to London from Australia, and with the members of Throbbing Gristle they formed a small community of like-minded performers.✿ Included in this cadre—

---

disbursed £17,000 pounds to Dimehart, including Coil's royalties, which Dimehart ought to have forwarded to the band.[15] However, Dimehart's Chung denies having received payment for publishing: "As Stevo/Some Bizzare has never paid any monies owed for publishing rights . . . he cannot have paid any monies for Coil. I have spent years trying to get him to at least pay the writers if he didn't want to pay the publishing company he co-owned. . . . It's frankly a nightmarish mess and underneath all that maybe a sad story too."[16] With both Balance and Christopherson now deceased, the dispute may never be fully resolved. Einstürzende Neubauten and Genesis P-Orridge have also claimed that Pearce owes them money. In his defense regarding Einstürzende Neubauten, he paid for months of studio time beyond their album budgets. Chung and the band acknowledge that the expenses lavished on their albums allowed them to experiment and develop as a band.

✿ In 1979 SPK's Graeme Revell had been living in Paris; 1980 was also, incidentally, the same year that Nick Cave's Australian punk band the Birthday Party moved to London. Blixa Bargeld would play in Cave's later band, the Bad Seeds.

more a clique than a scene—were also Nigel Ayers of Nocturnal Emissions and Lustmord's Brian Williams, who joined up with SPK early the next year. To this day, Williams still works with Graeme Revell on film soundtracks.

SPK's musical origins are outright punkish; Australian musician Ian Andrews writes that they "emerged out of the extremely abrasive guitar and electronic noise post-punk typified by [Australian] groups Voigt/465 and Primitive Calculators," and indeed at their first gig in 1978, they covered "Panik" by French synthpunk act Metal Urbain.[17] Initially a duo, SPK was formed by Revell and Neil Hill at a psychiatric hospital in Sydney, where they were nurse and patient, respectively. This relationship led the culturally curious Hill to research the Sozialistisches Patientenkollektiv, a radical group of patients and former caretakers in Germany from whom SPK would initially take their name and inspiration.✿ The Sozialistisches Patientenkollektiv believed that individual sickness was a proper and revolutionary response to a sick modern world, and that curing or isolating the ill served only to hide the evils of capitalism. Founded in 1970, the group disbanded a year later and was largely absorbed by the Red Army Faction. SPK's embodiment of the movement is most clearly enacted in their 1979 song "Slogun," which chants, "Kill, Kill, Kill for inner peace! Bomb, Bomb, Bomb for mental health! Therapy through violence!"—a lyric lifted decades later in KMFDM's "Rubicon."

As discussed, SPK eventually veered heavily toward pop, but the band's sound was decidedly clanking, droning, metallic industrial music when the first LP was recorded in the midst of the 1981 Brixton riot.✿✿ Customers who bought *Information Overload Unit* received with it a political pamphlet and a capsule of semen.[20] Revell illustrated his polymorphous artistic tendencies and simultaneously demonstrated that the I-word was in the subcultural air by February 1981 when he said, "I don't want to be labeled as futurist, just like I don't want to be labeled with Industrial."[21]

Whitehouse was also based out of London and was at the center of a small group of bands who made sheer noise—usually blisteringly high-pitched and rhythmless. Some tracks featured distorted vocals screamed over them, usually

---

✿ To Neil Hill (who was called Nihil), interest in subversive politics verged on the paranoid. In 1980, *Slash* magazine boasted he was "a certified schizophrenic."[18] More reliably, onetime SPK bassist David Virgin recalls, "Nihil was like a Joseph Conrad character, I'm thinking, Secret Agent. He always had a carry bag filled with vitally important documents. One had the strange feeling that at any moment we would all be blown to pieces."[19]

✿✿ Hill didn't participate in making the record, having stayed behind in Australia; he would commit suicide in 1984, days before his wife succumbed to anorexia. It's potentially troubling that former nurse Revell and Dr. Wolfgang Huber were the public figureheads of SPK and the Sozialistisches Patientenkollektiv, given that these were ostensibly pro-patient groups.

barely coherent. The style is called "power electronics," but like many gradients within the noise continuum it's often grouped within industrial music when most broadly defined. Whitehouse's ceaseless scream is annoying when played quietly, but overwhelming when played loudly—and extreme volume was always a part of noise gigs.

The power electronics faction, which also included such acts as Ramleh, Con-Dom, the Grey Wolves, and Whitehouse side projects Consumer Electronics and Sutcliffe Jügend, has been more consistently grouped by its politics and iconography than by its music. Occasionally similar in sound and paratext to Boyd Rice's NON project, Whitehouse and groups like them consistently invoked extreme violence, social Darwinism, and fascist-derived politics. Some of these acts have claimed this was all done in irony. Gary Mundy of the band Ramleh explains:

> At the time, this all fitted in with the audience-baiting and obnoxious attitude of the band—deliberately taking opposite standpoints just because it was irritating to do so. We enjoyed getting up people's noses and found it amusing to be accused of things which were simply untrue. We were never a racist or right-wing band. Indeed, no members of Ramleh ever had any affiliation with any political party, but this kind of game is ultimately futile and childish and I became more aware of the danger involved and decided to call a halt. We had made our point although, I guess, it's very easy to see why nobody understood it . . . there was no right-wing viewpoint to any of the stuff—we made an error in judgment in testing out the bounds of offensiveness.[22]

Fascism and racism vis-à-vis industrial music receive an extensive discussion in Chapters 13 and 14, but it suffices here to say that when sometime Whitehouse member Philip Best advertised Ramleh's 1982 *Onslaught* through his tape label Iphar as "a cassette of agonizingly dominant hate, sheer contempt . . . The first in the new Iphar era of White Power," then simple irony cannot adequately account for the possibilities in this music.[23]✿ Nor, however, is it easy to read these bands' constant conflation of fascism, murder glorification, and extreme pornography as unblinkingly earnest, as Mundy's quote indicates; to their apologists, the idea of a supposedly genuine evil so consistent and totalizing simply strains credulity, especially when its reach is limited just to music.

---

✿ If there's any conceivable defense to be offered here, it would include the mention that Best was fourteen years old at the time. He has since earned a doctoral degree in English literature, for what that may be worth. His unspoken thought processes, however, bear little functional impact on the way these words, sounds, and symbols behave once turned loose to the public.

At any rate, Whitehouse and the apparently right-wing noisemakers of the early 1980s are constantly derided as having missed the critical message of acts such as Throbbing Gristle, Laibach, and SPK, instead latching onto only their violent imagery at face value. Whitehouse were frankly hated by many of their contemporaries, despite having worked in their early days (when the band was called Come) with Daniel Miller of the Normal (and founder of Mute Records) and Jim G. Thirlwell. In more recent years, Whitehouse frontman William Bennett has gradually shifted his image, with the help of some sympathetic publications, to that of an elder statesman of noise music. He has accomplished this in part through an alarming self-awareness, using his post-2000 records as a platform to critique noise, its fans, and its opponents, shining a thousand-watt strobe on his own political shortcomings and paradoxes, offering ceaseless questions with no possible answers.

Similarly interesting in their exploration of noise were the New Blockaders, who in their 1982 manifesto declared themselves to be "anti-music, anti-art, anti-magazines, anti-books, anti-films, anti-clubs, anti-communications."[24] Their recordings and performances—songless, endless, grinding noise—are demonstrations of their total nihilistic purpose. By refusing meaning itself (and by also refusing to participate in either the social aspects or the imagery of early 1980s industrial music), they have managed to remain a willfully obscure and impenetrable artifact. As Paul Hegarty, author of *Noise/Music: A History* writes, it "was never about listening."[25]

Prerequisite across early 1980s English subcultures was a disdain for Prime Minister Margaret Thatcher, whose conservative economic and labor policies went hand-in-hand with the ruling classes' regressive and repressive views on all things social, sexual, and artistic. The industrial scene was far from Thatcher's only pop critic: punk band Wah! recorded "The Day That Margaret Thatcher Dies (A Party Song)" and Morrissey's "Margaret on the Guillotine" is a minor indie classic. This sentiment can serve as a common thread, helping to connect industrial music's distant political corners. Whitehouse, whose name is a smearing cooption of anti-pornography activist Mary Whitehouse, crosses paths with socialist act Test Dept. when the latter title a brassy song "Long Live British Democracy Which Flourishes And Is Constantly Perfected Under The Immaculate Guidance Of The Great, Honourable, Generous And Correct Margaret Hilda Thatcher. She Is The Blue Sky In The Hearts Of All Nations. Our People Pay Homage And Bow In Deep Respect And Gratitude To Her. The Milk Of Human Kindness."

One of the great metal-banging acts, Test Dept. was among London's most important industrial groups of the 1981–1985 era. Originally a six-piece band,

Test Dept. included Londoners and Scots, gay and straight men, drama students, unemployed artists, and a few trained musicians who (as so often) decided to set down their instruments to create a new noise with the junk they found lying around. Like Einstürzende Neubauten, the band staged many site-specific performances that relied on their surroundings: under a railway arch at Waterloo station in 1983, at Cannon Street Mainline station, in an underground parking lot. The theatrics might easily have been considered "atmosphere" by some spectators, but don't overlook the importance of that idea: "atmosphere" describes a dialogue between a performance and its surroundings, and so a good atmosphere means this dialogue is consonant, or at least interesting. Test Dept. was committed to these ideas, having endured a police raid at their unlicensed "November Reprisal" performance in 1983. Band members were arrested and their instruments were confiscated.

Music critic John Gill remembers the band's live show:

A band who had given us a tape of their music, crashing industrial gamelan music battered out of steel springs, oil drums, sheets of metal, vast tanks, drills and buzzsaws, had invited us to one of their performances. The precise address of the concert had to be kept secret. They hired industrial premises—railway arches, warehouses, industrial depots—under the guise of anonymous charities in case the owners and the authorities got wind of what they intended to do in, and sometimes with, this property. . . .

As they drummed up metal thunder on an adventure playground's worth of industrial detritus, violent electronic noise was bled into the mix and grainy Russian revolutionary films were projected on to band and stage. . . . The smell of oil was everywhere, and when they began applying cutting machinery to their instruments, producing volcanic spurts of sparks 20 feet across, people stubbed out cigarettes and backed towards the door.[26]

More important than the audacity and the access to structural percussion that site-specific performances allowed was their role in the band's ongoing commentary on the collapse of England's industrial age. As the band themselves say, "We feed off the corpse of British 'culture' . . . Utilising the waste of a dying civilization to create a new pure and honest music."[27]

It's fitting, then, that Test Dept. squatted and rehearsed among a community of antiestablishment punks and ex-hippies living in a row of old houses on Nettleton Road in New Cross. Author Tony Allen argues that in living thus among the waste, squatters such as Test Dept. in fact saved London's industrial age architecture: under the city's late 1960s policies, those buildings would have been torn down to make room for highrises had they not been occupied.[28]

With Test Dept. more than nearly any industrial act of the era, every action was political—not merely in a punkish negation, but in unambiguous, partisan terms. The band, who preferred to identify collectively, declares, "We wanted to make very direct, confrontational music that used ideas driven from deeply rooted social and political issues."[29] They continue, stating that people have "seen what the Conservative government has done to this country and [Test Dept.] have become increasingly relevant through that. If there had been a socialist government it would have been a completely different story."[30]

The band's socialist agenda took them so far as to join in the 1984–85 UK Miners' Strike in solidarity with the workers. They recorded an entire album, *Shoulder to Shoulder*, with a choir of striking miners from South Wales. Actions like these caught the attention of the leftist press, and by the end of the 1980s Test Dept. were receiving more performance and collaboration requests from arts groups (including the Royal Scottish National Orchestra) than from industrial venues and labels. By 1989, they were staging massive events such as *Gododdin*, in which "hundreds of tons of sand, dozens of trees and wrecked cars, and thousands of gallons of water" flooded an abandoned car factory in Wales, paying elegy to a lost valuation of human labor.[31] "The God in Britain now is efficiency," the band laments.[32]

Test Dept.'s unambiguous political tone and their earnest, literal take on "industrial" music may ultimately have led to their somewhat lesser standing in the industrial canon than, for example, Einstürzende Neubauten, to whom the press compared them constantly, if only superficially. Even in their much later concession to dance pop, "Pax Americana," Test Dept.'s members can't quite bring themselves to use political signs in a cryptic, classically "industrial" way: after they chant, "We love Saddam Hussein," the band starts reciting William Butler Yeats's poem "The Second Coming," that most modernist of all verse. In doing do, they suggest by proximity that at the time (late 1990), any understanding of the coming Gulf War was only fragmentary, and to suppose otherwise was to commit intellectual colonialism—even as armies and governments enacted military imperialism.

It's true that their music is occasionally overripe with nineteenth-century English brass choirs and sloganlike admonishments of "a government that conspicuously favours its wealthy, its corrupt, its immoral citizens, but denies basic human rights to the majority." But Test Dept.'s musical commitment to change and its members' postdisbandment investments in social and political progress through art suggest that the group's significance has as much to with their development of a musical and political mission as it does with banging on drainage pipes.

South London was also home to the band Portion Control, a trio of John Whybrew, Ian Sharp, and Dean Pianvanni, who lived and recorded at Kennington Road, just a quick tube ride away from Test Dept.'s stomping grounds. Portion Control had begun as a band in 1979, and their first recordings, the *Gaining Momentum* cassette, saw the light of day in 1981. A combination of analogue synth noises, found object drumming, and a Greengate digital sampling card powered by an Apple II gave much of their earliest work a sound that blends innocuously with the moodier moments of Cabaret Voltaire and Throbbing Gristle, although there were also inspired aberrations like the hip-hop infused track "In Pursuit of Excellence." At times, Portion Control demonstrated a gift for gritty, teeth-grinding distortion, not unlike Esplendor Geométrico. What makes the group important, though, were two things: first, by the time they made songs such as "Bite My Head" and "Chew You To Bits" in 1982 and 1983, they were using verses and choruses—"Our punk grounding meant we often worked within conventional song structures."[33] For better or for worse, this element of pop songwriting was becoming gradually more pervasive within industrial music. Second, Whybrew's singing style quickly developed into an animal sneer that was more expressively theatrical than were his contemporaries in the scene, but also more focused than the unhinged wailing that characterized songs such as Throbbing Gristle's "Discipline." It was a bestial and confidently nasty growl from a tight throat through a drippy echobox. The sound is an unignorable precursor to the work of Skinny Puppy. As Bill Leeb of Front Line Assembly writes:

> It made you feel you were witnessing a total transformation of human liquid form to a devastating alien. So barbaric, cold and hard, but a thing of brutal beauty. What hard, pure clean sound with devastating vocals. I have never ever heard such vocals. At first I wasn't sure whether it was a monster being tortured or a total maniac trying to tear the world apart with his voice.[34]

Portion Control never reached the same level of popularity as many of their contemporaries, even despite landing a session appearance on John Peel's BBC Radio 1 show. Portion Control, like many of London's bands from this era, instead found their most enthusiastic audiences in the Benelux countries. As Whybrew says, "The whole industrial, wild planet electronic music movement was always small in England with most bands playing across Europe for any recognition at all. The movement was about obscurity."[35]

## 3. Beyond London

There were rumblings elsewhere in England too. Ben Ponton of the group Zoviet France made droney, quiet, cut-up noise from acoustic samples of home-made instruments and started releasing records in 1982. He recalls:

> We never felt we were in the industrial tradition which was very much the contemporary movement from which we sprang. It was round about that time where everybody seems to have arrived at the same point and started lots of things, like Nocturnal Emissions, and what Throbbing Gristle were doing, and Test Dept.'s early days, and everybody else . . . 23 Skidoo. We were aware of what everyone else was doing, but because we were in Newcastle, which is quite a cultural island in itself, we didn't feel any bonding to that at all, we didn't feel any attachment to it. We saw ourselves as very isolated and very much out on a limb. It didn't worry us, we were quite happy in that situation, quite happy to continue fiddling about with the ideas we had. We didn't feel that we had to conform to any kind of preconceptions about what we were doing at all.[36]

The power of geography persists here. This kind of isolation similarly allowed Essex teenagers Douglas McCarthy, Vaughan "Bon" Harris, and David Gooday to bring in musical and conceptual ideas from far outside the London-Manchester-Sheffield axis in creating their band Nitzer Ebb in 1982.

The three schoolmates shared a socialist worldview and a passing fancy for the occult, and although it's tempting to suppose they embarked on music out of these interests, the reality is that their first love was skateboarding. From there, Harris says, "Music was very closely knit with skateboarding culture. It was only a matter of time before we segued into music."[37] Their hometown of Chelmsford was a decidedly third-rate city in the eyes of Londoners, and so the band members' exposure to postpunk entailed not only musical excitement but a risky, cosmopolitan flair with midnight trains and immersion in an older, cooler set. "When we saw these groups, we were 13 or 14 years old. You'd go to one of these shows and people were just beating each other up in the name of dancing. Just having fun. That release was something we wanted to tap," says lead singer McCarthy.[38] The youth of Nitzer Ebb's members almost certainly played a role in their interpretation of this music. For them, it was no information war; it was the logical extension of dancing, skateboarding, and sex; "we were pretty much preoccupied with expending energy."[39]

Despite their status as one of the premier industrial dance bands of the 1980s, Nitzer Ebb eschewed drum machines for much of their career, instead basing their live and studio setup on only a Roland SH101 monophonic synth, an incomplete drumkit, and a microphone (they would later expand their sound and also use drum machines). The band's early live gigs—enormously and immediately popular—were reminiscent of Deutsch-Amerikanische Freundschaft, with McCarthy's ultramasculine shout and Harris playing hype man over the quarter-note kick-snare alternation of the drumkit. A rowdy showmanship was needed to cover the time between songs, during which Harris literally had to reprogram the band's next number from memory. He says:

> There was a built-in sequencer in the SH101, so in fact on stage, I had to pull the main plug out and program each song before it played because it could only hold one song in memory. I managed to get this down to thirty seconds, roughly. We would play a song and then stop. I'd pull out one cable, plug in the headphones, program the bassline, switch back over again, and then press Play.[40]

Nitzer Ebb's songs throughout their career have been based on simple loops of the sort that one could indeed program quickly, but Harris maintains this wasn't because of the technology: "I think we chose the means to fit what we wanted to achieve. We were very interested in funk and disco taken to a further degree."[41] Despite choosing repetition consciously as a musical device (as opposed to stumbling upon it technologically), Nitzer Ebb built their loops and designed their songs improvisatorily:

> That's the blues connection right there. It's complete instinct. It was a desire to express youthful angst and emotion and those were the sounds. If you press this key after that one, that's how I'm feeling. It wasn't any preconceived thing. Later on I actually went back and I did study music and I understand a lot of theory now, and it's interesting to go back and look at what we did and see how close to blues it is.[42]

England's postpunk scene was fond of Jamaican reggae and dub—important African diaspora styles that found their way into industrial through such artists as Mark Stewart and Adrian Sherwood—but very few industrial acts openly acknowledge roots in blues-derived musics. Between these nods to disco, funk, and blues, we can hear in Nitzer Ebb a pleasure-based use of pop's rhythms and harmonies at work. In their 1984 song "Isn't It Funny How Your Body Works?" Douglas McCarthy's words serve up a typical industrial juxtaposition of "a hammer and stars, a sickle and stripes," but melodically, he repeatedly bends the third scale degree—a hallmark of the blues. All this happens over the synthesizer pattern's alternation from C to F and back, emphasizing the plagal cadences that separate blues from classical music. Their 1983 song "Tradition" from their *Basic Pain Procedure* demo tape has identical features (and is even in the same key).

With some care not to oversimplify the meanings and contexts of blues inflections, we might argue that Nitzer Ebb, through these musical signs (and bolstered by their youthful, bodily exuberance) helped offer an alternative to the meditative (if loud) music of Coil or Einstürzende Neubauten. Nitzer Ebb employed the same propaganda savvy that guided Throbbing Gristle and Laibach—"We tended to mix and match from both political extremes and different political eras to confuse the issue . . . the system is not designed for our benefit"—but Nitzer Ebb was ultimately instrumental in developing electronic body music, a separate strain of industrial music that would become the genre's dominant form from the mid-1980s to the present.[43] Although SPK's "Metal Dance" and other acts' excursions into pop language were heard by most as embarrassing concessions, audiences interpreted Nitzer Ebb's disco angst (at least through the 1980s) as uninhibited and natural, as if there were no other way it could have sounded.

A lot of this had to do with their fixation on the body: though acts like NON and Factrix had attempted to drown out conscious thought through overbearing noise, early EBM (and indeed bands such as Deutsch-Amerikanische Freundschaft) attempted to do more or less the same by highlighting, disciplining, and exhausting the body at the expense of explicit intellectual discourse. McCarthy pants and wheezes throughout Nitzer Ebb's songs, suggesting exercise, sex, and physical overload. Their chant of "Let your body learn—let your body build" not only indicates that the body possesses subconscious understanding but suggests that access to this understanding can be something instinctual and animal: *let* your body learn—don't *make* it learn.

Whether Nitzer Ebb's members realize it or not, this idea is in line with the philosophical approach called phenomenology, which argues among other tenets that all our knowledge is derived from our perception, and that all perception is necessarily mediated through our bodies. Music can play an interesting role in the whole equation because it foregrounds the body in its creation and reception—the physical exertion of singing or strumming, and the act of dancing or playing air guitar, respectively.

The sounds of electronic music aren't the sounds of arms pounding or throats singing, though, and so it can short-circuit listeners' assumptions about the bodies of its performers. Traditional rock music favors a working-class body with callused hands and a whisky-rough voice, and by denying this particular brand of physicality the body of electronic music was easily heard as lazy, weak,

    **ASSIMILATE**

undisciplined, and effete. The criticism in the 1980s and 1990s that electronic musicians were fake or talentless, then, is a response to a perceived threat against a specific bodily identity as encoded in sound—an identity within a narrow range of class, gender, sexual orientation, and race. As Front 242's Patrick Codenys says, EBM was "a reaction to the fact that people say electronic music is just for faggots behind keyboards . . . EBM takes exactly the opposite angle and says, Listen, this can be as fast and physical as you guitar guys."[44] If we recall how electronic music demands that we learn new relationships between the body and sound, then this physicality in Nitzer Ebb and Front 242 can teach a different sort of body. As phenomenologist and dance theorist Alva Noë writes, "The body is the substrate of our understanding. But as we learn to do new things, as we learn to use new tools, we extend and transform our body, just as we extend and transform our understandings. Electronic music doesn't take the body away. It gives us a new body."[45]

As we'll soon see, the particulars of this new body retain certain rockist features—maleness and whiteness, to be sure—but they recast other parts of identity, and these changes are closely connected to industrial music's historical place within modernism. As scholar Deniz Peters explains, "The hopes of this modernist aesthetic were on the machine, not only on the noise machines make, but, just as importantly, on the mechanistic production of sound; that is, the hopes were tied to the image of the generation of sound using a perfectly suited, untiring and infallible body. . . ."[46]✿

Nitzer Ebb thus heard in disco and funk's pleasurable bodilyness the Burroughsian possibility of returning to a state unmediated by language, uncontaminated by the separation of mind from body that so much western Christianity and culture has relied on; they heard a physical state of being that was prior and immune to mind control—integrated and impregnable.✿✿ With an emphasis on pleasure and an eye toward the transhumanist improvement of the body through cybernetics, this is a more optimistic take on dance rhythms than

---

✿ Peters adds to the end of this passage, "or, in stark contrast, no body at all"—an idea potentially applicable to some musicians' attitudes, although Noë, writing in the same book, argues that regardless of intent, such a decorporeal music is impossible; in either case, the issue of bodilessness is all but intrinsically inapplicable to EBM.

✿✿ Contrast this approach with the more fluid equation of metal and flesh that Psychic TV offered. As stars of RE/Search Publications' book *Modern Primitives*, which addresses body modification, band members Genesis and Paula P-Orridge had extensively explored piercing. Jean-Pierre Turmel's liner notes to 1985's live album *Descending* pontificate: "What is to be thought of this masculine sex pierced by a ring (the feminine symbol)? A desire for the feminine sex to become 'the penetrator' and the phallus 'the penetrated'? (the fact that the ring on the photo enters by the urethra seems to confirm this) A desire not for castration but for reunification."[47]

Laibach's insistence that in response to the beat's unifying power audiences must reenact their own submission in order to cleanse themselves of it. A vital issue implied in these two approaches to pop rhythms within industrial music is whether bodily pleasure is a personal empowerment or a collective opiate. As with industrial music's ambivalent view of technology, the ambivalence it displays regarding this bodily pleasure only increases the tension over the issue. It's a central question to keep in mind throughout the next chapter, on the origins of electronic body music.

**ICONIC:**

Chris & Cosey – "October (Love Song)" (1982)

Coil – "Panic" (1984)

Nitzer Ebb – "Warsaw Ghetto" (1985)

Psychic TV – "Just Drifting (for Caresse)" (1982)

Scraping Foetus Off the Wheel – "I'll Meet You In Poland, Baby" (1984)

**ARCANE:**

23 Skidoo – "Porno Bass" (1982)

Portion Control – "If I Could Spit" (1982)

SPK – "Twilight of the Idols" (1983)

Mark Stewart – "Hypnotised" (1985)

Test Dept. – "Hunger" (1983)

# 10.
## Body to Body:
## Belgian EBM 1981–1985

### 1. A Satellite State

The amount of significant electronic music to emerge from Belgium in the early 1980s suggests a vibrant scene: there were acts that went on to become major players in industrial music, notably Front 242, the Neon Judgement, Luc Van Acker, à;GRUMH…, Absolute Body Control, and Vomito Negro, as well as bands whose following was more regional but whose music deserves continued attention, such as Parade Ground, Snowy Red, Polyphonic Size, the Names, A Blaze Colour, Siglo XX, Pseudo Code, and Kuruki. Later in the 1980s a hoard of new, important Belgian acts (and the entire New Beat genre) would follow. Because of such a density of electronic dance music in the small country, it's surprising, then, to learn that in the first half of the decade these musicians had very little mutual contact. For example, Dirk Ivens of Absolute Body Control and the Klinik flatly states, "We didn't know about each other."[1] Other Belgian EBM bands of the early 1980s were collegial with but fundamentally wary of one another. Collective ambition was muted, and there's almost no hint of Belgian nationalism in this music, nor even in the efforts of alternative Belgian record companies such as Antler or Play It Again Sam. As à;GRUMH…'s Philippe Genion says, "Belgium doesn't really have national pride. We are an area; it's not even really a country."[2]

The city of Leuven is only a twenty-minute train ride from Brussels, and Antwerp is less than an hour from both, but Belgian cities remain nonetheless socially detached from one another in important ways, a lingering relic of a time when it might take the better part of a day to cross such a distance. Add to that these musicians' bedroom-recording mentality and the linguistic divide that cordoned off Francophone acts such as Front 242 and à;GRUMH… from Flemish bands such as Absolute Body Control or the Neon Judgement, and the isolation starts to make more sense. The few hangouts of the day included the DNA bar in Brussels and Arno's in Leuven, but punks outnumbered synth aficionados in these dives.

In the 1970s, there had been one or two Belgian bands to find success in electronic music, most notably the disco-tinged act Telex, who debuted in 1978 and represented the country in the 1980 Eurovision contest. But at that time, most of Belgium's incubating industrialists thought of themselves chiefly as fans, reading *Sounds* and *Melody Maker* to learn about groups such as Wire from the UK and Suicide from New York. Joy Division and the Cure especially found larger audiences at Plan K or Beursschouwburg in Brussels than in most English clubs. Philippe Genion was a music journalist in Belgium in the late 1970s, and he recalls, "Brussels was considered the second base from London for all bands. They would tour England and the UK, and then the first stop they would do on the continent was Brussels. It was the most hip place."[3]

Having drawn record collections from abroad, it was natural for a lot of Belgium's amateur synth tinkerers to connect more with the global cassette network than to join a mutually supportive urban music scene. For example, Sandy Nijs, a sometime collaborator of early EBM act Absolute Body Control, was exceedingly plugged into the network; the entire output of his band Maniacs is scattered across cassette-only compilations from Norway, the United States, and Belgium. In fact, it was directly through Nijs's mail scene connections that the Klinik and Absolute Body Control received an offer to tour Norway in 1985. It was common for these acts to be bigger abroad than at home.

## 2. Luc Van Acker

The musician Luc Van Acker is both historically important and a good example of what sort of efforts laid the groundwork for EBM. Van Acker is a founding member of Revolting Cocks and a hired hand for Shriekback, Arbeid Adelt, and My Life With the Thrill Kill Kult. It's useful to see how his desire to participate in music culture at a very young age was subject to the journalistic and technological tastes that he and his family, as Belgians, had access to. It's also curious to see how Belgium's peculiar milieu of artistic isolation at that time affected a musician who is known more today for his collaborations than his solo efforts.

At just six years old in 1967, Van Acker took an active interest in rock band photos on the cover of *Melody Maker* at a newsstand in his hometown of Tienen. Musically hungry from the beginning (if decidedly untrained), he asked his mother for a subscription, and she obliged. "I couldn't read English. I just looked at the pictures and slowly found words I understood, but the magazines were the only thing available that had to do with music."[4] No Flemish rock magazines of any traction existed at the time.

Van Acker taught himself a little guitar and bass early in his teens, but the synthesizers he read about in *Melody Maker* in the mid-1970s instantly appealed to him more than any rock instrument:

I was 14. It was 1975. At school we had two weeks of Easter vacation. I bought this train pass that you can use every day and go on any train, and for two weeks I traveled all over Belgium to any music store that had a synthesizer. I was there at 9 in the morning when they opened up, and I just plugged in with my headphones. I didn't eat, didn't drink, just asked to use the toilet. I'd be kicked out at 5 o'clock. I was at these places so much that Korg Belgium asked me to give demonstrations in stores.[5]

This love of electronic instruments may have been idiosyncratic to Van Acker; his father was a computer programmer, so he'd been raised around technology. However, across EBM there's a pervasive belief that the synthesizer itself somehow resonates with the Belgian experience. As Patrick Codenys of Front 242 puts it:

Being Belgian was very particular because I'm not Anglo-Saxon; I don't feel rock in my veins, or blues, or jazz, or whatever. It's not part of me. I'm living in a country that's very mixed: cinema is very mixed—a lot of movies are shown in original versions. Flemish people live alongside French people, and there are German parts. It's the center of Europe, a melting pot, really. . . . So here you have a machine that does sound and noise, sort of an orphan or a bastard machine. It is very interesting for me to associate that with my origins as a Belgian. We don't have a strong past; we don't have a strong inheritance.[6]

As discussed in Chapter 8, analogue synthesizers and drum machines suggest and enable certain kinds of music, and the fact that Belgian industrial musicians chose these tools more frequently than metal percussion or Throbbing Gristle-esque distortion contributes heavily to the preponderance of industrial dance music in Belgium, noise acts Etat Brut and Club Moral notwithstanding.

Fittingly then, the small collection of gear that Luc Van Acker assembled prioritizes harmonic and rhythmic features. At age seventeen, he was using a Korg MS-500 synthesizer, a Roland TR-505 drum machine, and a polyphonic Korg PS-3100, which his father had bought for him shortly before the latter's death. Van Acker soon thereafter added a Korg MS-20 keyboard and a sequencer. This musical setup favors pitch-controllable sound generators instead of keyboardless modular devices and processors. This fact alone all but necessarily differentiates Van Acker's music from the recordings of Throbbing Gristle and Cabaret Voltaire, in which effects units and uncalibrated oscillators paint a sonic landscape where timbre rules, not rhythm and pitch. This distinction is important in understanding EBM's signature features within the industrial genre.

It also goes without saying that although Van Acker played some guitar too, his dominant reliance on this electronic setup further differentiated his music from the metal-banging likes of Einstürzende Neubauten and Test Dept.

Because Van Acker was still in high school when he began recording his first album *Taking Snapshots* onto a Tascam four-track, he had basically no contact with other electronic musicians. He was a bedroom recordist, and even as the 1980s dawned he knew of few kindred spirits nearby, especially once he started attending art school in Hasselt—essentially the boondocks compared to Brussels and Antwerp. Van Acker tuned into the tape scene, however, which was on the art school radar thanks to its connections with Fluxus and mail art. He particularly became a fan of Z'EV. Playing occasional concerts and exchanging tapes both abroad and within Belgium, Van Acker landed a spot on a 1981 compilation record assembled by Roland Beelen, who would later found Antler Records and take up the overdue task of fostering a collective Belgian musical scene.

In September 1981, Van Acker finished and self-released *Taking Snapshots*, a throbbing mix of ambient tracks and clattery dance songs. For a year, he drove his Renault R4 to every record store he could find, hoping to hawk his album—an endeavor reminiscent of his teenage synthesizer quest. It worked, and he built a small following on the strength of songs like "Find a Way," even landing a live set on the liberal Dutch radio network VPRO.✿ In Van Acker's case, it's hard to assert that the lack of an organized scene hindered him, because in fact he was able to attract attention and play shows partially because he was one of Belgium's only all-electronic acts.

He recalls, "My first show was a Revox tape recorder and vocals, and that was it."[7] Without any keyboards to hide behind, Van Acker emphasized the physicality of his music. The 1981 song "What's Downtown" verges on funkiness as he sings, "Everybody's moving and they're dancing to the beat." The song is admittedly a shade or two removed from the sound of classic EBM: the drums rhythmically emphasize syncopation, the snare sound outweighs the kick, and Van Acker's intonation flails toward the high end of his vocal range. The cumulative effect is one of insufficient masculinity for modern EBM standards, but seen in retrospect the beat-driven aggression that intersperses the more ambient moments of *Taking Snapshots* points directly toward a particular reckoning with the body that would soon develop more fully in the music of fellow Belgians such as the Neon Judgement and A Split-Second.

Regarding the emergence of the dance-driven EBM from the industrial scene, à;GRUMH...'s Jacques Meurrens says, "In '85, the people who liked industrial

---

✿ Songs were untitled on the original release of *Taking Snapshots* but were later named.

and the people who liked EBM were mostly the same crowd," but even by that time, audiences were starting to form subgenre-based expectations.[8] Bandmate Genion explains:

à;GRUMH… started as an industrial band and separate rhythmic EBM band. The writing of the names on the records was different. . . . It was a gothic font for the industrial ambient thing and it was a bold Helvetica font for the EBM style. After the first album, produced by Daniel of Front 242, was such a big thing, the second album was the industrial one, and then another rhythmic album followed. Then the record company [Scarface, owned by Play It Again Sam] said, "The people are confused, because they all thought your second album would be rhythmic as well. They bought it and then we had a reaction from the record shops, so you have to change your name for the industrial stuff."[9]

## 3. Front 242

In grappling seriously and historically with EBM, let's turn to the subgenre's most formidable name, Front 242. Launched in late 1980 as the project of Aarschot-based Daniel Bressanutti and Dirk Bergen, Front 242 had expanded its lineup within a year to include Patrick Codenys and Jean-Luc De Meyer, who'd previously worked on a project together called Under Viewer. They'd given their demo tapes to Bressanutti, who worked at a record store, and he was impressed enough to invite them aboard. Bressanutti was something of a mastermind behind the scenes with the band, frequently absent from press photos, and more focused on the intricacies of recording than on performance. Prior to launching Front 242, he'd released a few one-off tracks as Prothese, including one on a 1981 compilation curated by Michel Lambot, later the founder of the hugely important label Play It Again Sam.

As with the music of Luc Van Acker, the earliest recordings by Front 242, Under Viewer, and Prothese all prioritize simple diatonic harmonies, rigid drum patterns, and the discrete identity of every instrumental timbre in the mix. Codenys confirms, "Each album we made was linked with the technology . . . every new synth in the house was a reason to rethink the whole aesthetic, including the imagery."[10] This wasn't simple consumer techno-determinism, but Codenys and Bressanutti, in their cerebral focus on media and interface design, wandered a virtual Situationist dérive through the architecture of their synthesizers, looking for an ethical path of musical behavior beneath the knobs and keys; it's fitting thus that their debut album is called *Geography*.

More than any other industrial act, Front 242 analytically embraced the unspoken expectations that machine design placed on humans. In this way, they differed somewhat from earlier industrialists who celebrated technical ineptitude and rule breaking. Codenys explains, "Our system was questioning the truth of the image, which is something you find in some postmodern philosophy. It's a little different from the Throbbing Gristle philosophy. For us, it was a need to put our music together with those [given] elements."[11] This didn't mean simply dialing up a machine's factory settings. Instead, the band built sounds from the ground up by scoping out a machine's systemic parameters: "Erase all the factory sounds for sure, and try to get at the guts of the machine." If Cosey Fanni Tutti and Genesis P-Orridge's hippie background contributed to Throbbing Gristle's tactics of confronting and reversing cultural signs, then we might likewise see Codenys and Bressanutti's respective backgrounds in architecture and history as a driving force behind Front 242's critical exercise in mapping the psychogeography of technological interfaces—assessing and "questioning the truth of the image." This is part of why postpunk historian Simon Reynolds says "Front 242 have an *amoral* fascination [with the] future."[12]

The group's early music avoids washes of noise, the clatter of reverberant simulated space, and tuneless, gritty drones; instead, every song features a repeating drum machine pattern and pulsing synth chords. Under Viewer's "Trouble" foregrounds De Meyer's unprocessed vocal in a Beatles-esque major key melody—a far cry from Industrial Records' standard fare, despite Codenys's insistence that "Throbbing Gristle's noise [and] chaos" was a "trigger" for their music.[13] Most of Front 242's earliest songs are instrumental, though, and their repetition naturally foregrounds those few elements not based on cyclicity—oftentimes an individual drum hit that stands out, or a single reverberating note. In this way, the music suggests a kinship with dub reggae and with the 1970s experiments of Brian Eno, whom the band cites (along with krautrock) as another significant "trigger."

Shortly after self-releasing *Geography*, Front 242 signed a deal involving the Belgian indie-label consortium Les Disques du Crépuscule, which was co-founded by Annik Honoré, mistress of Joy Division's Ian Curtis. With the 1982 single "U-Men," the 1983 re-release of *Geography*, and the 1984 album *No Comment*, Front 242 began garnering significant attention across northern Europe.

It's evident in listening to the music from their 1981–1984 period that the band was developing a more finely honed aesthetic: progressively fewer songs were instrumentals, and when Bergen stepped down to manage the group in 1983, he was replaced onstage with Richard 23 (Jonckheere), a second vocalist and drummer who echoed De Meyer's tight baritone declarations in an unhinged bellowing tenor. As Jason Hanley points out, this counterpoint between singers both reflected and suggested the band's move into more differentiated song structures. Though most Front 242 tracks of this era eschew simple verse-chorus behavior, patterns of alternation increase steadily in their oeuvre throughout the 1980s.

The other significant change contemporaneous with Richard 23's joining the band was an increasingly overt focus on the body. Taken on its own, the doubling of vocal duties plays a small part in this change, but duly contributing were two other facets: first, the combination of these humanizingly familiar new song structures with the volume and compression of percussion in the mix, and second, the confrontational live act that Front 242 began staging in which they employed smoke, military camouflage, and riot armor—or to be more precise, athletic padding made for baseball catchers.

The former, inspired in part by the hard-edged Spanish and Italian dance music of the early 1980s, unambiguously issues the sound of force: a man drumming as hard as he can, or alternatively, being hit with that same aggression. The more compressed the sound is, the greater the impression that the ear—and by extension the body itself—has reached its limit of shock absorption. On a song like "U-Men," the particularities of timbre conjure metal, even electrocution.

The latter approach to centralizing the body in this music, a military-themed live show, was partially a response to the aforementioned popular belief at the time that electronic music was not only geekish, but impotent—that it could never compete with rock's capacity for visceral power. This is of course a highly gendered criticism: the implication was that electronic music lacked balls, and indeed, the music press at large was not kind to Front 242 even as they were becoming one of Belgium's most popular acts. Thus the band's response was one of masculine overkill. Codenys explains, "We needed to impose the genre. It's the kind of music that needs to be played loud, so that we could slam people somehow."[14] To that effect, the band's military goggles and body armor stood as an open invitation for the audience—or critics—to slam back; the band presented itself as ready for the physical assault. While they were largely successful in asserting their music's forcefulness, the results that these efforts had on their crowd makeup did little to attract women to the already male-dominated electronic scene. To Codenys, the connection between their adopted aesthetic and their audience demographic was clear: "Between '81 and '85 there weren't any girls at the shows, only guys. It was really a very martial music."[15]

Throbbing Gristle and NON had taken similar visual approaches a few years earlier, but never with the beat-driven sound that Front 242 made. Here, the body was not the site of experimentation via infrasound, or disgust via performance art's grossness; it was instead neutrally responsive to technological control, just as Front 242 instinctively directed their music through their machinery's design ethos. Although Deutsch-Amerikanische Freundschaft called their music *Körpermusik* ("body music") in 1980[16] and Kraftwerk used the phrase "Electronic Body Music" two years earlier in a radio interview,[17] Front 242 independently coined the term again to describe their music in terms of this combined physicality and techno-centrism; the liner notes of their 1984's *No Comment* boast "ELECTRONIC BODY MUSIC COMPOSED AND PRODUCED ON EIGHT TRACKS BY FRONT 242."[18] This coincidence reveals a common conceptual thread between these predecessors and Front 242's music.

In particular, it is Front 242's lineage of EBM that has inarguably found a home in the endless labyrinth of electronic and industrial subgenres. In 1988, the band's sometime label Play It Again Sam released a compilation called *This Is Electronic Body Music*, with a remix of Front 242's "Body to Body" as the leadoff track. This seminal compilation both solidified the style's popularity in the underground and also—perhaps unfortunately—erected walls around what was and was not EBM, possibly delimiting the genre's future musical potential. The record also reinforces EBM's geography; more than half the featured bands are Belgian.

## 4. Musical Order

Reviewers over the years have consistently referred to the sound of EBM and especially Front 242 as "clean." This is in keeping with the style's aesthetic of *order*, where the grid of a song dictates its construction and its hearing alike—both horizontally in terms of quantized timing and vertically in terms of stacked instrumental parts.

"In architecture, they work with rosters," Codenys says, referring to precalculated construction plans. He continues:

> There might be a roster for air circulation set at 90 degrees, a technical roster for the lighting at 45 degrees, and then 45 degrees the other way for all the water pipes. This way to work with layers or rosters fit perfectly at the time with our approach to synth programming. On a structural level, the architecture was very interesting . . . it's got a balance between a bassline and a drummer. It's layers and layers.[19]

In EBM's 1980s configuration, the bassline was generally a two-measure synth pattern, sometimes with chromatic inflections (for example, the bass in Nitzer Ebb's biggest hit "Join in the Chant" can't seem to make up its mind about whether the song is in F minor or F major). These timbres might be muted, emphasizing low frequencies, or they might be made up of square and saw-tooth waves for a brighter, more in-your-face sound, but as a rule synth parts were undistorted and staccato, making it easy for the ear to distinguish one sound from another. This is a big part of the style's supposed cleanliness.

Rhythmically, EBM is based around an incessant quarter-note kick drum pattern, often with a backbeat snare. Drum machine hi-hats fill in the rhythmic gaps, but percussive ornamentation varies from artist to artist: Bressanutti would meticulously festoon Front 242's drum tracks, for example, while the Klinik's Dirk Ivens opted for a bleaker, emptier aesthetic. At any rate, the four-on-the-floor beat became a monolithic presence in the style by 1985; syncopation was rare and always quantized to a grid.

Moving beyond the Italo-disco of Giorgio Moroder, these drum sounds were not quiet Kraftwerkian blips or TR-808 thumps but were usually either based on white noise generated from an analogue synthesizer or more often they were samples of drums, car crashes, doors slamming, or "environmental" percussion, to borrow a phrase from Die Krupps. Samplers were expensive; Codenys was able to purchase an E-MU Emulator II only because his family won the lottery in 1984 (his father wanted to buy him a car instead). Prior to that, however, his sampling was done on tape: on Front 242's 1982 "GVDT," listen for the telltale sound rewinding before the sample of "What's wrong?" from *THX-1138* is replayed.

Structurally, most EBM songs of the early and mid-1980s contain repeated texts and melodies (even if tuneful singing was something of a rarity), but seldom did repeated modules of a song manage to take on the feel of verses or choruses. This has a lot to do with musicians' desire to escape the rock paradigm and their lack of training in pop music's structure. In some cases, it also reflects the collaborative back-and-forth of composition in a group without a singular vision of a finished work. The emphasis that many of these musicians place in interviews on the synthesizer as a tool quietly demonstrates how much more concerned they were with sonic exploration than songwriting, an industrial practice common since the days of Cabaret Voltaire. There was also the reality that some of the lower-budget EBM acts could still not afford sequencers that held more than one loop in RAM at a time, limiting the melodic and harmonic variety across a song.

## 5. Bodily Order

The preceding chapter mentioned the fascination with the body in the music of UK band Nitzer Ebb. Indeed, themes of kinetic exertion are everywhere in

EBM. In Nitzer Ebb's video for "Let Your Body Learn," singer Douglas McCarthy glistens under torrents of sweat and the camera repeatedly ogles a male gymnast's efforts on the parallel bars; similarly, Patrick Codenys graces the cover of Front 242's *Tyranny >For You<* album gasping in mid-breaststroke, water cascading over his goggles. Thus, when Jean-Luc De Meyer shouts, "If you're physical youth, you say you're moving youth, so why don't you feel the beat?" on the 1983 cut "Take One," the notion of "feeling the beat" is neither vicious cruelty nor beatnik metaphysics, but instead it's about undergoing a productive regimen. The tense-gutted shouting that characterizes EBM is always expulsive, safeguarding the body against any penetration, crafting an impregnable, fit machine of a man.

Musicologist Suzanne Cusick invites us to hear this kind of antimelodious singing as a performance of masculinity in which a vocalist effectively declares, "I have chosen not to re-learn the deep-body disciplines required to produce a 'singing' voice, as such voices are described by the gatekeepers of middle-class culture . . . the borders of my male body cannot be penetrated by Culture."[20] In this way, classic-era EBM acts an exercise in improvement through order and self-denial. Driving the point home, leather scene favorite à;GRUMH… applies this idea to sexual reality in the song "Danger Zone," asking, "Are you a clean boy? Are you the AIDS toy?" The song's culminating declaration that "Rubber is better than death!" explicitly advocates this bodily purity. When Front 242 chant "Divine body! Look right!" in "Take One," they similarly idealize a self clean in its proximity to godliness as being "right." This message would later reach its fullest lyrical articulation in Die Krupps' 1993 "Iron Man":

Weakness—these days are over
Old flesh—replaced by shiny armour
New thoughts—the mind expanding
Real tasks that are demanding
This body is invincible
Perfection is the principle

This consistent message of bodily strength and military neatness in EBM easily appealed both to gay and straight musicians and audiences; especially in the 1980s, industrial music was very closely linked with gay male culture (reaching an apotheosis with the early days of WaxTrax! Records), and it certainly helped to empower new possible identities within and beyond sexuality for men who made and enjoyed music that wasn't cock rock. In Front 242's classic track "Headhunter," the chant of "I'm looking for this man!" drives home a potential interpretation of same-sex desire already suggested by the title.

ASSIMILATE

Most industrial music prior to 1985 functionally excluded women, even if EBM (unlike power electronics) rarely actually articulated this idea. We briefly discussed this discrimination in Chapter 7, but it's worth mentioning again here for two reasons. The first is that EBM forces the issue by centering its discourse—even its name—on bodily difference, whereas previous industrial music was at least plausibly about something else (though no doubt there's a lot to be said about it through a gender-aware lens). The second reason to bring this up is that it was precisely during this era—1981 to 1985—that industrial music began attracting female fans and participants, and so EBM stands in opposition to such a change. This development is very closely linked with an industrial aesthetics decidedly concerned with an unclean, disorderly conception of the body. Delving fully into this will be a bit more meaningful, however, after a brief theatrical interlude.

**ICONIC:**

Front 242 – "U-Men" (1982)
Front 242 – "Take One" (1983)
The Klinik – "Sick in Your Mind" (1985)
The Neon Judgement – "TV Treated" (1982)
Luc Van Acker – "Fear in My Heart" (1984)

**ARCANE:**

à;GRUMH... – "New Fashion" (1985)
Absolute Body Control – "Weaving Hands" (1981)
Arbeid Adelt – "De Dag dat het Zonlicht Niet Meer Scheen" (1982)
Snowy Red – "Never Alive" (1982)
Vomito Negro – "Radio Silence" (1985)

# Industrial Music as a Theater of Cruelty

## 1. Artaud-Damaged

Industrial music's parading of staged authority relationships is theatrical by nature, but its relationship and its debt to theater as an art runs deeper than merely acting out spectacle and the détournement of twentieth-century governments. The name most useful here is Antonin Artaud, who has already popped up a handful of times in this book. Artaud was a French actor, artist, and writer who grew frustrated with theater that "limits itself to showing us intimate scenes from the lives of a few puppets, transforming the public into Peeping Toms."[1] In his 1932 essay "The Theater and Cruelty," he proclaims, "In the anguished, catastrophic period we live in, we feel an urgent need for a theater *which events do not exceed*, whose resonance is deep within us, dominating the instability of the times."[2]

What Artaud offers us in "The Theater and Cruelty" is a way to bring together a variety of industrial music practices that might otherwise seem disconnected, and to see them in service of a common goal that's consonant with the political self-proclamations of industrial musicians, fans, and critics. In this way, the focus here isn't so much on Artaud's influence on industrial music (though it certainly exists, as we'll see) but more on the usefulness of his ideas in making sense of industrial performance.

A handful of industrial musicians are aware of Artaud's ideas and acknowledge their importance: Mark Spybey of Zoviet France cites him,[3] and in 1984 Blixa Bargeld of Einstürzende Neubauten said, "I can't say any author has an influence, well, apart from Antonin Artaud."[4] But more often, the understanding is a superficial one, kind of like the genre's relationship to avant-garde music; for example, Angus Farquhar of Test Dept. says, "I like the imagery with which he wrote. But we're not intellectuals."[5] That said, Artaud's 1932 first manifesto serves as a prescient blueprint for industrial performance, particularly in its celebration of the abject and its distaste for camp.

The first part of this book privileged Futurism and Burroughs because they both help to paint the world that industrial music sees as its inheritance; Artaud helps us to see how the genre communicates this worldview to others. Futurism avails new artistic frameworks through technology, culminating (for the genre's purposes) with Russolo's technophilic noise-as-music, and the techno-paranoid Burroughs provides the cut-up logic as a means to disrupt the all-surrounding, invisible control machines; for his part, Artaud empowers an aesthetic means of shock, calls on the grotesquery of the gothic, demands the bodily, and implements this all in a political framework.✿ For these reasons, and also because his work has remained underappreciated in previous assessments of industrial music, Artaud is worth quoting here at some length.

## 2. Theatricalities of All Kinds

For art to exceed the unrest of political reality, Artaud writes, theater needs to reassert and make public "the internal world, that is, of man considered metaphysically," in hopes of reawakening such a world within audiences.[7] By focusing on what audiences keep internal but don't recognize themselves, Artaud calls on everything a person dares not admit to thinking or secretly enjoying: "the truthful precipitates of dreams, in which his taste for crime, his erotic obsessions, his savagery, his chimeras, his utopian sense of life and matter, even his cannibalism."[8] Industrial music follows a near one-to-one correlation in its exorcizing these themes, from an obsession with the dreamlike (as in Mind. In.A.Box's *Dreamweb* album or the music of Oneiroid Psychosis), its fascination with the celebration of serial killers (such as Whitehouse's album *Dedicated to Peter Kürten* or Suicide Commando's "Bind, Torture, Kill"), a pervasive theme of sexual fetish (nearly every song ever by Die Form), to yes, even cannibalism (think here of Ministry's "Cannibal Song," Wumpscut's *Cannibal Anthem* album, and Nox's "Cannibal Night").

Simply using words to achieve this reawakening isn't enough, because to Artaud verbal descriptions of our inner experience verge on academic psychology, lacking real punch; indeed, he advocates that performers give words "approximately the importance they have in dreams."[9] A good example of this is Z'EV's early 1980s Uns project, which explores directionless, crazed ranting.

Rather than focus on semantic clarity, the Theater of Cruelty's tools are instead "Cries, groans, apparitions, surprises, theatricalities of all kinds, magic beauty of costumes taken from certain ritual models; resplendent lighting . . . concrete appearances of new and surprising objects, masks, effigies yards

✿ Bringing these intellectuals into dialogue is hardly new. For example, David Sterritt in *Screening the Beats* observes, "Antonin Artaud's pursuit of a Theater of Cruelty . . . anticipated key elements of Burroughs's ethos."[6]

high. . . ."[10] The screams, ghostliness, and elaborate costumes and props that Artaud describes here call to mind Skinny Puppy's live performances in which lead singer Ogre, cackling a gothic cut-up text, dons long-beaked plague masks or vivisects a distressingly realistic stuffed animal. It might just as well apply to the infamous 1981 Survival Research Laboratories/Monte Cazazza/Factrix performance *Night of the Succubus*, for which Mark Pauline constructed a multi-carcass mechanized chimera, whose teeth Joseph Jacobs drilled out onstage, all to a flashy lightshow and a soundtrack of echo-drenched madness.

As for the nonstandard venues favored by the likes of Survival Research Laboratories, SPK, Test Dept., and Einstürzende Neubauten, Artaud's got them covered too: "Thus, abandoning the architecture of present-day theaters, we shall take some hangar or barn, which we shall have re-constructed according to processes which have culminated in the architecture of certain churches or holy places."[11] The desire here is to erase the division of performer from audience that traditional theaters encode in their very being.

Artaud is similarly instructive with regard to sound itself, overlapping with Russolo in a desire for new sound, but expressly seeking to pain the audience:

> The need to act directly and profoundly upon the sensibility through the organs invites research, from the point of view of sound, into qualities and vibrations of absolutely new sounds, qualities which present-day musical instruments do not possess and which require the revival of ancient and forgotten instruments or the invention of new ones. Research is also required, apart from music, into instruments and appliances which, based upon special combinations or new alloys of metal, can attain a new range and compass, producing sounds or noises that are unbearably piercing.[12]

Not only does the inventive percussion of Z'EV, Test Dept., and Einstürzende Neubauten apply here, but so too does the work of Monte Cazazza and Throbbing Gristle. Cazazza relates the story of driving away gypsies from the backyard of Genesis P-Orridge by blaring "this sound-wave generator which produced high frequency sounds almost (but not quite) above the range of human hearing . . . they made you really nervous." Echoing Artaud by fifty years, he goes on, "Infrasound can be used to make people really sick . . . what's needed is a thorough, scientific study."[13] Indeed, some industrial bands such as the Hafler Trio and the Anti-Group Company explicitly present their recordings as acoustic research, rather than art.

Artaud frames much of his manifesto with the desire to restore the power of theater so that it might forcibly pull viewers out of themselves by denying the decorum that differentiates private thought and behavior from public, by silencing the language that reduces inner experience to mere words, by alienating these audiences through summoning the otherworldly, and by upsetting their physical comfort with sound's tactility. This invasiveness, despite ecstasy as a possible goal, is the cruelty in Artaud's theater. He points out the numbness of common audiences when he writes, "Without an element of cruelty at the root of every spectacle, the theater is not possible. In our present state of degeneration it is through the skin that metaphysics must be made to re-enter our minds."[14]

These precise strategies are also the tools of most of the early industrial music discussed so far. In seeking to shock listeners out of themselves, industrial music often attempts to expose the needless, arbitrary, and complacent trappings out of which those audiences are being shocked, treating people to a view of hegemony from the outside in. Artaud helps us to articulate the aim of so much industrial music to birth the audiences into their new selves, replete with both the freedom and the agony of maternal separation. (Its efforts to do this can be earnest or a put-on; the social and aesthetic aspects of the genre give it an overwhelming tendency to preach to the converted, as we'll discuss later.) This notion is perhaps made most famously visible in the ultra-industrial cyberpunk blockbuster *The Matrix*, when Keanu Reeves's character Neo chooses to be shocked out of his comfortable reality and reborn naked into a constant warzone against machines. Industrially enacted by acts like Wumpscut, Unit 187, Pain Teens, and Rotersand, this metaphor of rebirth was staged explicitly by Artaud—albeit with scorpions and Swiss cheese—in his 1925 Oedipal nightmare *Jet of Blood*.

To lovers of surrealism, to the dedicatedly paranoid, and to many self-declared freethinkers, Antonin Artaud is a symbolic figure not merely for his writing and theater but for what they perceive to be a self-sacrificing commitment to the pan-revolutionary. After a series of drug experiences, hallucinations, and run-ins with the law, Artaud was placed in an asylum. Late in his life, he received electroshock therapy, and was effectively silenced.

In the upcoming chapter about the Canadian industrial act Skinny Puppy, the legacy of Artaud looms large. Importantly, the shock, disgust, and unreason that he embraces also take on a gendered duty—hardly surprising in light of Artaud's fascination with birth and chastity, and given the important critiques of his work by feminist thinkers Susan Sontag and Julia Kristeva. Through a peculiar logic, these aesthetics of cruelty historically served in part to unlock industrial music to wider audiences.

# "She's a Sleeping Beast": Skinny Puppy and the Feminine Gothic

## 1. From Pop to Puppy

As the story repeated in Skinny Puppy interviews goes, cEvin Key (born Kevin Crompton) and Nivek Ogre (born Kevin Ogilvie) met at a party in Vancouver in late 1982, went and recorded the song "K-9" on a lark, and saw the next day that in their drunken session they'd written the name "Skinny Puppy" on the tape. It's not exactly true, though; Key had thought up the band name a least a year beforehand, and he'd already composed many of Skinny Puppy's earliest tracks on his synthesizers at home before he asked Ogre to sing, moan, and cackle over them. Ogre, a Calgary native, was nineteen or twenty when Key first heard him growl along to the jukebox at a diner, and his manic dourness— somehow both gregarious and cagey—seemed a good match for the demos Key had been cooking up.

Key himself was foremost a drummer and had played in some trash rock bands in the mid-1970s—Bastille and Illegal Youth. He was now busy with Images in Vogue, a primped new wave act that was starting to attract some serious popular attention in Canada. The band's roots reach back to the surprisingly fertile Vancouver punk scene of the late 1970s, but instead of relentless live playing, Images in Vogue spent most of their energy programming synthesizers and tweaking demo recordings in the isolation of a warehouse on the south shore of Vancouver Harbour.

Early on, the group exhibited some experimental leanings, but by 1983 Key was already wary of the upbeat pop concessions they were starting to make in their music. Though he would stick with Images in Vogue through August 1985, touring with the likes of Bryan Adams and Duran Duran, Key's heart and creative energy belonged chiefly to the Skinny Puppy project once it launched in earnest during the summer of 1983. Ogre remembers, "He was looking for something to break out of [Images in Vogue], and maybe I was it."[1] It was then that Key and Ogre (who was rooming with Images in Vogue member Gary Blair Smith) composed most of the songs for their debut tape *Back and Forth*.

*Back and Forth* finds its clearest musical precedents in the dublike delay effects of Cabaret Voltaire; in the hollow, mean, analogue synth and drum machine grooves of Portion Control and Nocturnal Emissions; and in the roomy sadness of Chris & Cosey's not-quite-pop. But Ogre's voice is consistently treated with digital echo, tweaked so that instead of a tasteful one-beat repetition effect, it spawns choirs instantaneously—a short delay time with a low decay rate high in the mix, in techspeak. As Key recalls, the Lexicon PCM41 (borrowed from Images in Vogue keyboardist Joe Vizvary) was central to Skinny Puppy's sound: "Everything we made was run through it. I had no idea what it was actually doing at first, other than what I heard, so I felt like it was the perfect machine."[2]

Although this kind of processing to some degree mechanizes Ogre's voice, it also gives the impression that every lyric careens in an imagined space and through the gaps between the sounds of Key's Roland TR-808 drum machine, itself run through a Korg SDD-1000 delay. There are other elements at play in the sound too: Key would tape background noise and ambience from movies—sometimes minutes at a time—and simply play them in the mix as a thickening layer. On "Intro (live in Winnipeg)," the opening track of 1992's "Series Two" rerelease of *Back and Forth*, you can hear Key's primitive method of cueing these ambiences: the sounds of his pressing Stop/Eject and switching out a tape on a cassette player are unmistakable. Similarly, the long, legato synth tones that cascade over songs like "Sleeping Beast" show that even though Skinny Puppy was making beat-driven dance music, they weren't quite marching in sync with EBM's rule of tightly contained, pulsing rigidity.

Key and Ogre dubbed just thirty-five copies of *Back and Forth*, sending many of them to the addresses they'd seen printed in *The Elephant Table*, which was one of the most popular compilations to come out of the tape trading scene. This helped them connect with musicians like the Legendary Pink Dots, Nocturnal Emissions, Die Form, P16.D4., and Bourbonese Qualk. They made a quick splash in this network (Dave Henderson reviewed *Back and Forth* in his "Wild Planet" column in *Sounds*), and the group was sufficiently encouraged to go to Vancouver's famous Mushroom Studios in 1984 and cut the *Remission EP.*

Ric Arboit, sometime mixing engineer for Images in Vogue, worked at Mushroom, and he and his buddy Terry McBride footed the recording bill and signed Skinny Puppy as the second act on their indie label Nettwerk Records—an imprint born from McBride's experience with his failed label Noetix. Nettwerk's first signee had been Moev, whose earlier debut single was Noetix's sole release. Moev was a chronically underappreciated dark synthpop act whose bombastic initial recordings smacked of Siouxsie and the Banshees and Depeche Mode—hovering around the edges of industrial music but never really taking part in it. Skinny Puppy, though, fully embraced and embodied industrial's snarling aggression. "We were interested in the Throbbing Gristle scene, but they hadn't made enough rhythm," Key says.[3] Like a lot of second-wave industrialists, Skinny Puppy's attraction to rhythm wasn't consciously political, but based in the pleasure of making and moving to a beat; Key was, after all, a drummer.

## 2. Vancouver's Fertile Ground

The band's first show was in February 1984 at a perpetually empty art gallery called Unovis. Key remembers, "Our friend who had the key to the place went away that day, so we broke in and set up . . . at three a.m. we played to about 300 people, including [the UK Batcave band] Alien Sex Fiend," who was in town on tour.[4] The band took the makeshift stage just as they were peaking on MDA, a hallucinogenic amphetamine. The publicity for the show was all word of mouth, quite a bit like Test Dept.'s early unauthorized performances.

Less than a year later, Skinny Puppy had picked up a third member—Vancouver über-scenester Bill Leeb (then known as Wilhelm Schroeder)—and recorded "Smothered Hope," *Remission*'s lead track and as close to an industrial hit as any North American act had scored by then. A lot of the support for Images in Vogue, Skinny Puppy, and Vancouver's underground music in general came from the University of British Columbia's student radio station CiTR and from late-night clubs (mostly unlicensed) such as Mr. Toast and Club Soda. The most popular and influential venue of Vancouver's underground was the Luv-a-Fair, a former gay club that turned into a punk hangout in 1980. DJs such as Steven Gilmore were dedicated to bringing cutting-edge oddities and soon-to-be classics to the little city. "The first time you ever heard, say, 'Love Will Tear Us Apart' by Joy Division was there," Key recalls; "[Y]ou heard it at this club because some DJ went all the way to Seattle and picked it up. And so it was like, 'Oh, my god!' You'd run to the DJ booth so many times it was tiring."[5]

If some of the names in the Vancouver scene sound familiar, there's a reason. The city's crop of musicians and engineers would become major players both within and beyond the industrial community in the years that followed: in addition to Leeb (who would found Front Line Assembly), Key, Arboit, and McBride, Dave "Rave" Ogilvie (no relation to Ogre) was a soundman for Images in Vogue and went on to produce Skinny Puppy's first seven studio albums, later recording Marilyn Manson and Killing Joke; Steven Gilmore would go beyond DJing and become Nettwerk's in-house graphic artist, helping to shape industrial music's look; Greg Reely, another engineer for Images in Vogue, continues to work with Front Line Assembly and has production and mixing credits for Coldplay and Sarah McLachlan (who, before she was mother of the Lilith

Fair, was immersed in Canadian ethereal and goth music); Images in Vogue guitarist Don Gordon later launched the gritty industrial band Numb; Al Nelson was road crew for Images in Vogue (and younger brother of keyboardist Glen) and recorded a few albums with Skinny Puppy's members under the collective name Hilt; Anthony Valcic was briefly in the band Moev and later engineered records by Front Line Assembly, Manufacture, and Download. Others such as youngster Rhys Fulber (of Front Line Assembly, Conjure One, and later the producer of Fear Factory), Chris Peterson (of Will, Decree, and later Front Line Assembly), Michael Balch (of Front Line Assembly and Ministry), and Carylann Loeppky (graphic designer and former wife of Leeb) were also lurking in the Vancouver scene in the mid-1980s as DJs, club kids, and clerks at record stores such as Cinematica.

## 3. Disrupting Maleness

Skinny Puppy's quick rise in 1984 and especially 1985 (when they toured more widely and released their first proper album, *Bites*) didn't just serve to place Vancouver on the map of industrial history, and it wasn't simply the inevitable product of an uncommonly talented musical community. Rather, Skinny Puppy's recordings, performance, personality, and fan base together helped to open up industrial music to female audiences—and by extension female musicians. It's hard to overstate the importance of this.

Certainly there were some women in industrial music before Skinny Puppy, but generally as makers, they played an ultraconfrontational role that took their power from the fear they inspired in male audiences with their sexual assertiveness. To participate in early industrial music, women were expected to be formidable and ultimately inaccessible. This was the case with Cosey Fanni Tutti's dabbling in porn or with Diana Rogerson and Jill Westwood's London-based act Fistfuck, whose live shows featured "a female dominatrix ritually humiliating men, pissing on them and tying them to chairs, all to a soundtrack of extreme noise and sound collage," according to author David Keenan.[6] Industrial music's phallocentrism almost seems a tactic of sexual intimidation, given the names of its champions Throbbing Gristle, Meatwhistle, SPK's incarnation as Surgical Penis Klinik, and later acts such as Revolting Cocks. Perhaps not surprisingly, then, female audience members in the early 1980s (rare as they were) more often listened to industrial music casually as merely one of many post-punk genres popular in the underground. SPK's Graeme Revell admits, "I was always concerned that there was something kind of macho and therefore pathetic, about what we were doing because we couldn't quite access it to females."[7]

Desire and fulfillment are effectively invisible in early industrial; in the words of Throbbing Gristle, even if the music occasionally trails "hot on the heels of love," it never obtains it.

Key supposes that "the female followers—I think they came maybe because in Canada, we were seen as a followup to Images in Vogue." But this is at odds with the fanaticism that so many young women—previously locked out of industrial music's cult—felt specifically toward Skinny Puppy.[8] Beyond devoted fans' deep emotional engagement (more on this later), Ogre's appeal was sexually tinged: Michael Balch recalls that when Bill Leeb (Skinny Puppy's keyboardist at the time) worked at a punk clothing store called Black Market, "Little goth girls would come in and stare at him and ask him about Ogre."[9] Owing in part to the simple demographics of the subculture, Skinny Puppy, by merely reaching out to goth fans, fostered an audience that, despite remaining mostly male, was far more gender-inclusive than any previous industrial fan base.

A self-professed fan of the iconically goth English band Bauhaus (who, incidentally, titled a song "Antonin Artaud"), Ogre took a cue from that budding scene and steered the makeup and teased hair look that Key had picked up in Images in Vogue toward a gaunt androgyny that occupied a fluid, pansexual arena of expressive desire that scholars such as Paul Hodkinson and Carol Siegel describe as central to goth culture.[10]✿ As Key recalls, "We kind of also attracted the people from the gay community, who were very sexless by that point. We were kind of all androgynous."[11]

Beyond the band's image, though, there's an argument to be made that Skinny Puppy's music itself takes on aesthetics and forms that resonate with more inclusive ideas about gender and identity than did other industrial music of the era.

## 4. Feminine Gothic

Skinny Puppy's appeal has a lot to do with the band's invoking of what some scholars call the *feminine gothic*, with *gothic* here referring not to modern goth subculture per se, but to an older set of artistic themes and practices. The gothic in art is most often identified with certain eighteenth- and nineteenth-century literature, but it applies here as well.

---

✿ This brand of androgyny is a different sort from that which proliferated in hair metal, which Robert Walser reads as patriarchal and misogynistic in *Running with the Devil*. Joshua Gunn explores this aesthetic's simultaneously empowering and oppressive gender politics.[12]

(As suggested by Balch's story, it might also be said that Skinny Puppy's popularity among female fans has to do with Ogre's good looks and charisma; but even so, this charisma is tied in with his self-presentation through lyrics, voice, and image, which is filtered through this lens of the gothic. Indeed, Ogre wasn't the first good-looking industrial frontman, but given that the Los Angeles Times has called him "the first industrial rock star," it's worth asking what Skinny Puppy did differently from other bands.[13] It's likely that most of the band's directly acknowledged influence has to do with their sound, their lyrics, and their visual presentation, but again, these facets embody and demonstrate a treatment of gender and politics different from other industrial music of the day. Being thus set apart from European EBM or noise, Skinny Puppy was both popular and enduringly influential in ways that are difficult to divorce from their gothicism.)

Now, the gothic, as literary scholar Kelly Hurley explains, is fundamentally concerned with the body—specifically its ruination. Rather than glorify the ordered body of fascism and EBM, the gothic "offers the spectacle of a body metamorphic and undifferentiated . . . continually in danger of becoming not-itself, becoming other."[14]

Hurley explains that the gothic as a practice speculates about questions of what it means to be human, and so it makes sense that Skinny Puppy highlights this with dehumanizing vocal processing effects and a political invective that prioritizes animal life above human life. In their undulating, voice-deforming, endlessly echoing dance music, Skinny Puppy raise these questions by wallowing in the danger of becoming other—Ogre's image is of a thing drenched in blood, his voice is bestial, and his lyrical subject matter is a mix of confession and alienating rants about the world through the eyes of animal test subjects. Even Key has felt revulsion and surprise at his bandmate: "I was shocked the first few shows—they were heavy duty. He was doing a lot of simulated effects of cutting. Heavy, scary shit: razor blades, broken glass, heavy blood."[15]

Ogre's visual performances, his lyrics, and his vocal delivery perform *abjection*, a depraved self-purging—physical or otherwise—that Chris Bohn (writing as Biba Kopf) claims industrial music dedicatedly enacts and understands.[16] According to literary theorist Julia Kristeva in her important book *The Powers of Horror*, abjection is a response to the realization that a peaceful and primordial kind of meaning—one of a unified, fully knowable world-womb—is necessarily unrecoverable, severed at birth as a precondition of being.[17] Remember industrial music's modernist recognition that we're born into a hierarchical network of control systems from which it's our impossible duty to escape? Well, abjection strives for an Artaudian rebirth into a new flesh uninterrupted by the real world and untouched by that most fundamental logic, the subject-object division. Abjection is a gross attempt to counteract the inescapability of the control machines. It rages against the irreconcilability of the exterior with the interior. And because abjection seeks to erase the borders between the inside and outside of bodies and objects, it shows up in human art and action as willful bleeding, vomit, and excretion. By refusing bodily order and behavioral rationality, abjection is a model for rejecting the fact that any experience of worldly meaning begins with an act of differentiating.

Skinny Puppy's 1986 song "God's Gift (Maggot)," is a good musical metaphor for bodily indifferentiation. The drums don't rely on a four-on-the-floor kick but are instead syncopated, and a shaker (instead of a hi-hat) keeps time, its sonic attack more of a fade-in than a hit—the swirling noise of an eggshell's contents. Behind them is a bongo drum loop that more closely resembles a porn soundtrack than a drum corps. The synth bass uses a low frequency oscillator that makes it sound like a worm being squished underfoot, not a plucked string. Film and choral samples are pitch-shifted down, taking on a direly evil and linguistically incomprehensible quality. Ogre, mutated as always with distortion and reverb, swaps between a nasal-voiced declaration and a gagging whisper; recorded in alternating takes, these two misshapen voices collide and overlap. Lyrically, he takes on the misapprehension of all meaning by interlacing references to Plato's allegory of the cave, but he keeps coming back to the permeability of the body: "Knives in the eyes, maggots fill the brain."

A song like "God's Gift (Maggot)" can be usefully understood as an *abreaction* (to borrow a term from psychology), which means the reenactment of trauma in order to purge its effects. Within this theoretical framework, the original trauma of losing one's harmonious unity to the harshness of the external world is recast musically as the grotesque blending of inside and outside, back and forth, in order to reclaim some kind of symbolic integration.

From a gender-informed perspective, there's an easy connection to be made here to the physical experience and grossness of birth, and indeed Kristeva writes a fair amount about that. She specifically aligns abjection with the female body, and similarly, the gothic is often understood as representing a threat to patriarchal ideas of control that rely on the absoluteness and differentiation of identities—hence the term feminine gothic.❋ Similarly, the liberating female potential to disrupt male-enforced order is a hallmark of the previous centuries' literature that informs what we mean by "gothic."

❋ The "male gothic" as a literary practice also exists, as described by Anne Williams in *Art of Darkness: A Poetics of Gothic*, but instead of it being an opposite coding of the body, it concerns the panopticon of the male gaze, which she asserts (by way of Luce Irigaray) is incapable of perceiving anything genuinely outside of its maleness.

Equally relevant to Skinny Puppy is that Kristeva also sees abjection's attempts to reclaim undifferentiated wholeness as connected to the control system of language. One way that we can think about Skinny Puppy is to view them as constantly reenacting the trauma of *coming to be*. The near incomprehensibility of Ogre's voice (as routed through the Lexicon PCM41) and the antisyntactical weirdness of his stream-of-consciousness lyrics perform a therapeutic function: an abreaction in attempt to reclaim preverbal harmony. Ogre's textual and vocal affectations are strategies that he partially developed in his theater and mask-making training with artist Myra Davies and playwright-director Morris Panych, and in that verbal reenactment of a formational violence and meaninglessness he attempts to find a space for peace and understanding. In this way, abreaction serves as another explanation of the reversal tactic that so much industrial music applies to control systems (indeed, Burroughs's famous assertion that language is a virus serves to conflate it with the genre's other targets of critique). And the idea that the breakdown of language is connected to the grotesque is a basic tenet of the gothic: as literary scholar Anne Williams explains, "A 'definition' of 'Gothic' thus outlines a large, irregularly shaped figure, an irregularity that implies the limitations of language—appropriate for the category containing the unspeakable 'other.'"[18]

Tying this together, when Kelly Hurley says that gothic strategies "function maximally to enact the defamiliarization and violent reconstitution of the human subject," it's easy to see how abjection as an act can play an explosive, transformative role in this.[19] Significantly, how Skinny Puppy acts out abjection is theatrical—video of a 1986 hometown performance shows Ogre wielding a television set, attempting to eat a hamburger and vomiting (recall their animal rights advocacy); later, he holds aloft a severed head by its hair and serenades it in front of a backdrop video of a burning car, *Hamlet* by way of J. G. Ballard. In this theatricality, Skinny Puppy offers not merely a spectacle of heavy critique, but an overt, sexualized delight. There is, of course, a perverse thrill in finding the animal within; as Ogre hisses, "She's a sleeping beast."

Most ideas of the gothic, especially older literary and architectural ones, focus less on a preoccupation with the body and more on the invoking of the hidden, the dark, the ghostly. Though these aspects are less directly relevant to the argument here, it's worth acknowledging that Skinny Puppy also engages with these topics, sometimes in ways that other industrial acts hadn't previously done. For example, whereas early industrial music took interest in the occult as a study of mass control, a chastisement of Christianity, or an earnest attempt at magic, Skinny Puppy's treatment of the haunted more closely resembles the ghost story as a convention: the undead are as good at mood setting as they are at critical commentary. Characteristically Ogre names as a favorite author

*Figure 12.1: The cover art of Skinny Puppy's single "Dig It" is unambiguously gothic in multiple senses of the word. Drawing by Gustave Doré; design by Steven R. Gilmore.*

Comte de Lautréamont, arguably the most macabre and abjectly gothic writer of the nineteenth century.✿

Similarly, on the cover of Skinny Puppy's 1986 single "Dig It," the choice of an illustration from *The Inferno* (of a man ascending from an open tomb, drawn by the nineteenth-century romantic artist Gustav Doré) drives home this additional compatibility with the literary gothic.

### 5. Gothic Femmes

To bring this all back to Skinny Puppy's disruption of industrial music's male genderedness, the point here isn't necessarily that abjection and gothicism translate positively into Canadian girls wanting to dance to "Assimilate" or tattoo the band's logo on their shoulders. Instead, it's that Skinny Puppy took a music that had been (ironically or otherwise) militaristic and impenetrable and recast it as permeable, ectoplasm-drenched, and borderless. Their music embodies nonrigidity, overflow, theatrical spectacularity, birth, and irrationality. It creates a metaphorical space that welcomes real, visceral bodies—not body armor.

Though it's essentialistic and crass to declare these qualities intrinsically feminine, they nevertheless transgress the values of fitness, organization, clean-

---

✿ Comte de Lautréamont, the pen name of Isidore-Lucien Ducasse, was also the inspiration behind the title of Nurse With Wound's 1979 debut *Chance Meeting on a Dissecting Table of a Sewing Machine and an Umbrella.*

liness, and discipline that the overwhelmingly male industrial scene chose to privilege. As Rhys Fulber recalls, "The big thing about Skinny Puppy was that they had a huge female audience," and a connection is evident when we consider that this coincided with the band's unique invocation of the natal and linguistic abject, the monstrous, and the grotesque.[20] Ogre's good looks and Key's history with Images in Vogue would likely have done little to attract women to industrial music and retain their attention if Skinny Puppy's music itself hadn't conjured and given voice to ways of being that extended beyond the genre's agenda up to that point. Fulber says, "They certainly turned the scene into what it is now, by glamming it up a little bit, because it wasn't like that before."[21] He highlights the lasting importance of Skinny Puppy's gothic subversion of gender on account of the social, political, and ultimately musical possibilities that it made newly available.

Did Ogre and Key think of their music in these theoretical terms? Not likely, though they did read up on critical theory—laughing, Key says, "We had to find an intellectually stimulating way to say we like horror films."[22] The purpose of theoretical constructs like the gothic or the abject, though, is to give a generalized explanation that can be applied to actual events; they give us *ways to understand what people do* more than they tell us what those people think. This is useful because when makers and listeners viscerally latch onto a sound and want to be part of it, that subconscious negotiation is wrapped up in how the music resonates with their understanding of their social, intellectual, emotional, and sexual identity—sensibilities more deeply rooted than any premeditated creative strategy.

As a concluding illustration of the real gendered effects of Skinny Puppy's gothicism, consider the case of Jolene Siana, a fan who documented her self-harm and teenage rebellion in confessional letters to Ogre, later published as *Go Ask Ogre*. She writes to him:

> I wanted to be raised differently. I wanted to have a father and sisters and brothers. I didn't want to be teased in elementary school. I wanted to be special. I wanted to cry less. I wanted to be disciplined. I wanted to be safe. I look in the mirror. I know myself. I don't like myself and I know you can't like myself. I don't want to die. I don't want you to dislike me. I don't know you well, but you matter. Kristy tried to tell me that I write to you because she says you're good-looking. That's so shallow and untrue. I'd write to you even if you looked like David Lee Roth but still had your thoughts. I like all nice people. I have no right to say anything to you. I have no right to care. I don't know myself and I'm sorry about everything. Really I am.[23]

Stepping beyond the sort of sexual teenybopper appeal that Images in Vogue fostered, Siana proclaims a gendered but nonsexual yearning that situates Ogre's "thoughts"—his lyrics and self-presentation via the band—as solace for her inability to understand herself. She's able to use Ogre and Skinny Puppy's music here as a stand-in for some missing piece of her own identity: "This may sound strange, but the only means of me getting my feelings out is on paper to you," she wrote in 1987.[24] Not only is this an act of personal relation (imagined or real) across genders, but given her own private abjection—her book's subtitle is *Letters of a Deathrock Cutter*—it's also a case of her using the band's theatrical bodily ruination as a way to abreact her own.

In the mid-1980s, industrial music for the first time opened up to a level of emotional engagement that recognized its community's personhood as well as its politics.✿ In live performance and on record, Skinny Puppy's music introduced an aesthetic approach that both in theory and in practice proved crucial in this change, and by extension they helped ensure the social viability and longevity of the genre.

Also, it's good for dancing.

### ICONIC:

Diamanda Galás – "Wild Women With Steak Knives" (1982)

Moev – "Cracked Mirror" (1981)

Skinny Puppy – "Assimilate" (1985)

Skinny Puppy – "First Aid" (1987)

Skinny Puppy – "Worlock" (1989)

### ARCANE:

Bauhaus – "Antonin Artaud" (1983)

Doubting Thomas – "Blowfish" (1989)

Front Line Assembly – "A Decade" (1986)

Images in Vogue – "S&M" (1982)

The Tear Garden – "You and Me and Rainbows (parts 1–6)" (1987)

---

✿ As just one instance of this wider event, consider the first all-female compilation record to emerge from the underground scene, 1986's *Femirama*.

# Part IV

# INDUSTRIAL
# POLITICS

THE NARRATIVE UP TO THIS POINT HAS ALLUDED TO A VARIETY OF POTENTIALLY alarming aesthetic and political themes in industrial music without really stopping to offer them fuller consideration. What are we to make of allegedly anarcho-leftist music that takes inspiration from serial killers, from European militarism, from Mussolini-loving Futurists, and from obsession with order, or replication, or disgust? And beyond questions of how we today are supposed to react, what have fans and political ideologues historically made of this music?

Having looked at industrial music through the mid-1980s, we're at an apt moment in the story to pause and ask these questions, because, as we'll see in Chapter 15, the late 1980s functioned as a vital period when the genre's popularity expanded rapidly beyond the urban underground of Europe and the United States. Given industrial music's use of polarizing and totalizing signs, the mere fact of its public spread is remarkable, and to get more specific, the way that audiences both shape and are shaped by the confounding messages of extremism and détournement makes for a telling case study in music and marketing, in race and resistance.

The following section's two chapters consider the intentional extremism and inadvertent blind spots of industrial music. Although the genre's characters and musical tools have changed over time, concerns over its political goals prove perennial. Both to illustrate the continuing centrality of these issues and to address them comprehensively and with relevance, these chapters temporarily step beyond the book's chronology thus far, opting to include examples from industrial music's more recent years alongside earlier ones.

# 13.
# Back and Forth:
# Industrial Music and Fascism

## 1. Extremism as the Norm

Industrial music's pan-revolutionary streak isn't just fond of extreme imagery; it relies on it. The Debordian tyranny of the spectacle, with its aligned control machines and hegemonies, is perceived as so all-encompassing that industrial music often takes neoliberal moderation as useless. In particular, the genre's imagery of totalitarianism is pervasive enough to have rightly become a recurring topic of curiosity, caution, prurience, and debate within industrial music's communities of fans and commentators. Graphically in videos, performances, and on record sleeves; sonically in the music's unforgivingly quantized march rhythms and samples of political events, news, and films; and discursively in bands' lyrics and interviews, industrial music borrows from, enacts, mocks, documents, and embraces signifiers of political and ideological extremism from seemingly every corner of human belief. This makes a certain sense given that the purported enemies on whom the genre fixes its crosshairs take so many forms. Instead of surveying and cataloguing industrial music's extremist rhetoric, this chapter looks deeply at how and why musicians use these signs (both theoretically and functionally), as well as how audiences have interpreted them.

Throughout its entire history, the industrial music scene has been home to socialist ideologues, Randian libertarians, anarchists, academics, mistrusters of western intellectualism, utopian mystics, racial purists, nihilists with nothing to lose, and a substantial crowd who either hold aestheticized and underdeveloped ideologies or deny any interest in politics, culture, and the discourse thereof, and who just want to dance. With this apparent variety in mind, it's useful to turn to Slavoj Žižek, a savvy theorist of extremist politics and mass culture, who says, "The fundamental conflict today is no longer Left versus Right, but rather, liberal openness versus neoethnic closedness."[1] This perspective helps us move past some of the picky distinctions between one band's particular brand of sloganeering and another's. Nearly all industrial music falls to the "open" side of Žižek's new division, advocating for collective transparency and individual free action, if not always for ideological fluidity and open-mindedness. Indeed, Jon Savage's assertion that industrial is concerned with "access to information" rings true across the genre's history. From Throbbing Gristle's insistence that the cut-up reveals hidden truths behind cultural texts to the 1990s' glorification of the hacker figure within cyberpunk and beyond, the music deals with exposing secrets hidden by the powers that be.

Industrial music resists these powers, and it prioritizes resistance above the particulars of politics, a sentiment illustrated by Fifth Colvmn Records' oxymoronic and only slightly tongue-in-cheek 1996 compilation album title *Fascist Communist Revolutionaries*. Industrial groups' reactive resistance has frequently made them slower to offer solutions than to point out problems—most notably that authoritarian powers of any stripe exert more control over us than we realize. It's true that some unambiguously leftist acts call for specific political engagement: the band Consolidated springs to mind, with their vegetarian advocacy, their use of second-wave feminist Barbara Kruger's art on the cover of their *Business of Punishment* album, and their featuring of African American separatist rapper Paris on 1992's "Guerillas in the Mist." But Consolidated are the exception to the rule here, for two reasons. First, on the theoretical level, any positive alternative to a totalitarian regime or a commodity-based economy risks being superficially appropriated and defanged by the system—recall Debord's phrase "the recuperation of the spectacle." Second, on a practical level, industrial audiences have historically rejected preachiness; Consolidated's album *Play More Music* kicks off with a recording of an audience member angrily declaring to them at a live show, "If you don't like fascism, don't play industrial music."

Despite the actual antifascist beliefs of most industrial musicians, then, how is it that a fan could conclude that "Industrial Music is Fascism," as Consolidated's track title suggests? How is it that at a 2001 VNV Nation concert in Montreal, a fervent skinhead fan saw fit to offer the hardline leftist lead singer Ronan Harris a Nazi salute in a mistaken presumption of solidarity (to which Harris responded with a communist salute)?[2] The first part of the answer is in the aforementioned tendency of most industrial music simply to critique and tear down authority rather than to verbalize a utopian replacement for it. The second part has to do with the fact that this critique comes coded in industrial music's now familiar and often intentional language of ambiguity. We'll return to the first issue in some depth, after this question of ambiguity has been addressed.

## 2. Silent Politics

In an essay on industrial music videos, Jason Hanley expresses concern that fans might sometimes misunderstand musicians' uses of totalitarian imagery.

ASSIMILATE

Specifically, Laibach built their reputation by declaring themselves to be a nation (Neue Slovenische Kunst—New Slovenian Art) and then staging their concerts and videos as unblinking state military rallies, driven with tactics that were all too familiar in Cold War Yugoslavia, such as constructivist graphic design, formation marching, and domineering one-way demagoguery.✿ The band's embodiment of an oppressive regime "makes no attempt to subvert this image [so] it has the aura of authenticity."[3] According to Hanley, as a result, "Many Laibach fans began to revel in the evils of the band and to take their stage act at face value."[4]

Hanley grants, "Perhaps that is what these bands are hoping for, that the origin of the sign is so powerful that it immediately connects with the audience, shocking them, awakening them, violently attacking them. Then once the image has grabbed the audience, the band can do its work."[5] But as we'll explore more thoroughly in this book's final chapter, the *fact* of shock gives way to the content of shock with near inevitability—especially upon its less shocking repetitions—and so we oughtn't fall prey to Artaud's error of treating shock as an end unto itself. The uniformity of Laibach's provocation seems to insist that we grapple with fascism specifically—or at least with the way that pageantry itself can dress up fascism and democracy with identical ease.

Taken literally, "provocation" means inciting a verbal response; it asks questions. Laibach, for example, is referred to as an "interrogation machine" by scholar Alexei Monroe because their actions target the tyrannical and demand a response—to the degree that this reply (whatever it is) can be seen as part of the artistic work itself. The nationalism they stage is so extreme as to become *overidentified*, and it effectively calls a bluff: for example, the Yugoslav government in the 1980s either had to take a position affirming the band's obviously dangerous national zeal (aligning themselves through silence or advocacy with unambiguous tyranny), or they could denounce it, thus revealing nationalism (and thereby the state itself) as limited and flawed. It can duly attempt to dismantle any patriotism born of listeners' unspoken (even unrecognized) desire for totalitarianism by "traversing the fantasy," preemptively exorcising that longing.

---

✿ In the early 1980s, the Neue Slovenische Kunst outraged Slovenia's government and culture at large. However, Laibach have since attained significant stature and commercial heft in their tiny home country; prior to the fall of communism, they were, in western countries, the top-selling Eastern Bloc band of any genre, and today their largest markets are in Germany and the United States. In 2003 they began receiving financial support from the Slovenian government. The practice of anti-authority acts receiving government funding is arguably paradoxical, but within the industrial scene it dates back to COUM Transmissions, to whom the Arts Council of Great Britain repeatedly awarded grants.

The context of industrial music's extremism can ask other important questions too. Noise journalist Mikko Aspa convincingly argues that social shock is no more the goal for acts like Whitehouse or Brighter Death Now, who sing about murder and pedophilia, than it is for murderers or pedophiles themselves—which is to say not really at all.[6] Rather, this extremist music instead asks the question of how ordinary people become such monsters, suggesting an underlying paranoia that it could happen to anyone, that our free will is illusory. In a way, that's what's going on with Throbbing Gristle's commentary on normality in "Very Friendly," as discussed in Chapter 4. And if we listen carefully, we might hear that this music answers its own question, musically portraying oppression and evil as the unforeseen fallout of a technologically modern, (post)industrialized world—a claim supported by the violence that pervades Futurism, the obsession with virus and addiction in the work of Burroughs, and the Sozialistisches Patientenkollektiv's argument that mental illness is a symptom of capitalism.

But it's rare for industrial music actually to verbalize questions and answers of this sort. And moreover, the music almost never takes the step of suggesting what we might productively do about tyranny or the postindustrial political condition.

Here's why. Hanley worries that "audiences can still interpret [fascist] signs in many ways," leading him to argue that the music shouldn't merely insinuate questions about the roots of violence and control, but in the name of discouraging real totalitarian politics it should ideally clarify its stance.[7] "Education is so important to Industrial music," he insists, effectively siding with the outward partisanship of bands like Consolidated and Test Dept.[8] But this is easier said than done, for reasons that both underlie and supplement the avoidance of preachiness and the diversity of specific politics across the genre's breadth.

First, direct attempts at "education" are frequently misinterpreted; recall Genesis P-Orridge's recognition that "revelation and education" reach only a fraction of the industrial audience. For example, at each concert on their 1990 tour, American industrial rock juggernauts Ministry launched into a rant against George H. W. Bush's government before performing their classic "The Land of Rape and Honey"—a song that contains a "sieg heil" sample from the 1979 film *The Tin Drum*. Hanley singles out this onstage rant as good education, but even explicitly moralizing gestures like this get lost in music's noisy reality: Ministry's concert footage shows sweaty fans deliriously singing along to their songs' ironically sampled dialogue, which raises the question of whether a "sieg heil" is really successfully détourned when the audience joins in without visibly distinguishing it from earnest lyrics. (Certainly Ministry's record company didn't "get" their politics when they shipped the band's CDs to Desert Storm soldiers who used them as psych-up music for bombing raids on Baghdad.[9]✿) In short, there's a conflict between the verbal intellectualization of industrial music and its desire to bypass conscious thought.

Second, and more importantly, dictating the social meaning of one's music not only renders the music redundant but goes against the individual autonomy that industrial music so privileges in its directive for people to "think for themselves."[10] The fact that telling an audience to think for itself is paradoxical and offers a pithy but effective summary of why so many industrial acts resist both utopian proposals and self-explanation. An artist who instructs audiences in the imperative becomes another authority to behead, which is certainly one reason why industrial vocals are traditionally cloaked with distortion: singers reject the signal clarity that aurally identifies authority.

The endgame of didactic preaching is dogmatic tyranny, and any ideological specificity becomes a fixed point to be pinned down and coopted by control machines. In the name of individual liberty, then, industrial music's ambiguity risks misinterpretation; hence we get situations like the gay, leftist Deutsch-Amerikanische Freundschaft in 1981, hot on the heels of the success of "Der Mussolini," accepting a gig in Middlesbrough UK only to discover at show-time that they'd been billed as a neo-Nazi act—and had drawn an audience of more than a thousand amped-up skinheads.✿✿ However, not only do these risks diminish bit by bit over time as the music insinuates its subversion, but to the pan-revolutionary frame of mind they are outweighed by the ambiguity's vital rewards: an apparently airtight consistency of ideology and a resistance to assimilation.

## 3. Loud Apolitics

Some would say that audiences' conscious misinterpretations of industrial music are hardly the biggest problem of its flirtations with extremist symbols—that the real political troubles are more complex. This makes sense, because although 1980s audiences sometimes identified certain bands as fascist (often

---

✿ More recently, the post-9/11 industrial scene's reception of songs like Dutch act Grendel's "Soilbleed" even hints at a new air of genuine reverence for the specific reality of the United States military. The song was ubiquitous in clubs from 2005 to 2007, and its samples of *Full Metal Jacket* (which Ministry also pillages on 1989's "Thieves") were contextually heard by more than a few agreeable dancers as a pep rally cheer for the United States Marine Corps.

✿✿ In one interview, the band says the number was more like three thousand skinheads—and not one woman among them.[11]

incorrectly), since that time such controversies have become more the stuff of press releases and scene boasting than of reality. After all, industrial music is historically contemporaneous with—and in its small way, part of—the trickle down of popular postmodernism, in which mass audiences over the last several decades have become at least dimly aware that a sign's past use and its present interpretation need not bear a one-to-one correlation. Willful public misreadings of Laibach's rally-esque concerts, of Skinny Puppy's staged animal testing (on a stuffed dog named Chud), and of Rammstein lead singer Till Lindemann's emphatically pronounced rolled "r"—reminiscent of Hitler's mannerisms—have all become part of those bands' purported danger: fans get off on the music's supposed political extremism because they feel safe in their belief that these bands are secretly on "the right side."

This kind of enjoyment presumes that the music bearing quasi-totalitarian imagery doesn't in fact promote totalitarian beliefs. There are a lot of questions to ask about this presumption, though. It's useful to bear in mind the long communicative chain that a piece of music is a part of: an artist has a set of subconscious beliefs about the world, which feeds into a conscious identity, which feeds into an impetus to create a song, which feeds into a piece of packaged music, which is then heard and seen by innumerable individuals who all bring their own political identities and unspoken beliefs to its interpretation. And chains like this aren't just lateral; they run parallel and they intersect in webs. Amidst the multitudes of artists and songs and identities and images, people assemble repertoires and genres, and they congregate into subcultures, and all the lattices in this web connect back to the individuals, their politics, and their silent fundamental worldviews, mutually reinforcing, coaxing, or uprooting them. It's how culture works, and it's why we can't reduce a discussion of totalitarian imagery in music to a game of spot-the-fascist.

Certainly very few musicians publicly and un-ironically advocate genocidal totalitarianism (though some in the White Hardcore and National Socialist Black Metal scenes do, as 2012's Sikh temple shooting in Wisconsin soberly reminds us). However, a hoard of industrial acts—particularly in the offshoot "martial industrial," "dark ambient," and "neo-folk" genres that first arose in the mid-1980s—present what scholar Anton Shekhovstov considers a more insidious cultural threat than bands like Ministry or Nitzer Ebb, who stage totalitarianism as pageantry to expose how western culture and economics still use fascist control techniques. The artists that Shekhovstov writes about instead insist that their music is apolitical and spiritual (often invoking elements of northern European paganism). Calling it *apoliteic*, he explains that this music "does not promote outright violence, is not related to the activities of political organizations or parties, and is not a means of recruitment to any political tendency";

nor is it a direct critique of modern government per se.[12] Instead, apoliteic music saturates its surrounding culture with, and accustoms its audience to, what many consider an aesthetic and poetic core that fertilizes fascism.

This makes sense when we consider that fascism isn't just an authoritarian form of government; it's genuinely rooted in and inseparable from aesthetics. As many theorists conceive of it today, rather than explicitly referring to Mussolini's Italian regime in which government, corporations, and the military operated in lockstep, fascism can indicate broader alliances of cultural, media, military, and commercial powers—the techno-paranoid specter incarnate. Political historian Roger Griffin asserts that fascism's "mission is to combat the allegedly degenerative forces of contemporary history (decadence) by bringing about an alternative modernity and temporality (a 'new order' and a 'new era') based on the rebirth, or palingenesis, of the nation," where "nation" may be ethnically or culturally imagined.[13] Fascism, then, like industrial music, is resistant by nature. It exists to exert itself against an other; it exists to discipline. Žižek puts it more plainly: "Enough of enjoyment, enough of debauchery: a victim is necessary."[14]

Therefore, when we see an instance of fascist aesthetics—like the straight unambiguous lines of military uniforms, parading social and athletic demonstrations, or in the case of industrial music's appropriations the architectural cleanliness of EBM—we can start to reconstruct and thus identify the purported decadence to which these aesthetics respond. Fascism invokes the spirit of corporate manufacturing, technological reproduction, and military enforcement to issue an *ethical* mandate, via *aesthetics*, against alternative ways of being. Musicologist Sean Portnoy goes deeper into this:

> Fascism stridently foregrounds the inherent aesthetization of politics (rather than destroying the gap between the supposedly separated spheres of art and politics), [so] there is no such thing as a "fascist aesthete," instead merely a fascist, and this fascist does not "borrow" from the aesthetic realm but sees the intrinsicness of that vocabulary in politics.[15]

In fascism, aesthetics are the necessary, visible means by which the conspiratorial unification of force, technology, and commerce is culturally endorsed and maintained. Through their purity, fascist aesthetics socially safeguard fascist politics by instantly singling out deviance, squelching resistant attitudes before they can become resistant action.

To this line of thinking, then, it's not much of an excuse to embrace only the fascist aesthetic while claiming to be apolitical—indeed how else would a world saturated with supposedly nondoctrinal imagery "spontaneously give way to the spiritual grandeur of national reawakening," in the plan of postwar fascist philosopher Armin Mohler?[16] As Shekhovstov says, "Fascism is definitely not confined to the realm of politics. One can be a metapolitical fascist without being drawn directly to politics."[17] As such, he observes:

> Significantly, all the movements and groups that, in one way or another, turn to Neo-Folk/Martial Industrial bands in an attempt to infiltrate certain youth subcultures are metapolitical, rather than political . . . these New Right groups focus on the cultural terrain in their attempt to influence society and make it more susceptible to undemocratic and authoritarian ways of thinking.[18]

The reasons for this boil down to a disdain for sullying the perceived purity of the spiritual and national—ethnic—ideal with the dirtiness of modern practical politics, as well as an understanding that one can't be vocally pro-fascist today without severe social repercussions. Nazi sympathizer and philosopher Ernst Jünger thus explained the need after World War II for fascist ideologues to "retreat into the forest" to safeguard, in Shekhovstov's words, "'a secret Europe' . . . hidden in the interregnum, while the Europe of the 'deadly' liberal democratic order and of 'homogenizing' multicultural society triumphs."[19] As such, there are very few open neo-fascists in the industrial scene, but rather than assuage antifascist worries, this points to a useful extension of Shekhovstov's argument: recalling the weblike nature of people, politics, music, and meaning, it's not so much that we ought to worry about the self-declared fascists and racists. Instead we should question the effects of fascist symbolism on our own instinctual, unvoiced oppressive urges.

These apoliteic tactics of symbolic bombardment in the absence of stated politics are evident in some industrial music. For example, consider Boyd Rice's choice of the wolfsangel rune as the logo of his band NON.

*Figure 13.1*

Rice insists that the symbol's runic origins represent a balance between death and life, overlooking the functional reality that the symbol has also been the emblem of the Wolf's Hook White Brotherhood, and that regardless of its history, the wolfsangel's visual similarity to the swastika is unmistakable.[20] Inasmuch as meaning is a process that involves human interpretation, words and symbols mean what people interpret them to mean, and thus the wolfsangel is de facto a racist symbol.✿ A charitable interpretation of NON's logo is that Rice is reclaiming the wolfsangel from the perceived racism that it predates, but his glee in provoking listeners is well documented and teeters on the abusive. (To offer but one example, 1975's "Hazard Music" is a conceived but never performed piece that involves heating bullets on a grill until they explode, firing in all directions through suspended plate glass, and into the audience—"It wouldn't give them time to run, just maybe time to know it was coming."[21])

Rice, who can be disarmingly charismatic and charming, personally rejects clear political interpretation of his own music. Asked directly if he would go on record stating that he is not a Nazi, Rice's reply—notably not "I am not a Nazi"—is that "there's no such thing as Nazis. If you think people with jackboots are going to be kicking in your doors, it's going to be a long fucking wait."[22]✿✿ Indeed, in his book *No*, Rice relegates Nazism exclusively to its original historical context, claiming that the term "has lost its specific meaning, becoming instead a word applied to any person with whom one disagree[s]."[23] Rice justifies his position by asserting that using the word *Nazi* ahistorically disrespects the real victims and survivors of the Holocaust, but this line of reasoning also conveniently offers plausible deniability to any rebranding of Nazi aesthetics. Additionally, it self-righteously defangs the vocabulary of those who would critique aestheticized extremism. This is particularly useful to the likes of Rice, for whom aestheticism is a tradition and a way of life—a little reminiscent of such bygone dandies as Oscar Wilde and Radclyffe Hall. Indeed, Rice tells us today that he's more concerned with his own immediate happiness than with politics. He has written for *Modern Drunkard* magazine and he is blasé in his dismissals of public opinion: "I don't care about a lot of the things that people care about. If I were upset every time someone did something that I thought was wrong or ugly or misguided, I'd be a nervous wreck."[24] Might this detachment serve as part of a Jüngerian "retreat into the forest?"

Through these tactics, Rice asserts that his interest in Nazism, for example, is strictly an intellectual and spiritual one. It was a revelation to him when as a young man he read Louis Pauwels and Jacques Bergier's *The Morning of the*

---

✿ Lest this essay blindly vindicate what might be the baiting of "puritan leftist" politics (for which most crypto-rightist industrial music has little patience), another perspective on this type of provocation is offered in a few pages through the lens of Žižek.

✿✿ Incidentally, a long fucking wait is not quite the same thing as never.

*Magicians*, which probes the curious fact that Hitler had merely been "some weird artist who lived down the street" but within a few years somehow became "the most powerful man in the world, through his use of occult imagery and strange ideas."[25] Notions like this are undeniably compelling, if prurient, and they're in keeping with the idea stated earlier that industrial music questions how such monstrosities come to be. But there's hardly a case to be made for inquisitive detachment or ironic reversal when it comes to Rice: he is the self-appointed head of the mostly defunct Church of Satan (which advocates hedonism and personal gain, rather than devil worship or intentional evil), and as such, a study of Hitler's acquisition of power stinks less of "how can we prevent this?" than "how can I do this too?"

Rice rightly complains that few reviewers really address his music. His lounge-inspired spoken-word recordings are at times poignant and funny, and his noise-based NON material is often sonically appealing in its tape-loop sensibility, where colossal roars of din form long rhythms that refuse to subdivide rationally. The largely undifferentiated nature of NON's sound can often turn the audience's attention, in their grasping for the work's identity, to Rice's lyrics and imagery (he is a visual artist too). In fan favorite "Total War," a military drum pattern provides a soundbed over which other musicians might choose to scream, but Rice instead interrogates his audience with calm, serious authority; the song's muffled, lo-fi patina situates the affair not in a recording studio but at an outdoor political rally, where a Socratic sermon of eternal violence becomes a listener's reward for actively straining to hear. Sonically difficult or cloudy music seems to demand listeners' exerted engagement, investing them in its meaning.

Verbal declarations of "Might Is Right" and symbols like the wolfsangel make it hard to interpret NON's whole package purely aesthetically. The mythic and political vocabularies that this and nearly all martial industrial noise draws from is so uniformly one-sided that through most lenses it simply doesn't hold up as a general critique of power itself. Beyond that, its participants' real politics impede an ironic reading; neo-folk singer Tony Wakeford (of Sol Invictus), for example, was once a member of the National Front.✹

Ideally, to artists like Boyd Rice, an audience's difficulty in experiencing this supposedly apolitical music as purely aesthetic ideally becomes a critique of listeners' political assumptions and indoctrinations—Laibach's old trick of provoking a response that completes the art work. But it's hardly a fair move for crypto-rightist music, a little like saying that a driver who stops at a red light is

---

✹ He has since declared this "a big mistake"—the worst of his life.[26] Some journalists and music fans have continued their criticism of him despite this.

**ASSIMILATE**

a slave to authority signs. If indeed these artists want to challenge the fundamentals of cultural semiotics, then why do symbols linked to racism occupy so specific and central a role in so ostensibly broad a critique?

Appraisals like this can also apply to acts that pervasively invoke a mythic imagery of pre-modern Europe, as with Von Thronstahl, Blood Axis, or Der Blutharsch—this last group having been blocked from performing in Israel by government officials in 2004. Within more popular industrial circles, Feindflug, This Morn' Omina, and even Wumpscut have all been dogged by similar political suspicion. None of this is to say that any band invoking Euro-pagan imagery or reappropriating military aesthetics is unwittingly fascist; indeed if that were the case, then practically the whole industrial genre would be guilty by association. As Shekhovstov argues persuasively, though, a lot of music that treads this line of controversy acclimates its fans, scenes, and surroundings to an aesthetic whose dominant twentieth-century use was in creating an ethic of exclusion and oppression, and many musicians doing this may be more aware of the potential role they play in Mohler's "interregnum" than they let on.

## 4. The Effects of Fascism's Specter

Let's look more specifically at the roles industrial music plays in laying an aesthetic and political groundwork for oppressive attitudes and behavior. Hanley quotes a Laibach fan responding to a 1989 concert: "I felt pride in a country I did not belong to. . . . I liked it, I just want to know if they are serious or not."[27] But beyond the fact that Laibach's tactics surpass mere ironic reversal, their "seriousness" is almost a foregone conclusion if the fan has already felt the swell of aesthetically induced pride in a content-free, spurious nation.

There's an unexpected flipside to the fan-level interpretation of fascist signs in music, though. On the Stormfront messageboards, the internet's central meeting place for white nationalists and neo-Nazis, the user "English Celt" witnesses the undermining of real fascist expression by the industrial music community's familiarity with détournement:

> I went to a Blutharsch gig in Camden a couple of years ago. The audience consisted of a good handfull [sic] of blatant homosexuals, a couple of ethnic goths, the Nazi memorabilia fetish brigade (some very Jewish looking) and a couple of Nationalists in the corner wondering if we where [sic] in the right place or not.
>
> Like NSBM [National Socialist Black Metal], another weirdo genre designed to attract freaks to a once honourable movement! Why the

hell would patriots want to associate themselves with "industrialism" anyway? I thought these Evolian types rejected the modern world?✿ Not that you have to be an Evolian to revolt against the modern world of course.

Sorry to say all of that, I just can't understand why we'd want association with that crowd?[28]

Just as "English Celt" questions his own native belonging (or at least Der Blutharsch's belonging) when confronted with the possibility of its ironic cooption, the confused Laibach fan is upset with the possibility of earnestness; optimistically, he might now know that the next time he feels such pride as Laibach inspired, it's potentially the product of yet another imposed aesthetic political theater, and not of any native belonging. (Certainly no one has ever accused Laibach of expecting too little from their fans.)

Ultimately, Shekhovstov's concern isn't that audiences will misinterpret anti-fascist bands' cutting-up and recasting of fascist symbolism as hateful; as discussed, audiences don't really do this very often anymore. Instead, a greater danger might be that fans will assume the motivations behind actual fascist displays to be harmless. Despite the potential victory of "blatant homosexuals" and "ethnic goths" overtaking white nationalist space, Shekhovstov would worry in the case of Der Blutharsch's concert that the band's message and iconography have become less politically shocking and are thus more naturalized, one aesthetic step closer to becoming acceptable ethics.

One of the west's most important public intellectuals of the late twentieth century, Susan Sontag, says, "Shocking people in the context also means inuring them, as Nazi material enters the vast repertory of popular iconography usable for the ironic commentaries of Pop Art."[29] Sontag focuses on the aforementioned idea that fascist aesthetics are indelibly linked to fascist ideology, and as such she believes that even an ironic recontextualizing of this imagery contributes to this naturalization, and ultimately to oppression. Through her lens, even bands such as Ministry or Front 242 who are decidedly advocates of liberal openness give power to evil by fetishizing it: in her influential 1975 essay "Fascinating Fascism," she comes out swinging against the day's semicomedic genre of Nazi exploitation porn, among other enemies. She points out that in these films the aesthetics of fascism are beautiful, appealing, even sexy.

Never before was the relation of masters and slaves so consciously aestheticized. Sade had to make up his theater of punishment and delight

✿ Julius Evola was an Italian philosopher influential in postwar fascism.

from scratch, improvising the decor and costumes and blasphemous rites. Now there is a master scenario available to everyone. The color is black, the material is leather, the seduction is beauty, the justification is honesty, the aim is ecstasy, the fantasy is death.[30]

Sontag's last sentence applies as easily to industrial music as it does to Nazi propaganda. (Needless to say, it also reasserts industrial music's connection to BDSM—as she says of Hitler's rapturous hold over his audiences when speaking, "The expression of the crowds in *Triumph of the Will* is one of ecstasy; the leader makes the crowd come."[31]) The extension of her argument is that neither artists nor fans can meaningfully criticize fascism while reveling in its aesthetics and values (which Sontag, like Portnoy, argues are one and the same). Black, leather, beauty, honesty, ecstasy, and death: regardless of whether the genre's telemetry of this constellation was originally intended ironically, one can't deny the embraced vitality of these aesthetics in such songs as Neuroticfish's "Black Again," My Life With the Thrill Kill Kult's "Leathersex," and Laibach's anthem "Smrt za Smrt" ("Death for Death"), which was among the last of the band's songs with original vocalist Tomaž Hostnik prior to his December 1982 suicide.

Beyond these specific signifiers, to Sontag the very act of aestheticizing power is itself a fascist gesture. In light of this, the only industrial musicians who might escape the fascist trap are those like Nigel Ayers of Nocturnal Emissions, who tried scrupulously to avoid even hinting at totalitarian imagery; with grave doubt, Ayers rhetorically asks in a 1992 letter to the industrial zine *Electric Shock Treatment*, "At what point does the imagery 'turn around'?"[32] Can industrial music, in its central discourse of control and technology, avoid serving the goals of its authoritarian enemies? The chant of "Smash this fascist racist bullshit" by the 1990s Seattle-based industrial act Kill Switch... Klick swaggers to a decidedly unwhite shuffle beat—a smart musical call, considering— but ultimately it comes across as naïve and easily appropriated. This sort of explicitly antifascist disclaimer rings especially ineffectual when we take to heart Ministry's Burroughsian belief that capitalism and democracy—often purported as an antidote to totalitarianism—merely privatize the role of a fascist state.

## 5. Who's Assimilating Whom?

So if "Everything Provokes Fascism," as Slavoj Žižek and coauthor Andrew Herscher assert, then is any attempted revolutionary move by industrial music doomed to be rejected by its own community, to champion either intentionally or "apolitically" a regime of punishment, or to fuel the machine against which it rages with even more power still? This question, decidedly central in industrial music's iconography and politics, is directly connected to the old problem of assimilation that Marx, Adorno, and Debord all grappled with, wherein revolution's grand duty is to be endless and ever-changing, even amidst the potential futility of any single revolutionary act. Did industrial music misstep at some point, as some purists such as Jon Savage believe? In the isolation and insularity that, as we'll see, the genre takes on in the late 1990s, does it play the deluded soldier, clutching his gun in the jungle decades after the war's end? Let's consider what it means to say yes or no to these questions.

Remember that fascist aesthetics by nature identify and seek to reprogram the decadent and the degenerative, confining social expression until, in Sontag's words, "Masses are made to take form, *be* design."[33] Imagine a narrative in which an ever-assimilating economic and cultural fascism succeeds in regimenting industrial music like this—a history that compels us to answer yes to those questions of whether industrial music's political game a losing one:

The *amorphous strangeness of the early music—Throbbing Gristle, Chrome, Cabaret Voltaire, Z'EV—lost a degree of its effluent sonic variety when its second wave—Laibach, NON, SPK—started to militarize their image and sound. The media industry named the genre and began to market it in an attempt to bring it under epistemological and economic control. This wasn't just the result of big business descending on the music—the musicians themselves took on the form and image of business and government in détournement and protest, but that ultimately served only to inure industrial music to the language of the controlling economy. As the dance beat became more standardized, the limited space on club playlists and record label rosters enforced simultaneous competition among bands where there had previously been a communal ethic. Even as the music attempted organizational autonomy and informational warfare, the foisting to popularity of the most verse-chorus-centric acts of the 1980s illustrated that industrial music as a whole was being sculpted to the rigid patterns of pop, despite—or perhaps because of—EBM's preemptive efforts to inoculate industrial against pop cleanliness by exposure. What's more, these popular acts became the public faces of industrial music (as we'll see in the coming chapters), marginalizing the uncategorizable degeneracy of acts such as the Hafler Trio or Muslimgauze. Today, even the shape of the industrial scene is a fascist confining of force—a subculture with formulaic music whose military aesthetic goes beneath the surface, informing not just the stomping of dancefloors but the homogeneity of output. The whole move-*

*ment is thus known, replicated, and sold. Ultimately its power to upset—once extending to the British parliament and the RIAA—is now contained culturally by its size, by its circularity, and as far as the arbiters of youth culture are concerned, by its cyclical uncoolness. Industrial music has over time gone beyond subscribing to an aesthetic of fascism and now instead can "take form, be design."*

This is of course just one way to tell the story, but it's a sobering one. A more complete and honest narrative would (and will) note that from the musicians' perspective, some creative developments within the broader genre have suggested new if less bombastic ways for industrial music to explore resistance. From the audience's perspective, not every approach to industrial music's totalitarian borrowings lies on the Hanley-Shekhovstov-Sontag continuum. It is still thankfully possible to read the dialogue of power in redemptive ways that ultimately can help us answer no to the questions asked a few paragraphs ago.

To this end, Žižek is not so quick as Sontag to assume that if it looks like fascism, it must be fascism. A fan of some industrial music himself, Žižek has written a fair amount on his fellow Slovenians Laibach, and in his 2010 book *Living in the End Times* he turns his attention to the German act Rammstein. Rammstein is not strictly industrial by most definitions, but the style of metal they play (the German press call it Neue Deutsche Härte) couldn't have happened without the likes of Laibach, Die Krupps, and Ministry.

Of Rammstein's flirtations with Third Reich aesthetics, Žižek writes, "Not only are such mass performances not inherently fascist, they are not even 'neutral,' waiting to be appropriated by Left or Right—it was Nazism which stole them from the workers' movement, their original home."[34] From this perspective, first, it's merely an empowerment of Nazism (or whatever -ism last appropriated a given sign) for an audience to align those symbols with evil; by doing so, listeners vindicate their own paranoia, effectively carrying out their enemies' dirty work. Second, by demanding a moratorium on using certain symbols (either legislatively as the German government has done with the swastika, or artistically as Nigel Ayers has), people effectively leave these symbols unquestioned in the hands of the bad guys. This type of reasoning also contributes to why Žižek has been critical, for example, of political correctness. Giving new meaning to an old cliché, he says of the political panic that Rammstein set off in Europe, "The only thing we have to fear here is fear itself."[35]

And some even insist that the point of it all lies well beyond fear or reclamation or acceptance. SPK argues in an early manifesto, for example, that besides "completing" the provocative artistic act, any kind of audience response at all is freeing because of its incited visceral honesty: "To use overpowering force is not, in itself, fascist. Fascism is the *lack* or *limitation* of choice; so to use intensity/confusion as weapons to actually force a choice (instead of leaving pre-coded rationalism intact) is necessarily anti-fascist."[36] They mean here that when a reaction to art is instinctual and not premeditated, it's not subject to the limited behavioral options preselected by culture. (What they don't acknowledge here is the link that some see between this honesty and the revelation of a supposedly "true nature," which all too often devolves quickly into social Darwinism.)

Going backwards from Žižek's point, though, if it's the do-gooder leftist critics of (and within) industrial music who are actually empowering fascism by fearing its presence and signs, then it's no surprise that some figure the purpose of industrial music is not just to reveal the fascist in and among us, but additionally to reveal the prejudiced fascist hunter. From this point of view, think again about NON's wolfsangel logo: a response to the accusation that Rice's use of it is racist would be that it's in fact the sensitive neoliberal who's reaffirming the symbol's racism, that the accuser is the real threat to equality. As Lisa Crystal Carver, Rice's ex-partner and the mother of his child, sums up, "It's everyone else who's sick. That's always his art piece."[37]

It's worth saying, incidentally, that the people who feel most shafted in these disputes are the fans who merely like how the music sounds. Out of all this theoretical debate, they're effectively asked to justify their own pleasure from a selection of hopelessly flawed political positions.


## 6. Battle Scars

Because both fascism and industrial music are resistant by nature, their relationship is in some ways a constant back-and-forth where the reversal of signs' meanings can become dizzying. The strange misapprehensions of Ministry, Laibach, and Der Blutharsch in this chapter are testament to that. The very nature of these overlapping political reclamations emphasizes an element of truth in both Žižek's and Sontag's positions: we can indeed subvert the signs and methods of tyranny, but we can't whitewash the fact that in doing so we become desensitized to (or even drawn in by) the aesthetic seeds of casual bigotry.

Consider UK-based Pauline Smith, whose mid-1970s mail art appeared alongside the work of industrial VIPs Cosey Fanny Tutti, Genesis P-Orridge, Monte Cazazza, and Vittore Baroni in *Vile*. In 1974 Smith launched a mail art project called the Adolf Hitler Fan Club. As she explains, "All the hostility encountered during the time of the 'Adolf Hitler Fan Club' was part of the event and where-ever possible incorporated into it."[38]✿ Unambiguously prefiguring Boyd Rice, Smith considered the retaliation against her work to be the real art: a display that the enemies of tyranny were the ones responsible for its persistent power. By packaging Hitler into a teenybopper "fan club," she may have succeeded to some degree in critically emphasizing how mass culture cares more about celebritizing than it does about what sort of people it celebrates—a compelling statement, for sure, and one well within Rice and Žižek's territory. But Smith's project also ultimately validates Sontag's concerns about abyss staring.

As Smith explains, she began ironically aestheticizing Hitler as a figure of provocation in 1970,

> but I did not read *Mein Kampf* until 1971. At that time I was struck by the way Hitler's description of decadent Austrian democracy prior to WW1 could equally well suit the last few British governments. In 1971 ruthless destruction of the community in which I lived was being carried out by commercially minded people whilst those who had the power to stop this happening stood by like reeds in the wind.[40]

The frustration that Smith vents on her 1983 CV should look awfully familiar:

> I am preoccupied with Adolf Hitler's involvement in the occult, the mediumistic nature of his public speaking and the mystery of his charismatic appeal to the multitudes. He may have been a bad man but he knew very well that people do not live by bread alone—a fact our leaders seem to have forgotten, and probably forgotten precisely because Adolf Hitler thought so deeply about meeting a people's need for inspiration.[41]

By criticizing those whom her project shocks, Smith seems on one hand to mock audiences for spending too much energy thinking about Hitler, but at the same time she plainly suggests that England would be better off if its leaders paid closer attention to him. Somewhere in the reasoning behind Smith's provocation, she seems to stop focusing on the public's enslavement to its own fear of tyranny, and instead she starts recommending tyranny to them, insisting that it should be embraced, not feared. What may have begun as a détournement of propaganda's dictatorial voice becomes a mere echo of it. In Smith's

---

✿ The attributed author of the source from which this quote comes, "Klaos Oldanburg," is a pseudonym for Stewart Home. A mid-1970s pamphlet by English mail art duo BLITZINFORMATION (Stefan Kukowski and Adam Czamowski) declares, "it has become one of BLITZINFORMATION's foremost projects to change everyone's name to Klaos Oldanburg."[39]

work, fascism ceases to be a mere bogeyman the moment she casts accusations of decadence and proclaims the virtues of inorganic rigidity by comparing her enemies to reeds in the wind; her words tellingly drip dangerous disdain when she pouts, "It seems that Jewish people in this country had become worried that the 'Adolf Hitler Fan Club' may be a front for some kind of pressure group building up against them."[42]

Similar to Smith's provocations, industrial music's extremism is a screen on which grand struggles are acted out in shadow. Stepping back, we can explain the genre's ironic use of fascist imagery by (at least) two verifiable models that, significantly, don't actually cancel each other out. One indicates the power of the artist to repossess the images of tyranny while the other points to the simultaneous power of tyranny to diminish the impact of any artwork that takes up its symbols.

This dual action is especially clear when we move beyond theory and look at some actual events within industrial history. In 1988, Nurse With Wound released the track "A Precise History of Industrial Music," which is little more than the sound of a dot matrix printer's whine, presumably as it spits out the song's titular narrative. By offering just the noise of machines while suggesting that all of the genre's history can be inked in forty-two seconds, Nurse With Wound snidely asserts the genre's reducibility. In 1990, the Killer Tracks series of generic radio advertising jingles published *Power/Industrial*, a synth-plus-guitar collection of instrumental ditties for high-tech tough guy commercials. Two years later, the Evolution Control Committee released "The Industrial Polka," affirming the commodity attributes of a style as only parody can do.

Now, these events aren't condemnations of industrial music, but we might consider them as battle scars. As part of what Chapter 3 calls the revolutionary class, industrial music has never operated alone politically but has assembled at the front lines of little revolutions. It's therefore no surprise that industrial music has lost some nuance and taken some symbolic damage. As part of a duly resistant multimedia (sub)cultural effort, it has helped to deal a kamikaze blow by weakening the signs of authoritarian control machines through overidentification and exposure to unresolvable debate. By agitating the dialogue over totalitarianism outlined in this chapter, industrial music has helped to belabor certain cultural tools of tyranny into blandness and affixed permanent red flags to others. In this narrative, industrial music's imagistic language has indeed forged progress, helping to render strong-arm politics and authoritarian censorship neither effective nor culturally tolerated anymore.

Some of the cultural and technological changes to which industrial music has contributed are hard to see today because they've become normalized. Think, though, of the giddiness with which industrial-aligned magazines such as

*Mondo 2000* fetishized the near future in the early 1990s. The promise was one of a free, anarchic, grassroots society in which technology would level the playing fields of gender, appearance, language, location, and disability. The dizzying, aggressive collages that hip-hop created before the advent of sample clearance lawsuits, those few years of endlessly experimental online self-presentation in the mid-1990s before the web's social networking lock-in, or Napster's pirate free-for-all in the summer of 2000—these were brief moments of victory for technology-driven "liberal openness," harbingered by the anti-authority victories of the tape scene long ago. Inevitably, the desire of copyright holders, governments, entrepreneurs, and lawyers to control and monetize these situations ended the celebrations, but that's simply how power responds when threatened. It assimilates.

The back-and-forth volleying of meanings or accusations between a resistant culture (like industrial music) and a resistant controlling force (like fascism and its analogues) serves to reify extremist signs and their contexts into mere commodity attributes. In other words, the historical moments just mentioned above reveal the game of resistance and recuperation that industrial music and its enemies both play, chipping away at one another's armor, with the overdetermined signs of fascism a weapon on both sides. Just as a musical gesture such as vocal distortion can be reduced over time from an ideological claim to a mere advertisement for a genre, the propaganda techniques of media politics are understood by the public through increasingly savvy and cynical lenses.

It's more useful and correct to think about industrial music and totalitarianism in this way than as an either-or proposition. To the question of whether, in tragic self-deception, industrial music ultimately serves its enemies, this deeper understanding affords us a productive way to answer no. Whatever the punishment, stepping out of cultural ranks to assume degenerate victimhood under fascism exposes its tyranny. It's therefore fitting with the genre's thematic proclivity for self-destruction that the whole of industrial music behaves as a suicide commando.

Here the question posed by neo-folk act Death In June takes on new poignancy: "What ends when the symbols shatter?" Writing about Survival Research Laboratories and their giant robot demonstrations, technoculture scholar Mark Dery says, "The problem of SRL-inspired fantasies of a techno-revolution by garbage pail kids is that they're underwritten by an incongruously Weathermenesque faith in the power of a well-placed bomb to 'strike at the heart of the state' as the Red Brigades put it."[43] In general, though, industrial music doesn't seem to expect a lasting victory. A single bomb—COUM Transmissions' *Prostitution* exhibit or Einstürzende Neubauten's riotous "Concerto for Machinery and

Voice"—can't explode eternally, although Marinetti's Futurist fantasies resonate with Survival Research Laboratories' hope to the contrary. Instead, Front 242's directive "Never Stop!" applies: industrial music is most effective and vital as a program of revolutionary work, continuing the back-and-forth of assimilation that Guy Debord and the Situationists pioneered. Both as an historical reading and as advice to today's musicians, this ceaselessness is necessary not just to the existence of the music but to the hopes of the pan-revolutionary.

## 7. The Hidden Reverse

Interpreting industrial music's use of extremist imagery as part of this ultimately productive struggle against authority doesn't serve as a blanket justification of its every artistic gesture. The genre's extremist flirtations call into question our preconceptions about propriety, the functions of music, and our internalizing of institutional signs, but recall how they spur what Shekhovstov and Sontag see as the preconditions of prejudice. Despite the genre's purported antihegemony, its unchecked battle wounds weaken its already shaky stance on some key social and political grounds.

As previous chapters mentioned, industrial music has had gender problems. Skinny Puppy took some important steps toward opening the genre to women, and we'll see that Nine Inch Nails did too, but it wasn't until the 1990s that many people started asking questions about industrial music and sexism. Examples of this questioning include the *Diva Ex Machina* compilation series organized by Kim "X" Nguyen of Cop International Records, which highlighted female industrial musicians, and more recently the label machineKUNT Records was founded on a policy of signing only female artists. The gender-dissolving Pandrogyne project has also raised awareness of the issue, but even as of 2012's Kinetik Festival, the year's largest industrial event in North America, troubles persist. Taking the stage as Ad•ver•sary, Canadian rhythmic noise musician Jairus Khan used video projection to issue "a public service announcement regarding the use of racist and sexist imagery by two of tonight's performers," juxtaposing Marie Shear's definition of feminism as "the radical notion that women are people" alongside the band Combichrist's lyric "All you feminist cunts, you know that you want it. Give head if you got it."[44] Khan's screen declared, "We are not offended by this toxic language. We are contemptuous of it," and after reinforcing the industrial credentials of his antibigotry politics with a quote from Peter Christopherson of Throbbing Gristle and Coil, he concluded, "Reject Sexism . . . We demand better."[45] The genre still largely works under the assumption of maleness. At least some are asking why.

The audience at Kinetik had been primed for half of Ad•ver•sary's message by decades of liberal voices within industrial music addressing and inviting gender difference—albeit with slow progress. But it was a bigger surprise when Khan also seized the moment to criticize Combichrist's use of the Confederate flag. He effectively revealed just how infrequently the topic of race comes up among the community; indeed, industrial musicians and fans mostly see themselves as socially progressive, and direct racism in industrial music's most trafficked corridors is exceedingly rare. Instead of calling out any one band, then, the question we should ask is how race had become such a blind spot within the genre that using a Confederate flag seemed like a good idea to anyone—especially in a context apparently devoid of any attempted détournement. Within this broad discussion of how industrial music has handled politics, the upcoming chapter asks why the particular issue of race reveals an incongruous glitch in the genre's supposedly omnidirectional mission of radical empowerment.

It's no doubt tempting for some to declare, exasperated, that race has absolutely nothing to do with industrial music. There are two important reasons, though, why it should.

First off, whether or not one shares Shekhovstov's concerns about Europagan themes incubating fascism, to reveal this kind of blind spot is absolutely in keeping with—even necessary to—the industrial idea of questioning hegemonies. The spectrum of genders, abilities, and sexual orientations in industrial music communities means that even though there is certainly attitudinal work yet to be done, these differences are not invisible. Race, on the other hand, is basically unplumbed in the genre, owing in no small part to industrial music's near homogeneity of whiteness.

The other reason is because despite the tactics of ambiguity that industrial music embraces, its wide-angled revolutionary politics can significantly benefit from the specificity that certain nonwhite musics have voiced. It's an obvious springboard for industrial music's thematics of enslavement and liberation. Let's move forward, now.

# 14.
# White Souls in Black Suits:
# Industrial Music and Race

## 1. Whiteness

In light of industrial musicians' purported concern with the politics of control, one might expect them to engage with the topic of race. This happens only rarely in a direct sense, though. A close look at this music over time nonetheless helps us not just understand its racial attitudes but also explain why these attitudes matter, and how they relate to the music's past and future.

By the numbers, the overwhelming majority of industrial musicians and fans are caucasian. The low level of minority participation in the music might have something to do with the already rich body of protest music in Latin America and the African diaspora; one could argue that there's an abundance of protest musics more welcoming of diversity. But beyond that, there's a more insightful set of reasons for industrial music's predominant whiteness (and perhaps its maleness). This book notes early on that a lot of industrial music embodies the enraged response to "waking up" from a supposed hegemonic enslavement. For example, Paul Lemos of the band Controlled Bleeding wrote in 1985 that his output "reflects the frustration that comes in realizing one's own inability to affect a political system, and one's own insignificance in the scope of the masses."[1] But waking up to a cataclysmic personal shock like this is only possible to those lulled into slumber to begin with—a condition predicated on certain privileges, such as the promise of adequate earning power, correct fluency in the dominant language, and an inheritance of social autonomy, trust, and belonging.

To many people who aren't socially granted these privileges of identity, it's self-evident that the system is rigged. Although the cultural conversations of racial disenfranchisement might not be overly concerned with exterminating all rational thought, it's yesterday's news that western culture's particular brand of rationality sometimes offers limited benefit to outcasts. Industrial music's privilege, along with its post-1990 surge of lyrics about romantic relationships gone bad (more about this in the coming chapters), largely accounts for the occasional journalistic criticism of the genre as being whiny.

Industrial music's mission of exposing western control systems has the greatest potential significance to those for whom such controls and their categorizations are least visible. Put plainly within the specific context of race, this means that industrial music presumes a white audience. This doesn't mean that the music is racist; nor does it preclude deeper, more nuanced articulations of racial politics within the genre. It does suggest, though, that a genre concerned with recognizing and combating social hegemonies could potentially learn and gain strength from an ongoing dialogue with other racial expression and critique.

This chapter looks closely at how industrial music inadvertently operates within, and reinforces its presumption of, identity. It also acknowledges and analyzes the genre's engagement with racial otherness, highlighting both some actualized moments and some missed opportunities in the dialogue just mentioned.

## 2. The Inheritance of Blues, Jazz, and Dub

Before delving into how industrial music assumes and responds to whiteness, let's begin by locating some of its nonwhite origins. Recalling Chapter 3's differentiation between industrial and classical values in music, we should reiterate that industrial is a form of western popular music, and that broadly some of the most ubiquitous features of modern popular styles derive expressly from African American music. A kick-snare backbeat and a pervasive syncopation in vocal rhythm are just two practices that have become so normalized across rock and dance music that, taken on their own now, they convey only faint traces of any markedly African music. With a few exceptions like the power electronics subgenre, most industrial music has spoken with—or at least spoken about—this pop language since 1980 or so. In the overwhelming majority of industrial music and pop styles, rhythms are looped with consistent tempo and beat emphasis, harmonic progressions repeat cyclically (often in patterns of two or four chords at a time), key changes are rare, and melodies recur unchanging. The modern use of these musical building blocks is remarkably consistent on records by Al Green and à;GRUMH… alike, and it all stems unambiguously from the collision of African musical practices with the historical Euro-American soundscape.

Beyond industrial music's prerequisite (and occasionally resented) pop heritage, it intersects in a few more meaningful and specific ways with African American music. For example, Chapter 9 noted the pleasure that Nitzer Ebb took in the blues; Douglas McCarthy's voice constantly slides between a song's tonic and its minor third, a hallmark gesture of the style. As more influences from rock filtered into industrial music in the 1990s, borrowings like that spread; Sister Machine Gun's "Cut Down" is a prime example, with a flatted fifth in its melody, a jivey offbeat emphasis in its drums, and a brass-filled, zero-irony chorus about "the middle of the big ol' night."

From a chronological view, though, the first important junction we should acknowledge between industrial music and racial otherness is in the genre's early connection to experimental jazz. The pop and blues idioms just outlined are so ingrained in modern western music as to be plausibly transparent, but industrial music's invocation of jazz comes from a self-aware position of musical understanding. In most cases, it's a nod of kinship to a shared revolutionary moment when musical worlds were bridged by commonalities of improvisation, (Afro-)Futurism, and organizational independence.

The heavily improvisatory nature of early industrial music, combined with its literate self-inscription within a twentieth-century political tradition, compels connections to the Englishman Cornelius Cardew. Cardew was a former protégé of Stockhausen who, with a Maoist focus on equality, formed the radically improvisatory Scratch Orchestra in 1969. Like Genesis P-Orridge, Cardew was involved with the Fluxus art movement in the 1970s and saw the bounds of musical composition as extending well beyond traditional performance: in addition to his fascination with the recording studio as an instrument, he studied graphic design to allow his nebulous, abstract musical scores to stand as art themselves.[2]

Outside this European intelligentsia, however, the fundamental improvisatory force in music was the free jazz that Ornette Coleman and others had been playing since the early 1960s. Free jazz (a loaded term that, like nearly any good subgenre name, was largely disavowed by its practitioners) is wilder and less populist than Cardew's music, and it thrives on the tension between players' responsive musical dialogue and the loud tantrum of their individual, isolated monologues, warring for the listener's ear.

Both of these approaches to improvisation hung fresh in the air when early industrial acts like Clock DVA got their start. Their debut *White Souls in Black Suits* offers a panorama of thin, reverberant soundscapes devoid of steady rhythm and littered with saxophone whines; bearded band member Charlie Collins was a self-described Ornette Coleman fan.[3] Remember also the choking, frantic saxophone that pervaded early performances of Deutsch-Amerikanische Freundschaft (the 1979 live version of "Gib's Mir" on *Die Kleinen und die Bosen* is particularly ferocious); it becomes clear that the innovations of jazz music in particular were important to industrial musicians, especially because so many of them had been weaned on the jazz inflections of the prog-rock scenes of the 1970s—even Kraftwerk's first records were full of flute solos.

This jazz crossover is evident in the media surrounding early industrial music as well. The November 1984 issue of *Artitude* magazine boasts in-depth artist profiles of both Coleman's guitarist James "Blood" Ulmer and NON's Boyd Rice, unblinking in its juxtaposition. In 1987, the Jazz Composers' Orchestra Association took out full-page ads for their New Music Distribution Service in San Francisco's industrial zine *Unsound*, hawking records by Coleman, goth-blues shrieker Diamanda Galás, turntablist Christian Marclay, and John Zorn, a jazz wild man from New York's No Wave scene.[4]

It was in this downtown sensibility that the connections between industrial and jazz are most clearly forged, and their mutual encounter is still visible today in crossover magazines such as *The Wire*. Although Zorn, for all his clattering abjection, never had much to do with the industrial scene, he and his New York contemporaries (notably Glenn Branca, Lydia Lunch, Elliott Sharp, and bands like Bill Laswell's Material and Sonic Youth) were similarly concerned with moving beyond punk's rockabilly trappings and exploring noise. No Wave scene historian Marc Masters writes, "No Wave's deconstructive approach drew on other ancestors from the 1960s and '70s: the radical noise of free jazz musicians like Albert Ayler and Sun Ra, the experimental blues-rock of Captain Beefheart and the Magic Band, the trance-inducing rituals of German groups like Can and Faust."[5] The majority of industrial music however, had generally seemed to jazz-descended hipsters in the 1980s a bit too white both in its inability to achieve a relaxed coolness and in its real (if rare) pockets of racial extremism. Recalling the geography of industrial music's earliest years, we might even posit that at the turn of the 1980s the genre's relative silence in New York (and for that matter, Chicago, Bristol, and Paris) had a lot to with the degree to which African-descended populations contributed to the urban dialogue of cultural innovation.✿ Despite this, a few important No Wave–related acts managed to appeal both to the ever-trendy offspring of the New York scene and to the industrial milieu. Prominent among these are Michael Gira's occasionally gothic band Swans (later joined by tape scene chanteuse Jarboe); some projects by Jim G. Thirlwell (of Foetus), whose *York (First Exit to Brooklyn)* album, for example, employed No Wave's session players and its spirit; and Jon Spencer's pre-hardcore band Pussy Galore, arguably most known for their raucous 1988 version of Einstürzende Neubauten's "Yü Gung."

The rare direct borrowings from jazz in later industrial music reach back to a cultural moment when cacophony bleated a pruriently appealing threat to the

---

✿ By the middle of the 1980s, nearly all of these cities had developed industrial scenes, but this was more an effect of the music's growing popularity at large than of the cities' particular racial politics.

western status quo. (This jibes particularly well with industrial's debt to Burroughs and beat poetry.) Such nods include Trent Reznor's modal saxophone improvisation in "Driver Down" from the soundtrack to *Lost Highway*, whose auteur David Lynch stands at the crux of industrial extremism and 1960s cool cat Americana. Or take Nettwerk Records signee MC 900 Ft Jesus, whose career's odd shape owed heavily to the fact that neither he nor his record label could seem to figure out whether he was an industrial musician, a rapper, a comedian, or a jazz man; he delved deep into Coleman territory on his third album, 1994's *One Step Ahead of the Spider*, on which he traded out Steven Gilmore's cyber-cool graphic design for a whiteness-obscuring, neobiblical portrait by graffiti artist Greg Contestabile. Or consider 2004's "Sex With Sun Ra (Part One—Saturnalia)" by old school industrialists Coil; Sun Ra was among the most daring and opulent performers in free jazz, and in this marimba-driven song John Balance narrates an imagined religious experience with the man (who had in fact been dead since 1993). Within later dance industrial music, Haujobb's 1996 "The Cage Complex" concludes with a thrillingly earnest saxophone solo, full of altissimo squeals and multiphonic squonks directly from the bebop language of the 1960s, and Mona Lisa Overdrive's 1993 "It's Time" opens with a faux Miles Davis moment of trumpet cool. The message in all these songs' close brushes with jazz is at the very least a recognition of its musical power, both in the notes themselves and in its stylistic connotations— a consideration inextricable from race. To most musicians (and likely many audiences), these borrowings function as musical admiration or homage.

Production effects and recording techniques are other touchstones that have connected industrial music across racial lines in ways that don't immediately strike one as problematic. Dub music—a 1970s reggae-derived experimentation with beats, textures, and effects—has especially close ties to industrial, both historically through a handful of individuals who straddled both scenes and conceptually through the idea of Afrofuturism, which is the practice of reclaiming and controlling the dialogue of one's racial otherness by becoming "out of this world" through technology and sheer strangeness. By recasting disenfranchisement as literally alien, Afrofuturists tap into science fiction's treatment of the alien as awe-inspiring and plainly superior. Musicians such as Sun Ra, Afrika Bambaataa, Janelle Monae, and Kanye West have all invoked Afrofuturism, and production practices like sampling and remixing (first practiced live by African American DJs) are inextricably associated with it. Scholar and electronic music producer Steve Goodman asserts that it's a driving force behind jungle, dubstep, and nearly every major innovation in recent dance music, and its compatibility with industrial music's technophilia (if not its technoparanoia) is self-evident.

The closest continued acknowledgment between Afrofuturism and industrial music occurred in the mid-1980s with the racially mixed Bristol UK–based dub reggae scene that Adrian Sherwood and Mark Stewart helped to kickstart. Assisted intermittently by New York–based compatriots Doug Wimbish and Keith LeBlanc—both backing musicians for first-generation rap acts such as the Sugar Hill Gang—Sherwood and the On-U Sound collective applied dub production techniques to records by Nine Inch Nails, Ministry, and KMFDM. The Bristol scene, which also included Tricky and the future members of Massive Attack, effortlessly applied what they called "dub logic" to reggae and harsh dance music alike.

Dub involves the spacialization and blurring of musical events through looping, equalization, and reverberation; in the hands of Sherwood, dub owed nearly as much to Brian Eno as it did to Jamaican production and DJing. In the 1980s, Sherwood and his buddies produced and played on literally hundreds of albums—mostly for Jamaican artists—while maintaining a relationship with industrial music. For example, as Keith LeBlanc cut tracks for World's Famous Supreme Team's 1986 album *Rappin'*, he was at the same time assembling his own underground hit single "Major Malfunction," sampling the *Challenger* shuttle explosion and looping Ronald Reagan's intonation that space was "pulling us into the future." Similarly, Mark Stewart's band at the time, the Maffia, felt at home crafting straight-up reggae tracks such as "None Dare Call It A Conspiracy" alongside the classic industrial assaults "Hypnotised" and "The Wrong Name and the Wrong Number"—tracks beloved by cEvin Key of Skinny Puppy.[6] For these musicians, the path between Black Uhuru and Big Black was clear and open: "I don't see race," Stewart says flatly.[7] Jamaican reggae and dub are the sound of a culture transplanted from Africa across the ocean and forced to adapt; the sound that Sherwood, Lee "Scratch" Perry, and Mark Stewart crafted is that of a culture now twice transplanted, echoing the cold of England and its postindustrial techno-ambivalence into the old song. Displacement itself is the subject here, and it follows the trade routes of slave ships.

It should be noted that Sherwood is white, which in the 1980s led to a few members of the Rastafarian sect Twelve Tribes accusing him of appropriating a sound that was "rightfully theirs." However, to most of the musicians he worked with, his commitment to and respect for reggae was in no conflict at all with his race and his industrialist tendencies. In Sherwood, industrial music and Afrofuturism mutually absorb one another; On-U Sound's releases used to be stamped with a copyright date of ten years into the future, boldly reclaiming the music's displacement with sci-fi panache.

But On-U Sound is an anomaly, and after the 1980s Sherwood only occasionally popped his head into the industrial scene. Even then, it was just to remix a twelve-inch version for old friends like Skinny Puppy and Nine Inch Nails. In the dub-meets-industrial world, there are remarkably few descendants of this bloodline: Godflesh and Scorn both mixed noise, reggae, and metal together, Legendary Pink Dots bassist Ryan Moore founded Twilight Circus Dub Sound System, and the French act Treponem Pal broke modest ground with some rootsy industrial rock records in the 1990s, but these endeavors had limited impact on industrial music as a whole.

### 3. Exotica, Caricature, and the Techno-Oblivious

Although the previous examples suggest a symbiosis between industrial music and African-derived traditions, the relationship is usually more parasitic. Beyond the aforementioned blues, jazz, and dub inflections, industrial music's connection to race is less a dialogue than a monologue: as mentioned at this chapter's outset, industrial music tends to presuppose whiteness—that is, hegemonic non-otherness—on the part of audience and musician alike. This manifests in its use of racial caricature and its engagement with certain technologies as racially incidental rather than intentional. In what follows, the point again is not to brand any music or individuals as racist, but to look at how industrial music seldom acknowledges racial otherness.

Part of industrial music's vocabulary is its "Third World tribal rhythm mentality [that] was thrown in to add a sense of disembodied cultural yearning," according to tape scene historian Scott Marshall.[8] Some industrial musicians feel a genuine empathy with the ritual and trance elements of specific foreign musics, but this is in nearly every instance an outsider's projection, not a case of "going native." Marshall refers mostly here to the influential lineage of 1950s exotica, which manifests musically in certain recordings by Throbbing Gristle (the song "Exotica," unsurprisingly) and NON. It lurks behind the band names of Pygmy Children and Voodoo Death Beat, and with varying degrees of irony it's also an undercurrent in the music of 23 Skidoo, Hula, and other postpunk acts. Masked as world beat, this exotica was the entire foundation of the Italian pseudo-Inca band Atahualpa, whose "Ultimo Imperio" was a hit on industrial dancefloors in 1990.

Musicologist Phil Ford connects exotica to Futurism in its ability to relate simultaneously to modernity and also to an imagined world that offers an alternative to the military-industrial control of culture, "Seeking a residue of the primitive in a present cluttered with our machines."[9] In this way, it occupies a role similar to the "fallen Europe" trope that martial industrial music has centralized, or more recently, the playful vintage aesthetic that the industrial-turned-steampunk act Abney Park invokes. Exotica, Ford says, "is a kind of pictorial music, broadly representational though not necessarily narrative," and thus (again, not unlike steampunk) inasmuch as exotic sensibilities feed into industrial music, its no surprise that they're most evident in the visual component of the genre.[10] Recall, for example, Monte Cazazza's forays into Mondo-derived filmmaking, or consider the record sleeves seen here.

*Figure 14.1: The cover sleeve of Hunting Lodge's 1985 "Tribal Warning Shot" single uses a photograph of African tribespeople from a 1935 text-book. The rear sleeve quotes the book, "The little people are very good to us when they learn that we do not mean to harm them. They listen with great curiosity to our small radio, which seems like magic to them."*

*Figure 14.2: The Fair Sex's 1987 "Bushman" single exoticizes the southern African people by name while its cover obscures the German quintet in a gauzy jungle of otherness.*

*Figure 14.3: Bizarr Sex Trio's 1990 self-titled record closely resembles (and overtly sexualizes) the Congolese Pende tribe's Gitenga mask art. Art by Paul B. Hirsch.*

*Figure 14.4: The Neon Judgement's 1986 Mafu Cage, inspired by the 1977 film of the same name. Frontman Dirk Da Davo says, "We wanted to do an album that fit a voodoo kind of feeling. We wanted to use monkey sounds, earthy sounds."*

It's apparent that there's a dimension of cultural and racial border crossing at work here. Ford explains, "The exotica imagination is orientalist . . . whether or not the places it envisions are literally oriental, or even belong in the real world."[13] Westerners' use of these racialized images then isn't specific but is instead based on the *otherness* of the supposed cultures it portrays; it illustrates a sexual, safarilike, dangerous fun that's presumably absent from the white post-

ASSIMILATE

*Figure 14.5: The visual theme of* We Came to Dance *(12 vols., 1993–1999) derives from the Mexican Día de los Muertos celebration. Art by Margit Tabert, Charly Rinne, and Nadine Van Den Brock.*

*Figure 14.6: The back sleeve image of Dance or Die's 1991* 3001 *is of a Javanese puppet.*

industrial world. Here this manifests beyond the African diaspora and includes the near eastern flavor one hears in SPK's *Zamia Lehmanni* album, Laibach's version of "God Is God" (originally by Juno Reactor), and A Split-Second's 1988 "Mambo Witch," a catchy single that freely conflates "the Hindu curse"—whatever that is—with Cuban mambo.

Ford characterizes exotica as "a libidinous fantasy stocked with conventionalized others. The human objects of orientalist perception are unreasoning, instinctual, indolent, childish, cruel, sexual—the old colonial hand's half-wishful

*Figure 14.7: Neither the name of the American coldwave band Clay People nor their 1995 EP title* Iron Icon *quite clarifies the use of a Japanese porcelain figurine on the record's cover. The image was selected for use by the band's record label owner.*

inversion of his own self-understanding."[14] And so for industrial music, this wishfulness takes the form of the Burroughs-esque wild boy persona to whom abjection comes laced in gross whimsy, more clownish than miserable. Good examples of this are 1992's "Do the Monkey (Hitchhike to Mars)" by Swedish act Peace, Love & Pitbulls and 1995's "Hey Fuck Da' World" by Klute, a side project of the Danish EBM powerhouse Leæther Strip.

The critical considerations of exotica lie well beyond its aesthetic intent. Ford concludes, "When intellectuals handle this music with the hermeneutic equivalent of tongs and a HAZMAT suit they are in a sense *not hearing it at all*. The moment we insist on the interpretive priority of colonialism and commodification, fun time's over."[15] Certainly this chapter is guilty as Ford charges, but nevertheless, in order for exotica's fun to work at all, one needs to assume a collective self-identity against which to frame the otherness portrayed. From its Tiki theater, exotica gives free rein to the white imagination—but perhaps *only* the white imagination—to roam outside the western responsibilities of culture and privilege.

Another possibly contentious way that industrial music interfaces with race is in its use of gestures from traditional African-derived musics as a source of irony, reading them as kitsch. A clear case of this is KMFDM's 1995 "Juke Joint Jezebel," whose chorus features a massive gospel choir erupting out of nowhere, rhyming "sister salvation" ridiculously with "my cremation." In addition to the backup singers, the chorus's harmonic use of the flatted seventh within a major key (the Mixolydian mode, as it's called) immediately sets the song apart from industrial conventions. It's a send-up, to be sure, but of what? At once sleazy and exuberant, the chorus takes pleasure in self-destruction (as the lyrics describe), tapping into shallow perceptions of religious fervor and lasciviousness. Is the musically encoded sense of African American stereotypes the point, then, or is KMFDM using it as a genuinely expressive meeting ground for the old industrial warhorse topics of Christianity, sex, and hypocrisy? Both interpretations are problematic. And there are other examples too. Nearly the exact same reading is available to 1985's "The Only Good Christian Is A Dead Christian" by Scraping Foetus Off the Wheel, a foot-stomping jive song that in gospel harmony declares, "I'm payin' for the price of sin," while simultaneously, "The time is ripe for satisfaction." Or for that matter, Revolting Cocks' "Beers, Steers, and Queers" is plainly a rap song about (among other things) "sex in barns," proclaiming, "Texas has religion: Revolting Cocks are God!" Are industrial musicians taking pleasure in African American tropes while simultaneously turning their nose up at those for whom such music is a genuine expression, or are they shooting holes in minstrelsy by parading it as absurd? If the latter is the case—a charitable reading—then the tactics of reversal here share the same pitfalls as industrial's treatment of fascism, as discussed in the preceding chapter.

In this industrial tackiness (which seems to have all but died out since the mid-1990s), racial borrowings are a source of humor. Even if this humor might not expressly come at the expense of African American culture or its music, it's worth asking whether the joke would work in the same way if the musicians were not white. Describing a similar kind of borrowing in language, anthropologist Jane H. Hill talks about what she calls "mock Spanish," as when Arnold Schwarzenegger's badass cyborg character learns to say "no problemo" and "hasta la vista, baby" in *Terminator 2*. But, as Hill argues, "It is only possible to 'get' 'Hasta la vista, baby' if one has access to a representation of Spanish speakers as treacherous," and by extension, "getting" the caricature thus reinforces it.[16] So although there is real musical pleasure and power in these industrial borrowings, and despite their arguable status as "crossover" gestures ("curiously indeterminate" in their politics, Hill says), they nevertheless occupy an uneasy position, their value relying to a degree on the genre's baseline assumption of whiteness.✿

✿ Here the use of "crossover" is adapted from Geneva Smitherman by way of Hill.

## 4. Technology and Racial Engagement

Not all connections between industrial music and race are borrowings. Technology provides musical similarities across genres that can be both historically incidental and ideologically loaded. Prior to the advent of the sampler as an instrument, musicians who wanted to make electronic pop of any kind had a decidedly finite choice of sounds, due to the limited number of synthesizers and drum machines for sale. Thus the drum and bass sounds we hear in the mid-1980s work of Chris & Cosey come in some cases from the same presets on the same gear that was used on disco records from the era. For example, musicologist Robert Fink has traced the use and history of the "ORCH5" preset on the Fairlight CMI workstation, replete with appearances in the music of Kate Bush and Afrika Bambaataa alike.[17] As hinted at in Chapter 8, it makes for a sonic sameness across styles that might optimistically be read as kinship: it's part of why clubs like Antwerp's Ancienne Belgique and Chicago's Muzic Box could play breakdance records alongside Cabaret Voltaire. It's also why on Front 242's first U.S. tour they attracted massive audiences of African Americans who heard a connection between early EBM and the electro to which they regularly danced; a quick listen to 1983's *Enter* album by Juan Atkins's band Cybotron drives home the point nicely. Through the first half of the 1980s, neither these electronic sounds nor the gear nor the production practices were particularly racially coded.

But the way people enjoyed this music could indeed be racially coded. As this book's discussions of beat-driven industrial and EBM have suggested, much of the musical pleasure in repetition is rooted in bodily pleasure, most directly connected to dancing, but also mapped as an analogue for sexual expression. Pop scholars have pretty conclusively demonstrated that a lot of the repetition and bodily-ness that we hear in popular music today takes funk and disco as its basis, and that because those musics share a common cultural and racial origin, there's an associative cultural element in dancing to the harmonically static and the rhythmically relentless. This is certainly the case in America, Africa, and Western Europe by virtue of their long, often ugly history in which music, culture, money, and slaves repeatedly crossed the Atlantic.

Beyond the shared sounds across electronic musics in the 1980s (racially imprinted or not), we can talk about repetition in popular music as a potential function of technology. Recall, for instance, the loop-based songs of Deutsch-Amerikanische Freundschaft discussed in Chapter 5. The technological repetition of a groove, digitally precise in its sameness, resonates naturally both with this somewhat racialized bodily pleasure and with industrial music's ironic fetishization of technology and uniformity. This is another reason why the musical phrase lengths in à;GRUMH...'s "Ayatollah Jackson," addressed in Chapter 2, are of seemingly arbitrary duration: in the recording studio, a singer who belts lyrics over a looping beat doesn't have to memorize a predetermined timing but instead can start and stop as the mood strikes. The coldness of technology and the human "feel" of music's structure find a common ground here. As Skinny Puppy's cEvin Key says, it "wasn't intentional to throw in time changes as much as it was a hunch, like what sounded right at the time."[18] Again, this hearkens back to the improvisatory nature of the music and its connections to jazz.

As the 1980s moved along, sampling became an affordable reality in record production, and this started to differentiate electronic styles that had previously shared sonic profiles. The records and sounds being digitally reproduced reflected musicians' taste, culture, and physical surroundings. Samplers made first by AMS and later by Akai and Yamaha allowed multisecond snippets of sound to become building blocks of production, and musicians used them no longer just to capture a drum hit or a guitar pluck; now they were lifting entire one- and two-measure segments from records and looping them. Probably the most impressive work done with this technique occurred in hip-hop between 1988 and 1991, where Public Enemy's producers the Bomb Squad aligned old funk loops in tempo and layered them with one another amidst horn jab samples, nonverbal funk grunts, and gospel choirs to create a veritable curriculum in African American music history. The Dust Brothers, who helped assemble the Beastie Boys' *Paul's Boutique* album in 1989, used their samplers with similar cultural savvy, highlighting the group's white boy wackiness.

Loop-based sampling is especially well suited to hip-hop and industrial music because both styles tend to downplay traditional melodic and harmonic concerns, thus minimizing the degree to which a producer might worry about clashing tones in the sampled measures. Jon Savage recognized in 1983 the connection between hip-hop's sound collage and the "anti-music" of the industrial movement: we "hear cut-ups played freely on the radio, in popular 'scratch' and 'rap' music. . . ."[19] With the sonic retooling of the past being a tenet of industrial and hip-hop, it's no surprise that they both reached the boiling point at the same time in the late 1980s, driven in part by the availability of sampling.

Simon Reynolds writes, "Sampling is enslavement: involuntary labour that's been alienated from its original environment and put into service in a completely other context, creating profit and prestige for another."[20] In this distant way, sampling allows musicians to turn the tables on the slavery narrative, or alternatively to abreact it; the racial power in this act is clear, but industrial music's themes of authoritarian control and sadomasochism resonate here duly, if with less historical force. And as exemplified by Meat Beat Manifesto, Consolidated, the Beatnigs, the Disposable Heroes of Hiphoprisy, MC 900 Foot

Jesus, and other moments of crossover such as Ministry's 1989 guest vocal rap "This Is A Test," industrial music and rap found common ground in their anger and the practice of sampling. It wasn't that Burroughs-reading anarchists were expressly concerned with racial struggle, or that the Bomb Squad had been necessarily listening to Test Dept., but rather the sampler was a vital, shared tool in the political expression of all contemporary urban cultures. Thus the modes of production between these musics overlapped as a result of political similarities, emphasizing certain common musical characteristics.

Legal battles and shifts in technology and trends toned down the sampling-as-politics practice in hip-hop and industrial music by the mid-1990s. This move away from reliance on the sampler was simultaneous with the mutual distancing of industrial and hip-hop, though technology may have played less of a role in this divide than suburbia's remarkable repackaging of hip-hop as a marker of coolness and toughness for dominant white social groups; as an emerging soundtrack to high school jock culture, hip-hop became a flag of outcasts' enemies. Nevertheless, postmillennial industrial rap groups such as SMP and Stromkern serve as a reminder, if only as a throwback, of this hinted-at kinship.

In terms of sonic artifacts on industrial recordings, the connection to African American musics via sampling also means that hip-hop sounds are all over records by the likes of Front Line Assembly: for example, 1992's "The Blade" samples James Brown's classic "Funky Drummer" beat, while 1997's "Sado-Masochist" samples NWA's Eazy-E. Nine Inch Nails similarly sample Prince's "Tamborine" on 1990's "Head Like A Hole (Opal mix)." This indicates both some cross-stylistic ideologies and tactics and also the simple fact that industrial musicians were listening across racial lines; for example, Paul Lemos of Controlled Bleeding boasts his fandom of Public Enemy and Ultramagnetic MCs in a 1989 interview.[21] This crossing of lines was largely a one-way practice, though: industrial DJs in the UK, Germany, and America could spin rap records, but the days of the left-field crossover into hip-hop culture had effectively ended with the advent of its explicitly political self-awareness, around 1987.

One of the reasons for this unidirectionality was that despite a common attraction to the cut-up and a desire to subvert and confront, industrial music, on the rare occasions when it grapples with race directly as a topic, has a tendency to misunderstand or naïvely misuse elements of racial discourse.

German EBM act Funker Vogt offer a politicized racial context in their fascinating 2000 song "Black Market Dealers," which seeks to capture the experience of German children following their nation's defeat in 1945: "The first black men they ever saw were among the foreign soldiers. Some of them were really kind," states the lyric. There's a noncommittal strangeness to this passage that goes beyond Funker Vogt's frequent infelicities with English. Rather, the careful mention of the soldiers' kindness hints at a consciously civil response to racial otherness that may reflect the band's modern politics as much as the experiences of the children they sing about.

Belgian project Holy Gang evidently felt the need to comment musically on the 1992 rape conviction of boxer Mike Tyson. The one-off group, which included Front 242's Richard 23, titled their 1994 album *Free! Tyson Free!*, explaining to industrial zine *Music from the Empty Quarter*, "We felt if there was a rape, it was the rape of Mike Tyson more than anything else . . . he was black in America."[22] But any racially savvy critique that the trio offered of "New York City's ghetto streets" badly misfired with the title track's chorus chant of "Free Tyson! Fuck that bitch," obliquely attacking submerged racism with direct and senseless misogyny.

This off-kilter treatment of race plays out elsewhere. Consider, for example, three industrial songs that sample the voice of Martin Luther King Jr.: Swedish act Covenant's 1994 "Voices" replays a segment of his American Liberties Medallion acceptance speech, but incongruously it is a song about a man's individual paranoia and regret; German electro-industrial band X Marks the Pedwalk transforms King's cry of "Free at last!" from a dream of racial equality into a personal escape from "emotional lies" on their 1992 "Repression" (notably not "Oppression"); Australian act Snog's "Born to Be Mild" of the same year critiques yuppie culture's "Rick Astley look" and then confusingly throws in a sample of "I have a dream," reframing either King himself or his dream—or in a less likely reading, perhaps commenting on yuppie suburbia's coopting of King's legacy. Regardless, in all of these songs artists play fast and loose with race. The industrial information war means cutting up the signs of the control machines, but in some of these cases artists are instead destabilizing other victims of that same control. Even when KMFDM aims for camaraderie across racial lines, enlisting Adrian Sherwood's friend reggae singer Morgan Adjei to implore "Black man [and] white man" to "rip the system," the message falls a little flat in its simplicity.

The industrial artists mentioned here hail from countries outside what cultural studies scholar Paul Gilroy calls the Black Atlantic. As such, the cross-racial interactions in their work are different from those of American, African, Caribbean, English, or French artists. Indeed, nearly every nonwhite industrial musician lives in America, including Charles Levi and Jacky Blacque of My Life With the Thrill Kill Kult, Ministry engineer and keyboardist Duane Buford, the members of Code Industry, Noise Box's Dre Robinson, and members of Hawaiian Cleopatra Records signee Razed in Black. Brit Dean Dennis of Clock DVA and Amadou Sall of the French act Collapse are among the only exceptions.

Industrial acts from within the Black Atlantic region—especially American musicians—comment musically on race less frequently than those based elsewhere. Generally, by the late 1980s in America leftist white musicians, regardless of genre, shared an understanding that, however benevolent the intention, their overt critiques of racial power dynamics contributed little to what was an already exceedingly rich discourse in African American and Latin American music, and in fact many felt that by speaking they risked silencing other voices in this dialogue. This, combined with a few particularly mortifying public instances of white attempts to co-opt hip-hop (including rapping commercials for Chicken McNuggets and Fruity Pebbles), contributed both toward the relative lack of white American music expressly about race (including industrial music) and toward the perception that genre lines were racially enforced. The difference of approach to race in music between Europe and North America has a story all of its own, and it includes, among other chapters, a white British fascination with reggae in the 1970s and some often-overlooked German forays into rap idioms in the early 1980s, among them Spliff's "Das Blech" and Die Toten Hosen's "Hip Hop Bommi Bop."✻

## 5. Black and White

There are a few important exceptions to the rule that American industrial music avoids race as a lyrical topic. As discussed in the preceding chapter, San Francisco's ultra-Marxist industrial rap act Consolidated often invited confrontation, and they delighted in interspersing their album tracks with live recordings of their political sparring with concertgoers. In one such encounter, documented on the 1991 track "Murder One," an African American man expresses concern that the band is speaking on behalf of minorities despite "not going through what I'm going through." This leads to their inviting him on stage to speak and rap for himself. More noteworthy in this category is the band Code Industry, who were probably the first (and perhaps the only) all African American industrial act to release a record. On their 1990 debut, released only in Belgium on Antler Subway, racial politics are submerged, but 1992's followup (distributed by Caroline Records in the United States) was called *Young Men Coming to Power* and boldly asserts a revolutionary stance, complete with Malcolm X samples.

---

✻ Not only did this 1983 song featuring American rapper Fab Five Freddie predate the canonically "first" rap/rock crossover of "Walk This Way" by Run-DMC and Aerosmith, but in an unsettling commentary on race, its video portrays the band as jungle-dwelling cannibals in blackface, cooking Freddie in a cauldron as he raps—into a banana.

ASSIMILATE

A few years later, Seattle-based Noise Box released "Monkey Ass." The song begins auspiciously with a sample of Black Panther founder Bobby Seale declaring, "We're gonna walk on this racist power structure and we're gonna say to the whole damn government . . . motherfucker, this is a hold up." Both "Monkey Ass" and Code Industry's later oeuvre invoke a militant language reminiscent of Public Enemy—at once a call to political action for racial minorities, a scathing exposé of institutional western racism, and a celebration of collective expression.

If these are exceptions, though, then we can at this point summarize the racial politics of the genre. What follows are tendencies, not rules, and they are based on past industrial practices, not necessarily current or future ones.

Like nearly all western popular styles, industrial music derives its rhythms from African Diaspora music, but notably it also celebrates a political and musical kinship with postwar experimental jazz. However, industrial music more readily appreciates this music's experimental status than its racial origins. A few exceptional figures aside, industrial music in general passively presumes whiteness, as evidenced by its cavalier use of caricature and exotica, both of which declare racial otherness to be a playground. Thus, despite its ostensibly parallel ideals of freedom from oppression and technologically rewriting the past, industrial music has been largely oblivious to its own potential for a radical discourse of real politics, resulting in its consistent use of African-derived signifiers as barely differentiated from any other.

It's possible that this presumption of whiteness is inextricable from the genre's central debates. To move beyond empirical history and into a bit of theory, recall that a large amount of industrial music is concerned with mechanically replacing the body. This move is much easier when the body is hegemonically invisible—when it's "normal" enough to be blindly assumed, and thus inessential to one's identity. Questions of the body—like whether it's necessary or outmoded, or whether it's a site of pleasure or a site of discipline—are available to industrial music largely *because* of the normativity of whiteness within the western culture it participates in (or rails against): in the west, the white body is not a site of constantly reinforced difference, and so it can be ambiguous and amorphous in industrial music. A body of another race, however, is almost always fixedly at the center of hegemonic attention, demanding definition. In turn, because industrial music has so privileged these debates over the body's different meanings, it tends to be a poor stylistic fit for racial otherness, in which one has less control over the dialogue of social identity that surrounds one's own body. It's therefore no surprise that most moments indebted to free jazz within the genre don't happen within electronic body music. Front 242's Patrick Codenys cautiously explains: "We were asking what 'white rhythm' meant, because people talk about black rhythms or Hispanic rhythms. That idea of EBM, the physical body, white rhythm—it comes from something very mathematical and very tribal."[23] In short, industrial music's politics themselves are in conflict with the otherness of the body; if racial status is culturally foisted upon a body as its primary concern, then the issue preempts both Skinny Puppy's abject destruction of the body and Laibach's commanding it in salute.

## 6. Addendum: Repetition and the English Ballad

As an appendix to this chapter, let's explore one final intersection, considering industrial music's largely Anglo-Saxon heritage for the time being not as a hegemonic blind spot but as a meaningful source of musical traditions. Scholar Peter Webb has correctly connected the dots between industrial music and the neofolk genre. Sometimes called apocalyptic folk, this style freely employs the noise textures, military soundscapes, quasi-totalitarian imagery, and thematic direness of Throbbing Gristle and Whitehouse, but unlike those acts neofolk bands such as Death in June, Current 93, and Sol Invictus are also steeped in the folk music revival and psychedelia of the 1960s. Neofolk's antecedents use modern technology to comment on the past; industrial music arose in response to the postindustrial society, and as folk music historian Britta Sweers makes clear, the electric instrumentation of hippie-era revivalists such as Fairport Convention and Steeleye Span was directly tied to how they explored "the exotic and grotesque . . . mythic topics."[24] Both industrial music and electric folk are also rooted in the imagery of (and occasionally the participation in) pagan belief systems.

Although the development from early industrial music into neofolk has been made clear through shifts in personnel and musical practices, not much has been said about how archaic folk derivations have fed back into industrial music's dance-oriented strains. Earlier in this chapter and in this book, the idea of repetition in pop music was cast in terms of the African diaspora and technology: machines make possible a never-ending groove. Consider here a partial supplementary explanation for this repetition, one that stems from the ever-present repetition in the British Isles ballads so favored by late-1960s electric revivalists and neofolk bands alike.

In his book *Origins of the Popular Style*, Peter van der Merwe writes:

> In European folk music, as in African music, the repeated cycle remain[s] the standard form. It might be closed, that is, come to an end in the fa-

miliar way, or open (or, as it is sometimes put, circular), where instead of coming to a close, the tune simply repeat[s] itself indefinitely.[25]

A clear example of this is "Twa Corbies," an English-Scottish ballad with a text dating to 1611 and a melody adapted from the old Breton song "An Alarc'h." After being popularized by electric folk band Steeleye Span in 1970, "Twa Corbies" became a mainstay in the repertoires of neofolk acts Sol Invictus (1989) and Omnia (2006). "Twa Corbies" consists of a repeated melody, with every line in every verse based on the same melodic ascent of a third. In the earliest printed version of the melody (1839), thirty-two verses were to be sung, though in most later versions this number is reduced to five.[26] The ballad's lyrics (about crows in a tree), its modal tune, and the brightly majestic arrangements that bands drape around the song all emphasize repetition within the modern context of a mythic, lost England.

Even if neofolk acts themselves seldom make industrial dance music, one could reasonably suspect that the highly repetitive old northern European melodies and texts that so compel them have assuredly crossed back into the central vocabulary of industrial music. In certain industrial songs, the cyclical relentlessness we hear is not merely technology's resonance with blues-derived musical practice but an arcane assertion of a pre-modern tradition.

Among the clearest examples of British Isles balladry in industrial music is 1993's "Soldiers Song" by the Swiss act Spartak. The track is a highly appealing EBM cover of "The Kerry Recruit" (also called "The Irish Recruit"), a ballad about the Crimean War of the 1850s, first collected in an 1870 issue of *Putnam's Magazine*.[27] The band's interest in folk music had been evident in their earlier song "Volkstanz." On "Soldiers Song," Spartak's vocals are arranged as a unison male choir, which suggests a certain workmanlike solidarity—a sound that the band Funker Vogt would later make their trademark.

We might also consider the 1989 club hit by Controlled Bleeding "Words (of the Dying)." Though the band has at times identified as a noise act, this song comes from a period when they were signed to WaxTrax! and were releasing a fair amount of dance music. The song's rhythm loop is built around a flammed drum pattern, the snare rolling just enough to militarize the beat. Harmonically and melodically, the song is almost entirely composed with the black keys of a synthesizer, giving it a folky modal sheen while perhaps suggesting the band's limited comfort with keyboard performance. The chorus of the song is a two-measure sequence with alternating G-flat and A-flat major chords, one per measure, and this pattern continues six times as the chords rock back and forth, resolving indifferently to E-flat minor. It's in this repetitive chorus pattern that the influence of old music filtered through electric folk and neofolk is heard: the upper vocal part is an unsyncopated leaping gesture whose lower note, instead of fitting into the sounding chord, follows a melodically determined sequence.

*Figure 14.8*

The effect of the straight rhythm, its short repeated cycle, and the modal emphasis on melody (in the absence of harmonic consideration) is unambiguously folkish. Paul Lemos, who cowrote the song, doesn't recall specifically channeling folk music in its composition—"If anything, it was our attempt to sound a bit like D[epeche] Mode, whose music Chris [Moriarty, his bandmate] was really digging at that time." But influence is seldom a one-to-one correlation; Lemos does grant that during this time "I came to really like Fairport [Convention], Nick Drake and others in this genre."[28] The band's pronouncement that "We're very interested in the music that was developing in Europe, from the period of 1100 or 1200 to 1400 or 1500," speaks loudly of an openness to old forms like the English ballad—the first of which ("Judas") appeared in the thirteenth century.[29]

A third convincing example might be the 1998 song "Genetik Lullaby" by the Pennsylvania-based act THD (or Total Harmonic Distortion). The melody of the verse follows a logic identical to "Words (of the Dying)," in which a two-note cycle—as before, played just on black keys—is transposed upon repetition (Figure 14.9).

*Figure 14.9*

This pattern repeats eight times before the chorus ever arrives, again always guided by melodic considerations that effectively ignore the unchanging harmony. Despite the aggressive dance beats of the song, its compositional seed was this melody, which as frontman Shawn Rudiman explains immediately sounded like a lullaby when he first thought it up.[30] Verses commence with "Hush little baby, sleep," and "Hush little child, don't you cry"—derivations of

"Hush-a-by baby" from the English book of children's folksongs *Mother Goose's Melody*, dating back at least to 1796.

Even stranger is the case of "Little Black Angel," which began as "Brown Baby," a 1958 spiritual by African American activist Oscar Brown Jr. and was subsequently rewritten as "Black Baby" in 1973 by Marceline Jones, the (white) wife of Rev. Jim Jones, whose cult's nine-hundred-member suicide in 1978 made headlines. In 1992, Death In June rewrote the song's lyrics to address an angel (note the bodiless-ness here) and altered its music, replacing the vibrato-rich organ, free rhythm, and melodic glides with majestic acoustic guitars in rigid 3/4 time and Douglas Pearce's declamatory British baritone. The effect is specifically a channeling of the English ballad style, almost completely replacing the soul of the original. Then in 2011, to the delight of goth club DJs everywhere, synthpop act Ladytron released their own cover of Death In June's rewrite of Marceline Jones's rendition of Oscar Brown Jr.'s song. Filtered through Death In June's über whiteness, the song's transformations make musically clear the stylistic influence of the British Isles ballad on music from outside its tradition. Ladytron's end result is appropriately befitting an industrial club, complete with pounding kick drums and synths in an unflinching 4/4 meter and a vocal performance so compellingly sterile as to be creepy.

Ladytron found their way to Death In June's ballad-esque catalogue, Controlled Bleeding captures a particularly northern sense of nobility in their alternating chord progressions. THD channels the lullaby tradition, and Spartak directly recreate an Irish ballad: these examples are evidence that industrial music, almost certainly more so than most other pop, is in meaningful dialogue with British Isles folksong. This is hardly a surprising claim, given how often industrial musicians play concerts and share record labels with faux-medieval and neofolk acts, but it's an important point.

It's also important to remember that the conversation between archaic folk music and industrial goes two ways: plenty of acts have straddled the stylistic line successfully. For example, sometime WaxTrax! artist In the Nursery had, on one hand, made a name for themselves by recording orchestrally tinged military new age music and scoring silent films that directly depict a "lost England," while on the other hand they've packed club dancefloors with remixes by Flesh Field, Haujobb, and Assemblage 23. More recently, the French act Dernière Volonté has similarly hybridized industrial dance and neofolk. The upshot of all of this is that in the songwriting and production of industrial music, when we hear repetition, we should recognize not merely the confluence of technology and African heritage that pervades nearly all western dance styles of the late twentieth century but also a rare strain of something expressly European, conjuring the past through its relentless repetition.

Part V

# PEOPLE AND INDUSTRIAL MUSIC

IN THE SECOND HALF OF THE 1980S AND BEYOND, INDUSTRIAL MUSIC'S STORY IS less about devising an ultramodern war against authority itself and instead about how that long-planned campaign took shape once it spread to people who might have wanted something other than revolution. Having looked up close at industrial music's politics, warts and all, we can now step back into the timeline with a better understanding of the relationship between radical music, those whom it seeks to liberate, and those whom it overlooks.

# 15.
# Wild Planet: WaxTrax! Records and Global Dance Scenes

## 1. Industrial Music and Pop

By the mid-1980s, industrial was selectively crossing over into other genres, including more widely popular ones. A notable moment was Fad Gadget's 1984 single "Collapsing New People," in which singer Frank Tovey teamed up with Einstürzende Neubauten to make an attractively off-kilter pop song. Other bands adapted industrial imagery or production techniques to dance and rock music; for example, Anglo-French synth brooders Hard Corps landed a deal with Polydor, and Germany's Belfegore layered hair metal vocals and guitar atop oildrum banging and big analogue keyboards on their 1983 and 1984 albums. Similarly, established bands such as Shriekback, who'd had an indie hit in 1982 with their funky "My Spine (Is the Bass Line)," began introducing industrial elements into their music. The sampling and percussion that fills their 1985 *Oil and Gold* album makes the record a clear sonic predecessor to the likes of Nine Inch Nails.

Probably the most high-profile act to graze the edges of industrial music during this time was Depeche Mode. The flagship act of Mute Records, they were labelmates with Liaisons Dangereuses, Mark Stewart, and Fad Gadget (and by the end of the 1980s, Nitzer Ebb and Laibach would join the family too). Depeche Mode had begun as a lite synthpop act, but when guitarist Martin Gore took over songwriting duties after founder Vince Clarke left the group in 1981, they developed a progressively darker and kinkier tone. The Synclavier-made albums *Construction Time Again* (1983) and *Some Great Reward* (1984) are both packed full of sampled junkyard banging and quasi-socialist themes; their song "Pipeline" is the most blatant example of this, built around the literal sounds of construction and pitched percussion on metal pipes. On stage, the group would dress in bondage garb and clang hammers on noisy percussion rigs, taking a page directly from the Test Dept. playbook. Rumors eventually circulated that Depeche Mode was using second-hand samples and loops that Einstürzende Neubauten had created in the studio, although Gareth Jones, who produced both bands during this time, convincingly denies this.[1] Nevertheless, the change in the band's sound and the ascent of industrial music seemed no coincidence; one writer points to Depeche Mode's November 1983 TV gig with SPK as a particularly important cross-pollination. In any case, Depeche Mode has been enduringly popular—every studio album of theirs has reached the UK top ten—and in the 1980s this popularity gave mass audiences a reference point for industrial music's clear influence, even if they'd never heard the genre's name.

At the same time, some industrial acts had gone pop, with Cabaret Voltaire being probably the most significant example beyond SPK. Despite making small inroads toward mass appeal (check out the *Micro-Phonies* poster in *Ferris Bueller's Day Off*), they managed to lose almost all their original fans while picking up middling numbers of new ones with their brassy, quasi-house music of the middle and late 1980s; their biographer Mick Fish writes a bit cruelly, "Perhaps it's best to stick to what you're good at. Maybe if over the years the Cabs had obliged a few more people with that version of 'Nag, Nag, Nag', who knows?"[2] And as we've discussed a few times, some selective elements of popular styles had worked their way into industrial music's dominant strains.

Recall that popular music and its genres are defined as much by their consumption as by their production. Concerning the conversation between industrial music and popular audiences in the second half of the 1980s, it's much less interesting and useful to speculate about influence or selling out than to address the real fact that industrial music—and not just its secondhand borrowings—was acquiring increased public visibility, to the point where the occasional savvy suburbanite could find records and share them with friends. Some of this spread has to do with the swelling quantity of the music: industrial acts were popping up around the world, in small towns and nonwestern cultures alike. Fans and musicians of a certain generation also frequently assert that the music made during this time was of especially high quality—a golden era. Opinions aside, it's certainly true that far more industrial records made in the second half of the 1980s have endured in subcultural canons than those from the genre's first ten years.

But these considerations are only part of the reason that the genre gained so much popular ground. Cultural proliferation is about successfully distributing images, messages, and ideas so that people care about and respond to them. Although this chapter does deal with music itself (especially the band Ministry), arguably the biggest stories in industrial music during these years belong to record labels, distributors, dance clubs, radio, and finally the audiences whose participatory engagement inadvertently gave the music new possibilities. This chapter doesn't catalogue every step in the scene's growth during this time, but it uses a few particular instances of this growth to show the many ways that industrial music and its audiences mutually empowered one another. Starting with a short history of the U.S.-based label WaxTrax! Records and one of its figurehead musicians, Al Jourgensen, this history of the 1985–1988 period looks at how participatory culture in Europe gave new purposes to industrial music and then concludes by revisiting WaxTrax! and Jourgensen at the decade's close.

## 2. The Beginnings of WaxTrax!

At least in America, WaxTrax! Records was the most widely beloved operation within industrial music's cultural expansion during the late 1980s. When industrial fans and musicians think of WaxTrax!, most recall a time when as a label it was feverishly hot and the culture it purveyed was at its most contagious and thrilling. But WaxTrax! was more than a record label; it represented a particular sound, and to kids in Denver and Chicago, it was a bricks-and-mortar store. At the heart of WaxTrax! were the people behind its brand—and their story starts well before the company's high point in the late 1980s.

Jim Nash and Dannie Flesher met in 1971 at Gage Park in Topeka, Kansas, a popular cruising spot for young gay men—though initially neither knew the other was gay. They quickly formed a deep bond that was both enduring and perpetually risky: Nash, twenty-three at the time, was married and had two children. "I didn't want anything to do with breaking up a family," Flesher insisted, but after Nash came out to his wife, she gave him her blessing to be with Flesher.[3] The duo moved initially to California and then to Denver, where they could more easily live uncloseted. After three years, their love of psychedelic and strange music drove them to open Wax Tracks, a used and new record store on Ogden Street. They funded the store with money from working in carpentry and occasionally dealing drugs. Tom Nash, Jim's brother, also helped to manage the business in its earliest days.

As Jim's daughter, Julia Nash, has carefully documented, the pair honed their tastes and aesthetics through a correspondence with UK glam scenester Mike Smyth.✿ After a visit to London left Nash and Flesher disillusioned by its lack of grassroots fan-driven gigs and events, they and Smyth envisioned that the Denver store could be more than a place to buy records: it could be a venue, a hangout, and a recognizable name that meant *something was happening.*

This was a prescient ambition in light of the DIY ethics of punk's emergence in 1976 and 1977. After they attended a Ramones concert in January 1977 (also witnessed by Ministry's Al Jourgensen and Dead Kennedys' Jello Biafra, none of whom knew each other yet), Nash and Flesher enthusiastically did everything

---

✿ This entire narrative of the WaxTrax! history is heavily indebted to the recollections and writings of Julia Nash and the dissertation work of Stephen Lee.

they could to immerse themselves in the punk scene, even if it meant regular road trips to California and Texas. In 1978, though, they ultimately decided that Denver's geographic isolation was holding them back from centrally participating in the cultural and musical energy of punk and new wave, so they sold the store and moved to Chicago, opening their new location at 2449 N. Lincoln.

In Chicago, Wax Trax (as it was now called) quickly became one of the country's premiere spots to buy postpunk and experimental music. A 1980 issue of *Billboard Magazine* said the store "probably carries the Midwest's largest stock of independently produced 45s."[4] The ceilings and walls were plastered with press photos of obscure bands, televisions blared bootleg punk shows, and the clerks were infamously snarky in their hipster elitism. Continuing the vision that Nash and Flesher first tested in Denver, the store emerged quickly as the daytime hangout for Chicago's counterculture and a nighttime sponsor of films, clubs, and gigs.

As Nash said in 1985, "We got involved in the label not because we're great business people but because we're really enthusiastic."[5] In fact, he and Flesher were notoriously loose with their bookkeeping, and they paid little attention to licensing and legality; their first record release was a totally illegal re-pressing of Brian Eno's "Lion Sleeps Tonight" single in 1979.

Julia Nash recalls, "Jim had one of the most infectious and charismatic personalities, while Dannie was the strong quiet presence that would do anything for you. With a true Southern work ethic, Dannie wasn't afraid of working hard to get things done."[6] Together, Jim and Dannie (everyone used their first names) made Wax Trax as much a family as it was a hangout or a brand. As onetime employee Sean Roberts remembers, "They really had a very Mom-and-Dad approach to the label," adding that "Dannie was more Mom."[7]

The store itself—and by extension the label, whose headquarters were in the back rooms—was a party, an R-rated love-fest. The smile-and-a-handshake practices made for artistic collaboration, not competition. As Michael Toorock (lawyer for Skinny Puppy, Nine Inch Nails, and others) has said:

> These artists have a sense of community that is unprecedented. . . . Not only are they not suffering by going into and out of each other's projects, they seem to be rejuvenated by it, to become better musicians. The rest of the industry, which says you live or die as a band, would be aghast.[8]

A lot of the congenial attitude was coded into the physical space at the store. Revolting Cocks singer Chris Connelly writes, "The WaxTrax! aesthetic, or rather Jim Nash's aesthetic, was a celebration of 50s & 60s Americana, his domain was filled with gorgeous furniture, lamps, mirrors and knick-knacks from another era. His walls were covered with Communist propaganda posters, and his television ran 24 hours-a-day, fed on a diet of unusual and bizarre video tapes."[9]

With ever-adventurous taste in music, Nash and Flesher had begun helping out some of the young artists who frequented the store. "I feel it's sort of a civic duty to carry a lot of local product," said Nash, and indeed the store stocked dozens of Chicago-made records. But the two wanted to go further; they wanted to make new records happen.[10] Most of the first releases that Wax-Trax! put out were indeed locally recorded, like Strange Circuits' 1980 "Industrial Living" and Ministry's 1981 goth-tinged "I'm Falling," but soon the label widened its net, landing a deal to put out the campy disco of cross-dressing icon Divine, with 1981's "Born to be Cheap." Of the label's output prior to 1985, Nash said that most of it sold "in the area of 5,000 records."[11] A few releases were disappointments in this regard; the Blackouts' debut, recorded, at the Cars' Synchro Sound Studios in Boston, sold only three hundred copies, for example. (It was produced by Ministry's Al Jourgensen, at the insistence of the Blackouts' manager Patty Marsh—the future ex-Mrs. Jourgensen.) At the other end of the scale, though, Ministry's "I'm Falling" moved well over ten thousand units.[12]

Jim Nash and Dannie Flesher also brokered licensing deals with European acts because, amazingly, they were selling so many import titles that it was cheaper to reprint them stateside than to pay for shipping. The company's ability to move so staggeringly many foreign releases has a lot to do with how adeptly Nash in particular straddled the line between Chicago's postpunk scene of mostly straight white kids (at venues such as Metro and, for the underagers, Medusa's) and its growing house music scene of mostly gay and African American clubgoers (based foremost at the Warehouse, later called the Muzic Box), which orbited around pioneering DJs Frankie Knuckles and Ron Hardy ("Quite simply the world's greatest DJ," according to a popular book on clubbing history).[13] Through the alternately familial and bacchanalian ties that WaxTrax! fostered with every racial, sexual, and subcultural corner of the city, Nash and Flesher made sure that both scenes were hearing the likes of Front 242.

### 3. Ministry

The history of the band Ministry is closely entwined with WaxTrax! and as a symbiotic pair they're best understood in the context of one another. When frontman Jourgensen first came to Chicago (from Denver, like Nash and Flesher), he was an unstylish rock fan with a humble, pliable personality. The earliest Ministry recordings had an occasionally grim anger to them, but they were decidedly pop music; Jourgensen was immersed in disco as a DJ at Club 950 and as a musician for hire; an early gig had him singing a jingle for Shasta soda.

In 1981, Nash had paid for Ministry to record at Hedden West studios in Chicago after hearing a demo of "I'm Falling"—a boppy Killing Joke-esque number that Jourgensen had made at home with an ARP Omni, a drum machine, and a reel-to-reel. The song's B-side, "Cold Life," was the real success, though; it took off on UK dancefloors, did well on college radio, and topped the charts in *Rockpool* magazine (whose editor Andy Dunkley would later work for WaxTrax!). Riddled with jazzy bass slaps courtesy of session player Lamont Welton, "Cold Life" was about Jourgensen's experience living in a Chicago neighborhood that "was about one per cent white—[a] very low, low class depraved neighborhood . . . all my friends and everything else were black."[14]

Though Ministry variously branded themselves as funk, electro, and politically aware goth pop, Jourgensen was in those early days basically willing to become whatever it took to have a hit. "Everybody is striving to have a #1 record . . . anyone who tries to tell you otherwise is either a fool or they're lying," he told a reporter in 1982.[15] In his quest for success, he landed a six-figure, two-album deal with Arista, after which his music and persona became a degree more powderpuff. In interviews he namedropped ABC and the Cars and proclaimed, "I'm *petrified* of humiliation . . . I'm basically pretty sensitive."[16] He was also quick to tell reporters how distasteful he thought drug abuse and public misbehavior were. Jourgensen has long since disowned this entire phase of his career (especially the Arista album, *With Sympathy*, which is a pretty good New Romantic record, actually), but the claims that his record label was to blame for his image as an American Howard Jones don't sit easily with how earnestly he threw himself into the affair.

By late 1984, however, Jourgensen and his music were at odds. A review of Ministry's October 12 gig at the Ritz in New York (opening for APB) declares:

> The band's hits, generated from last year's debut album for Arista, were very familiar to the crowd, which was as enthusiastic for them as for APB. Lead singer Al Jourgensen made it tough for the fans, however, as he kicked refuse off the stage into the crowd, hurled his mike stand dangerously close to the front row, and threw cups of water over the audience. Jourgensen played the tough-guy stance to the hilt. . . .[17]

The following year produced the moody, antiauthority dance club hits "All Day" and "Everyday is Halloween" for Jourgensen, now accustomed to wearing black nail polish and hanging out with Siouxsie Sioux in Europe. By 1986, when he first met Chris Connelly (who was at the time in a Scottish dance act called the

Fini Tribe), "Al was still trying to earn his bad boy image, and build this new Al that ate children and injected drugs into his eyeballs."[18] Connelly recalls that their first impromptu recording session together outside the little London office of WaxTrax! at Southern Studios was mostly "an excuse to go out drinking at 11 in the morning."[19] Before long, Jourgensen's drug-crazed egomania would become the predominant identifier of his personality. Sometime collaborator Trent Reznor of Nine Inch Nails recalls, "He was always the last one standing."[20]

Jourgensen's retrofitting has turned out to be a functionally earnest metamorphosis, and it's one with a clear musical component. Few have ever called Ministry's pre-1985 music "industrial," but Jourgensen was nevertheless networking within the scene at the time; in between tours, he was a buyer and co-manager at Wax Trax!, meeting Front 242 and other bands the label distributed. In 1985, when he first collaborated with Belgians Richard 23 and Luc van Acker on Revolting Cocks' debut single "No Devotion," Jourgensen had begun to identify a sound and a community through WaxTrax! that enabled his musical aggression to match his growing personal brashness.

We can hear the first footsteps down Ministry's path to industrial-metal hybridity in the transformation of the 1985 WaxTrax! single "All Day" to its remixed version released a year later on the album *Twitch*, co-produced by Adrian Sherwood. Between the two versions of "All Day," plenty remains the same. Lyrically, the song takes up what was fast becoming standard industrial subject matter: a man toils thanklessly within an inescapable machine, "Break[ing] his back without nothing to gain while the boss man sits around and drinks champagne." Reminiscent of Nitzer Ebb, Jourgensen layers the song with heavy breathing that thematically centralizes the body at work, and just maybe suggests the possibility of sex. Harmonically, the whole song is just one transition between E-flat minor and D-flat major, repeated endlessly, synth bass and faux analogue strings lushly voicing the chord succession. But while the 1985 single keeps time with a constant quarter-note hi-hat—a choice unambiguously indebted to disco—the remix omits this timekeeper, leaving the song's tom-tom fills to clatter starkly in syncopation, demanding that the listener work at a constant rhythm to understand their pattern within an unpunctuated temporal grid. The absence of the hi-hat allows us to hear the remix's opening clapping sound—now exposed—not in the context of a funky drumbeat but with reference to the sample of a barking drill sergeant: the sounds become the loading of rifles, the stamping of feet, the noise of war. In addition to this change and to the general thickening of the musical texture (essentially by turning up the bass, even to the point of distorting the kick drum), the later version of "All Day" uses constant distortion on Jourgensen's vocals. Crucially, this mechanizes him, its square waveform gives the impression that he is screaming (and thus it makes him aggressive), and it taps into a developing trope within industrial music: the distorted vocal today, despite being pioneered by late-1960s psychedelic bands, is more associated with industrial music than with any other style. Taken together, these subtle changes show a clear set of strategies by which Ministry parlayed their 1985 sound into something identifiably, even vitally, industrial.

A lot of this new industrial sound came from Adrian Sherwood's production work. Luc Van Acker recalls,

> Al stole some of Adrian's ideas when *Twitch* was mixed, and took them to Brussels to ICP studios and mixed [Revolting Cocks'] *Big Sexy Land*. It is very funny because I was in the studio with them and Al would go to the toilet and write on the toilet paper the setting of the effects. His pockets were full of toilet paper. Then we'd go back to the hotel and he'd dictate to me: "Yea, 6.1, 7.4," but they wouldn't make any sense. "Was that the delay time? Was that the reverb?" I don't know. "Just write it down! Just write it down!"[21]

Indeed, the brightly equalized slapback delay of the kick drum on Ministry's "Isle of Man (Version II)," "Stigmata," and Revolting Cocks' "We Shall Cleanse the World" is a veritable signature of the WaxTrax! sound—a timbral act of commercial branding.

Given that Ministry's studio albums of the era all came out on major labels (after Arista it was Sire and Warner Bros.), it may seem a little strange to tie the band so closely with WaxTrax! But Jourgensen maintains that although major labels helped with sales—from 1988 to 1992, Ministry was awarded three gold records and one platinum record by the RIAA—his affection, trust, and loyalty lay with Nash and Flesher. A 2008 exchange with Pitchfork Media's Cosmo Lee went like this:

> PITCHFORK: You've been on Arista, Sire, Warner, and Sanctuary. Did you have positive experiences with any of them?
> AL JOURGENSEN: No. None. They all suck.
> PITCHFORK: Did you know that when you went in?
> AL JOURGENSEN: No. But I should have known. . . Which is why I did Wax Trax. . . .[22]

And Jourgensen was literally at the center of their operations, working at the store's sales counter even as the *Twitch* album was on the shelves. He also fed the label a continuous stream of new material in its initial moment of expansion. Nash and Flesher had only released seven records from 1979 through 1984, but in 1985 alone they released nine, of which six were by Ministry, the Black-outs (from whom Ministry would acquire bassist Paul Barker and drummer Bill Rieflin), or Revolting Cocks, who were initially launched in part because Jourgensen was busy wresting the Ministry name free from Arista Records, whom he still technically owed a second album. Jourgensen's numerous side projects and pseudonymous releases have acquired canonic status on industrial playlists and mixtapes; in addition to Ministry and Revolting Cocks, there's 1000 Homo DJs, Lard, Pailhead, PTP, and Acid Horse, to name just a few. Nash recalled, "Every time Al sneezed in the studio, he wanted to put it out."[23]

## 4. Mixing and Merging

The rate at which this music came out was tremendous. Each of the projects mentioned above managed to put out at least one release in the 1988–89 period alone. Jourgensen and bassist Paul Barker—by this point his comparatively even-keeled musical primary partner—achieved this prolific rate by constantly recording grooves, basslines, and beats, then farming them out to a given project depending more or less on who was around that day to cut vocals at Chicago Trax Studios (not officially related to WaxTrax!).✿ Barker recalls, "Al and I encamped there, so we would just work on tunes. We would have rhythm section songs."[24] For some collaborations, such as Pailhead (with Minor Threat and Fugazi's Ian McKaye), they wrote songs dedicatedly, but their working style was more often such that "we could have a couple of different sessions cooking at the same time," as Chris Connelly says. This was also enabled by the layout at Chicago Trax: there was one main recording and mixing area and another smaller studio for MIDI sequencing and overdubs, which together made the twenty-four-hour-a-day sessions into free-for-alls where partygoers would wander between rooms, playing a bassline here or sequencing drums there. Albums took only two weeks to record, and in many cases songwriting credits and royalties were divided evenly in part because it was nearly impossible to piece together who had done what on a given song.✿✿

Another reason behind the rapid output was that Jourgensen's personality was domineering, if still affable. There was little doubt about who was in con-

---

✿ Also in Chicago beginning in 1985 was Trax Records, an important record label for house music, and in 1997, Dust Traxx Records, also for house music. If there's any urban pride in Chicago's repeated invoking of "Trax" as a spelling, it certainly began with Nash and Flesher.

✿✿ This led to a series of lawsuits between former band members in 2005 when Rykodisc reissued many of Jourgensen's side projects.

trol socially. This power was both a cause and an effect of his being the most successful of the musicians who hung around WaxTrax! throughout the 1980s. It meant he was in constant demand, and that others tolerated—and often enjoyed—his wild swings from slacker to slavedriver. Beyond this, the steady intake of cocaine and speed (among many, many other drugs) meant that records were made in a desperate blur, though Connelly notes that despite the wild stories, "If everyone had been completely bananas, nothing would have happened. . . . There were several level heads around who managed to keep a lid on things."[25] There are outrageous stories of Jourgensen bringing livestock and motorcycles into the recording studio, and much more sobering ones about his proximity to others' overdoses, but he maintains:

> If I really did all of the things that I'm given credit for, I would need a 48 hour day. There's no way I could have gotten all that shit done and still chased skirts and been the biggest junkie in the world since fuckin' Lou Reed and William Burroughs times 10. That's giving me credit as if I'm some superguy, and I'm none of the above.[26]

Regardless of how specifically depraved the recording process was, the output was a stream of records that all bore slightly different permutations of the same dramatis personae. Chicago-based rock critic Jim DeRogatis recalls, "You'd get this image in your head of some satanic cult at night all mixing and merging."[27] The sense of mystery was kindled further by the arcane pseudonyms Jourgensen and Barker took: Hypo Luxa and Hermes Pan. The collective cultishness was apparent from the inside too: Luc Van Acker declares, "At WaxTrax!, everybody lived on the same block. We were like a religion."[28]

The collaborative dynamic of the label's musicians in the second half of the 1980s closely mirrored the subcultural sense of family that the store's patrons had nurtured under Nash and Flesher. Specifically, Jourgensen's rising star at the center of these collaborations was one of the two most prominent factors behind WaxTrax! exerting a dominant force on industrial music. The other part of the equation is less glamorous, but certainly every bit as important: it has to do with the development of their licensing agreements.

## 5. The Business of Chaos

As mentioned, Nash and Flesher had been licensing a few European artists' releases from overseas labels in the early 1980s, but their foothold in pressing and distributing import industrial music got a big boost when Belgian indie powerhouse Play It Again Sam started distributing (and eventually bought) Front 242's European label, Red Rhino Europe (owned by Englishman "Tony K" Kostrzewa, an old tech-junkie friend of Chris Carter's and the manager of the Cartel independent record distribution network). In a 1997 interview, Flesher recalled, "When we heard Front 242 we tried to get it into the record store. We got two or three copies and it was like, Shit . . . let's start pressing this ourselves."[29] Front 242 had effectively allowed this to happen by turning down a lucrative but potentially soul-sucking offer in the mid-1980s from ZTT Records, who'd just had a mega-hit with Frankie Goes To Hollywood's "Relax."

In negotiating with Nash the details of Front 242's continued verbal contract with WaxTrax!, Play It Again Sam boss Kenny Gates opened up the distribution channel to more European artists such as Switzerland's the Young Gods. As Nash said, "One thing led to another, and other stuff developed."[30] This other stuff included deals with Third Mind Records to distribute music by Front Line Assembly and In the Nursery, as well as arrangements to license stateside releases by Laibach and Belgian EBM act A Split-Second. A band's newly recorded album would usually cost Nash and Flesher a $3,000 advance, but oftentimes the only up-front expenses in licensing these ready-made releases was the printing cost.

In addition to licensing (which meant the record got a WaxTrax! catalogue number and logo), the company also manufactured, marketed, and distributed an additional sixty titles for Play It Again Sam, including much of their Belgian EBM and bands such as Borghesia, Slovenia's "other" great industrial act. In turn, European labels began licensing Nash and Flesher's American signees. Further spreading the label's geographic reach was its mail-order business, which had begun with a one-sheet catalogue in 1983; by the end of 1987 WaxTrax! had issued forty titles of their own and distributed many more through a variety of companies and channels. The imprint was a recognized player in Europe and America alike. Though Nash and Flesher were focusing their efforts primarily on the label by 1987 (moving its headquarters to 1659 N. Damen Ave.), the store was also picking up speed, gaining the reputation as a Mecca worthy of pilgrimage among American industrial fans. Whatever coziness it lost was made up for in sales. Julia Nash remembers, "They were having upwards of $20,000 days."[31]

Into 1988, the numbers kept growing, despite Flesher's increasing unease with being at the helm of an empire. Front 242's "Headhunter" single dropped just a few weeks into the year, and it became a breakout success with a strange video that received regular MTV play (directed by Anton Corbijn, photographer for U2 and Depeche Mode). A thoroughly tuneful number, the song's quirky production detailing was initially a serendipitous accident: the band loaded the wrong sound diskette into their sampler, and suddenly the sequence they'd designed for a punchy bass sound took on a strange new character, as if played on a cello made of scrap metal. "Headhunter" is sung from the perspective of a bounty hunter, and its catchy countdown chorus helped it to become the most famous EBM track ever recorded. The album it supported, *Front By Front*, racked up ninety thousand sales through WaxTrax!—their highest numbers ever—and eventually sold an additional half million through Play It Again Sam and a later rerelease on Epic/Sony.

En Esch recalls that 1988 was the year that, at least in America, the genre label of "industrial" moved from the underground into common parlance. WaxTrax! that year effectively doubled the size of their catalogue, putting out thirty records. The label welcomed new artists quickly, a few of whom are worth naming here. KMFDM, whose debut had gotten a European issue in 1986, released their 1988 WaxTrax! album *Don't Blow Your Top*, a reverb-drenched samplefest of sparse beats and odd loops; within a year or two, they would find their groove with unabashedly saucy guitar-driven songs. My Life With the Thrill Kill Kult was an intentionally tawdry industrial act from Chicago (complete with pinup-esque backing singers the Bomb Gang Girls), and their 1988 debut captures an entertaining *Rosemary's Baby*-esque faux gothic. Pig was the project of former KMFDM member Englishman Raymond Watts, who had run a studio in Hamburg during the mid-1980s, where he recorded Abwärts, Einstürzende Neubauten, and Psychic TV; Pig's debut LP layered colossal orchestral samples over sneered baritone vocals and spacious dance beats. Nash and Flesher also managed to score new releases by longtime electropunk veterans Suicide and by a reinvigorated Clock DVA.

Although by 1988 WaxTrax! had become the most visible and successfully branded of any industrial record company—essentially responsible for introducing industrial music and America to each other—there were other record labels in the game too, notably Nettwerk, KK Records, Play It Again Sam, Third Mind, and Antler Records, to say nothing of the noisier, perhaps more authentically "industrial" distributors such as Tesco Organisation, Dossier, Staalplaat, ROIR, and the upstart Cold Meat Industry. But while the smaller labels got their music to those hardcore industrial fans who sought it out, Nettwerk, WaxTrax! and the higher-profile industrial dance brands worked to reach more casual fans, and in many ways the music they released served as a gateway to more esoteric fare. It's hard to imagine that a fan of Dirk Ivens and Marc Verhaegen's Belgian industrial dance act the Klinik would not own a Front 242 record, but one can't suppose the inverse. Big independent labels helped pay for music videos for their bands, which would air on MTV's late night alternative show *120 Minutes*. They had the budget to distribute promotional copies of their releases to hundreds of DJs and radio stations. Smaller outfits, on the other hand, might only press a thousand copies of a release, making that kind of promotion financial suicide. These smaller labels, regardless of the quality of the music they released, generally had to make safer bets with their money, advertising in industrial music magazines and servicing a smaller pool of more reliably devoted DJs.

A big boost to large and small labels alike in the late 1980s was the industry-wide shift toward CD sales. Staalplaat Records, for example, switched to the CD format in 1988 with the release of Muslimgauze's album *Iran*. As label head Geert-Jan Hobijn recalls,

> All of a sudden this whole flood of CDs came and then cassettes dropped. It was a balloon that popped and it was gone, and no one bought cas-settes. It stopped. This was 1987 or 1988. For us it was quit or shift, so we shifted. And besides, in those days, releasing CDs was like printing money. It was easy and it would sell like hell because everyone dumped his whole collection and they started rebuying what they already had.

It's important to keep things in perspective, though. To a boutique imprint such as Staalplaat, a record selling "like hell" still meant fewer than five thousand copies. Even so, this was enough to keep these labels in business as operations with one to four employees. Hoping to cash in similarly, it's no surprise that in 1987 the first CDs that WaxTrax! released were reissues of Front 242's early work. There were no costs for recording advances, and sales were all but guar-anteed by the success of the records the first time around. One of the only sig-nificant drawbacks of the shift toward CDs it that it effectively sounded a death knell for the cassette-based indies that had endured since the early 1980s. The tape scene continued (even to this day, for a devoted few), but it atrophied into a circle of willfully stubborn ideologues.

## 6. Clubbing and Participatory Culture

As mentioned at the outset of this chapter, a big part of the story behind indus-trial music breaking into cultural consciousness at large was the network that supported it, and this network extended beyond record labels. Young listeners who fancied themselves as nonconformists found this music through the boom of college radio stations in the United States adopting alternative music formats and an uptick in urban UK pirate radio (due to the new affordability of movable transmitters).

In cities, nightclubs were constantly opening and shifting formats, and as the genre's musical catalogue grew with every release, these clubs grew more able to draw from industrial, goth, and techno than had been previously possible. Rhys Fulber remembers that one of the top industrial clubs in the world at the time was Hard Club in London, which was held on Wednesday nights at Gossips in Soho: "The Hard Club was it. It didn't get better. . . . The guys from Depeche Mode and Nitzer Ebb would come down there. I remember hanging out with the guy from Pop Will Eat Itself. It was happening. It was a happening place."[32] Industrial music found a welcome home at other clubs across the United States, Spain, Germany, and the UK.

The role that industrial music played in clubs like these was more social and sonic than overtly political; it's hard to ponder a confrontational ideology when you're dancing and drunk, and though it's true that some industrialists were concerned with the subliminal and the subversive, the DJ's flow from one song to the next recast any individual political message as merely one in a parade of meaning. Artists themselves may have had reservations about this carefree blending, but club owners and new, casual fans were happy to employ industrial music as cyberpunk mood setting: an attractive evil twin to the cultish optimism of acid house and techno, a sexier update of pop-concrète acts such as Swell Maps and This Heat.✿

In 1986 through 1988, Hard Club DJ Dave Mothersole was in Goa, India's hippie capital, where pot was cheap. He recalls that at the clubs

> the music tended to be industrial and EBM during the night and then Italo [disco], cosmic and new beat as the sun came up. Because of the locations and the drugs and also because the DJs deliberately cut out all the vocals—only disembodied documentary style voices were considered acceptable—the music took on its own life and no one cared if a record was electro-goth or Italo or anything else. You would [hear] Divine, Front 242, Koto, Blancmange, Telex, Tantra, 16 Bit, Poesie Noire, Lazer Dance, Nux Nemo, Depeche Mode, and Alien Sex Fiend all in the same night. It's an unwritten story.[34]

The genre-free breadth of these musical selections makes a certain sense given Goa's uniquely eclectic history. Joining India in 1961 after 450 years of Portuguese rule, Goa buzzed with a distinctly global vibe, and ever since American hippie Yertward Mazamanian ("Eight Finger Eddie") set up a soup kitchen and party hut in Anjuna Beach in the mid-1960s, it had been a tourist destination,

---

✿ Martijn Voorvelt coined the useful term *pop-concrète*.[33]

a no-man's land where partiers from all over Asia and Europe mixed. By the 1980s, Goa was home to eight thousand westerners; as a state, it boasted India's highest average income and lowest alcohol taxes.

Goa's clubs have become chiefly known as a cradle for trance techno, but we can also think of them—along with those in England, Spain, and Germany that they directly inspired—as sites of *recontextualizing music according to its sound.* This sonic consideration especially makes sense in light of the instrumental edits that Goa's DJs were spinning. This contributes to our social understanding of industrial DJing: just as Kraftwerk's records in the late 1970s found new life in hip-hop culture when African American DJs in New York heard in them an untapped funkiness, industrial music's popular expansion in the late 1980s isn't tied just to the many changes in the music itself, nor merely to the commercial development of brands like WaxTrax! It has to do with the people who singled out the music's sound for dancing, fluidly riffing on individual and collective identity simultaneously.

The intention here isn't to situate Goa as a locus of industrial music's history per se; open musical attitudes had flourished earlier in Europe and America in postdisco clubs, and of course industrial music had blasted in dance venues since Stevo Pearce DJed his Futurist nights—but certain connections can't be ignored, and it's important that we see industrial music of the late 1980s as part of a larger shift in clubgoing behavior. First and most directly, DJs such as Dave Mothersole brought back much of what they learned in Goa to the industrial scenes of London and Europe. He notes that his playlists were "mainly stuff like Front 242, Nitzer Ebb, Depeche Mode, Skinny Puppy, ClockDVA, Chris & Cosey, Neon Judgement," but he and other DJs would spin synthpop, occasional punk records, rap artists such as Big Daddy Kane and Public Enemy, and even pop music with a sonic profile that matched the darker fare. He specifically recalls playing "Land of Confusion" by Genesis, which the crowd danced to even as the club's management roiled in panic.[35]

A more important (if less direct) connection between industrial music circa 1988 and the DJ-driven genre-blending sensibilities that Mothersole witnessed at Goa is that the rise of industrial music's popular profile coincided directly with 1988's "second summer of love," fueled by the newly available drug MDMA—ecstasy. Interestingly, one of the players in the UK house music movement was none other than Genesis P-Orridge, who had become enamored with the music in California and who in 1988 recorded an album called *Jack the Tab* with Fred Giannelli and some of his Psychic TV entourage, which was marketed as a compilation record having each track attributed to a different made-up band name. P-Orridge was among the first to use the word "rave" to describe an electronic dance event, and rock historian Dave Thompson writes, "P-Orridge is generally credited with creating the term 'acid house.'"[36] However, given the amount of important dance music coming to the UK from Ibiza, India, Belgium, Germany, Detroit, and Chicago, it's probably safe to say that P-Orridge's savviness with naming and with cultivating quasi-religious sentiment contributed more to the UK acid house scene than his and Giannelli's music did; indeed, Simon Reynolds calls any claim that P-Orridge jump-started the scene a "self-serving myth,"[37] a notion that Giannelli himself has corroborated.[38]

At any rate, the house music boom meant that new wave clubs and London's deathrock destination the Batcave came face to face with the steady throb of German and English late-1980s techno. Just as industrial was stylistically blended in Goa (and before that in Ron Hardy's Muzic Box in Chicago), now audiences heard proto-house music like Rhythim Is Rhythim mixed in with Front Line Assembly at places like the Hard Club in London, while Nitzer Ebb's "Murderous" would find its way into the rave mix across town at Sunrise and Shoom. It's not that the edges of genres became more permeable during this time—few mistook industrial records for techno—but rather, the edges of genres appear to have been less mutually repellant than at other times. This can be easily seen on the compilations that alternative music magazines and remix services assembled: a 1988 album by the DJ-only label Razormaid Records boasts the Frankfurt-based EBM act Bigod 20 alongside the industrially flirtatious Shriekback, Israeli chanteuse Ofra Haza, and the soulful onetime Peabo Bryson duet partner Regina Belle.

Industrial music easily partnered with other dance musics beyond England, too. Jeff Mills is a techno producer and DJ who had been a member of the Detroit-based industrial act the Final Cut. He remembers:

> It was what was happening in Detroit at the time. Techno and industrial. Front 242, Nitzer Ebb, the more danceable things. Shriekback, Love and Rockets. . . . At some stage in Detroit they used to mix: the techno crowd and the industrial crowd used to party together. It's a very segregated city so it didn't last very long. The club owner got threatened that maybe something was going to happen. The industrial scene was more suburban, more white. The techno scene was predominantly black. We were partying together for a time, so this is where we were integrating, and certain people, certain club owners, certain clubs didn't like it. They cancelled a lot of nights. They didn't like the fact that black guys were walking out of the club with white women, and vice versa.[39]

The musical pairing was much less contested in Germany, where the electronic dance tradition of Deutsch-Amerikanische Freundschaft and Kraftwerk fed into a techno style that toned down the African American influence of Detroit and Chicago house, instead playing up vast-sounding, reverberating minor-key synth textures. The most important club night of this sort in Germany was Technoclub in Frankfurt. Bigod 20's mastermind Andreas Tomalla (later called Talla2XLC) had started hosting regular techno-industrial Friday nights in 1984 at a venue called Dorian Gray (run out of the basement of the Frankfurt airport to remain immune to curfew laws). After a few sleepy years, its attendance quickly ballooned from 1986 to 1989, so much that Tomalla had to relocate it three times, always in a larger space, ultimately settling on a two-thousand-person-capacity megaplex that he managed to fill for a decade.

As a musician, club owner, DJ, and label head (of New Zone Records and the industrial powerhouse Zoth Ommog), Tomalla exerted an inestimable influence on the Frankfurt sound of the late 1980s. Spurred on by the growing audiences who were happy to dance to nearly any kind of electronic music, he helped to shape a blend of breakdance, techno, EBM, synthpop, and new beat with his bands Bigod 20, Axodry, Micro Chip League, and Moskwa TV. Not unlike Al Jourgensen's role as the common denominator of the Chicago industrial scene, Tomalla was ever-willing to team up with new cowriters and was astoundingly prolific. Though Tomalla's label Zoth Ommog (founded in 1989) and his previous distributor Westside Music were home to rotating casts of collaborators, they lacked the debaucherous atmosphere of WaxTrax! So if Tomalla is less venerated in industrial music now than Jourgensen, then it might have to do with his comparatively coolheaded personality. Some of his music was also prone to unabashed poppiness more reminiscent of the day's Stock Aitken Waterman's Hi-NRG productions than of Throbbing Gristle. His music during the late 1980s, however, was ubiquitous in Europe's dark clubs (especially his own). Micro Chip League even managed to score a minor hit in America with their 1988 single "New York" reaching number nineteen on the Billboard dance charts. Other Frankfurt producers, notably Sven Väth, straddled electronic dance genres similarly. Väth's short-lived band OFF (Organisation For Fun) sounds today like awfully lite fare for industrial audiences, but the song "Zak," an homage to "industrial kids," lets slip the couplet "Nitzer, Skinny, and 242—a few examples that speak for you."

## 7. New Beat

Belgium was home to the most remarkable example of a participatory culture in which audiences and DJs socially and sonically recontextualized industrial records. The innovation here was a style called new beat, which, like Goa trance music, began as a sound discovered within and insinuated by a variety of musics including new wave and instrumental hip-hop B-sides. But most notable among these ingredients was EBM, Belgian through and through. New beat essentially developed out of the DJing style circa 1986 of "Fat" Ronny Harmsen at the cavernous, two-thousand-capacity Ancienne Belgique club in Antwerp, a music selection and approach to mixing so distinctive as to have been called "AB" music after the club's initials. AB music was also broadcast on an electro radio show called Liaisons Dangereuses (named after the band) on Antwerp SIS, a low-watt radio station (103.9 FM). The music was popular enough that not only was the club full every week, but fans would drive from out of town to come within the broadcast range of Antwerp SIS so they could hear radio personality Paul Ward announce the name of the records that he and DJ Sven van Hees played; that way, fans would know which singles to pick up at USA Imports, Antwerp's main electronic music store.

What Fat Ronny and DJs at important clubs such as Confetti's did was to slow down largely instrumental records, smudging their uptempo pulse into a bassy, thick march in the 90–115 bpm range. As Ghent-based DJ Marc Grouls (of the club Boccaccio) explained in 1988, "Here in Belgium we can't dance to an Acid record on normal speed—we can't follow it because we don't take drugs or anything!"[40] The aesthetic they sought was an emotionless heaviness, a menacing calm. It was an idea that pointed directly toward industrial music's fascination with disciplining the body and silencing the mind, but here the idea was less about frantic motion than embodying the unfazeable, the unstoppable.

The debut track "Flesh" by Ghent's EBM act A Split-Second connotes these values well: a harmonically static bassline bores through the song, a steady kick drum restlessly thwaps, and after two patient minutes of instrumental preparation, lead singer Marc Ickx half whispers a brief lyric about "the duty of the beast," declaring that "the outcome is always the same." Aarschot-based Antler Records released it as a single in September 1986, but at just over 130 bpm, the song came across as a bit manic for the tastes of many.

Like Genesis P-Orridge's debated role within acid house, there's some disagreement as to exactly how and when "Flesh" set off the new beat craze. But if Marc Grouls was the first to call the sound "new beat" and to emphasize its Belgian-ness nationalistically, it was DJ Dirk "TeeCee" T'Seyen who first slowed down A Split-Second's song by playing the 45 rpm single at 33 rpm plus 8 percent, putting its tempo at a cool 106 bpm. T'Seyen had been slowing down records with his Technics turntables since 1981, and he recalls:

I wasn't the only one: several different Belgian DJs had the same kind of idea. The fact we met each other regularly at the USA Import had some-

**ASSIMILATE**

thing to do with it for sure. I can assure you that New Beat wasn't invented by one particular DJ in a certain club or that one single record started the whole New Beat-movement.[41]

But nevertheless, when he and DJ PC Patrick were spinning at a club near Ghent called Carrera in June 1987, he dropped "Flesh" and its mood aligned just right with the mean, slow trance that Belgian clubgoers had sought since Fat Ronny first hinted at it. "Everybody important from the Antwerp nightlife was there when I introduced 'Flesh.' That's how the whole thing got going," T'Seyen says.[42] There was real demand for new music that similarly captured this mood. As was the case in both Goa and the UK, DJs and casual fans here saw new potential in industrial music that musicians themselves had not intended.

To some EBM and industrial bands, new beat initially seemed like an opportunity to find wider audiences, and many began carefully to sculpt mid-tempo grooves for their 1988 releases; Front 242's "Circling Overland" is a good example. However, a trio of Belgian producers were already marrying the lurching beats of AB music with pop vocals inspired by the breakdance tracks that played alongside the industrial, and as owners of record labels and managers of nightclubs, they had better access to the growing audiences than any industrial band.

Morton, Sherman, and Bellucci (not their real names) flooded the Belgian dance market with hastily made but catchy releases, assuming a whopping thirty-four band names and putting out more than a hundred recordings in a year; they literally released a new single every week, having worked with a variety of quickly erected labels to do so—most notably Maurice Engelen's imprint Subway, which merged with the musically aggressive Antler in January 1989. (Bellucci, incidentally, was actually Roland Beelen, Antler's founder and a veteran producer in Belgium's new wave and industrial scenes).

Their style still used the heavy quarter-note sampled kick drum of EBM and a chugging bassline, often provided by an Oberheim Matrix synth and always of extreme harmonic simplicity, but the blankly undead vocals of EBM were exchanged here for callisthenic entreaties to dance and have sex. Women's voices became nearly as common as men's. Among Morton Sherman Bellucci's most successful new beat singles was "Move Your Ass and Feel the Beat" under the name Erotic Dissidents, which sold more than forty thousand copies in Belgium alone—the proportional equivalent of a million seller in the United States. As the title of the song might suggest, much of the trio's output (and indeed most of new beat) was lyrically and conceptually concerned with dancing as an end unto itself. Similarly, "The Sound of C," which was recorded by Confetti's (now a "band" as well as a club) is self-reflexive, its lyrics inanely stating, "This is the sound of C . . . this is a new style of music." That cut sold fifty-six thousand copies in Belgium. Without overstatement, it's easy to assert that new beat quickly became a genre *about* new beat. The deluge of tailor-made dance far outsold the industrial attempts at crossover (called "hard beat" by some), and it ultimately led in a traceable way to the technopop of early 1990s European club music. For example, new beat act Nux Nemo was the brainchild of Jo Bogaert, who would later mastermind Technotronic of "Pump Up the Jam" fame.

A 1989 article from the Belgian pop magazine *Fabiola* is incisive about the music's edgelessness: "The success of New Beat is therefore undeniable. There's actually talk about a 'movement' that's being compared to punk, but the one who's missing completely in this picture is the 'rebel'. New Beat seems to be quite conservative and very conforming to the established values. No better Yuppie-music than that."[43]

It didn't take long for the industrial musicians whose work had helped to spawn new beat to detest the genre. Though a small handful of lasting acts emerged from the craze, most notably Maurice Engelen's project the Lords of Acid, new beat was badly overexposed by mid-1989. As Fat Ronny says, "After some time you really had enough of it."[44] The Subway Dance sublabel of the newly merged Antler-Subway folded in 1990, with the scene effectively having run its course (Antler-Subway for the most part went back to putting out industrial records). New beat's movers and shakers largely split off into pop acts or joined in the growing rave bandwagon, which was much stronger in the UK and Rotterdam.

### 8. The WaxTrax! Heyday

Let's return once more to Chicago and grant for a few pages a bit more agency to musicians and music than we have thus far this chapter. An unignorable moment in the industrial boom of 1988 came in October with the release of Ministry's *The Land of Rape and Honey*. Jourgensen had been collaborating with Paul Barker, Bill Rieflin, and a host of European industrialists on his WaxTrax!-issued side projects for a few years, but this was the first proper Ministry album with an extended lineup, and even though 1986's *Twitch* had moved into full-on industrial territory, Jourgensen's new bandmates spurred on and facilitated his desire to make even harsher, louder music.

It's sometimes claimed that *The Land of Rape and Honey* was the first album to blend industrial music and heavy metal, but this is incorrect; beyond nods to such warhorse progenitors as Suicide and Killing Joke, antecedents include recordings by Swans, the French act Nox, UK-based Head of David, Texas acts the Pain Teens and Butthole Surfers (whom Coil's John Balance especially enjoyed), and Detroit's excellent Shock Therapy. But Ministry, by virtue of embracing sample triggers and quantization in addition to reverb-free guitar distortion, imbues EBM's cleanliness with razorlike precision where most of these predecessors conjured a billowing swampiness. More directly relevant in Ministry's case were the sound and recording techniques of Swiss act the Young Gods, whose overwhelming debut single "Envoyé," released on WaxTrax! in 1986, sampled a ferocious guitar lick and looped it over the virtuosic drumming of Patrice "Frank" Bagnoud. Even though the Young Gods—alternately jazzy and Neanderthal in their ecstatic furor—tried to steer clear of the industrial scene, the song was prescient of Ministry's emerging sound. Lead singer Franz Treichler even traded production notes with Jourgensen: "He invited us out to his place, he was really cool, he had a cool attitude. He wanted us to tour with him last fall with Ministry. But it didn't happen because they hadn't finished the album in time. . . . He liked the fast metal stuff."[45] Also important to note here is Big Black, whose guitar-plus-drum machine formula in the mid-1980s was rooted in an ultramasculine aesthetic; Rapeman was the dubious name of the band that frontman Steve Albini later went on to form. Chris Connelly remembers that as Big Black played shows at Chicago venues across town from WaxTrax! they

> threw down a gauntlet of piously heterosexual indie rock to WaxTrax!'s gay dance club overtones, and it had a trickle down effect that never went away, at least that's the way I read it (one thing is for certain, Albini and Al: not about to go fishing together). Al had something to prove.[46]

Albini corroborates with his characteristic brand of derision, "I'm pretty embarrassed that Ministry keeps putting out our records."[47]

What Ministry had that Big Black and the Young Gods lacked was a major-label deal. The contract that Sire/Warner Brothers had drawn up was with Jourgensen himself—not Ministry—and it granted them first right of refusal on all projects (though a gentlemen's agreement meant that most non-Ministry recordings went to WaxTrax!).[48] Jourgensen in turn arranged with Sire label head Howie Klein to have total creative control over his own music. The big labels didn't know initially how to market *The Land of Rape and Honey*, but they nevertheless provided a large promotional budget, and the album landed in the Billboard Top 200 at 164, eventually selling more than six hundred thousand copies in the United States. Most of this was on the strength of its lead track "Stigmata," a song that skyrocketed the heart rates of pill-popping club kids and metalheads alike on account of its 152 bpm tempo and a snazzy pitch-bending guitar riff—"That's played guitar, with a sax sample and a didgeridoo sample slowed down really low and bent—portamento. The guitars are real. We've never used sampled guitars," says Jourgensen.[49] Many of the album's other songs followed a similar trajectory. Borrowing neither the postured constructivism of EBM nor the amorphous spookiness of Skinny Puppy, Ministry foregrounded the act of rocking out where previously it had lurked as a secondary, even shameful pleasure within industrial music.

Whether we're considering the initial boom surrounding WaxTrax! or the role that industrial music played in spawning dance scenes and styles, or its new overtures toward metal subcultures, the cachet that the genre acquired in the late 1980s is rooted in the social process of its creation (e.g., collaboration in Chicago, Frankfurt, and Antwerp), in the music's centrality at cultural hotspots (such as the WaxTrax! store or Goa's clubs), and in the way that casual and fanatic new listeners and musicians heard different possibilities in the sound (its contributions to trance techno and new beat, or Ministry's adaptation of rock via the Young Gods and Big Black). Simply saying that the music grew in popularity suggests that somehow the music itself exerted its own agency and was acting on the wider public; to the contrary, the music itself was in many cases the object of public action. Industrial music's cultural role, which its early makers staunchly asserted and attempted to control, was now in the hands of people who sometimes barely knew what it was and who were happy to treat it as just another way to party; hence it's no surprise that after 1988 some derided industrial music as essentially the sum of techno and metal.

A number of the post-1985 musical changes were indeed connected to attitudinal changes, but the bigger shift during this era was in genre negotiation: as cachet translates to cash and the musicians start to matter less than labels, clubs, and DJs, an artistic genre can exchange the power to shape culture for the popular privilege of being shaped by it. Recall the discussion of genre in this book's introduction, and how industrial music passed from being an avant-garde genre where aesthetics are negotiated to being a scene-based genre in which social roles within the larger community are at stake. Well, if there was ever a moment when industrial music became an industry-based scene—one that, according to genre theorists Lena and Peterson, appeals to hundreds of thousands of fans, engages with external sponsorship, and is culturally controlled by multinational corporations—then it would be the years that all this led up to, the decay of the 1980s into the 1990s.

## ICONIC:

Clock DVA – "The Hacker" (1988)

Ministry – "Everyday Is Halloween" (1985)

Ministry – "Stigmata" (1988)

A Split-Second – "Flesh" (1986)

The Young Gods – "Envoyé!" (1986)

## ARCANE:

Fini Tribe – "I Want More" (1987)

Moskwa TV – "Generator 7/8" (1985)

Organum – "Horii" (1986)

Pig – "It Tolls for Thee (Pig Breath)" (1988)

Thug – "Fuck Your Dad" (1987)

# 16.
# Q: Why Do We Act Like Machines?
# A: We Do Not.

## 1. Pretty Hate Machine

In March 2011, the publisher Continuum released Daphne Carr's book *Pretty Hate Machine* as part of their 33 1/3 series of think pieces about significant albums. A good number of Nine Inch Nails fans bought Carr's volume, hoping to learn more about what happened behind the scenes in writing and recording the 1989 debut, such as what equipment frontman Trent Reznor used, which records he sampled, how he got his contract with TVT, and the presumably juicy stories of the failed relationship(s) that inspired his angsty tunes. What these readers got, much to the outspoken online annoyance of many, was instead Carr's meditations on Rustbelt Americana in the 1980s, depression and masculinity, white suburban pride, the Hot Topic mall store chain, and the 1999 shootings at Columbine High School. Huh? How dare she write a book about *Pretty Hate Machine* and not interview its A-Team lineup of producers John Fryer, Flood, Adrian Sherwood, and Keith LeBlanc? Or track down Reznor's ex-bandmates and manager? However, what Carr succeeded in doing through her ethnography and interviews with *Pretty Hate Machine*'s enthusiasts was to suggest that beyond the album's blipping synths, cut-up guitars, and hip-hop samples, there's an important story waiting to be told about why modern suburbia so desperately needed an industrial music to call its own. It's an elegant illustration of the previous chapter's suggestion that an album's public life after its release date can be every bit as important as the private gestation that preceded it.

Because this is a critical history of industrial music, let's consider Nine Inch Nails' debut album in terms of its relationship to the industrial genre. Remember that social negotiations determine genre as much as musical ones do, and so we'll start by looking historically at how *Pretty Hate Machine* and Nine Inch Nails were publicly conveyed to industrial audiences. This approach offers the added clarity of largely removing Trent Reznor himself from the needlessly loaded debate of whether *Pretty Hate Machine*'s tuneful pop structures are a subversive victory for industrial music or its death knell.

Reznor had slummed around Cleveland playing in synthpop bands for a few years when he started writing and recording angry dance music with an E-mu Emax SE synth and a Mac Plus during the unscheduled nighttime hours at the Right Track, a studio where he'd gotten a job as a technician. In an uncommon move within industrial music, the twenty-three-year-old hired a manager in 1988, figuring that he'd "put out a twelve inch on some European label [and] see what happens," but Reznor found himself with more options than he'd anticipated for his Nine Inch Nails project—essentially a solo endeavor. His demos caught the interest of eight labels, from majors like Warner Brothers to industrial home bases Nettwerk and WaxTrax! both of whom offered deals, but ultimately Reznor took a gamble by signing with TVT Records.[1] TVT had previously been a label for novelty albums of television theme songs and a few eclectic releases (notably the Connells and the Timelords—aka the KLF), but the odd little company enticed Reznor with their willingness to shell out money to hire his favorite producers and send him to Boston and London for recording. These extravagances weren't entirely unheard-of within industrial music—WaxTrax! flew Jourgensen and his entourage overseas semiregularly—but by doing this, TVT immediately placed Nine Inch Nails in a cadre with Front 242, Ministry, and Skinny Puppy well before their debut album was even made; such was the negotiating power that Reznor had leveraged along with his manager John Malm Jr. Prior to the album's release, there was an understanding among those in the know that it was poised to be big. Certainly Reznor was aware of the possibility, having at the time referred to himself in a letter to TVT president Steve Gottlieb not so humbly as "Your Paycheck."[2]

When *Pretty Hate Machine* dropped in late 1989, Reznor and Gottlieb were already having big interpersonal troubles, but TVT nonetheless prioritized the record, marketing it aggressively with television spots, radio servicing, and vast print advertising. Sean Roberts, who worked sales and marketing for TVT (after a short stint with WaxTrax!), affirms, "A lot of NIN's early success was—I hate to say this—due to what TVT did for Trent."[3]

All this publicity is evidence that TVT and Reznor's manager wanted to find a fan base beyond the industrial world. Reznor himself sells the talking point in a 1994 interview: "We have very little to do with [industrial music] other than there is noise in my music and there is noise in theirs."[4] Exasperated, he adds, "I'm so tired of thinking about it can't even tell you."[5] But consider that he said this at the steepest moment in his fame's ascent; as this book's introduction notes, once musicians reach a critical level of popularity, delimiting their genre means limiting their sales, and so it was strategic for Reznor to issue this denial. Pushing implicitly against the public power of fans and media to dictate Nine

Inch Nails' genre, Reznor apparently situates sound and music as central to his supposed nonindustrialness. In contrast, by 2005—a very different moment in his career—he acknowledges retrospectively:

> I felt like I was part of the scene, certainly as a fan of the WaxTrax! stuff and Ministry and Skinny Puppy and all the classics. And that was the music that I related to on a number of levels—I liked the sound of it, I like the way it was made, I liked the message, which seemed fresh at the time.[6]

In a revealing counterpoint to his 1994 protestation, this recognition of industrial kinship is expressed entirely in social measures: a sense of belonging, fandom, and relating. In this odd way, both comments serve to reinforce a social alignment of Nine Inch Nails with industrialism.

So regardless of how *Pretty Hate Machine* actually sounded, Nine Inch Nails' image was publicly and socially constructed as industrial, and Reznor's initial burst of in-scene activity makes it easy to see why. In 1988, he had thrown together a live band (sans guitarist) and rehearsed a handful of times at the Phantasy nightclub in Cleveland before playing ten shows with Skinny Puppy—a gig secured with help from Nettwerk Records, whose offer of a record deal Reznor and Malm were weighing at the time. Once the album came out, Nine Inch Nails toured with opening acts such as Meat Beat Manifesto, Die Warzau, and Chemlab. Reznor spent a day or two recording in Chicago with Martin Atkins's industrial supergroup Pigface (along with Steve Albini, En Esch, Paul Barker, and others) and also put in some work with Ministry side projects Lead Into Gold and 1000 Homo DJs. Through visibly aligning himself thus with industrial bigshots, Reznor secured an important foothold with the scene's musicians and audiences alike: in a career plan to accumulate fans and allies eventually across genres and subcultures, the easiest converts at this early stage were the people already in the industrial community. This was how Nine Inch Nails' music got grouped alongside that of older industrial ideologues in clubs and record stores—even if their similarities were sonically limited, politically nonexistent, and, in light of the tension between Reznor's management strategies and the industrial tenet of organizational autonomy, economically out of whack.

## 2. Industrial Harmony

We shouldn't chalk the popularity of Nine Inch Nails entirely up to marketing, management, and the savvy navigation of subculture. Their live shows, for example, eventually gained a reputation for mixing punkish kinetics and spooky atmospherics, complete with artsy backing films. In particular, the band's performances during the first Lollapalooza tour of the United States in 1991—a gig that TVT facilitated and that Reznor initially balked at—popularized them to a wide hard rock audience.[7] *Pretty Hate Machine*'s 1992 metal-tinged followup EP *Broken* acknowledges this in its liner notes: "The sound on this recording was influenced by my live band in 1991."[8]

But going further back to Reznor's demos for *Pretty Hate Machine*, we know there must have been something in those recordings that all those courting labels heard as marketable. It's therefore worth moving beyond the album's strictly social history and asking what *Pretty Hate Machine*'s music specifically offered that was otherwise not readily available to the would-be industrial fans of suburbia. This alchemical something derives both from the industrial dance of WaxTrax! circa 1988 and the emasculated abject of Skinny Puppy's fluidity— all seasoned with a taste for corporate new wave and a pseudoclassical interest in modality. Understanding it more specifically starts with a look at the music's harmonic features.

Around the time of *Pretty Hate Machine*'s release, most industrial music fit into a narrow range of harmonic practice. The genre's emphasis on process, repetition, and the timbres of found sound and distortion all downplay the role of traditional melody and harmony, and inasmuch as industrial music is at heart a modernist endeavor, its suspicion of goal-oriented chord progressions and tunefulness makes sense. Recall from Chapter 3, however, that actual atonality in industrial music is rare, despite the word's common misuse in the industrial community (for example, a 1985 issue of the zine *Artitude* describes Hunting Lodge's catchy "Soul Vac" as atonal, even though it's unambiguously in B minor).[9]

The most common harmonic approach in industrial music is stasis. As a general rule, a given repeated pattern in the genre's music uses just one or two chords. There are countless illustrations from this era, but give a listen to some high-profile examples. The opening song of Front 242's 1988 *Front By Front* album, "Until Death (Us Do Part)," uses precisely one chord, C minor, through its entirety, over a looped bassline. Ministry's classic "Thieves" from their 1989 *The Mind Is A Terrible Thing To Taste* shifts gears rhythmically from section to section, quadrupling its tempo, but of its 138 measures 118 are all on the same E minor chord (the other 20 are on F). Al Jourgensen sings only one note, G, throughout the whole song. On the same album, "Burning Inside" has all but eight measures with A minor on the downbeat, and "Dream Song" never once departs from B-flat minor. Skinny Puppy's *Too Dark Park* album of 1990 features the harmonically static "Convulsion" (not once leaving G-sharp minor) as well as "Grave Wisdom," which holds steady on D minor for all but six measures. Einstürzende Neubauten's brilliant 1989 club hit "Haus Der Lüge" is similarly singleminded, never fundamentally altering its D minor stomp.

In nearly every case, industrial songs are in minor modes, usually either Aeolian (using pitches in the natural minor scale) or Phrygian (like Aeolian, but with a flatted second note that pulls downward). Musicologist Karen Collins goes to great lengths to show that these modes typically connote the mythic, the mournful, and the technological. The music's tonal stasis also aligns with what she calls the genre's harmonic predilection for the "megadrone" and the "persistent pedal point": "The sound could be said to resemble a bell tolling, or a heart beat, but is perhaps most clearly like footsteps."[10]✿ Her mentor Philip Tagg has shown this practice to connote all things "large, heavy, dark, catastroph[ic], threatening, ominous, brutal, unremitting, intractable, slow, and unpleasant."[11]

On *Pretty Hate Machine*, Nine Inch Nails present alternatives both to the harmonic stasis and to the rigidly minor modality of industrial music. Though some tracks on the album do focus on stasis or two-chord alternation ("Sanctified," "Ringfinger"), other important moments are based on four-chord patterns, which are the bread and butter of pop music from doo-wop to Depeche Mode. This offers greater tonal variety over a short time span, which inflects melodies with more tendency, tension, and expectation. This hearkens back to a tradition of classic pop in which harmony is the songwriter's primary means of shaping resolution, reward, and narrative. Important parts of Reznor's songs "Sin," "That's What I Get," and "Terrible Lie" are all built on compellingly poppy cycles of four chords.

Reznor is also keen on mixing modes, hinting at major and minor inflections of the same key in sometimes peculiar juxtaposition. Some of his deviation from strict Aeolian and Phrygian writing is blues-derived, like most of the hit "Head Like a Hole"; other pitch-based gestures are more exotic. In "Sin" and "Something I Can Never Have," he crushes the major third scale degree simultaneously against its minor version, giving a sense of overripeness and self-contradiction. You can hear it in each song's chorus: a grainy tension between Reznor's voice and the synth parts.

It gets stranger. Reznor's "Big Whole mix" demo of "Down In It" prominently highlights a whole-tone scale, a peculiar artificial mode used by early-twentieth-century composers such as Stravinsky and Debussy. On later recordings like "La Mer," Nine Inch Nails would explore these ideas even further.

---

✿ The term *megadrone* was coined by Anders Wintzéus in a seminar.

*Pretty Hate Machine*'s harmonic and melodic features owe both to Reznor's schooling in jock-pop bands and to his classical curiosity. Some of the album's idiosyncratic pitches clash badly against industrial music's antipop tendency of stasis, while others manage to impart the genre with a lasting melodic vocabulary audible in the chromatic synth playing of bands such as Haujobb and Oneiroid Psychosis, respectively channeling watery impressionism and gothic eeriness. The most blatant copycat use of Nine Inch Nails' harmony comes from the industrially tinged rock bands who found brief popularity in the second half of the 1990s. To offer a particularly telling example, compare the original melody in New Order's 1983 synthpop classic "Blue Monday" with the melody that the band Orgy used on their 1998 cover of the song. On the lyric "I thought I was mistaken," Orgy diverges from the original tune, briefly suggesting a major key within the overall minor milieu. It is the sound of New Order refracted through the lens of Nine Inch Nails. The melodic gesture is unmistakably Reznoresque, and it has become part of the language of industrial music, and indeed of rock at large.

### 3. Language, the Self, and Gender

The identity markers of Nine Inch Nails extend beyond the notes of the music. One of the band's devotees interviewed in Daphne Carr's book, Greg from Cleveland, notices a certain emphasis in Reznor's lyrics: "When you're singing a song with 'I' and 'you' in it, if it conjures an emotion that people can relate to, it's almost like it's your song. . . . Trent's lyrics do that."[12] Greg hints here that "people can relate" to Nine Inch Nails' songs because they come across as *personal*—an attribute that not much industrial music of the 1980s shares. To illustrate what a significant departure this album was from its industrial forebears, consider a statistical analysis of its lyrics. As it turns out, Reznor uses "I" and "you" with overwhelmingly greater frequency than other industrial bands. More broadly, by considering an artist's lyrical use of personal pronouns, we can get a numerical impression of how "personal" an album is.

In Figure 16.1, the printed lyrics of *Pretty Hate Machine* are compared with thirteen earlier records that are foundational to industrial music: Throbbing Gristle's *20 Jazz Funk Greats* (1979), Einstürzende Neubauten's *Kollaps* (1981), You've Got Foetus On Your Breath's *Deaf* (1981), Big Black's *Bulldozer* (1983), Coil's *Scatology* (1984), Skinny Puppy's *Remission* (1984), Severed Heads' *Stretcher* (1985), Revolting Cocks' *Big Sexy Land* (1986), A Split-Second's *Ballistic Statues* (1987), Nitzer Ebb's *That Total Age* (1987), Front 242's *Front By Front* (1988), Ministry's *The Land of Rape and Honey* (1988), and Front Line Assembly's

| | I | We | You | She | He | They | Total % Personal Pronouns |
|---|---|---|---|---|---|---|---|
| *20 Jazz Funk Greats* | 5.7 | 0.7 | 6.3 | 0.3 | 0.8 | 0.5 | 14.3 |
| *Kollaps* | 6.5 | 2.0 | 2.2 | 0 | 0 | 0 | 10.7 |
| *Deaf* | 7.6 | 0.3 | 3.5 | 0.1 | 0.1 | 1.3 | 12.9 |
| *Bulldozer* | 7.4 | 1.8 | 0.9 | 0.4 | 1.1 | 0.9 | 12.5 |
| *Scatology* | 1.9 | 0.2 | 3.5 | 0.2 | 1.1 | 0.4 | 7.3 |
| *Remission* | 3.0 | 0 | 1.0 | 0.1 | 0 | 0.7 | 4.8 |
| *Stretcher* | 5.1 | 0.2 | 2.1 | 0.5 | 2.5 | 0 | 10.4 |
| *Big Sexy Land* | 2.6 | 1.0 | 2.4 | 0.2 | 0 | 1.9 | 8.1 |
| *Ballistic Statues* | 1.6 | 0 | 3.0 | 2.2 | 0.4 | 0 | 7.2 |
| *That Total Age* | 0.2 | 2.7 | 4.0 | 0 | 0.1 | 0.3 | 7.3 |
| *Front By Front* | 3.5 | 2.2 | 3.2 | 0 | 1.1 | 1.2 | 11.2 |
| *The Land of Rape and Honey* | 6.3 | 1.1 | 5.9 | 2.4 | 4.2 | 1.1 | 21.0 |
| *Gashed Senses & Crossfire* | 1.7 | 0.7 | 4.3 | 0 | 1.5 | 1.8 | 10.0 |
| **AVERAGE PRE-PHM** | 4.1 | 1.0 | 3.3 | 0.5 | 1.0 | 0.8 | 10.6 |
| *Pretty Hate Machine* | 12.6 | 0.2 | 4.8 | 0.9 | 0.4 | 0.2 | 19.1 |

*Figure 16.1*

*Gashed Senses & Crossfire* (1989).✿ Personal pronouns have been grouped broadly into the headings *I*, *we*, *you*, *she*, *he*, and *they*; all numbers are percentages based on the total word count of a record's lyrics, which fall between 500 and 2,400.✿✿

First note that the total of *Pretty Hate Machine*'s lyrics that are some kind of personal pronoun is 19.1 percent—nearly twice the other albums' collective average of 10.6 percent. Only Ministry's *The Land of Rape and Honey* (certified gold by the RIAA) tops that number.

When we look at the use of "I" in particular, though, the difference between *Pretty Hate Machine* and the rest of this representative cross-section becomes much clearer. If word usage is any indicator, Reznor sings about himself *over three times more often* than the industrial norm. More than one out of every eight words on *Pretty Hate Machine* invokes the first person.

This is markedly different from what happens in other industrial music. Consider Nitzer Ebb's classic *That Total Age*, whose paltry 0.2 percent incidence of first-person pronouns comes from just four uses of "me" and, amazingly, not a single instance of "I." In comparison *Pretty Hate Machine* has 40 mentions of "me" and invokes "I" an egomaniacal 157 times. In this case, we might attribute this to Nitzer Ebb's use of the imperative "you" and the collective "we," both of which reinforce their callisthenic military image. Alternatively, Skinny Puppy's

---

✿ The lyrics analyzed for *Kollaps* are the English translation published by the band itself.

✿✿ The words tallied and grouped are: *I* (including its contractions), *me*, *my*, *mine*, *myself*; *we* (including its contractions), *us*, *our*, *ours*, *ourselves*; *you* (including its contractions), *your*, *yours*, *yourself*, *yourselves*; *she* (including its contractions), *her*, *hers*, *herself*; *he* (including its contractions), *him*, *his*, *himself*; and *they* (including its contractions), *them*, *their*, *theirs*, *themselves*.

near-total avoidance of any personal pronouns on *Remission* is readable as a move away from personhood itself (into monstrosity, perhaps?). Going further, we might see Einstürzende Neubauten's texts as a reflection of Berlin's aesthetic of cramped isolation, where *I*, *you*, and *we* exist, but not *she*, *he*, and *they*: there is no outside.

There's also a dialectic of gender going on. Though explicit references to "him" and "her" are generally uncommon across these recordings, male pronouns show up twice as often as female pronouns in pre–*Pretty Hate Machine* lyrics. Similarly noteworthy but not appearing on the chart is that these records collectively mention "man" and "boy" (along with their plurals) fifty-five times, compared with ten mentions of girls, one of women, and two of bitches. Reznor flips this bias, favoring female pronouns by a factor of two, most notably on "Sanctified"—a love song to a girl, or perhaps a drug.

Thus at the lyrical level, the tone that *Pretty Hate Machine* offered was strikingly new within the genre at the time. It's an album about people as they relate to each other, one-to-one. It opens itself to the "I" and "you" dialogue that fans such as Greg in Cleveland can plug themselves into. It makes room (if not political equality) for the subjectivity of listeners across the spectrum of gender.

The female space in Nine Inch Nails' music and fandom extends beyond Reznor's lyrical word counts. Although Skinny Puppy give voice to a monstrous gothic that erodes the maleness of all involved, offering, as Anne Williams says, "a kind of vicarious contemplation of patriarchal horrors," Reznor presents himself as a clear-cut heterosexual masochist with remarkable consistency.[13] Of the nine music videos he released from 1989's "Sin" to 1994's "Closer" eight portray some kind of sexualized bondage; he longs for "your fist" and "your kiss" in "Sin," and he won a Grammy for declaring "I have found you can find happiness in slavery."✿ This inflection of abjection and the gothic, according to feminist scholar Carol Siegel, "allows for identifications that disrupt the idea that the victim must always be female and that sadistic pleasure must always involve thrilling to the spectacle of a woman's pain."[14] Both the literary gothic and the modern subcultural goth scene are expressly concerned with sexual otherness and ambiguity, Siegel argues. To this effect, like KMFDM's En Esch before him, Reznor's adoption of fishnet stockings and go-go shorts onstage circa 1994 probably functioned more as a queering of gender binaries than a dominant restaging of oppression (which is how some have read the spandex-clad hair

---

✿ Some of these early videos were directed by Chicago's H-Gun Labs, who from 1988 to 2001 helped brand industrial visual style, making clips for Ministry, Front Line Assembly, KMFDM, LaTour, Pigface, and many others. They also helped insinuate this aesthetic into mainstream media in their later work with clients such as Nickelodeon, Fox Networks, and Animal Planet.

metal scene of the late 1980s). However, this kind of performance does behave similarly to hair metal in that the visual questioning of totalizing masculinity functionally opened doors to female fans.

Chris Connelly calls *Pretty Hate Machine* "industrial music for your girlfriend," and indeed Nine Inch Nails resonated with more women than even Skinny Puppy had. But this isn't only by way of a sexualized, submissive self-presentation; nor does Reznor's collaboration with Tori Amos on her *Under the Pink* album account for the number of the band's female fans. Instead, *Pretty Hate Machine*'s "pretty"-ness and its lyrical emphasis on the personhood of everyone involved serve to address the listener as an individual. Music by Laibach and Manufacture intentionally speaks with a one-way broadcast of unassailable authority, and in doing so it necessarily addresses a paralyzed mass audience. This denial of individuality is built into the mechanization and the totalitarian imagery that characterizes so much industrial music. In contrast, *Pretty Hate Machine* speaks—and sometimes whines—with the voice of a single heartsick suburban kid; the album's audience, then, is not a proletarian mass but instead likely just another heartsick kid. Probably a girl. Maybe you.

### 4. Get Me an Industrial Band

With this potential for mass appeal and the marketing push that TVT offered Reznor, *Pretty Hate Machine* crept steadily beyond the borders of the industrial scene, with high school outcasts, tech-savvy thinkers, and hip MTV viewers latching on to the record. This happened first in America, culminating with the band's twenty-five successful gigs on the first Lollapalooza tour in 1991; partially in light of the band's success, the festival would take on a token industrial act for the next few years, with Ministry in 1992 and Front 242 in 1993. The Nine Inch Nails buzz then spread to Europe, where following Lollapalooza the band opened up for Guns 'n' Roses on tour. *Pretty Hate Machine* was certified gold more than two years after its release, but long before that day it had both saturated and exposed the industrial scene.

Major labels quickly decided they wanted a piece of this action. The gold rush on industrial bands came "because Trent and Nine Inch Nails had started to break—*Pretty Hate Machine*,"[15] confirms Sean Roberts. "Labels did what they did, which was, 'Get me one of these. Get me an industrial band.' There were so many at the time, but unfortunately most of them were on the same label."[16] That label was WaxTrax!

WaxTrax! played loose with paperwork, especially when it came to the Chicago-based artists whom they considered family. The price of Jim Nash and

Dannie Flesher's familial bond of trust was that they risked losing their musicians to major labels who wanted to cash in on industrial music, the "Madchester" boom, or the surprising breakout success of Depeche Mode's 1990 *Violator* album. Taken together, the blows that the WaxTrax! roster suffered in the early 1990s are gut-wrenching.

Some of the label's losses were through licensing deals. In 1990, Sony/Epic picked up Front 242 as their own EBM act, taking away Nash and Flesher's top seller. Stunned and angry over the loss, Nash severed ties to Play It Again Sam. That same year, Al Jourgensen's bands had collectively sold 350,000 records; sniffing the money, Sire/Warner Brothers leveraged his contract in 1991 to buy out the entire stable of Ministry side projects once and for all.[17] Relations between Jourgensen and WaxTrax! had been uneasy ever since the budget for Revolting Cocks' "(Let's Get) Physical" single and *Beers, Steers, and Queers* album had ballooned more than threefold to $30,000 in early 1990, owing heavily to copyright troubles over the band's covering Olivia Newton John's hit.[18]

Out of necessity then, WaxTrax! was increasingly putting more eggs in fewer baskets. Take the example of My Life With the Thrill Kill Kult's 1991 *Sexplosion!* album. Shortly before its release, Nash told the *Chicago Tribune*, "I expect and hope it will account for 33 percent of my revenue this year."[19] He and Flesher put considerable promotion behind the release of *Sexplosion!*—even hiring an outside marketing agency for its publicity. Six weeks after its June 1 release, the record was selling impressively well, having moved more than sixty-one thousand units (as compared with the forty-one thousand that their previous effort, 1989's *Confessions of a Knife*, by then had sold).[20] But the record's success made the band too tempting for major labels to ignore, and they signed with Interscope Records in mid July, even as they toured for their WaxTrax! release. If it hadn't been Interscope, it would have been someone else; the aforementioned *Chicago Tribune* article notes, "Warner Brothers and several other major labels are courting Nash in an effort to get their hands on records by as many as five Wax Trax artists each year."[21] It was during one such effort—a visit to WaxTrax! from Atlantic Records's A&R team— when it slipped that the label operated on handshake deals without enforceable contracts. Though the majors had previously looked into buying WaxTrax! outright in order to acquire certain acts, from that point on they knew it was just as easy to snipe the bands directly. According to Flesher, bands "would leave the label after I poured in $100,000 for their latest tour."[22]

The label's shoddy paperwork meant not only that it lost bands, but it leaked money. A lot of cash was coming in, but most of it was kept at the physical store, where staff, musicians, and their nameless friends were freely dipping into the register. The volume and sloppiness of the sales made it hard for WaxTrax! to know how many copies any release sold, how much was owed to the artists (Nash and Flesher often erred on the generous side), and how much was reasonable to budget for the advance costs and promotional expenses for upcoming records.

Like most other industrial labels, WaxTrax! also lacked bureaucratic savvy. Employee and eventual vice president Matt Adell handled some of their business and legal affairs in the early 1990s, but in his own words, "Everything [was] done wrong. . . . And the things that weren't done wrong were done totally differently than the industry tends to do them."[23] In fact it's safe to say that the staff and artist roster generally resented the very presumption of law's necessity. Nash's fondness for intentionally bad taste and his disdain for contracts were a good match for the largely anarchistic music WaxTrax! put out. But as media scholar Stephen Lee writes, when the organization was in desperate straits over money and contracts, "Wax Trax's employees faced a crisis of contradictory belief systems. They actively attempted to recontextualize both their company's business practices and the ideological readings they brought to those practices."[24] These attempts were basically unsuccessful, because the company's choice was one of clinging to its misfit familial identity while bleeding money at a lethal rate, or staying afloat by conforming to the dictates of big business and law—both among the vilest of the pan-revolutionary's enemies.

On one hand, when WaxTrax! tried to persevere in its anarchic idealism, the results were often disastrous. A telling example of this was the release of KMFDM's 1990 *Naïve* album, which Nash and Flesher had hoped would be the band's breakthrough record in the wake of their tour with Ministry. The album's cover, cartoonishly drawn by Aidan "Brute!" Hughes, depicts a grinning man having sex with a terrified woman, naked with a nipple in full view. Hughes maintains that the depicted woman's fear is not on account of rape (as most interpret the drawing), but of the nuclear bomb exploding in the scene's background. Either way, the label didn't want to limit the band artistically for their questionable taste, but as former label manager John Dennett sighs, "That nipple kept it out of all the major stores."[25] Although WaxTrax! may have scored a vague moral victory in its decision to respect KMFDM's artistic freedom, not only did they lose valuable sales, but amidst the internal struggle over *Naïve's* cover art WaxTrax! and KMFDM crucially failed to address an uncleared sample of the famous "O Fortuna" from Carl Orff's 1936 *Carmina Burana* that appeared on the album's seventh track "Liebeslied"—a legal oversight that resulted in the album being deleted altogether under threat from Orff's publisher. The record failed to give KMFDM the breakthrough they'd hoped for, not only because of its cover art and its deletion but also from the bad planning of its release during the Christmas season, when kids stop buying albums in the hopes that their parents will give them the ones they want—and parents opt for safe bets over unknown, nearly pornographic ones. In Dennett's hindsight, it was "a really dumb time to release a record."[26] WaxTrax! had projected 44,000 sales of *Naïve*, but a year after its release the album had moved just 22,528 copies.[27]

On the other hand, when WaxTrax! tried to play by the conventional rules of law and finance, it rang sour with the label's artists and its conscience. After losing My Life With the Thrill Kill Kult, WaxTrax! hired an outside consultant to help them computerize their records, draw up contracts, and compute sales projections and budgets for each release. This meant that employees (Dennett and Adell) had to convince the label's longtime family to sign contracts that damaged the implicit trust on which the whole operation was based—a trust that was already compromised by the first bands' leaving. These contracts were also not nearly as generous as the verbal deals Nash and Flesher had once offered. Chris Connelly remembers it was

> something they were making all of their artists do as the label's profile had grown. The lights illuminating the roster had brightened, and major labels were sniffing around, signing up many of the acts and there wasn't a lot Jim or Danny could do. Along with the heightened popularity of the label, there came a new crop of employees; a cloying, mealy-mouthed bunch who fancied themselves on the cutting edge of the business. They were full of casual put-downs of us old-guard, apparently the future lay with the young hotshots they were signing—laughable, as not one of the acts they signed ever went anywhere. . . . I signed, of course, like an idiot, there was no excuse except it was under duress.[28]

The acts that Connelly refers to were mostly techno groups. Nash and Flesher's roots had always been more in disco than the Death Factory, and when Meat Beat Manifesto jumped ship to Elektra Records complaining that they had been unfairly labeled "industrial," the label's heads admitted that they felt some empathy. Journalist John Bush says of Meat Beat Manifesto's alleged industrialness, "Simply appearing on Wax Trax! Records was enough to do the trick," but if industrial acts were now signing on with major labels, then WaxTrax! didn't have much bargaining power to land new ones, and so Nash and Flesher attempted to invest in their longevity by signing dance musicians whose style had not quite yet become the Next Big Thing.[29]

Even when this idea seemed like it might work, though, the company still ran into trouble. Their biggest success in this new crop was the KLF, a radically political UK acid house act who had bounced around a few U.S. distributors, including TVT. Their 1991 Euro-dance single "What Time Is Love (Live at

Trancentral)" found its way into the hands of DJs and tastemakers (via non-WaxTrax! import sales) even before its official U.S. release. The buzz surrounding the song was tremendous, but because WaxTrax! hadn't projected sales figures, "We couldn't supply demand on any level," says Dennett.[30] The label had bad credit with its manufacturers, meaning that they were unable to place large orders; "On a retail level, we couldn't produce enough copies. Four or five thousand copies would come in from the manufacturers and would be shipped pre-sold."[31] WaxTrax! ultimately managed to print and sell thirty-five thousand copies of the single, but the band left the label for Arista, where their next two releases both went gold in the United States and charted top five in the UK.

WaxTrax! soldiered on under their new, businesslike approach, and they did manage to push KMFDM's profile a bit higher in 1991 and 1992 (despite the band having nearly broken up in that period). They also scored a minor hit with the debut album by the bluesy industrial rock act Sister Machine Gun. By this time, though, Nash had actively been trying to sell the whole label to a major in hopes of ending his business headaches so he could focus on A&R. Interscope had recently bought up all of TVT just to get Nine Inch Nails, and New York–based Roadrunner Records bought a 50 percent stake in Gary Levermore's Third Mind label, so Nash's hope was that WaxTrax! could bargain with its back catalogue and its admittedly reduced stable of artists. With the help of Jourgensen, a deal had almost come through with Sire Records in late 1990 but then collapsed. Similar near misses occurred with Zomba, Restless, and Island Records. Failure after failure to save the company effectively destroyed the morale among staff and artists. In looking back on the close of 1991, Chris Connelly says, "It was definitely the end of something."[32] Even the ever-loyal KMFDM, whose frontman Sascha Konietzko was personally renting his apartment from Nash and Flesher above the WaxTrax! store, began negotiating with Interscope in 1992. In a last-ditch effort to free up some cash and save the imprint, WaxTrax! filed for bankruptcy on November 20, 1992. Most of the label's staff were laid off at this point. By the year's end, the once-independent TVT stepped in and bought the label with a production and distribution deal that left Nash theoretically in charge, but with little functional power. For the people behind WaxTrax! the label, the store, and indeed life itself was no longer the party it had been. Though he hadn't spoken to many others about it, Nash learned in 1992 that he'd had HIV for several years; it almost certainly contributed to his desire to return to a life less nagged by the banalities of business.

## 5. Resembling the Machine

If this chapter is a downer compared to the story of the wild early days of Wax-Trax! then consider how one might reconcile these ruinous early 1990s with the snapshot that began this book, where ecstatic crowds in 1991 heard Front Line Assembly's music as something entirely new. Which story of those years is the "real" one? The answer, as ever, depends on whom you ask. Scenes by definition are always host to newly energized participants.

The number and the demographics of those who've cared about industrial music over time—along with the ways that they've used the music—correspond not only to the progressive stages of its genre development but also to how it engages the recurring metaphor of the machine. This is one basis of the decline-and-fall narrative that some impose on industrial music.

The music's early emphasis on process as a compositional method above any assessment of its sound points toward the music's *structure enacting the machine*. The subsequent negotiation of the genre's aesthetics entrenched samplers and drum machines as sonically industrial; the music was no longer a process, but a construction that *connoted the machine*. Once recognized as a sound, industrial music then became available as a stylistic imposition—a signatory feature to adorn songs and make them *resemble the machine*. From enactment to connotation to resemblance, the genre's important signification of the machine has thus grown more distant and tenuous over time; it's a tough fact to deny.

Socially, it makes for a disconnect between industrial generations. For example, Jason Novak and his industrial rock group Acumen (later Acumen Nation) nearly signed to WaxTrax! in 1992, and at the time they had essentially no sense of the headiness that early industrial music so explicitly emphasized.

> I was not at all aware of the first wave. We always said we were industrial, but thinking about it now, we were nowhere near. What industrial music originally meant had nothing to do with what it's identified with now. You almost have to say specifically it was industrial dance music, because with those first acts, there was no desire to pound a four-on-the-floor kick. It was about the sounds of industry; it was about the geography—taking those sound effects that they woke up to and heard in those industrial European cities or whatever. *That* became music. Then it was co-opted by people who wanted to put a dance beat behind it. I knew what their t-shirts and album covers looked like, but I never owned a single Neubauten record or Throbbing Gristle record until I was older and wanted to hear where some of this stuff came from.[33]

Not only does Novak's experience illustrate the disconnect between industrial music's eras, but his assumption that early industrial music's foremost concerns were "the sounds of industry"—as opposed to the social conditions they heralded—is instructive. It demonstrates that even if young musicians of the early 1990s had been in dialogue with early industrial music, their takeaway message was sonically derived, and not the stuff of social theory. To be fair, this interpretive gap isn't just created by time; recall Genesis P-Orridge's perception that Whitehouse and similar bands wrongheadedly appropriated industrial aesthetics without understanding industrial politics.

This disconnect doesn't derail industrial music's alleged mission, because as this book has repeatedly shown, one can readily hear its ideological echoes and undercurrent encoded aesthetically. It does, however, cloud certain ideas behind a haze: rare is the musician today who articulates the pan-revolutionary with the same clarity that SPK and Nocturnal Emissions once did.

Musically, the changes over time progressed, as noted, from process to construction to songwriting. This latter approach to making music supposes that the song is separable from its production, and it was still relatively new to industrial music in 1992, partially because neither samplers nor even cheap step sequencers could easily privilege harmonic variety and large-scale form, favoring timbral variety and groove construction instead—recall the workshop mentioned in this book's introduction on how to *build* an EBM track.

There's an undeniable question of personality too. In the 1980s, musicians most interested in the craft of songwriting were seldom attracted to the strangeness and alienation that was culturally assigned to electronic music; songwriting had long been entwined with authenticity in the wake of figures such as Bob Dylan, Joan Baez, and Bruce Springsteen. "[A]uthenticity works as a strategy to mask the commercial aspects of popular music," Nathan Wiseman-Trowse writes, and given industrial music's frequent agenda of revealing the ubiquitous tyranny of all things commercial, it's thus no wonder that so many electronic pop musicians in the late 1970s had fetishized glam rock, which flaunted artifice.[34]✿ Indeed, those who chose to use synthesizers were often tech heads or intellectuals uninterested in expressions of traditional authenticity, and frankly, many of them were incapable of writing what were traditionally deemed "songs"; for example, Martyn Ware says that one reason Adi Newton was kicked

---

✿ It's worth noting that this might be one reason behind rock critics' long historical distaste for industrial music, glam, and even pop. Critics like authenticity because it keeps them employed as interpreters; when an artist is self-analytical, the critic becomes redundant. Whether feeling that his or her territory is threatened or simply thinking the artist's self-analysis is wrong, she or he reacts badly to the music in either case.

out of the Future in 1977 was that he "doesn't really understand or really like pop music."[35] Electronic music's distance from songwriting also helps explain why so many early popular synth records were cover versions: Silicon Teens' *Music for Parties*, Soft Cell's "Tainted Love," British Electric Foundation's *Music of Quality and Distinction Volume 1*, the Bollock Brothers' *Never Mind the Bollocks '83*, Giorgio Moroder's "I'm Left, You're Right, She's Gone," and even Walter/Wendy Carlos's *Switched on Bach*.

But with an aura of coolness newly lit in the early 1990s, industrial music had begun attracting a varied, more "normal" clientele who were comparatively versed in traditional songwriting. Many of these musicians and fans flowed toward the industrial genre from adjacent styles like goth rock and synthpop.

We'll come back to songwriting in a moment, and we'll address goth music in the next chapter, but it's worth delving momentarily into synthpop, whose early-1990s encounter with industrial music has, in retrospect, increasingly proven to be significant. Granted, there'd always been some dialogue between industrial music and synthpop—acts such as the Leather Nun and Twice a Man, both Swedish, straddled these sonic lines in the early 1980s—but a second cross-pollination in the early 1990s produced more lasting effects on industrial's sound and creative process.

After the Futurist synthpop movement of the early 1980s was largely swept up by the major-label New Wave and Neue Deutsche Welle frenzies, a junior class of synthpop arose, savvier and decidedly swimming against the tide of the mainstream. The veil between underground electronic genres was particularly thin in Germany, where acts such as Celebrate the Nun and Camouflage specialized in minor keys and abrasively compressed percussion. These bands' songwriting was of a sadder stripe than the pop-made-on-keyboards that characterized the chart hits of the day, and as such synthpop records circa 1990 began wallowing in timbres that connoted the weighty and the epic: faux choral synth presets, huge single-note piano basslines, sustained string sounds, and lugubrious male vocals. Just when bright, brassy pop records began dominating western airwaves (to say nothing of hair metal and rap), synthpop musicians and fans peeled away and spawned a new generation of independent acts and labels. An odd collection of lovelorn nerds started filling European goth club dancefloors whenever Wolfsheim was played, and in America the synthpop scene heavily centered on the west coast and was an unlikely meeting ground for Christian and gay youth—a curiosity worthy of a book in itself. By 1992, such acts as Anything Box and Cause & Effect had gained small but religious followings, while Depeche Mode and New Order were outright gods.

The upshot was that the tenuous lines separating EBM from other electronic dance genres further dissolved. Industrial-friendly acts such as And One and

De/Vision were using the same sound palettes and song structures as synth-poppers Camouflage and Depeche Mode, and a band's relegation to one genre or another effectively relied on how traditionally tuneful the singer was and what record label they signed with. By 2000 or so, the line between synthpop and EBM-derived industrial had in many cases fully disappeared, as acts like Seabound illustrate today.

Returning now to the idea of songwriting in industrial music, one may well recognize its ascendancy in the 1990s as a fairly direct outgrowth of synthpop's path crossing. The interrogative chorus lyric of Die Krupps' 1992 hit "Metal Machine Music" barks, "Why do we act like machines?"—but inasmuch as industrial music was signified in production and thus chiefly *resembled* the machine during this time whereas it had previously *connoted* the machine, and even earlier had *embodied* its structure, we might answer that question with the admission that we don't, really. Not anymore.

This is one of the reasons why there is so much tension in the self-evident pleasures of the early 1990s' rock- and synthpop-derived industrial music. It is the sound of musical honing (if not development), but industrial music's encounter with the commercial phase of genre is so problematic in light of industrial politics that, as the next chapter explores, many felt it to be genuinely deadly.


**ICONIC:**

And One – "Technoman" (1991)

Ministry – "Thieves" (1989)

My Life With the Thrill Kill Kult – "Sex On Wheelz" (1991)

Nine Inch Nails – "Terrible Lie" (1989)

Nitzer Ebb – "Join In the Chant" (1987)


**ARCANE:**

Brighter Death Now – "Great Death" (1990)

Leæther Strip – "Antius" (1991)

Out Out – "Admire the Question" (1991)

Think Tree – "Hire a Bird" (1989)

Will – "Father Forgive" (1990)

# 17.
# Death

## 1. Death as Event

HIV-positive and weakening, Jim Nash saw a few last successes at WaxTrax! after the TVT buyout. 1994's *Black Box* retrospective was an instant classic, and in fitting ineptitude, the company was unable to print enough copies to keep up with demand. For a few years, KMFDM flirted with actual rockstardom: their song "Juke Joint Jezebel" headlined the platinum-certified *Mortal Kombat* soundtrack, and their albums *Angst* (1993) and *Nihil* (1995) each sold more than a hundred thousand copies. 1996's *Xtort* would top two hundred thousand copies. But Jim Nash died in October 1995, taking the face and the heart of the label with him. The Chicago store closed its doors in the first weeks of 1996.

TVT soon after played a big role in pressuring the label to become a techno imprint, though to be fair, overtures in this direction had begun as early as 1992. Flesher retained nominal control of WaxTrax! for about four more years, squeezing out a handful of significant industrial records by UK aggro-EBM band Cubanate, the moody supergroup C-Tec, and the still-incubating future-pop flagship VNV Nation. There was no doubt, however, that the WaxTrax! era had been over for some time. When TVT retired the WaxTrax! name in 2001, nobody noticed at all. Flesher quietly stayed in Chicago for a few years before moving back to Arkansas in 2005 to be with his family. His death, also AIDS-related, followed in 2010.

Just as there was a turnover of industrial personnel in the mid-1980s, the early and mid-1990s saw a second wave of departures. However, industrial music's first push had been a small, modernist endeavor to move forward and its petering out owed in many cases to musicians moving on in search of the new; this second death played out on a larger stage, as industrial music was more public and more populous than ever. Stakes were high: not only was money involved, but many believed the integrity of industrial music's anticorporate stance was in crisis.

Though Jim Nash's passing was singularly monumental, in the 1990s a number of other high-profile deaths chewed away at the scene's collective reverie.

In October 1990, Chicago scenester poet Lorri Jackson overdosed on heroin. Jeff Ward, the drummer for Ministry side project Lard (and occasionally for Revolting Cocks and Nine Inch Nails), committed suicide via carbon monoxide poisoning in 1993, distraught over being unable to kick his own heroin habit—the details are ugly. These two events hung particularly heavy around Al Jourgensen, who was close with both and was a heroin user himself. The Ministry camp was further hounded when River Phoenix overdosed in October 1993 at a performance by the band P, with whom Jourgensen performed that night. Within the next year, AIDS claimed both singer Dean Russell of Moev and Hans Schiller (born Michael Gutierrez) of the San Francisco–based EBM act Kode IV. Then in 1995, Lee Newman of former WaxTrax! band Greater Than One died of cancer. That same year, newly anointed Einstürzende Neubauten member Roland Wolf was killed in a car accident, and Damon Edge, founder of the band Chrome, was found dead in his apartment. In January 1996, another wreck took the life of Shane Lassen, the keyboardist (as "Rev. Dr. Luv") for the Electric Hellfire Club. Rod Pearce, whose Fetish Records had put out records by Throbbing Gristle and Clock DVA, was murdered with a machete in Mexico in 1997. A year later saw the suicide of Rozz Williams (born Roger Alan Painter), whose main body of work was with goth act Christian Death but who recorded ambient industrial with his project Premature Ejaculation. In the decade's last year, Bryn Jones of Muslimgauze died of a rare blood infection, and guitarist William Tucker of Ministry, My Life With the Thrill Kill Kult, and Pigface committed suicide. The respective deaths of Timothy Leary and William S. Burroughs in 1996 and 1997 imparted to industrial music a spiritual and ancestral loss.

It's crucial to note that through many of these deaths and through the scene's changes and attrition, industrial music's community at large became proportionately more heterosexual during the 1990s; as such its connections with fashion, house music, retro-raunch, and literary dandyism all atrophied.

## 2. Death as Metaphor

Though not a direct result of the commercially predatory atmosphere surrounding industrial music, all these events were, to many people, emblematic of the endings and changes in the music, its business, and its meaning. Beyond its makers, something about industrial music seemed to be dying—possibly of exposure.

Ministry was shedding all acknowledgment of its industrial past in lieu of a metal identity, and Nine Inch Nails had achieved completely unprecedented popularity with 1994's *The Downward Spiral*, selling more than four million copies in America alone. Its single "Closer" found regular rotation on MTV with a chorus hook—"I want to fuck you like an animal"—that appealed to a generation of teenagers looking for a quick way to enrage their parents. The backlash among defensively exclusionary industrial fans was immediate: no self-respecting DJ would play a Nine Inch Nails record at an industrial club between 1995 and 1999.

In addition to the major labels' gutting of WaxTrax! described in the preceding chapter, other veteran acts were picking up more exposure. German EBM act Armageddon Dildos, who had released their first album with Andreas Tomalla's Frankfurt-based Zoth Ommog records, managed to score stateside distribution through Sire in 1993. They would later sign with BMG. Tomalla himself had forged the relationship with Sire when his own band Bigod 20 had attracted their attention with the 1990 club hit "The Bog," featuring Front 242's Jean-Luc De Meyer on vocals; this record paved the way for bigger deals, including one with Warner Brothers, who in 1992 released Bigod 20's cover of Madonna's "Like a Prayer." Similarly, Sony put out Foetus's *Gash* album in 1995, hoping likewise for an industrial hit (it didn't come). Simply put, not only had a dozen musicians died, but the independent spirit—Jon Savage's old idea of industrial music's "organizational autonomy"—seemed only a weak undercurrent. In a move that earned Trent Reznor some grudging credibility from the industrial old guard, he set up Nothing Records, a vanity label within Interscope over which he and his manager had autonomous control. Nothing Records offered U.S. distribution to critical lynchpins of the 1980s industrial scene such as Einstürzende Neubauten, Coil, and Pig, as well as veteran crossover acts Meat Beat Manifesto, The The, and Pop Will Eat Itself, but it was no secret that Marilyn Manson—universally reviled within industrial music—was the imprint's real cash cow.

The death whose reverberations were most widely felt throughout industrial music was Skinny Puppy's. To understand its significance, let's back up a bit in the timeline.

By a lot of measures, the late 1980s had been good to Skinny Puppy. The band's world tours, their high-profile activism against animal testing and censorship, and several outstanding singles such as "Testure" and "Worlock" had given them not only massive popularity—1989's *Rabies* album sold 150,000 copies—but also a critical integrity that Ministry and Nine Inch Nails lacked in having gone pop in the eyes of many. Front 242 and Einstürzende Neubauten moved comparable numbers and were still making engagingly confrontational music, but neither act was so opulent; once Skinny Puppy was bolstered with a budget, the band's monstrous Artaudian aesthetic became a high water mark of industrial spectacle.

Their last album with Nettwerk, 1992's *Last Rights*, was in some ways an attempt to reunify the dance-oriented strain of industrial music with the genre's heritage in experimental collage, noise, glitch, and magic. Aware of other industrial acts' ventures into techno and metal, keyboardist Dwayne Goettel commented in an interview, "You know, there's pressure out there for us to make a dance album. But . . . I need to make records about how living in 1992 really fucking feels."[1] Though the album did produce "Inquisition," a 120 bpm club single, its overall tone was lugubrious and lumbering.

The murky opening track "Love in Vein" both lyrically concerns and musically simulates a heroin high gone wrong in progressive stages: first, time is unsettled through a warped marching band record, the lack of a chorus, a constant backwards piano sound, and a sample declaring "Everything around me seemed to move in slow motion"; second, blood sickness comes with a bubbling minor-key synth line and the accompanying lyric "Human heart explodes, attacking, pointed sticks in sores, the arms. Where's the warning? Shot the lights out . . ."; finally, an orchestral swell matches Ogre's vocal hysteria as he concludes the lyric, describing how "ants symbolize decay," bemoaning that he "missed the warning, missed the vein." The album also includes the song "Killing Game," which uses the harmonic and tempo conventions of a rock ballad to build to a loose, clattering climax in which "tortured animals wake up [and] time beckons death upon itself." The song's video is surprisingly artsy: a student dance troupe arrhythmically casts shadows in high-contrast black and white. Elsewhere, *Last Rights* is more abstract: its final track "Download" is a sprawling work of neo–musique concrète, cutting up white noise with the sounds of prepared piano for five minutes before concluding in a six-minute distorted drone (courtesy of the Legendary Pink Dots' Martijn de Kleer), carefully exploring the harmonics of a single pitch—an EKG flatline to end the record's experience. As Key recalls of the track, "Dwayne and Anthony [Valcic, mixing engineer] sat up for like 14 hours just editing, and that's not including the manufacturing of the sounds they did. They had collected that over a period of two months."[2]

The band was tense and unhealthy while making *Last Rights* in late 1991. During the day, cEvin Key and keyboardist Dwayne Goettel (who'd joined in 1986 to replace Bill Leeb) would smoke pot and record instrumental tracks, sequenced through their Atari 1040STs. They had little notion of what Ogre would add when he came in to do vocals at night, after they'd gone home. Overseen by his personal manager and by Skinny Puppy's longtime producer Dave Ogilvie, Ogre was not on steady speaking terms with Key. Nettwerk exec Ric Arboit recalls, "They couldn't even stand to be in the same room together."[3] Key says, "Through drug situations, I would end up on Ogre's paranoid delusional side, and I would become more or less the victim,"[4] while the band's one-time producer and Invisible Records head Martin Atkins pointedly contests that "in Skinny Puppy, the dynamic was to suppress Ogre."[5] It's undeniable that Ogre was difficult to deal with: he told *Spin* that during the recording,

> I was seeing things that I thought people were projecting into my room—like three-dimensional objects coming out of the walls. I'd go in the studio after incredible nights of hallucinations and hauntings. Those were the best sessions, but I was falling-down drunk. They'd stop the tape and say "Ogre, are you okay?" and then go "He's down," and put me in a cab. Everyone was concerned about me dying. I was off my head way too much—there's no way I could ever do that again.[6]

That the album bore a handful of instrumental tracks may have been less a planned decision than the result of Ogre's failure to record vocals for them.

The finished record, however, was powerful. The *All Music Guide to Rock* declares it "a hailstorm of electro-distortion ten years ahead of its time . . . a sonic masterpiece that undoubtedly influenced sound manipulators from Autechre to White Zombie."[7]

So when the band's contract with Nettwerk and their U.S. distribution through Capitol ran out in 1993, hip-hop megaproducer Rick Rubin began courting them to sign with his Def American label (later American Recordings), home of Sir Mix-a-Lot and the Black Crowes. Seeing Rubin as a potentially powerful advocate for their music, the trio accepted a three-album contract and set up camp at Shangri-La, a digital studio in Malibu whose equipment wasn't familiar to anyone involved. To helm the recording, the band's new label company brought in Roli Mosimann, a Swiss producer who'd worked with the Young Gods, Swans, and Foetus, but Mosimann bred trouble when he insisted that the band write and record no longer in shifts but together. The studio environment was hostile, exacerbated by Ogre's refusal to write lyrics and sing, and more importantly, by everyone's drug problems—which they each kept hidden.

In the face of industrial music's now-established sound and media presence, there was also a tension over the band's musical direction: Key and Goettel's interests were growing increasingly abstract and techno-driven, while Ogre felt compelled to make "songs . . . that's what we wanted to do, even though [cEvin] will say otherwise. That's why we signed a deal with a major label, that's why we went to these measures. I—as a singer—wanted to get some songs to perform live."[8] He had immersed himself in more guitar-driven material through his involvement with Pigface.

The band reached a standstill, and so Mosimann was taken off the project and replaced by Martin Atkins, with whom Ogre was already good friends. Sensing that the band needed additional artistic guidance, Rubin also brought in Genesis P-Orridge to spark them into creativity. P-Orridge recalls:

> They were at an impasse with their new album. They wanted me to persuade Ogre into doing vocals. We went down there and were living with them in their huge bungalow with this beautiful studio in it. We said why don't you all just fucking jam? And we put the whole studio through my box of tricks [Chris Carter's old Gristleizer] and then yours truly turned all these knobs and so on. Then we tried to get Ogre to do vocals and he was being very reluctant. And we hit him in the stomach—Guh! But it didn't work. He couldn't sing.[9]

Later, that Gristleizer—one of the remaining original two—melted in an electrical fire at Rick Rubin's recording studio and mansion, where P-Orridge was staying along with the members of Love and Rockets. P-Orridge was injured in the fire, and received over $1.5 million in damages from Rubin and American Recordings.

Amidst the difficulty surrounding Skinny Puppy's album, which also included several emergency evacuations for wildfires and flooding, the band racked up expenses of $650,000. To give a little perspective, compare that with two industrial albums distributed by Sire Records: Ministry's 1992 ΚΕΦΑΛΗ ΞΘ cost $329,000 to make,[10] and Armageddon Dildos' 1995 *Lost* had a budget of just $15,040—still quite a lot more than most indies could offer.[11] With Skinny Puppy's album still not done, Key asked the label to pay out their advances for the band's next two records. Rubin, worried that this had become a money pit, cut the contract down to one album and replaced producer Martin Atkins with Mark Walk, who had helped to run a studio in Minnesota where Pigface's albums were mixed.

Amidst all this, Dwayne Goettel's heroin problems got much worse. Ogre recalls,

> My girlfriend and I were in our room. I heard this bang on the door. The door was blown off the hinges. There was blood all the way down the fucking hallway. [Dwayne Goettel had] wrapped barbed wire around his arms, shaved his head, his eyebrows were gone, and he'd pulled a fucking stunt like Pink Floyd's *The Wall*.

After two days of him walking around very uncomfortably, I went up to him and we talked. This is why I'm at peace, in a lot of ways. . . . We talked and we hugged and kissed, 'cause we could do that, and the rest is history.[12]

The "rest" referred to here is Ogre's leaving Malibu and announcing to Rubin that he was quitting the band. With the frontman gone, Rubin was able to enact a clause in the contract that froze the album's funds altogether. Goettel returned to Canada and went through several weeks of rehab, but shortly after getting out, he died of an overdose at his parents' house in Alberta on August 23, 1995. He was thirty-one.

Rubin at this point begrudgingly funded the completion of the album, which amounted to Key reuniting briefly with former producer Dave Ogilvie in Vancouver to mix down the incomplete tracks into a record of what might have been. American Recordings released *The Process* in February 1996.

"The Process" refers both to a 1969 novel of hallucinatory discovery by cut-up inventor Brian Gysin and to the Process Church of the Final Judgment, a religious group of the 1960s and 1970s that worshipped both Christ and Satan. P-Orridge helped title the record and, together with Ogre, planned an online community that would attempt to combine the spirit of the early mail art networks with the mystical sensibilities of Thee Temple ov Psychick Youth, which had splintered a few years earlier. P-Orridge explained in 1996 that this new "process" would be

> like the old zeroxs [sic] and cassette tapes, [but] now it's going to happen on the computers. You can swap information to people across the world. The tactics and strategies are the same—slogans and cryptic remarks about behaviour. Initially people accessing the sites will be Skinny Puppy fans . . . but there's also a lot on "The process" as well which will direct them to other databases.[13]

Lyrically, the album's title track is an alarmingly self-aware statement of purpose.[14]

> The process
> aims to make individual freedom
> . . .
> to heal the wound of separation
> to question the unquestioning of the mind

The process
offers an alternative to mass control
the center of the information war

we have progressed

This clarity and self-analysis invite one to ask whether its function is to awaken a sleeping audience and inspire revelatory freedom or to archive the methods of doing so. Is talking about an internal revolution the same as doing it? At this point in industrial music history, when in fact most bands had not "progressed" in the dialogue that Throbbing Gristle initiated, did Ogre's lyrics serve as a renewed call to arms, or a throwback? Or worse, an obituary?

To many, rather than reinvigorating industrial music's "alternative to mass control," *The Process*'s annunciated ancestry within industrial culture functionally only highlighted Goettel's death and Skinny Puppy's demise as an end to this lineage. Goettel himself was not the band's most central member—though his melodic synth parts are evident on "Worlock" and "Mirror Saw"—but within the industrial music community, his death took on a sacrificial air.

Skinny Puppy's members were emotionally extroverted in interviews; Jolene Siana gushes in a 1987 letter to Ogre, "You're sensitive aren't you? You seem like a sincere person. It's really cool how you guys (cEvin Key and Dwayne) aren't secluded from your fans. It shows how human you are."[15] This publicly raw personhood of Skinny Puppy's members and their relentlessly abject imagery and sound meant that the band exuded both empathy and radicality, which taken together allowed fans to plug into honest emotional identities of theatrical extremity: no industrial band, excepting perhaps Nine Inch Nails, has inspired more fan tattoos, to be sure. Skinny Puppy was thus nearly sacred in the eyes of many fans on both sides of the Atlantic, and given their anticorporate, anti-exploitation politics, it was hard for the industrial scene not to connect the band's big budget dealings to their death. As Key said plainly of American Recordings in 1996, "They destroyed the band."[16]

The degree to which Skinny Puppy inscribed and influenced all that was "industrial" can be readily heard in the breathless slobbering vocal style of X Marks the Pedwalk or the monster-movie samples of Wumpscut. Daniel Myer of the German act Haujobb recalls, "When *Too Dark Park* was released by Skinny Puppy, this was the initiative for us to make this kind of music. We were blown away. . . . We wanted to sound like our heroes, we wanted to sound like Skinny Puppy."[17] The band's role is perhaps most plainly stated on the pages of the industrial scene's magazines of the 1990s, though: reviews and advertisements in *Industrial Nation, Under the Flag, Electric Shock Treatment, Zillo, Culture Shock,*

*Interface*, *Music from the Empty Quarter*, *Base Asylum*, and *DAMn!* draw more comparisons to Skinny Puppy than to any other act. As just one of countless examples, a 1997 print ad by Pendragon Records announces that the German act Kalte Farben "are the 'second coming' (SP being the first, of course.)"[18]

The top-selling industrial releases of the 1990s were all made by veteran bands formed in the 1980s, when indie labels were the order of the day: Skinny Puppy, Nine Inch Nails, Front Line Assembly, Front 242, Ministry, KMFDM and My Life With the Thrill Kill Kult. A few rock-plus-synthesizer acts signed with majors in the early 1990s and managed to sell reasonably well—Stabbing Westward and Filter, for example—but the major-label gold rush on industrial music peaked in 1995. By early 1996, modern rock radio stations were sandwiching vaguely industrialesque songs by Gravity Kills in between records by Bush, Sublime, and Alanis Morissette; the music was contextualized as merely another flavor in the "alternative" stew, which in some ways was fitting, because many of these quasi-industrial bands themselves used machinelike noises as just another instrument in what was at heart a rock band. Although this book's introduction notes that some supposedly industrial artists have spent their careers attempting to disavow the genre label, no such public pleas were needed with these acts: neither record labels nor fans nor the bands themselves ever thought what they were doing was "industrial," even if club DJs occasionally played a song from *The Crow*'s soundtrack to get the floor going on a slow night. No, as far as major labels and corporate radio was concerned, industrial music was a stepping stone to capitalizing on a demographic whose taste for Marilyn Manson, White Zombie, Rammstein, and Oomph (in Europe, at least) directly paved the way for the nü-metal of the early 2000s. Often derided as "mall-goth," this music claimed neither anticorporate ideology nor an aesthetic of genuinely challenging strangeness, and it was thus much easier to market.

## 3. Death as Fashion

"In the sense that Goth appropriates the mainstream's designation of everything that does not fit into its systems of signification as dead or deathly, Goth cultures are death cults extraordinaire," argues Carol Siegel.[19] In this regard, goth's embrace of the taboo is potentially consonant with industrial music's clandestine sensibilities. In the 1990s, a significant, less literal industrial encounter with death came in the form of the near convergence of gothic and industrial audiences and music.

Both as social scenes and aesthetic styles, the two had rubbed elbows since the early 1980s. The musics share a harmonic propensity for Aeolian and Phrygian modes and an instrumental default of the drum machine ("The Goth scene appropriated technological developments from an early stage," writes media studies professor Isabella van Elferen[20]). Aesthetically, there's also the inevitable categorization of both as "dark"; for example, both validate masochism as a critical experience, albeit for somewhat different reasons. Politically, it's true that goth's pro-androgyny expressive principles—and as some have argued, its brand of feminism—are of limited historical interest to industrial music, and likewise industrial music's militarized anarchy often comes across to goths as officious. But socially, it's hard to ignore the artistic friendships between, for example, KMFDM and goth rockers X-Mal Deutschland, or Al Jourgensen and goth empress Siouxsie Sioux, or ignore that Skinny Puppy's first performance was at an afterparty for an Alien Sex Fiend gig.

Part of what made the early 1990s a convergence point for these subcultures was that both had been effectively forced to stake out defensive cultural territory by the explosion of "alternative music" that was in full swing by the end of 1991, marked publicly by the establishment of a Grammy award for Best Alternative Music Album and iconically by the overnight success of grunge music like Nirvana and Pearl Jam. With "alternative music" now connoting by default a particular strain of college radio rock, goth and industrial bands—fantastical by nature—were misfits within an ascendant public taste for working-class authenticity, especially in America. Techno was in its own world by this point, and synthpop was a shrunken market. This consolidation and staking of subcultural territory brought to the surface those shared musical, visual, and social signs of goth and industrial practice. The scenes' potential differences with respect to gender and class were submerged as dance clubs increasingly specialized in crossover goth-industrial nights (often with respectively alternating DJs), purging the pop, techno, and the jangly alternative rock from their playlists little by little. Though some tension between hardline goths and industrialists quietly simmered, this communal state of affairs largely became the norm. A 1992 internet post in the alt.gothic Usenet group by Margaret Gates offers one perspective on the merge as it was happening:

> I have heard it argued that contemporary 'industrial' is the heir to the early-80s gothic cultural stream . . . and that current goth culture is more or less in the process of reclaiming that heritage, and in so doing absorbing part of the industrial stream. Tracing the roots of music is basically irrelevant and futile.[21]

Even if Gates's last claim here is plainly false, it nonetheless illustrates how entwined the histories of these genres are. They even became economically entwined in the early 1990s as record labels such as Cleopatra increasingly staked their credibility and financial success on audiences' free navigation between the subcultures.

Industrial music's mixing with goth gave rise to new musical possibilities and meanings, too. To illustrate, we'll consider a collaborative crossover whose particulars are unique but that ultimately uses a number of tropes common to goth-industrial music.

In the twelve years that followed their 1981 breakthrough *Stahlwerksymphonie*, Die Krupps reinvented themselves a few times, most recently as a heavy metal-tinged industrial outfit. Their 1993 album *II: The Final Option* was a massive hit with German teenagers, and so Rough Trade Records commissioned a collection of remixes with contributions from the likes of FM Einheit (of Einstürzende Neubauten), KMFDM, and Luc Van Acker.

Unlike most techno remix practices, industrial remixes nearly always emphasize and reframe a song's vocal; this is a simultaneous effect of techno and industrial club nights splitting off from one another in the early 1990s and of industrial music's increasingly songlike proclivities at the time. However, industrial practices do mirror techno and hip-hop in that remixes serve additionally to establish and publicly declare an artist's connections with other acts; by trading remixes with a bigger band, an act might insinuate itself into a higher caste within the scene. Indeed, Nine Inch Nails helped legitimize themselves to industrial insiders by recruiting Foetus, Ministry, and Coil for remixes, just as Die Krupps—older but less widely popular—aligned themselves with Reznor's gang by commissioning a mix from Nine Inch Nails' touring keyboardist Charlie Clouser and also by performing in Europe as the band's supporting act in 1994.

Track four on Die Krupps' resulting record, 1994's *The Final Remixes*, is a mix of "Fatherland" by Andrew Eldritch of the Sisters of Mercy, assisted by fellow Leeds native Rodney Orpheus of the early goth-EBM crossover act the Cassandra Complex. At this moment in subcultural history, Eldritch and the Sisters of Mercy held unrivaled goth cachet. Their version of goth rock, refined since the early 1980s, rejected the genre's typically watery, exotic musical textures in exchange for testosterone: instead of flange and echo effects drenching melodic guitars, they favored low, eighth-note power chord chugging over an incessantly unsyncopated kick-snare drum machine (which Eldritch named Doktor Avalanche). Their hits "This Corrosion" and "Lucretia, My Reflection" were (and still are) club classics. Eldritch channeled *Low*-era David Bowie with aviator shades and a vocal mumble that somehow bespoke singleminded hysteria and defeatist indifference at once. Ripping off the Sisters of Mercy's sound was the primary strategy for early-1990s male goth musicians who didn't look good in eyeliner. Given the time he'd spent pushing at the subculture's glass ceiling, it's no surprise that Eldritch fought loudly though futilely against genre classification, protesting that the Sisters weren't goth.

So by enlisting Eldritch to remix the decidedly masculine "Fatherland," Die Krupps recognized the subcultural value of the gothic-industrial crossover zeitgeist. Not only were they fans of the goth band's work—illustrating a latent kinship of musical genres—but the name and the sound of the Sisters of Mercy here served as a two-way signal whereby goth and industrial fans would find interest in one another's music. Most tellingly, the internal stylistic consonance of the "Fatherland" remix testifies that at least musically the genres were per- haps not so far apart as one might think—or at least that goth's inflections of the masculine and the epic overlapped with industrial music's new interest in melody and rockism. In either case, the popularity of this remix has endured, easily matching and probably exceeding Die Krupps' own original version.

In this track and in others, beyond merely revealing their compatibility, gothic and industrial elements come together to hint at a romantic transcen- dence within political ideology. A song lamenting the post-reunification rise of German neo-Nazi youth cultures, the original 1993 "Fatherland" is a lean dance number with a bubbling sixteenth-note synth bass and heavy metal guitar licks; singer Jürgen Engler's voice rides unambiguously atop the mix.

The 1994 remix commences with and repeatedly uses a sample of Senega- lese singer Baaba Maal, lifted from the 1988 film *The Last Temptation of Christ*. Maal's long, bellowed notes give both religious grandeur and a new sense of time's passage in the remix: over slow synth pads—halfway between choral and string sounds, thus amorphously epic—the religious chant carries the listener's attention for two measures at a time instead of the original version's most evi- dent divisions of quarter and sixteenth notes. The outright gothness of the remix peaks with the choir samples that Eldritch and Orpheus introduce in the chorus, more than a little reminiscent of the New York Choral Society's perfor- mance on the Sisters of Mercy's UK number seven single "This Corrosion." The overwhelming sense is of an organic, spiritual element superseding the drum machines and bass sequencer. In the overlaid hierarchies of time as demarcated by the song's rhythm and in the commingling of Engler's vocals with Maal's, this spirituality is one that embraces otherness, if imperfectly. Gothicized, "Father- land" is more than just words against Nazism's xenophobia; it's action, too.

The integrated goth-industrial sound (one of many styles called "darkwave") was also handy for tragedizing personal desire. It offered an inflection of long- ing that, in the meeting of the implicit male and female genderings of industrial and gothic music, suggests the abject male's entreaty to the angelic female. In the 1990s, programmer-plus-chanteuse acts L'Âme Immortelle (from Austria),

Kirlian Camera (from Italy), and Flesh Field (from the United States) all reiterated this pedestalization that otherwise pervaded the decade's self-deprecating indie rock. The gendered tragedizing of personal desire also translated into the particular goth-club emphasis on dancing alone, in which individual catharsis is theatrically performed as a mating call.

## 4. New Life

In light of the failed promise of success that at least temporarily swept up so many of the industrial scene's giants, the 1990s saw a rebirth of underground industrial music. Given that industrial music's wave of death-by-exposure had, in the scene's eyes, largely come at the hands of major labels, the role of new independent labels was a particularly important one, fostering an alternative to the poisonous ambitions of rockstardom.

A few underground labels championed the sneering, guitar-driven sounds that WaxTrax! and Ministry had pioneered—Re-Constriction Records and 21st Circuitry, for example. These Californian imprints attempted to brand their music with the subgenre moniker "coldwave," presumably unaware that the term had been used to describe French postpunk a decade earlier. Because this style was so close to what major labels were signing in hopes of scoring another Nine Inch Nails, the independent imprints risked being no more than proving grounds from which majors would snap up the most successful artists. Chicago's Slipdisc Records, for example, made a name for itself in the mid-1990s with industrial rock crossover bands such as 13 Mg., which led to its wholesale acquisition by Mercury/Polygram in 1998, which was then in turn bought up by Universal Music Group International.

Artists and labels in Europe saw the rat race of rock-based industrial and stepped in the opposite direction, by and large. Copenhagen's Hard Records, for instance, nurtured a lineup of Danish EBM acts such as Birmingham 6, who used modern synthesizers to make a shinier, faster, and more aggressive brand of dance music than their Belgian and German predecessors. Probably the day's most impressive stable of musicians belonged to Stefan Herwig's Off-Beat Records in Gelsenkirchen, Germany, not far from Dusseldorf. Off-Beat's lineup boasted Covenant, Haujobb, Suicide Commando, and the highly successful Project Pitchfork—bands who never really competed sonically or commercially with Ministry and Nine Inch Nails, but whose sound and image offered respite from the mid-1990s guitar craze. Haujobb, the project of East German–born Daniel Myer, was especially heralded as a cerebral, intricate alternative to the overtly bodily grime coming out of the States. Stefan Herwig's prescience is remarkable: the all-electronic sound that he fostered at Off-Beat starting in 1993 quickly became the initial blueprint for the Philadelphia-based Metropolis Records, whose synonymity with an all-electronic sound has since 1995 become positively dynastic.

Not all independent industrial labels created a trusted brand so easily. A cautionary tale is that of Los Angeles–based Cleopatra Records, who initially signed a handful of Californian acts, most of whom never escaped obscurity. Cleopatra managed to stay in business, however, by venturing outside its time and place, re-releasing hastily assembled editions of out-of-print albums by Psychic TV, Front Line Assembly, and Kraftwerk. They also served as American distribution for European bands, mostly from Zoth Ommog's roster. Their catalogue was made more eclectic by a deluge of goth rock signings, early punk reissues, and a glut of cheaply remastered space rock. Although some of Cleopatra's compilations were high-quality and sold well—the original *Industrial Revolution* set of 1992 remains a good introduction to the genre—the tactics they resorted to in order to create a name brand ultimately undermined their artistic integrity. Beyond the label's consistently trashy in-house cover art, they reduced themselves with a series of goth/industrial tribute albums throughout the second half of the 1990s, beginning reasonably enough with covers of the Cure, Depeche Mode, and Kraftwerk, and progressively venturing into embarrassing and utterly baffling territory, commissioning second-tier industrial acts to record the songs of AC/DC, Madonna, and Smashing Pumpkins. Cleopatra indeed became a go-to label, but for a product that eventually scared bands away from dealing with them. By the late 1990s, they had all but stopped signing new artists, not for lack of trying.

While industrial music was finding foothold in some new geographies (notably Mexico, Japan, and Russia), its online discourse was a particularly vibrant example of new life. Given the genre's fondness for cyberpunk themes, it's no surprise that the industrial community was internet-savvy long before the mid-1990s boom of the World Wide Web. The rec.music.industrial Usenet group, for example, organized and released a series of compilation CDs between 1992 and 1996 featuring its regular online contributors, including the bands Snog, Stromkern, Sphere Lazza, and Informatik—all acts who later achieved a measure of success in the scene at large.

The Usenet group was quickly filling the DIY roles left vacant by the decline of the tape scenes and by the pressure for zines to go glossy. Participants' conversations in 1996, for example, included a heated debate on the use of guitars, with headings like "GUITARS ARE DEAD," "HELLO THIS IS INDUSTRIAL, NOT GRUNGE ROCK!!!!!!" and the guitar apologist's response "Guitar Bashing (was: How to be cool in an 'industrial' interview)." Perpetually at stake in these online discussions was the nature of industrial music, the crowning of the best new and old artists, and the building of transcontinental friendships. The trading and recommending of music along with the public posting of DJs' playlists proved especially vital in giving bands exposure beyond local and regional audiences. Industrial music embraced its new virtuality with vehemence. Common was the situation of a band like THD, who hailed from Pennsylvania but whose first signing was with Hard Records in Copenhagen.

Beyond the internet, the middle and late 1990s reinforced the importance of danceclubs in popularizing industrial music. Bypassing the traditional model of building fan bases progressively from local to regional to national in scope, many bands throughout industrial music's history decided against playing live shows at all; it's neither physically practical nor performatively engaging to twiddle knobs onstage. Mechanical concerns over synth playback, live sound technicians' unfamiliarity with (or disdain for) electronic music, and the issue of whether to use taped backing tracks all made it hard for industrial music to play by the rock circuit's rules of authenticity. Plenty of acts managed to tour despite all this, but industrial music's marketing was channeled through taste-maker DJs and fans who negotiated small canons by region and subgenre through playlist construction and dancing.

This emphasis on the dancefloor reinforced industrial music's reinvention as a clean, electronic, European one. Frequently called electro-industrial at the time, the new music that Off-Beat and Hard Records peddled bore some self-conscious similarities to techno, which by the mid-1990s was the coolest music on the planet, the rave scene having danced into the limelight. EBM in the 1980s was characterized by crystalline timbres for melody instruments, oddly spatialized drum samples, and squonking FM bass sounds, but mid-1990s electro-industrial music by the likes of X Marks the Pedwalk, Haujobb, and Covenant was full of expansive analogue filter sweeps, muted echoing string pads, and vocoder effects.

To some, there was a nagging feeling that industrial, long assumed to be the self-evident vanguard of pop, had been surpassed not just in popularity but in experimentalism by techno— which was, after all, a largely instrumental genre that had, with the advent of jungle around 1994, managed to escape the pop treatment of the backbeat as prerequisite. Regardless of whether techno was cutting-edge, news magazines ran cover stories on it, and books were hastily assembled, offering supposed histories of electronic music that lacked any mention of industrial. The result within industrial music communities was a simultaneous chip on the shoulder and—whether out of genuine affection or in an attempt to capitalize—an intentional borrowing of techno sounds and gestures. Leætherstrip's 1997 pseudo-techno stomp "Kill a Raver" is representatively schizophrenic, indecisive about who its audience might be and whether they're supposed to dance, kill, or laugh.

Industrial music's shared sonic territory with techno in this era also owed to synthesizer manufacturers' tailoring their instruments for dance music to maximize sales. Industrial musicians bought these keyboards (certainly the most popular of the era was Roland's JP-8000 of early 1997) and when they used the machines' preset sounds, the washes and blips resembled the Prodigy more closely than Skinny Puppy. It is the sound of technology doing exactly what it was made to do; contrast this with early industrial music's intentional misuse of machines in search of the revelatory malfunction.

Beyond techno sounds becoming standard on keyboard presets and hence standard within industrial music, industrial itself was still enough of a buzzword that musical hardware and software makers developed tools to make it easier than ever to get certain aggressive sounds. For example, a pair of CD-ROM sound libraries for Akai samplers (released 1992 and 1994) was called *Dance Industrial.* If achieving the sound of banged scrap metal was as easy as loading a pre-made sample bank, then why go to all the trouble of finding, pounding, and recording an oildrum? The nativization, the taming, and ultimately the assimilation of once-transgressive musical practices into the entry-level consumer palette—editable and sequenceable—is almost certainly a reason behind industrial music's move in the 1990s away from technological misuse, found sound, improvisation, location-specific events, and urban provocation. A few astute musicians also worried that this shift silenced the little flaws of timing, the timbral changes from one percussive thwack to the next, and the musical spontaneity that flows from the body.

More than ever, the home studio became the location for industrial music making, as audio software such as StudioVision Pro (1994), SoundEdit 16 (1994), Cakewalk Pro Audio (1995), and FruityLoops (1997) hit the market and as dedicated digital recording machines became affordable. Recall that when Cabaret Voltaire set up shop in their own Western Works studio, they found themselves with enough time to tweak their sounds laboriously; the same effect applies here, with isolation, limitless time, and access to gear tailor-made for techno and industrial music leading to sonically cleaner, more detailed, mistake-free records. The increase from 1992 to 1997 in the audible fidelity and orchestrational complexity on industrial records can't be overstated, especially when it comes to independently recorded and released CDs. From album to album, bands such as Haujobb, Forma Tadre, and Gridlock unveiled a completely new cool sonic clarity, highlighting the aesthetic possibilities only just discovered in the digital era of home recording. In bedroom studios built out of hobbyists' desire to work more and pay less, the analogue grit of the WaxTrax!

sound was nearly impossible to recapture, but because sparse, single-synth timbres sounded immediately elegant, the songs that these bands made—Haujobb's
"Eye Over You" is a classic example—veered toward reverberant minimalism.
This music's breakbeat skittering of drums atop the surface of unchanging textures connoted an oceanic depth.

The dominant industrial sensibility that developed in the middle and late
1990s played up chic synthesizer mastery and ignored abjection. Was this un-
cluttered approach the confluence of death imagery, techno influence, and new
electronics? Was it a premeditated aesthetic shift? In any event, as the millennium neared, the genre's experience with death cycled through mourning and
gothicism, and as its tools revealed progressively more nuanced, home-designed
sounds that exchanged rage for meditation, rock 'n' roll swagger for European
flair, it was clear that, by chance or design, industrial music had begun to articulate new, subtle ideas—the stuff of wonder.

**ICONIC:**

Beborn Beton – "Another World" (1997)

Chemlab – "Codeine, Glue and You" (1992)

KMFDM – "Juke Joint Jezebel" (1995)

Project Pitchfork – "Alpha Omega" (1994)

X Marks the Pedwalk – "Facer" (1995)

**ARCANE:**

Gridlock – "From Zero" (1999)

La Floa Maldita – "Sorcière (Das Ich remix)" (1995)

Oneiroid Psychosis – "Box" (1996)

MindFluxFuneral – "Flesh" (1994)

Wumpscut – "Mother (Oral Staircase remix by Haujobb)" (1996)

# 18.
# Wonder

## 1. Covenant and the Ubiquitous Sublime

On January 13, 2000, Covenant released an exclusive European single of "Der Leiermann," a song that takes as its lyrics Wilhelm Müller's poem of the same name, most famous as the nihilistic closing text to Franz Schubert's 1827 song cycle *Winterreise*. Müller's poem concerns an old street musician who, as a wraith of the beleaguered narrator's bleak future, forever plays the same tune alone at the edge of a village, undying in an unchanging winter. In the context of Müller and Schubert's full cycle, "Der Leiermann" occupies the crushing moment at which death itself is revealed to be an insufficient escape from the narrator's terrible disillusionment, and where he instead resigns to fade into a numb, undreaming circularity. Both Schubert's and Covenant's settings of the poem are appropriately spare in their melody, but the harmony, rhythm, and timbral palette in Covenant's recording mismatches the stagnation in the text awkwardly.

"Der Leiermann" is built on an energetic quarter-note kick drum smash at 128 bpm, but although most electronic dance music fills its rhythmic space with eighth-note hi-hats, Covenant here subdivides the beat into three. Because the song never adopts a backbeat snare, we hear an intense phrasing where each kick drum pulse careens to the next with a suggestion of equal metric importance—a feeling emphasized by the handclap samples that eventually double the pounding. This, along with the song's consistent use of rhythmic triplets (as opposed to a two-step swing), differentiates it from the faux-blues shuffle of Skinny Puppy's 1989 "Hexonxonx" and from the menacing half-time arrangements of KMFDM's 1996 "Rules"—rare industrial digressions from squarely divided beats. Additionally, the triplet rhythms in Covenant's "Der Leiermann" skew slightly when we hear a delay effect on the lead synthesizer that doesn't quite fit into the song's metric grid. In short, the track achieves an airy yet forceful uncertainty that spins more than it swaggers. This is hardly revolutionary in pop, but within the industrial soundscape the opening moments of the song are undeniably fresh, befitting Covenant's Swedish minimalism, borne out by their black onstage business suits and white album covers.

The song's sense of the new and of the ever-emergent isn't merely rhythmic; undistorted synth timbres bubble in slower quarter-note triplets with filter sweeps that sonically distinguish each note's articulation from the previous, even on the same repeated F-sharp. The cadence that concludes the verses of "Der Leiermann" is the harmonic progression VI–VII–i, an Aeolian gesture that musicologist Philip Tagg suggests imparts not only dramatic flair[1] but also a signification of Northern European funeral music.[2] The alignment of Scandinavian industrial with funereality is no stretch: on the single "Call the Ships to Port" Covenant sings of Viking funerals, and fellow Swedish industrialist Roger Karmanik, founder of the noise label Cold Meat Industry, notes in an interview, "I love Christian funeral hymns."[3]

In Covenant's "Der Leiermann," Müller's text—dejected beyond suicide—fails in its intimate, eternally sad rot to resonate with the music's vibrant rhythms and grandiose harmonies. Significantly, however, Covenant released another song, "Like Tears in Rain," with identical instrumental parts but with a wholly new set of lyrics in English and a new distinct chorus melody, where previously the "Der Leiermann" refrain bore the same tune as its verses. "Like Tears in Rain" was initially a B-side to the single of "Der Leiermann," but in late February 2000 it was this English language take on the track that not only made the cut for their hugely popular *United States of Mind* album but was the record's opening song. Viewed as a commentary on their setting of "Der Leiermann"—or even a repositioning and correction of it—"Like Tears in Rain" is revelatory.

The lyrics to "Like Tears in Rain" capitalize on the song's clean brightness in a way that "Der Leiermann" does not. They do this with two significant poetic moves in juxtaposition.

First, the hopelessness in Müller's poem is so all-encompassing and bleak as to suggest that death, far from an escape, is meaninglessly undifferentiated from life: an eternally numb continuation of its misery. But Covenant's lead singer and sometime lyricist Eskil Simonsson repeatedly invokes death as forceful, totalizing, grandiose, and, as we'll shortly see, beautiful. In his chorus, featuring a new resolute melody with a syncopated hook, he sings, "Every man I ever knew, every woman I ever had is gone. Everything I ever touched, everything I ever had has died." The finality and the scope invoked here closely matches the harmony's epic flair. Tagg's likening of the "Aeolian pendulum" to the funeral music of Northern Europe finds apt consonance with Covenant's transformation of "Der Leiermann" into "Like Tears in Rain." The band was forging a new musical sensibility within industrial music, and through this public experiment they'd arrived on a lyrical sensibility to match, discovering and revealing what this new music was really about.

The second aspect crucial to "Like Tears in Rain" is in that aforementioned beauty—the way the song exchanges all its overstated loss and death for wonder and transformation. In light of the subject matter of "Der Leiermann," it's a funny twist of fate that among industrial music's only rhythmic predecessors to Covenant's quasi 3/8 rhythm is Wumpscut's tortured and swampy 1995 "Die in Winter," but there's a suggestion in the electronic bounce of "Like Tears in Rain" that instead of freezing to unchanging stillness, death here is a progression and a lens through which to revel in life: it is the moment at which beauty is shown to have been always present. This suggestion is voiced in the two verses' lyrics (we'll get to them in a moment) and is effectively understood through the heuristic of the song's title, which is itself never uttered in the recording.

Cyberpunk fans will immediately recognize the title "Like Tears in Rain" from the end of the genre-defining movie *Blade Runner*.✿ At the film's climax, the "replicant" android villain Roy Batty, suddenly aware that his predetermined lifespan is about to expire, opts to save the life of protagonist policeman Rick Deckard, whom only moments earlier he was trying to kill. Exhausted and mutually beaten, the two then sit atop a gothic skyscraper in a futuristic Los Angeles, pounded by a torrent of rain. Batty, fighting the throes of his inevitable death, holds a dove in his hand and speaks softly with a strange and wizened acceptance to his nemesis: "I've seen things you people wouldn't believe. Attack ships on fire off the shoulder of Orion. I watched c-beams glitter in the dark near the Tannhauser Gate. All those moments will be lost in time. Like tears in rain. Time to die."[4] Batty, played by Rutger Hauer, crumples and dies to the sound of a funeral drum, releasing the dove to fly into the blueness that only now begins to peer through the rainclouds. The major chords that Vangelis scores over the scene (framed aptly in an Aeolian mode) solidify Batty's redemption. His death makes meaningful all the wonders he has seen, but beyond that, the wonders themselves highlight the smallness of his life and his experience amidst their grandeur and perpetuity. On the screen, the sunlight that follows his death asks how meaningful life could really be in a finite world, or the underbelly of that question: How meaningful is the infinite possibility of experience without death? Death affirms the sublime nature of perception, the truth that our living minds and bodies are insufficient to withstand the world's present and full magnitude.

With this in mind, it's very easy to see just how, rather than reinforcing a mournful reading of the chorus, Simonsson's verses frame their loss and death as a gateway to beholding beauty:

✿ Covenant's *Blade Runner* reference here is nothing new; the first song they ever released was 1992's "Replicant," with its chorus "'Cause I am the replicant. To hell with the gods. The rain, always the rain."

Go to the Empire State and watch the city lights
Hear the noise of millions struggle in the sprawl
Stare into the sky, we're few and far between
Black eyes full of stars, wide with memories

. . .

Lie down in the park and watch the satellites
Hear the children sing just a breath away
Dance in the heavy air along the interstate
Black lung full of fumes, choke on memories

Though Covenant's music of this era typically walks a tuneful line between latter-day EBM and synthpop with an occasional excursion into analogue minimalism, their lyrics and public presentation sustain a fascination with the sublime. This reading of "Like Tears In Rain" is completely congruous alongside the rest of *United States of Mind*. In the song "Humility," Covenant is a notch less subtle: "Behold the beauty that surrounds us. . . . Turn your gaze towards the moon, even further if you dare."

The reason for this extended look at Covenant's song is that it typifies a postmillennial approach to the sublime in industrial music. The sublime exposes the limits of one's perception by markedly exceeding them. Classically, the human response to the sublime is a blend of awe and terror. The discussion here isn't whether listening to this music actually produces sublime experiences; such encounters likely depend more on the listener than on the music. Instead, the point here is that the sublime as a topic is an important one to industrial music; as an act of revealing heretofore unknown limits by exceeding them, we might understand it as dérive, or even as shock, and certainly as part of the industrial legacy.

Recall the genre's use of abjection and the gothic—qualities that break down the distinction between the inside and outside of bodies, spaces, and musical forms; examples include Skinny Puppy's fascination with slasher films and vivisection, Coil's "The Anal Staircase," and the genre's ubiquitous themes of the cybernetically enhanced body. Metaphorically speaking, this music forces open the body, exceeding the capacity of flesh to contain itself. This is also the musical impact of distortion, in which a sound's amplitude exceeds its medium's capacity to contain it. The sublime here is first, then, physical—even physiological. It's also rational, though, because not only is the body directly interrupted; this interruption makes it *irreconcilable*. (The irreconcilability is additionally part of a listener's supposed experience of unpredictable noise, as this book's postscript will discuss.) In the end, industrial music's traditional approach to a scorched earth sublime came by way of ugly disorder and irrational noise, or to use two of Jon Savage's characteristics of industrial music, shock tactics and "anti-music."

What Covenant attempts to enact circa 2000 is a sublime built on wonder, rather than abjection. They invite us to move past our own insignificance by embracing it, rather than recoiling from it. While their music may not particularly reach the heights to which the band conceptually aspires, it reinforces the lyrics' call to "feel the rhythm of time" and "be happy that you're alive." In their blend of hissing machine noise loops and lush, folkish harmonies, Covenant suggests that what we perceive as a tension between ugliness and beauty is only paradoxical because we are incapable of understanding their real relationship— certainly not binary. As noise theorist Joanna Demers writes, in musical moments of this sort, there resides "a pleasure that does not conform to Kantian standards of balance and semblance but nonetheless aspires to the condition of beauty. The sublime and the beautiful are thus not so much opposites as they are different destinations along the same trajectory."[5]

## 2. Apoptygma Berzerk and the Spontaneous Sublime

Covenant is only one of the many acts in a new wave of industrial around the turn of the millennium to take this approach. The same week that *United States of Mind* came out, Norwegian act Apoptygma Berzerk released their important album *Welcome to Earth*. For the previous ten years, the group had been putting out a goth-tinged brand of above-average dance industrial music; their early hits "Deep Red" and "Love Never Dies" narrated sadomasochistic bloodplay and sampled *Carmina Burana*, respectively—pretty standard stuff. *Welcome to Earth* was a marked change for the band, however. Aside from a cover of Metallica's "Fade to Black," Apoptygma Berzerk in 2000 jettisoned their goth murkiness in exchange for a focus on melody amidst Scandinavian tidiness. Hinting at the utopian social politics of rave, Apoptygma Berzerk uses "Hoover" synth chords and subtly swing their hi-hat timing to connote trance and house music. Here the lyrics again gesture unambiguously toward sublime wonder. Atop another Aeolian chorus progression nearly identical to Covenant's,✿ the album's first single, "Eclipse," declares:

> One day we'll awake by a bright light on the horizon
> In one second every eye will see the same
> And this blinding light will draw all our attention

✿ Instead of using Covenant's VI–VII–i, Apoptygma Berzerk uses VI–v⁷–i, which is the same upper-voice harmony but substitutes the dominant in the bass on the second chord.

Some day we'll catch a glimpse of eternity
As the world stands still for a moment
For the very first time and it's meant to be
We'll forget about ourselves and share the moment

Here, the wondrous sublime suddenly reveals itself, and "we" in turn reveal it in "our" actions: we forget about ourselves, unable to remain central in our own world—this, after only a glimpse of a light brighter than our eyes can withstand (blinding) and more enduring than our numbers can express (eternal).

*Welcome To Earth* dresses this sudden revelation of wonder as an alien landing. The album art features stylized crop circles, but perhaps more tellingly, the cover of the 1999 "Eclipse" single is the famous "I WANT TO BELIEVE" poster from *The X-Files* television show, which along with the Y2K computer virus scare was the west's the most culturally iconic reflection of pre-millennium tension. Sampled, referenced, and otherwise beloved by industrial acts in the late 1990s, *The X-Files* channeled into alien fascination the hope and fear of the future's arrival. Reversing this rubric, we might see then that *Welcome To Earth*, which was written and recorded in 1999, is less about science fiction and more about the potential of the future—in the form of the millennium—to solve our problems. The lyrics to the song "Starsign" make this clear.

I'm living on nerves last days of ninety-nine
Nightmare, conspiracy, depression, and lunacy
I need to feel more love inside
Locked up, messed up, maybe there is no tomorrow

Of course the turn of the millennium didn't solve much of anything, and despite all his hope, Apoptygma Berzerk frontman Stephan Groth aggressively turned away from industrial music to make pop after 2000, an apocalypse preacher searching for a new congregation after getting the date wrong. Despite this, *Welcome To Earth* (arguably alongside Haujobb's *Ninety-Nine* from the previous year) is a rare futurological moment of optimism in industrial music.

### 3. VNV Nation and the Unthinkable Sublime

Less than three months after Covenant and Apoptygma Berzerk's records dropped, Irish act VNV Nation released *Empires*, the final album of this triumvirate that would refocus industrial music on a synthpop-infused sound dubbed "futurepop" by VNV's Ronan Harris and Apoptygma Berzerk's Stephan

Groth.[6] Like the other two albums, *Empires* boasts a collection of tracks that are neither constructions nor processes but genuinely songs, with clear, singable vocal melodies and distinct harmonic progressions that largely delineate verse from chorus.

Sonically, *Empires* is less detailed and bright than its futurepop contemporaries; stereo imaging is minimal, drums are low in the mix, hi-hats are steambursts of dull noise, and the mixing pits Harris's quiet, husky vocals in the same frequency range as the synths' ever-lingering faux strings. The sense of sameness across the recording extends beyond the sonic and into a peculiar consistency of melody, harmony, tempo, and timbre from song to song.

Because the club dancefloor was industrial music's prime advertising space in 2000, bands were largely evaluated on the strength of singles. As an album, though, *Empires* took a surprising hold of the industrial scene: whereas tracks like "Standing" and "Kingdom" were club hits, the record was embraced and consumed as a unified entity. Other bands of the day aped VNV Nation's moody gothicism and muted trance techno borrowings, but beyond those superficial qualities, what makes *Empires* so compelling is the way its aesthetic unity interacts with its lyrical theme to expose the human limitations that the sublime exceeds.

The central plot of *Empires*, and pretty much of VNV Nation's entire oeuvre, is that of a solitary warrior fighting against unnamed, faceless, barbaric hoards. In an interview, lead singer Ronan Harris explains that it's "the battle for the control for one's own soul and destiny," though he expresses this lyrically as a quest against all odds to reclaim a paradise long lost—if indeed it ever existed.[7] It bears some readily apparent similarities to Kristeva's idea that we are unrecoverably severed from a perfect womblike state as a precondition of existence—a state to which we forever strive in vain to return.

The lack of vocal harmony on *Empires*, its dulled sonic palette, and the singlemindedness of composition don't distract from the image of a lone, fearless hero in a battlefield trench; they actually contribute to it. In the song "Darkangel," lines like "I'm in this mood because of scorn, I'm in a mood for total war" may appear to veer close to the anger and "Total War" of NON's music; in both, battle metaphorically depicts a struggle to assert one's individuality, but for the leftist Harris there's a world of difference.

First, the hero's fight in VNV Nation is to a large degree on behalf of the helpless; "Darkangel" continues, "Given time you'll understand what possesses me to right what you have suffered." To Harris, battle is the tragic but necessary path to an enlightenment whose merest glimpse would awaken the sleeping to wisdom. In NON's war, combat is its own thrill, and anyone not fighting (and winning) is complicit with the enemy—a waste of space.

ASSIMILATE

Second, and much more importantly, Harris's lyrics paint him as knowingly overconfident despite being insanely outnumbered; when combined with his humble production choices, it's too much to take at face value. The tragedy underlying VNV Nation's music is that the battle is a losing one. The hero doesn't stand a chance. Cinematically, he assures us (and himself) otherwise, but what choice does he have? Paradise can come only after the battle is won, and so whatever the odds, it's the only fight worth fighting. This perspective is revealed in the obsessively unchanging thematics of the band's other albums, whose titles include *Advance and Follow*, *Praise the Fallen*, and *Of Faith, Power and Glory*.

VNV Nation is perpetually stuck at the point of conflict, not because, like NON, VNV Nation glorifies violence or asserts dominance but because victory is such a distant hope that the music literally can't yet conceive of what the ensuing brave new world would even look like. The chorus of "Kingdom" sings of the heaven beyond battle, but the lyrics can couch it in only the haziest, most provisional way: "I believe that we'll conceive to make in Hell for us a heaven." To Harris, Heaven isn't here, and it's not coming on its own; the best that can be mustered is his belief in a collective future plan to build *a* heaven, despite the very real presence of *the* Hell. It's a fact of the lyric that an awful lot of words separate "I" and "heaven." VNV stands for "Victory, Not Vengeance," but instead of eyeing victory itself the band holds fast to the *idea of victory*—it's the closest they'll ever get. The gap between present war and future paradise is so pronounced here that, much to the credit of all involved, fans nearly universally understand VNV Nation's music as one of longing and peace.

Covenant suggests that a sublime paradise beyond life and death is already around us. Apoptygma Berzerk sees its glow in the future beyond the horizon. We cannot grasp the sublime by definition, but in VNV Nation's ethics, we—or at least the solitary "I"—must die trying. VNV Nation's sense that their efforts are simultaneously necessary and futile is closely in line with the information war of the old industrialists. As is, for that matter, the band's military imagery and garb—fascinations shared by neither Apoptygma Berzerk nor Covenant.

Futurepop is about yearning for wonder. Like nearly every previous incarnation of industrial music, it calls for an end to the invisible oppression that radiates from all authority structures. However, instead of invoking the abject sublime to glitch audiences into confronting their own assumptions about reason, power, and propriety, futurepop seeks to give audiences a glimpse of the wondrous sublime entailed by a life free from these quietly tyrannical assumptions. It focuses on that which lies beyond the battle, rather than on the ostensible enemy. It is victory, not vengeance.

Or so goes one line of thinking.

## 4. The Futurepop Backlash

Despite—or more likely, because of—futurepop's sudden and visible popularity within the global industrial scene, it was subject to harsh criticism in the early and mid-2000s. A musician in the subgenre himself, Tom Shear of U.S.-based act Assemblage 23 is quick to categorize it as "mostly people who can't sing, over 90s-era trance patches."[8] But criticisms of musicians' ability and genre borrowings mostly served to mask a deeper suspicion about futurepop. Its preponderance of melody and its avoidance of the abject both painted the subgenre's unspeakable wondrous sublime as awfully Christian. Indeed, early interviewers of Stephan Groth frequently probed him about his Christianity, and VNV Nation does little to shake the question when in the single "Genesis" they declare, "With you I stand in hope that God will save us from ourselves."

At almost every turn, industrial music is hostile to religion in general, and to Christianity in particular, viewing especially its organized forms as a control machine with a long historical and modern record of oppression; industrial music's anti-Christian discography is of nearly incalculable size. A few thematically Christian acts had managed to gain acceptance within industrial music over time—notably Blackhouse (active since 1984) and Mentallo & the Fixer (active since 1992)—but they were perennially underground groups who made challenging, sprawling albums of noisy strangeness. Futurepop, on the other hand, was easy to listen to, and with sales of at least fifty thousand apiece the breakthrough albums of 2000 were popular to the point of ubiquity within the scene. To those concerned with industrial music's impetus to escape musical, religious, and corporate dominance, futurepop's tunefulness, reverence, and popularity represented a major step backwards, and perhaps even embodied hegemony itself.

Related to this backlash was the gravitation of some industrial fans and musicians toward harsher styles. Though futurepop was a dominant strain within industrial music, acts such as Converter, Noisex, and Hypnoskull developed a sound they dubbed "powernoise," based on looped patterns of alternating noise timbres—pinching and abrasive—over a heavily distorted kick drum pulse. Largely instrumental and dance-oriented, powernoise was differentiated from techno styles on a structural level by its frequent absence of both harmonic content and timekeeping hi-hats. Powernoise is often more syncopated rhythmically than futurepop and EBM-derived styles, but this syncopation's pleasure is grooveless and cerebral. In the intros and breakdowns of songs like Winterkälte's 2001 "Green War Theme Three," there is a willful challenge issued to dancers: find the downbeat, if you can. This is what techno scholar Mark Butler calls "turning the beat around," but instead of playfully reframing rhythms, powernoise seeks first to disorient and then sternly to correct; it acts as provocateur, judge, and jailor.

On a broader aesthetic level, powernoise revels in sheer timbral ugliness and is a concentrated return after the 1990s to the aesthetics of the machine, replacing grungy guitars and EBM's futuristic computer blips with the mechanical roar of 1980s power electronics, now given hi-fi brightness and quantized to a beat in hopes of melding industrial music's old sense of formless dread with a rearticulation of rhythm's fascist undertones. Though powernoise predates futurepop (it was coined in 1997 by Noisex's Raoul Roucka), the redoubling of its club presence circa 2000 is best understood as an attempt by both musicians and DJs—typically connoisseurs and amateur historians of the genre—to reclaim an aesthetic of negation for industrial music.

If powernoise and futurepop staked out the poles of industrial dance music, then most of the post-2000 fare occupies the space between them. "Terror EBM" is one phrase that emerged to describe the new blend of harmonic simplicity, melodic synth riffs, harsh syncopated beats, and screamed distorted vocals, too angry to care about beholding wonder. Various inflections exist within this range, from artists influenced by Berlin minimal house music to mopey darkwave bands.

## 5. Clubbed to Death

In this era, it grew even more important that bands land club hits in order to sell records and concert tickets. This happened for a few reasons. The internet's rapid growth after 2000 helped put the industrial zine circuit largely out of business, but the websites that sought to replace the independent publications came, went, and were abandoned without warning. Thus advertising and interviews held less sway than they once did. The availability of CD burners and portable mp3 players also meant not only that music piracy was a growing concern but that fewer fans were listening to the already limited number of industrial-friendly radio shows—where DJs could play slower and newer music without the pressure to make people dance. The upshot was that artists started packing albums with 130 bpm dance songs, hoping that one would catch on; many releases of this sort don't hold up well to extended listening. And if a musician wasn't interested in making dance tracks and didn't want to appease DJs with a remix album—an increasingly common gimmick—then she or he simply risked oblivion. As such, the already appreciable divide within industrial music between dance styles and ambient, martial, noise, and found sound grew only wider after the 1990s.

This is a shame, because the esoteric corners of industrial music have made important advances and initiated productive artistic and political dialogues.

The arcane, magical sensibility of early industrial music's offshoot neofolk genre managed, after a twenty-year incubation, to find relatively hip exponents with the likes of Antony and the Johnsons, Devendra Banhart, and Joanna Newsom. Einstürzende Neubauten made a string of breathtaking albums beginning with 2000's *Silence Is Sexy*, and their family-friendly imitators Blue Man Group became a worldwide yuppie phenomenon. High-concept noise artists such as Matmos were churning out remarkable records under the spiritual influence of Throbbing Gristle, but none of this was even a blip on the radar for clubgoers.

In the midst of the wider culture's post-2000 retromania, hipster acts such as Cold Cave, Flux Information Sciences, the Knife, and the Horrorist lifted gestures of vintage industrial music, but they treated it as little more than yet another 1980s artifact to reframe. These acts felt affection for vintage Nitzer Ebb and Einstürzende Neubauten but were completely uninterested in the industrial scene's post-1989 family tree. They also embraced the idea that music could be fun—a notion almost completely missing from industrial attitudes, Tim Burton-esque carnival aesthetics aside.

The industrial community's rejection of all this music also had to do with branding: neither these acts nor the quieter, thinkier stuff were on EBM mega-labels Dependent Records or Metropolis, but instead they share imprints with techno DJs, alt. rockers, indie rappers, and electroclash bands—musicians from styles that were surpassing industrial music in coolness at that cultural moment. New acts would need baritone singers, songs about pain, and a lot of black clothes if they wanted to break into the industrial club scene, and given its insularity and apparent sales cap, many found themselves rhetorically asking, "Why bother?"

## 6. The Longevity of Industrial Bands

It's no surprise, then, that many of the musicians who've found success within the industrial scene since 2000—including Covenant, VNV Nation, and Apop-tygma Berzerk—have been veteran acts formed before the millennium. It's a rehashing of 1980s acts finding the widest audiences during the industrial gold rush of the 1990s. As a rule, industrial bands are long-lived. It might be nice to suppose that this has something to do with an unshakeable dedication to an ideological mission, but in many cases it makes less sense to call it persistence than failure to break up: the life of an industrial band, especially today, is one of minimal volatility.

For starters, there's the fact that a huge number of industrial acts are essentially solo projects. The physical and conceptual space of an electronic studio doesn't suggest collaboration: sequencers obsolesce live performance, and industrial music's focus on the materiality of technology and recording media gives musicians little impetus to emphasize live playing of any kind. Thus Nine Inch Nails is Trent Reznor. Android Lust is Shikhee D'iordna. Suicide Commando is Johan von Roy. Friends and hired musicians might contribute and help out in concert—sometimes if only to fill the stage with the illusion of a "band"—but the key arithmetic equation of interpersonal relations here is that with fewer members involved, there are fewer reasons for a band to break up. Artists do sometimes take breaks; for example, Claus Larsen's solo endeavor Leæther Strip was on hiatus from 1997 to 2006. But if the itch to make and share music returns, then a musician's choice is either to start all over again or to revive the brand, reclaiming its built-in fan base with minimal effort.

Because music is so central to identity in subcultures like the modern gothic-industrial scene, fans are unlikely to cast off their old records when they buy new ones. Goth club playlists in particular are endlessly nostalgic reinscriptions of identity, and sociologist Paul Hodkinson has noted that fans of gothic and industrial music tend to remain socially and sartorially involved in the subculture deep into their thirties and beyond. Thus it's no surprise that veteran industrial musicians periodically exhume their projects and take the stage at subcultural festivals. In 2010 and 2011, Leipzig's humongous Wave Gotik Treffen event featured performances by Clock DVA, Nurse With Wound, Leæther Strip, Kirlian Camera, Attrition, the Bollock Brothers, Lustmord, Deine Lakaien, and Front 242—all bands founded before 1985. The sense of history and myth is deep. For some in the scene, the ostensibly totalizing mission of industrial music suggests that these bands of the past still have something to say about the future: artists and fans use one another to hang on to a rebellious, hopeful youth. In turn, bands such as Einstürzende Neubauten, KMFDM, and Nine Inch Nails have launched particularly inventive fan-rewarding initiatives in hopes of attracting and retaining lifetime supporters.

At its heart, the choice of whether an industrial band calls it a day is one born of a certain privilege. Whether sales are a thousand units per album or ten thousand, it is and has always been nearly impossible to earn a full-time living from industrial music, and so at any time in the genre's history all but the most wildly popular, the most grant-subsidized, or the most independently wealthy artists have held day jobs.✿ The economic result is a normalizing one: industrial musicians almost never stake their livelihood on their band's success, and

---

✿ A remarkable number of industrial musicians have been teachers, professors, and academics, including members of Attrition, Controlled Bleeding, Stromkern, Clock DVA, Front 242, Seabound, the Cassandra Complex, Revolting Cocks, Razed in Black, and Cabaret Voltaire.

those musicians with traditional careers—seemingly more numerous as time goes by—similarly seldom compromise professional achievement for the sake of their art.

In a strange conflict with the music's oft-perceived sense of danger, there seems to be remarkably less personal risk taking among modern industrial bands than once there was. For example, heroin claimed the lives of a handful of important artists in the 1990s but is completely absent from the backstage area today.

## 7. Industrial Music Is Dead?

Despite the industrial scene's enduring institutions, there are persistent whispers among promoters, DJs, fans, bands, and labels that the social cachet, political relevance, artistic creativity, and subcultural vibrance of industrial music are not what they once were. Front Line Assembly's Rhys Fulber says the scene is now "akin to a comic book convention."[9] How seriously should we take him? Or the 2011 Sideline.com thread in which "Cyberium" declares, "Industrial is dead. . . . If the big name industrial bands had half the skill of these dubstep house guys we'd be in business"?[10] More seriously than the 1998 CD *Industrial Music Is Dead* by Polish EBM act Aggressiva 69? Or Jason Hanley's dissertation claim that between 1989 and 1996 John Fryer—producer of Nine Inch Nails, Moev, Die Krupps, and Stabbing Westwards—"ruined industrial music"?[11] Or the 1992 interview in which Bill Leeb declares, "Industrial music really was 8–10 years ago"?[12] Or for that matter Jon Savage's 1983 assertion that "'industrial' is now obsolete and useless"?[13]

On one hand, it's easy to dismiss these claims as perennial, a harmless noise in the system's works. However, as this book's preceding pages illustrate, 2011, 1998, 1992, and 1983 were all very different moments for industrial music. Between these moments, the ebb and flow of technology, politics, and subculture shape the music and its meaning in more dimensions than a simple rise-and-fall narrative can reveal; indeed, despite these repeated and grave pronouncements of industrial music's death, there's still a thing that people do called industrial music. To consider these recurrent concerns over industrial music's supposed death, one first needs to understand what the genre has been and what it has the potential to be.

This book's previous pages have presented a timeline of industrial events. As a history, we'll stop here; the present enforces its arbitrary law. But a few thoughts are worth reflecting on still, and the remaining pages offer a deeper interpretation of the genre's values and materials—an interpretation that directly addresses the questions of death, life, politics, and industrial music's legacy and future.

**ICONIC:**

Apoptygma Berzerk – "Kathy's Song (Come Lie Next To Me)" (2000)

Combichrist – "Get Your Body Beat" (2006)

Covenant – "Brave New World (Radio Version)" (2006)

Haujobb – "Grounds"/"Overflow"/"Doubleyou" (1999)

VNV Nation – "Solitary" (1999)

**ARCANE:**

Chrysalide – "I Do Not Divert Eyes" (2012)

Coil – "Batwings (A Limnal Hymn)" (2000)

I, Parasite – "Thirst" (2003)

Index AI – "Aerial Fossils" (2009)

Whitehouse – "Wriggle Like a Fucking Eel" (2003)

# Suture: From the Author's Diary

*May 13, 2011: My flight to London jetlagged me into a stupor, and now after four concerts already this evening, I walk dazed to the Roundhouse Studio Theatre. The room is hot and full of people in black, mostly German, here to see Carter-Tutti play. I go to the back of the room, where a pearl-haired girl is sitting in the only chair in sight. She indicates no intention to give up her seat, so I slouch against an eight-foot stack of disused folded tables at the back of the room. My feet hurt; I am still breaking these boots in. Chris Carter and Cosey Fanni Tutti are already on the darkened stage, along with the wiry Nik Void, whose huge drape of bangs covers her face. The three casually tool with their instruments while the mixing engineer speaks to them through his talkback mic, helping them to sound-check over the noise of the DJ's downtempo beat. Leaning back, I close my eyes, and my breathing slows. Sleep, almost.*

*After a minute or two, I hear the bass-heavy pre-show music recede, and the chattering around me sails into excited cheering. The band is ready to play. I open my eyes for a moment, but the shock of suddenly finding myself in physical space is repulsive—knowing the closeness of the crowd around me, the mean look the blonde's boyfriend gives me, the sheer not-infinity of this blackbox theater. The stage is now red as the band acknowledges the audience, and I close my eyes again, returning to the void, a quenching, zero gravity seduction of my fatigue's slow hunger.*

*A sharp, tight bass drum begins pounding in clockwork. Through the room's giant speakers, the sound blooms cavernous with every beat's attack, twice per second, hitting me in the chest first, then rumbling in decay down my hips and legs. A moment later Cosey and Nik begin scraping their guitars, filtered through Chris's harmonizers, ring modulators, and effects boxes. It is the sound of metal gouging metal, a scream that suggests the resonating of both source and filter, sawblades mutilating themselves against one another. And it is* loud; *recordings are mastered to ensure that no sound leaps out so aggressively, but the band is playing these noises live, impossibly painting the bass drum's already oppressive pulse as background to a clatter of extreme malfunction. The grinding is filtered so it locks to the beat's grid, echoes right to left, and excites an orgy of aching mechanical groans in antiphon. This is dub music's language, spoken with a mouthful of broken glass, I think to myself.*

But thinking is hard when music plays so loud and pervades my body so deeply, when I am already in a black, internal space, sleepy chemicals filling my brain and limbs. At this volume, when a bass frequency hits, its widening sine wave is amplified into squareness by the limits of mixing boards, subwoofers, and the human ear. It silences everything else, not just at the purely acoustic level, but in my head too. The sound drowns me over and over, and in the instant between the beats, I gasp for clarity, my head just above water, defenselessly receptive. Storm gods loom. High frequencies at this volume do something else. Either in some instinctive attempt to mimic the music's steely squealing and its sonic pre-conditions with my own body, or through an ancestral cochlear fight-or-flight response to danger, I cringe, tightening my face, clenching my teeth. Automatically I jerk my head away from the song's fiery birthing. I respond this way again and again, always a split second after each fricative machine growl. Half dreaming now and forced into pure response, I regress. The animal brain writhes sensuously in its own mere selfness.

I am at the edge of a pleasure rarely visited. The possibility of ecstasy—being out of myself—is nearly always either novel enough to marvel at (a strictly front-of-brain act) or strange enough to scare me back into my body. Dimly aware of this in my sleep-deprived trance, I raise my arms above my head and hang onto the edge of the top table in the stack behind me, my knees now about to buckle, my eyes still closed.

I will let go. Submit. Abject.

This choice is my last conscious act before I slip under.

My legs stomp, collapse, and wriggle to the pounding beat. My head and face twist at the high noise, now slamming in repetitive white-hot overexposure. When the screeching and the throbbing drums line up just right, I twitch harder, my head banging the tables behind me. It feels good so I do it more. Harder. I don't know if I'm awake. I don't know how many songs the band has played. I am an electrified thing, gnashing in spasm but not self-destructive, because there is in this moment no self to destroy. I am making noise now, resonating with the music, its collateral damage. Sex noises and fuck words. At some point my legs give way again and I am slumped, hanging from my hands, my wrists together. Not more than a dreaming body, I shake my head back and forth fast. I am drooling. There is no time.

Until the music stops, and amid the clapping I hear from everywhere, something touches me. I awake, a terrible reminder of where I am. It's only the blonde girl's boyfriend accidentally nudging me as he applauds, but that's all it takes to rip me back. Surfacing, I adjust my stance, fix my hair, and remind myself to clap for the band, whose set is finished. It's what one does in the social world of ugly buildings and plastic beer cups and other people.

　　　　　　　　　　　　　　　　　**ASSIMILATE**

# Postscript:
# Is There Any Escape for Noise?

## 1. Unpalatable Truths

Chapter 18 concluded by noting the recurring worry over industrial music's alleged demise—an accusation that in popspeak means not just that fewer people are producing and listening to the genre but that it's "irrelevant" to culture at large, incapable of meaningfully commenting on or changing people's shared experiences. Wholly biased by a personal affection for industrial music, this postscript attempts to frame the book in your hands as a musical reinvigoration rather than a eulogy. To do this effectively, we'll ask some big questions about noise, perception, and politics, reconciling industrial music's past and future with these reports of its death.

In the December 2010 issue of *The Wire*, editor Chris Bohn complains that "Most debates raised by [industrial] music still stall at its purportedly controversial nature. . . . The first generation claimed to be fighting an information war. Well that war's over, the underground lost, and it's high time nth-generation Noise and Industrial artists worked out new strategies for telling unpalatable truths."[1] Chris Bohn knows a thing or two about industrial music, having written in *New Musical Express* and *Melody Maker* about the genre since its early days. In 1987, under the name Biba Kopf, he was among the first writers to explore abjection as central to industrial music, and in 2012 he penned the foreword to a book about Test Dept. His 2010 claims ought to give us pause because we can easily see why they might be true: it's laughable to suppose that a band from the modern industrial scene could ignite the kind of public fury that Throbbing Gristle or Laibach once did, or that critics from across culture would lionize them as they had Einstürzende Neubauten, or that they might outsell Nine Inch Nails' *The Downward Spiral*. As *The Wire* and a generation of hip journalists celebrate new variations on darkness and noise in hauntology, witchhouse, dubstep, and whatever comes next, one is compelled to ask if the legacy of industrial music's past is all it can offer to the future.

Pointedly reassessing industrial music's goals will go a long way toward answering this question. If the music and its community have no investment beyond repeated and self-perpetuating pleasure in an unchanging aesthetic devoid of a shared larger politic, then we might as well reduce our discussion to musical formalism and social bookkeeping. But unless the preceding three hundred pages and the countless interviews, performances, and histories they dissect are completely misguided, then granting a consciously political dimension to the music's creation and consumption is an easy step.

Music is made by people whose motivations and goals differ individually, and in the industrial community there's of course a concern for sonic, bodily, and social pleasure, but taken broadly, the genre's revolutionary posturing calls the question: Does industrial music aim primarily to stake out the icy antipode conceptually furthest from complicity, tradition, and beauty, planting its flag atop that noisiest summit climbed simply Because It Is There, or does it seek the tangible, real-world dismantling of tyranny?

## 2. Noise as Noise

Within industrial music, a recurring tendency that we've mentioned previously is its nonspecific ambiguity. Whether we're talking about its attitudes toward technology or its politics, the open-endedness of the music consistently empowers (or burdens) listeners with its interpretation. This is strong evidence for the first of the goals just posited: the annunciation of extremes for their own sake, without regard to their specific practical implementation. One of the important ways that the genre offers up simultaneous extremism and ambiguity is through its pervasive use of noise.

Noise is sonically an extreme: pure white noise cannot get any noisier, and any signal amplified enough takes on qualities of noise. Noise is also shorthand in legal and engineering situations for any unwanted sound or data. Its extremeness and ugly undesirability makes it especially appealing to industrial artists and fans, and because noise is allegedly perceived as primeval, contentless, and random, these people can easily plug their own meanings into it. Noise is a wild card for bold metaphors, and it's so ubiquitous within industrial music as to be nearly synonymous with the genre. This one of the many ways industrial music lays claim to extremity itself.

If industrial music's goal is to stake out extremes, then it's important that noise remain noise, both as a metaphor and as a perceived sound, resisting assimilation into order, beauty, and "music." *Noise as music* gains access to cultural and economic legitimacy, fosters traditions and tropes, and can aspire to pleasure as a primary aim, but in exchange it forswears a certain absoluteness of autonomy and a position to critique music from the outside. *Noise as noise*, on the other hand, aesthetically underlies Genesis P-Orridge's admonition that "beauty is the enemy." It is an important strain of industrial music's resistance.

Artists sometimes attempt to retain noise as noise through sheer Gorgon foreboding, but a more common and successful approach is to use process-based composition to conjure unpredictability, and by extension to evade assimilation. Bond Bergland attributes the unpremeditated excursions of Factrix to "some sort of host situation . . . we kind of developed an imaginary friend," not unlike Coil's encounter with ELpH, or the Burroughs-Gysin idea of the Third Mind.[2] William Bennet of Whitehouse is infamous for mixing his albums by maxing out each channel's volume at every point in the signal chain. Dirk Ivens took the same approach on Dive's 1990 self-titled album, and to polish it off he slapped "To be played at maximum volume" on the sleeve. These practices fetishize noise as an act and a concept without regard to its sonic qualities.

Perpetually resisting assimilation means staying forever at the avant-gardes of art, which entails constant fluid change. This is in keeping with Chapter 13's assertion that industrial music's project is ideally an ongoing one. The spectacle's recuperation shouldn't stop artists from combating it; on the contrary, it's a call to keep up the fight. That's why Bohn wants musicians to develop "new strategies for telling unpalatable truths," rather than give up. Guy Debord, leader of the Situationist International, understood the need for constant change. He wrote of the pan-revolutionary struggle, "It must be understood that we will be present at, and take part in, *a sprint between independent artists and the police to test and develop the use of new techniques of conditioning.*"[3]

In reality, this is hard to do. Ever-flowing radical change is precisely what Fluxus sought—hence the name—and even that movement receded into an historical event rather than remaining an ever-current project. Fluxus used a panoply of aesthetics, attitudes, and media; industrial noise is both aesthetically confined to darkness—hence the divide between it and friendlier, less confrontational noise genres—and medially restricted more or less to sound and its visual window dressing. Industrial music's use of noise is basically a fixed, unmoving vision with static connotations of time and place—Europe in the 1980s, specifically. It may be an extreme of sorts, but it's hardly cutting-edge, nearly forty years on.

## 3. Preaching to the Converted

What's happened instead is that industrial noise has come to *signify* transgression instead of actually transgressing. Monte Cazazza's "Candy Man," an ode to serial murderer Dean Corll, may have shocked a few poor souls on its 1979 release, but by the time Pig put out 1995's "Serial Killer Thriller" the effect of such art relied on a willful suspension of disbelief: it signified shock while shocking nobody. To his credit, Pig's Raymond Watts knows this well:

> As regards to the whole thing about shock value, I haven't been shocked by a pop band or any kind of whatever the fuck you wanna call it industrial noise terrorist nah-nah-nah-nah-nah vomit-inducing bile-fucking shit-fucking fist-fucking super evil scary satanist fucking fuck band. I get a lot more scared by seeing the fucking National Enquirer than listening to anything on an industrial so-called subversive label. Forget the shock value stuff, I mean you're preaching to the converted, pal.[4]

"As much as the use of 'noise' in industrial music operates as a tag, so does the historical legacy of provocation," writes scholar Scott Lewis, affirming the genre's *indication of critique* above any critical directness.[5] The very notion of an historical legacy within industrial music is at odds with its supposed emphasis on innovation and revolution, encapsulating the central paradox of modernism: when the past has already been destroyed once, destroying it again is in fact reviving it. Philosopher Nick Smith puts a finer point on the issue: "Dissonance itself has become cliché. When the act of transgressing becomes 'hot', transgression no longer stands in a critical relation to culture."[6] How many times can we attend the Theatre of Cruelty and still feel properly violated?

Nick Smith makes the damning point that once radical art and protest are assimilated into mass culture, they're not destroyed but instead boxed into a known, controllable cultural space where they can do their thing, operating under a delusion of radicality. Citing Marxist theorists Theodor Adorno and Max Horkheimer, he writes:

> When noise becomes ensconced within commercial culture, it presents only an illusion of freedom and difference. As Adorno warned, where "the public does—exceptionally—rebel against the pleasure industry" it can only muster "the feeble resistance which that very industry has inculcated in it" (Adorno and Horkheimer 1972: 145). Crippled protests are integrated in the system and the status quo "embraces those at war with it by coordinating their consciousness with its own [because] what subjectively they fancy as radical, belongs objectively to the compartments reserved for their like" (Adorno and Horkheimer 1972: 46).[7]

Is the noise-as-noise paradigm sustainable on any scale, then? Smith is doubtful, and he in fact criticizes noise culture's self-importance as fundamentally misguided because of this: "Alternative music scenes and ideological move-ments have a history of generating delusional subcultures which stake out their territory and go to great lengths to defend their borders from attacks against their status as unique and liminal long after the gig is up."[8] Essentially, both he and *The Wire*'s editor Chris Bohn are saying that the large-scale process of as-similation bars noise and industrial music from actually doing the political work they lay claim to—and that if indeed the genre ever had the ability to translate its noisy metaphors for anarchic irrationality into real revolutionary moments, it certainly doesn't anymore.

## 4. Ways of Listening

Derived from the pessimistic, high-modernist "Frankfurt School" of philoso-phy, Smith and Bohn's argument is tough to contest. But within industrial mu-sic's project of unseating rationality, the vantage point of this critique has some important blind spots. In Smith and Bohn's view, noise's qualities of random-ness and ambiguity seem instrumental to its supposedly avant-garde aspirations because they act as a small-scale metaphor for a large-scale sense of revolution-ary resistance to assimilation—the logic being that if industrial noise resists any structural or hierarchical understanding when we listen to it, then it can't be fully grasped on the intellectual level, and hence it's subject to no expectations other than its own. As Nick Smith writes, "The very process of making sense of noise sterilizes it."[9] Plenty of musicians buy into this notion to varying degrees; it certainly helps explain why Japanese noise legend Merzbow puts out releases like the *Merzbox*, a truly overwhelming fifty-CD set of grinding, arrhythmic noise: its size practically guarantees that no disc will ever be heard more than once, and hence learned. This also helps explain why some of the most hard-core scenesters insist that noise and industrial music steps in the wrong direc-tion politically whenever it uses a steady beat—after all, what's more predictable and containable than a 4/4 kickdrum at 120 bpm?

This line of interpretation assumes that antirationality is attempted through *confounding* the conscious mind; it presumes that listeners are trying to under-stand and control the music, and that it's the music's duty to short-circuit this effort (whether such an attempted understanding is the will of the listener or of some parasitic control machine of hierarchical thought—remember Burroughs's idea that the virus takes over the host completely).

What if the path to irrationality isn't by confounding the conscious mind, but instead through *submerging* it? It's telling that Whitehouse's Bennet refers to himself as an Animal Response Technician: he believes that the musician's responsibility isn't to outsmart the audience's consciousness, but rather to stimulate a different mode of listening in which audiences willingly and preemptively disengage their rationality. As Jennifer Shryane writes in her book on Einstürzende Neubauten, "Listening to noise can take the form of a Dionysian experience during which individuality is abandoned and the limits of the senses are exceeded in the heightened state. The noise becomes a felt physical force—a physical phenomenon in space."[10]

## 5. Happiness in Slavery

The fullest political explanation of this idea within industrial music comes from Diedrich Diederichsen, a media scholar who edited the German magazines *Sounds* and *Spex* back in his punk days. He argues that with the age of visibly domineering top-down public governance largely behind us, by and large, modern social control is a diffuse and technological game of "forced participation and encouragement to join in."[11] By offering endless stimulation, communication, and distraction, media culture "seeks to produce an intolerable state and a condition of will-lessness."[12] Because it's much subtler, this advanced kind of control triggers far less resistance than brutality does, and it's every bit as effective for centralizing power.

The hegemonic function of media and technology is to pull us out of ourselves and into a shared state of responsiveness, where regardless of how we react we're all reacting to a controlled, external thing; we are summoned by the world's stimulations. This view discards the specific content of media as being superficial, and so Diederichsen posits that the way media most meaningfully communicate is through the *form* of the content over time—the rhythms of amplitude and extremity.

Like this model of technocultural media, industrial music privileges extremity and amplitude, both sonically and conceptually. When we also remember how often industrial and noise music claim that the partisan details of its political imagery, samples, and lyrics matter less than their juxtaposition and their visceral kick, it's easy to see why some artists find making and listening to noise so apt and powerful a commentary on the world today.

Diederichsen writes:

> It is no accident that the hard, asemantic aesthetic has been embraced wherever especially marginal, endangered, and dangerous subcultures have sought to establish themselves, from Muslimgauze to Whitehouse, from Hanatarash to the early Laibach, whether their content was politi-

cally left-wing or right-wing and whether it involved sexual politics or a "deviant" approach to diet and nutrition: clearly, a relationship exists between the noise of the asemantic and the precariousness of a highly specific semantic dimension with which it is then connected.[13]

This relationship he's talking about is one where the extremeness of the music's cultural signs lines up with sonic extremes in timbre and volume to make rhythms—either as beats or merely as temporal events in beatless tides—and the music's shape comes from these alignments of extremes. These coordinated "kicks" serve as metaphors to show us just how genuinely invasive the world's medial "noise" is, and in doing so they offer us a congratulatory sense in recognizing them, an aesthetic appreciation for the neat alignment of the sonic with the conceptual, and the dirty horrorshow delight that comes with witnessing real ugliness. It all adds up to a "passive experience of overwhelm[ing], masochistic pleasure."[14]

Diederichsen here is advocating a paradoxical kind of liberation, arguing that autonomy, subjectivity, and sovereignty over oneself aren't all they're cracked up to be. The rallying cry of most progressive social movements is "freedom," but the claim that he situates in this music is that modern freedom and the responsibilities of autonomy in fact only enslave and exhaust us: as subjects with free will, we choose and detail our identities from an artificially narrow, sanctioned range of media noise, or alternatively we might resist the invasive aggression of media, dogmatically asserting an autonomy whose parameters are in reality dictated by our fears rather than our desires.

Diederichsen proposes that in contrast, we can save ourselves a metaphorical beating by *choosing to become a thing*, by giving up on subjectivity and forfeiting that fight to control the noise and escape from it. This allows us to channel our attention toward a more sensorial, affective experience of feeling.

Throbbing Gristle's slogan "Entertainment Through Pain" means thus recognizing "all the things observed by the culture-industry thesis, along with the situations described by paranoid Burroughs-based theories of manipulation and conditioning, as a single, monolithic pain programme."[15] Struggling autonomously against this pain only reveals the tragic inescapability of the control machines (what Diederichsen calls "Pain Through Entertainment"), but submitting willingly to the "pain programme" reveals pleasures unavailable through other ways of listening and being. Diederichsen identifies three in particular: first, submission preempts domination, allowing the "kick" to be a masochistic thrill instead of a combative assault; second, the summoning call to conformity intrinsic in media and rhythm can now suggest a communal sensation, the carnival instead of the gulag; third, reacting to the amplitude and rhythm of media and noise is a simpler and more bodily immediate pleasure than reacting to the contradictory knots that tangle its content, affording listeners an instinctual dérive of sensory experience.

## 6. Internal Revolution (This Is How It Sounds)

These new possibilities are neither intrinsic to the music nor marked by tangible change in one's political surroundings; instead they emerge from a new way of listening, and by extension, of being. Following through on the familiar industrial assertion that perception shapes reality, the revolutionary potential of this submission is apparent only to those who consensually submit. The meaning and reward of this internal revolution is really only available, then, to people whose physical needs are already met and who possess enough subjective autonomy to render submission a *choice*. In short, it's the same kind of demographic blind spot that Chapter 14 exposed in industrial music. Historically (as Chapter 13's discussion of fascism and irony revealed), industrial music and noise avoided issuing political demands specific enough to change this situation, because doing so would be seen as a capitulation to the rigged game of partisan politics. Through this avoidance, however, industrial music's all-or-nothing politics suggests with grim entitlement that you're on your own: altruism is futile.

This is a problem.

The revolution in the mind afforded by a submissive response to the deep formal kick of industrial noise is as individually fragile as it is collectively limited. Effectively a change in perceptual attitude, it's prone to disruption during penetrating moments of self-awareness, and although Diederichsen differentiates between "an intellectual, ideological passivization and a sensory, nervous one," it's not clear that listeners consistently do.[16] The most obvious evidence of this is "the unholy alliance of industrial music with SS men or other bastards," born from the asemantic blankness of noise and from the focus on pure form that a submissive hearing requires.[17] This blankness is almost inevitably painted over (or at least tinted) by the extreme political content that so often parades at the music's surface; or alternatively it gives rise to an aesthetic of purity itself that is supposedly apolitical, troublingly close to the fascism that industrial music so often takes as window dressing, as we saw in Chapter 13.

Broadly, these are some of the problems that this book's first pages address in their discussion of the "vacuum left by deprogramming." These problems are enough of a reality that Throbbing Gristle saw fit to address them head-on when they bent weirdly into lounge music symbology on 1979's comparatively beat-driven *20 Jazz Funk Greats*. In fact, to Throbbing Gristle, providing listeners' blank submissive receptivity with an inauspicious foreground subject was the correction of a mistake; the quartet's sadness and vitriol toward the hopped-up thugs who mistook their systemic extremism for directed malevolence makes that clear. The commitment to this change is furthermore evident in Chris & Cosey's dance stylings and Genesis P-Orridge's championing of acid house music.

Despite elite noise fans' suspicion that drum beats indicate selling out, consider instead their potential to offer a steady division of time (or a topical presence of pop) as a semineutral way of filling the void where rationality used to be—a hole that extreme noise can otherwise leave open to hate-based politics. Diederichsen concurs:

> It was probably best for the pure effects to be directly hooked up to physicality in such a way that the bodies did the narrative themselves in the most compelling and accurate fashion: by dancing. In many respects, this is the best way to become a thing, an object buffeted to and fro, and still with sufficient headspace free to observe oneself and others with pleasure.[18]

Rhythm doesn't surrender the music's elusive power to heady apprehension, but in many ways it maintains the antirational industrial ethic by mapping itself onto the carnal, instinctual body in dance. Granted there's a danger here of pop itself overrunning the deprogramming, but if the drumbeat's suggestion that pop complicity is a lesser evil than tribalized violence seems milquetoast amidst revolutionary politics, then the abreactive commentary that EBM sculpted out of dance rhythms comes into focus as an important political turning point within the genre—yet another corrective measure over time. Thus from Throbbing Gristle and Cabaret Voltaire to the present, we see nearly unanimous functional agreement on the steady beat's political role in the genre, and more importantly by extension, *the valuing of industrial music's practical, real-world impact.* Pure noise bands and the power electronics subgenre might stand at the gateway to some unattainable, chaotic Eden with a flaming sword in one hand and *Might Is Right* in the other, but as Guy Debord and Situationist co-author Gil Wolman write, "Détournement by simple reversal is always the most direct and the least effective."[19]

## 7. The Future Happened Already

The potency of the pan-revolutionary against the control machines depends on contact between the two; noise can only redefine music when the two touch.

Noise is the grandest articulation of a process whose tactics, in order to succeed practically, *must be implemented at more nuanced levels*. If industrial music constructs a future hell-bent on combating the pan-systemic nature of control only with noise eternally placed outside of music (noise as noise), then its role will remain symbolic rather than real, remembered wistfully as an ideological dead end whose sole plan for growth was to turn the volume knob higher and higher.

Industrial music's relevance has changed because the world has changed. It's eye-opening to realize how suspiciously close modern reality is to the cyberpunk dystopia that industrial music sought to avoid by preemptively situating as its revolutionary arena. Cyberpunk's kinship with industrial music makes sense, given its roots in science fiction, and to a lesser degree, ecoterrorism—a radical defense of the last vestiges of a world free from economy, religion, language, and reason, essentially a Burroughsian dream.✿ A central narrative of cyberpunk and industrial music alike is that of a rogue abuser of technology unhinging the system with its own tools.

In her dissertation on industrial music, Karen Collins quotes Mark Hillegas, explaining that dystopia—central to Collins's notion of industrial music discourse—is formulated on "the cataclysmic war which precedes the new state . . . the standardization of men and women, including artificial faces and numbers for names, the substitution of the manufactured (plastic flowers and trees) for the natural, and the familiar revolt against the machine."[20]

But dystopia as fiction takes on an entirely less futuristic, if duller and more cynical, sheen when dystopia as reality is already in place. Between 1975 and the early 1990s, a cataclysmic war—the Cold War—ended, preceding a new global economy, and the academy and mass populace both gained admittance to previously limited telecommunications networks, ushering in a new era of internet access in which artificial faces and numerical names were the Usenet, BBS, and MUD standard. Today, email services prompt users to tack numbers onto their names, (comically) to avoid being mistaken for someone else. Furthermore, the musical revolt against the machine was a clear and polarizing benchmark of popular political culture, enacted both in the earnest antisynthesizer tirades printed on records by Boston, Queen, and Lou Reed and also

---

✿ In light of this, it's no surprise that Burroughs published *The Cat Inside*, which celebrates his love of animals. Similarly, it makes sense that author Neal Stephenson preceded his cyberpunk classic *Snow Crash* with *Zodiac*, whose protagonist is a radically anticorporate environmentalist, and for that matter that Merzbow, Skinny Puppy, Meat Beat Manifesto, and Nine Inch Nails have all publicly supported PETA.

through the sheer ironic mass of industrial music's history—to say nothing of the cyclical battles for "authenticity" in indie rock and pop.

Even though industrial music has always been ethically concerned with the present, the genre's aesthetics over its first decades expressly projected a future. However, the years leading up to and following the millennium have passed this future by, as Chapter 18 notes with regard to Apoptygma Berzerk. The genre's widespread momentary popularity peaked at that pre-millennial moment of eclipse, but since the dreamed-of future became the past, industrial music hasn't changed its tune much, which is why it can seem passé in the twenty-first century. As noise artist and media theorist Thomas Bey William Bailey writes:

> The "retro" fascistic elements utilized by Laibach—uniforms, banners, rigid discipline and Wagnerian symphonic clarity—are, paradoxically, the same elements which distance it from more modern . . . emanations of fascism. Leading ultra-rightist politicians like Jean Marie LePen and David Duke have made it a habit to court mainstream respectability, opting for crisp business suits and jeans instead of military uniforms, and insisting, at least publicly, that their followers claim power through the ballot box rather than through guerilla actions and violent intimidations. . . .[21]

As we might see over this book's preceding pages, the historical tides of industrial music's cultural relevance and visibility have ebbed and flowed with its outermost thematic content and the way it handles rhythm and form. There's actually no indication that its political tools of détournement and dérive ever stopped working; instead, industrial music's crisis of relevance both in pop and in politics comes from a bad miscalibration of these tools. It's no use détourning Hitler or dériving the battlefield for the umpteenth time. To become effective once more in revealing and reversing the meanings of controls signs, to undermine mediated communication and governance through ambiguity, confusion, and anger, industrial music needs to take on contemporary and specific signs. The Cold War is over. No, you can't use you a swastika. Yes, you can still wear combat boots.

Zeroing in on how a new, effective industrial music might work, we can look to other musics of resistance that have made a tangible difference. Chapter 14 demonstrated that despite good intentions industrial music has blind spots when it comes to race. For a variety of reasons, then, the genre might do well to learn from African American music and the protest histories of other racial minorities. Compare for example the détournement that industrial music hurls so broadly at cultural authority with the more issue-specific critiques that hip-hop voiced via noise and sampling in the 1980s and 1990s. Industrial concerns like technocracy, plutocracy, and theocracy haven't abated since Throbbing Gristle's day; in fact, they've considerably strengthened their grip on western culture. In contrast, though, hip-hop's concerns of racial politics in the west have taken clear if interrupted steps away from brutal tyranny over the last thirty years. This is not to assert hip-hop's direct causality in social change, per se, but the attention and influence commanded by the likes of Public Enemy and Ice-T derived from their specificity of critique and their willingness to work within major media systems—both tendencies that industrial music as a rule resists.

Thomas Bey William Bailey notes that no "contemporary power electronics artists have delved into the grisly specifics of the more recent genocides in Bosnia, Rwanda, Darfur etc.—making one wonder if these purveyors of brutality truly have a sense of history beyond Anglophone and Western European spheres of influence."[22] If industrial musicians were more willing to refocus and take a cue from the nonwhite subaltern repertoire, then the misdeeds of control machines might reveal themselves in greater specificity, visibly dislodging a single brick from the wall instead of imperceptibly loosening them all. Aptly, another advantage of this change is the expansion of industrial music's revolutionary potential beyond the internal revolution that Diederichsen describes, which depends frankly on a kind of class privilege. The politics of pan-liberation are relevant to all people.

## 8. Noise As Music

To some industrialists, topical specificity or willingness to engage with mainstream media and commerce—especially after industrial music's disastrous mid-1990s "sell-out"—might appear as unconscionable concessions to ephemeral culture or as assimilation by way of stooping to bleeding-heart electoral debate. As film historian Robert Ray argues incisively, however, "The avant-gardist's typical complaint about assimilation seems misguided."[23] In an essay called "How to Start an Avant-Garde," Ray points out, "To assume that increasingly rapid co-option will destroy the avant-garde ignores how much the avant-garde itself has, throughout its history, promoted its own acceptance," adding, "The Impressionists, [who were] the first avant-garde, understood almost immediately that assimilation was a necessary goal."[24]

Whether we're discussing impressionism, hip-hop, or industrial music, each in its moment of historical ascent sought to expand the number and breadth of ways in which people can interpret and behave in the world. By charting new, unexplored territory, the avant-garde can be seen as expanding that very mainstream against which it contentiously pulls. This tense dialogue and contact is essential for change, and if the tension is absent, artists beware: it's not because you've broken free of cultural controls, but because you're flailing in a supposedly "radical" playpen that has been cordoned off for you. To effect real-world improvement, artists must accept the risk of noise becoming music in the name of increasing the possibilities for musical meaning. Artists must resist isolation and open their own work to continuous change and motion as they remain a step ahead of the assimilating agents who in their pursuit—and in spite of themselves—expand the borders of cultural options, one momentous stride at a time. This is a vital and often-overlooked aspect of the noise-as-music approach.

Early in this book we saw a tension over the "I-word": exclusionist conceptions often delimit the genre in terms of sound, instrumentation, politics, era, or geography, while an inclusionist definition spans a wide range of highly varied so-called industrial music made for different reasons at different times. Whether exclusionists assert that "real" industrial music is Can or Throbbing Gristle or Skinny Puppy or Funker Vogt, this attitude denies the music's capacity then and now to be part of the ongoing operation described at the end of Chapter 13, resisting assimilation not to escape forever from the mediated world of hidden hegemonies but instead to stretch, overfill, and inoculate that world against itself bit by bit as it swallows down the stuff of the pan-revolutionary in each little, inevitable recuperation. On the other hand, an inclusionist view of the genre isn't just useful for writing a book about the history of music that people have called industrial; it's politically important to any future artist or fan who sympathizes with the industrial desire for change because it maps out a continued and still salvageable revolutionary program. Understanding the variety of industrial music over time—even the corners of it that are too poppy, or too noisy, or boring—reinforces Chapter 2's explanation of the music as process more than sound, but here we can understand the idea of process in the widest possible way. This approach safeguards against future industrial music merely sonically rehashing some favorite subgenre's moment in nostalgia. From this perspective, we can eye the future optimistically but also assess the past with honesty, reaffirming the simple but important fact of industrial music's continuity both in name and in pan-revolutionary attitudes and methods.

The industrial worldview casts reality as the perception of reality, and so we as audiences, performers, and scholars of industrial music have the chance to sculpt the music's meaning and potential, depending on what we perceive to be the answer to this chapter's opening question: What is industrial music's goal?

At this point, unless we deny the music's continuity, its technological prescience in the 1980s, its millennial concerns in the 1990s, its politicization of rhythm, and the limits of purely asemantic expression, then *staking out extremes for their own sake cannot and must not be the goal of industrial music*. The ideal of noise as noise—invariably linked to exclusionist views of the genre—comes from an incomplete understanding of industrial music's arguments, effects, practices, and history. Though we should eye carefully the manipulative economies of credibility, kinship, and lineage by which Cabaret Voltaire and VNV Nation somehow "sell" one another, a dose of inclusionism's political practicality informs this book's final idea.

## 9. The Third Mind

If noise stands in for the most irrational and revolutionary in art, and music is metaphorically the known, predictable, contained world of governance, then industrial music's power is neither simply a case of noise as noise nor noise as music; instead, industrial music can excite a sonic and symbolic frisson between noise and music, subversively rupturing their supposed border. In the spirit of Burroughs and Gysin, we can listen anew for a Third Mind between these two alleged positions, suggesting their binary opposition as a false one. Where raw noise à la Whitehouse or Merzbow reinforces the pairing with its in-or-out proposition, subtler uses of noise, both literal and figurative, can attack systems of control virally from within, and not just brutally from outside.

In her book *Listening Through the Noise: The Aesthetics of Experimental Electronic Music*, Joanna Demers writes, "In cases where some vestiges of conventional harmonic or melodic beauty linger, the role of noise, repetition, stasis, and distortion shifts to negative beauty . . . the desire for a return to conventional aesthetic language mixed with the knowledge that such a return is impossible."[25] And so it should be, as the likes of Susan Sontag and Genesis P-Orridge have warned us. Whether in worship of beauty or at war against it, the fundamentalist paths of purity are dangerous political roads. Consider then Snog's 2010 "Sleepwalk," a harmonically lush, slow song whose chorus slips unexpectedly to a major key. Over a breathtaking accompaniment from the City of Prague Philharmonic Choir, singer David Thrussell invites the listener to "Sleepwalk through this world with me, one nap at a time." Snog here recognizes still that beauty is the enemy, but instead of fighting it with ugliness Thrussell turns beauty against itself: the song is unmistakably gorgeous, and its beckoning call to blindness, ignorance, and complicity reveals more about the hidden reverse of consensus aesthetics—and hence ethics—than a litany of accusations or a wall of distortion.

Is the direction advocated here really industrial music? Surely some will say no, but ask what matters more. A pop genre or a war's end? A distorted TR-808 kick drum, or exposing the lies of broadcast media? Whether a song has guitars, or whether dogs died for your eyeliner? It's true that a victory of this sort is far from the sublime destruction of gods and governments, money and meaning, but it's a good start.

Beyond the stubborn obsolescence of simply reversing "music" and beyond the callous pessimism of purely internal change awaits this third option. It is a third mind: a future that has the potential to be more than the sum of music and noise, of the racial self and the other. It is the specific, the liminal, the absorbed extremity. It is the revolutionary.

# Sources Cited

Allen, Tony. *A Summer in the Park: A Journal of Speakers' Corner*. London: Freedom Press, 2004.

Andrews, Ian, in consultation with John Blades. "The Lost Decade: Post-Punk Experimental and Industrial Electronic Music." *Experimental Music: Audio Explorations in Australia*. Ed. Gail Priest. Sydney: University of New South Wales Press, 2008. 36–56.

Anonymous. Personal interview. Mar. 11, 2011.

Antrim, Doron K. "Music in Industry." *Musical Quarterly*, Vol. 29, No. 3 (July 1943), 275–290.

Artaud, Antonin. *The Theatre and Its Double*. Trans. by Mary Caroline Richards. New York: Grove Press, 1958.

Aspa, Mikko. "The Dark Side of Noise." *As Loud As Possible* Issue One (Fall 2010), 10.

Ayers, Nigel. Letter to the editor in *Electric Shock Treatment* 4 (Winter 1992), 62.

Ayers, Nigel. Personal interview. May 21, 2011.

Bailey, Thomas Bey William. *Micro-Bionic: Radical Electronic Music and Sound Art in the 21st Century*. London: Creation Books, 2009.

Baker, Cary. "Ministry: Ordained by Dance." *Illinois Entertainer* vol. 2, no. 103 (September 1982). Page numbers unavailable.

Barclay, Michael, Ian A. D. Jack, and Jason Schneider. *Have Not Been the Same: The CanRock Renaissance, 1985–95*. Toronto: ECW Press, 2011.

Barr, Stuart. "Helios Creed, Interview." *Convulsion*. 1993. Accessed Aug. 22, 2012, <http://under groundmusiclibrary.blogspot.com/2005/06/helios-creed-interview-convulsion-1993.html>.

Barr, Stuart. "Skinny Puppy." *Convulsion*. 1996. Accessed Aug. 22, 2012, <http://obsolete.com/convulsion/interviews/ogre1.html>.

Barr, Stuart. "The Young Gods." *Convulsion*. 1993. Accessed Aug. 22, 2012, <http://obsolete.com/convulsion/interviews/convulse/younggods.html>.

Beaumont, Roger A. *The Nazis' March to Chaos: The Hitler Era Through the Lens of Chaos-Complexity Theory*. Westport: Praeger, 2000.

Becu, Didier. "Interview with Portion Control." *The Original Sin*. Sep. 20, 2010. Accessed Aug. 21, 2012, <http://theoriginalsinfanzine.blogspot.com/2010/09/interview-with-portion-control.html>.

Beetz, Christian, and Birgit Herdlitschke, dirs. *Hör mit Schmerzen*. Zweites Deutsches Fernsehen, 2000.

Bell, Judith. "Interview with Monte Cazazza." *Slash* vol. 2 no. 5 (January 1979). Page numbers unavailable.

Benjamin, Walter. *Illuminations*. Trans. Harry Zohn. New York: Schocken, 1968.

Bergland, Bond, and Cole Palme. Personal interview. November 11, 2011.

Blake, Trevor. *SPK: Krankheit im Recht*. Heidelberg: KRRIM. 1995.

Boccioni, Umberto, Carlo Carrà, Luigi Russolo, Giacomo Balla, and Gino Severini. "Manifesto of the Futurist Painters." In *Manifesto: A Century of isms*. Ed. Mary Ann Caws. Lincoln: University of Nebraska Press, 2000. 182–184.

Bohn, Chris. "The Masthead." *The Wire* December 2010, 4.

Bonner, Staci. "Use Your Delusion." *Spin* June 1992, 14.

Boss, Katy. "Einstürzende Neubauten: Revolutionary Industrial." *Creem Magazine.com*. June 2004. Accessed Aug. 18, 2011, <http://www.creemmagazine.com/_site/BeatGoesOn/Einsturzende Neubauten/RevolutionaryIndustrial001.html>.

Brewster, Bill, and Frank Broughton. *Last Night a DJ Saved My Life*. New York: Grove, 2000.

Brewster, Bill, and Frank Broughton. *The Record Players: DJ Revolutionaries*. New York: Black Cat, 2010.

Brown, Adam, Justin O'Connor, and Sara Cohen. "Local Music Policies Within a Global Music Industry Cultural Quarters in Manchester and Sheffield." *Geoforum* 31 (2000), 437–451.

Burroughs, William S. *Electronic Revolution*. Göttingen: Expanded Media, 1971.

Burroughs, William S. *Junkie*. New York: Penguin, 1977.

Burroughs, William S. *The Letters of William S. Burroughs 1945–1959*. Ed. Oliver Harris. New York: Penguin, 1994.

Burroughs, William S. *The Naked Lunch*. New York: Grove Press, 1992.

Burroughs, William S. *The Western Lands*. New York: Viking Press, 1987.

Burroughs, William S., and Brion Gysin. *Colloque de Tanger II*. Paris: Bourgeois, 1979.

Burroughs, William S., and Brion Gysin. *The Third Mind*. New York: Viking, 1978.

Burroughs, William S., and Daniel Odier. *The Job: Interviews with William S. Burroughs*. New York: Grove Press, 1974.

Bush, John. "Meat Beat Manifesto." In *All Music Guide to Electronica*. Ed. Vladimir Bogdanov. San Francisco: Backbeat Books, 2001. 323–324.

Bush, John. "Last Rights." *All Music Guide to Rock*. Eds. Vladimir Bogdanov, Chris Woodstra, Stephen Thomas Erlewine. Ann Arbor: All Media Guide, 2002. 1019.

Butler, L. (Testure). *Music from the empty quarter—Sticky*. Mar. 13, 2007. Accessed Dec. 24, 2011, <http://www.hifiwigwam.com/archive/index.php/t-1338-p-2.html>.

Candey, Scott. *Worm Gear #4*, 1996. Via *MySpace*. Accessed Aug. 21, 2012, <http://www.myspace.com/brighterdeathnow/blog/106898228>.

Cardew, Cornelius. "On the Role of the Instructions in the Interpretation of Indeterminate Music." In *Treatise Handbook*. London: Peters, 1971. xiv–xvi.

Carr, Daphne. *Pretty Hate Machine*. New York: Continuum, 2011.

Carter, Chris. Email interview. June 29, 2011.

Carver, Lisa Crystal. *Drugs Are Nice*. London: Snowbooks, 2006.

"cEvin Key: See the Light, Feel the Heat." *Alternative Press*. October 1998. Via *Litany*. Accessed Sep. 26, 2011, <http://www.litany.net/interviews/ap123.html>.

Chainsaw, Charlie. "S.P.K." *Chainsaw* no. 11 (February 1981). Page numbers unavailable.

Chung, Mark. Email interview. Aug. 6, 2012.

Cigéhn, Peter. "The Top 1319 Sample Sources." Sep. 1, 2004. Accessed Feb. 4, 2013, <http://semi major.net/samples/sourcelist_20041019.txt>.

Clock DVA. Liner notes. *White Souls in Black Suits*. Industrial Records, 1980.

Coatts, Sarah. "Einstürzende Neubauten." *Grok* 7 (July 1984), 18–19.

Codenys, Patrick. Personal interview. May 17, 2011.

"Coil." *They're Coming to Take Me Away Ha Ha* 1 (1984), 11–14.

"Coil: Beyond the Eskaton." *Convulsion*. 1996. Accessed Jan. 4, 2010, <http://www.obsolete.com/convulsion/interviews/coil/2.html>.

Collins, Karen E. *"The Future Is Happening Already": Industrial Music, Dystopia and the Aesthetic of the Machine*. Diss. University of Liverpool, 2002.

Connelly, Chris. *Concrete, Bulletproof, Invisible + Fried: My Life as a Revolting Cock*. London: SAF, 2008.

Corbett, John. "Free, Single, and Disengaged: Listening Pleasure and the Popular Music Object." *October* vol. 54 (autumn 1990), 79–101.

*Culture Shock* 4 (January 1997).

Cusick, Suzanne. "On Musical Performances of Gender and Sex." *Audible Traces: Gender, Identity, Music.* Eds. Elaine Barkin and Lydia Hamessley. Zürich: Carciofoli Verlagshaus, 1999. 25–48.

Cyberium. "Industrial is dead . . . behold the future." *Side-Line.* Sep. 1, 2011. Accessed Nov. 27, 2011, <http://www.side-line.com/side-line-forum/topic/industrial-is-dead-behold-the-future>.

Da Davo, Dirk. Personal interview. May 17, 2011.

Daniel, Drew. *20 Jazz Funk Greats.* New York: Continuum, 2008.

Dasein, Deena. "Ministry Comes Clean." *Illinois Entertainer* 22/4 (February 1996), 26, 28.

de La Villemarqué, Théodore Hersart. *Barzaz Breiz.* Paris: Éditions Delloye, 1839.

Debord, Guy. "Detournement as Negation and Prelude." *Art in Theory 1900–1990: An Anthology of Changing Ideas.* Eds. Charles Harrison and Paul Wood. Cambridge: Blackwood, 1993. 697–698.

Debord, Guy, and Gil Wolman. "A User's Guide to Détournement." *Situationist International Anthology.* Ed. Ken Knabb. Berkeley: Bureau of Public Secrets, 2002. 14–20.

Demers, Joanna. *Listening Through the Noise.* New York: Oxford University Press, 2010.

Densmore, Frances. "The Music of the Filipinos." *American Anthropologist,* New Series Vol. 8, No. 4 (Oct–Dec. 1906), 611–632.

DeRogatis, Jim. *Milk It: Collected Musings on the Alternative Music Explosion of the '90s.* Cambridge: Da Capo Press, 2003.

DeRogatis, Jim, and Greg Kot. "WaxTrax! Records." *Sound Opinions.* WBEZ Chicago. July 8, 2011, <http://audio.soundopinions.org/podcasts/sooppodshow293.mp3>.

Dery, Mark. *Escape Velocity: Cyberculture at the End of the Century.* New York: Grove, 1997.

di Perna, Alan. "Nitzer Ebb: Analog Synths & Ambient Samples Put a Polish on the Industrial Grind." *Keyboard* February 1991, 56–62.

Die Krupps. Liner notes. *Volle Kraft Voraus!* Synthetic Symphony, 2008.

Diederichsen, Diedrich. "Entertainment Through Pain." *Cosey Complex,* Eds. Maria Fusco and Richard Birkett. Köln: Koenig Books, 2012. 25–33.

Dink, Phil. "Local Labels: A Practical Example." In *Cassette Mythos,* Ed. Robin James. Brooklyn: Autonomedia, 1992. 102–106.

Duguid, Brian. "Zoviet France: Look into Me." *Electric Shock Treatment* 2 (Winter 1991), 18–21.

Elitair, Pierre. "Fat Ronny." *Radio Ventraal.* Radio Centraal Antwerp. Nov. 29, 2009. Via King K. "Fat Ronny/Interview." *DJHistory.com.* Trans. King K. Dec. 1–2, 2009. Accessed Aug. 21, 2012, <http://www.djhistory.com/forum/fat-ronny-interview>.

Engels, Friedrich, and Karl Marx. *Manifesto of the Communist Party and Selected Essays.* Rockville, MD: Manor Thrift, 2008.

English Celt. "Nationalist Industrial Bands—Page 3." *Stormfront.* Feb. 28, 2011. Accessed July 27, 2011, <http://www.stormfront.org/forum/t771649-3/>.

'Enthal, Andrea. "Underground." *Spin.* May 1986, 38–39.

Esch, En, Mona Mur, and Günter Schulz. Personal interview. June 14, 2010.

Etat Brut. Liner notes. *EB001.* Etat Brut, 1980.

FatherWithHorns. "German Industrial." *Stormfront.* May 5, 2002. Accessed July 27, 2011, <http://www.stormfront.org/forum/t20990/>.

Faust. Liner notes. *The Faust Tapes.* Virgin Records, 1973.

Ferfolja, Gordon. "Laibach in Toronto." *Slovenian.* Nov. 2004. Accessed July 29, 2011, <http://www.theslovenian.com/articles/ferfolja.htm>.

Fink, Robert. *Repeating Ourselves: American Minimalism as Cultural Practice.* Berkeley: University of California Press, 2005.

Fink, Robert. "The Story of ORCH5, or, The Classical Ghost in the Hip-Hop Machine." *Popular Music* 24 (2005), 339–356.

Fish, Mick. *Industrial Evolution: Through the Eighties with Cabaret Voltaire.* London: SAF, 2002.

Ford, Phil. "Taboo: Time and Belief in Exotica." *Representations*, vol. 103 no. 1 (Summer 2008), 107–135.

Ford, Simon. *Wreckers of Civilisation*. London: Black Dog, 1999.

Fraser, Catherine C., and Dierk O. Hoffmann. *Pop Culture Germany!* Santa Barbara: ABC-CLIO, 2006.

Freel, Doug, dir. *Fix: The Ministry Movie*. Gigantic Pictures, 2011.

Friedberg, Anne. "'Cut-Ups': A *Syn*ema of the Text." *Downtown Review* 1.1 (1979), 3–5.

Frith, Simon. *Performing Rites*. Cambridge: Harvard University Press, 1996.

Front 242. Liner notes. *No Comment*. Another Side, 1984.

Fulber, Rhys. Telephone interview. Dec. 8, 2009.

Fusco, Maria, and Cosey Fanni Tutti. "Cosey and Maria Talk About Linguistic Hardcore." *Cosey Complex*. Eds. Maria Fusco and Richard Birkett. London: Koenig Books, 2012. 11–21.

Garcia, Sandra A. "The Guiltman Cometh." *B Side Magazine* October/November 1992, 38–43, 54.

Garcia, Sandra A. "Interview with Bill Leeb." *B-Side Magazine* September 1992. Page numbers unavailable.

Gardner, Neil. "Zen Paradox: From a Distant Land." *Music from the Empty Quarter* 11 (1995), 28–29.

Gates, Margaret. "Some girls . . ." *alt.gothic*. Nov. 24, 1992. Accessed Dec. 12, 2011, <https://groups.google.com/forum/?fromgroups=#!topic/alt.gothic/pEKrOmAfUbA>.

Gedge, Dave. "Helios Creed Interview." *Bad Acid Magazine*. 1998. Via *Helios Creed Tribute Site*. Aug. 22, 2012, <http://www.helioschrome.com/badacidinterview.html>.

Genion, Philippe, and Jacques Meurrens. Personal interview. May 18, 2011.

Geraci, Philip C. "The Home Recordist . . . Hobbyist or Hoodlum?" *Stereophile* 1/1 (September 1962): 3–6.

"Getting Down In It." *Alternative Press* March 1990. Page numbers unavailable.

Gill, Andy. "Cabaret Voltaire: This Week's Leeds." *New Musical Express* Sep. 9, 1978. Page numbers unavailable.

Gill, John. "Forgive Us Our Synths." *Sounds* Jan. 10, 1981. Page numbers unavailable.

Gill, John. "Interview with Damon Edge." *Sounds* May 10, 1980. Page numbers unavailable.

Gill, John. *Queer Noise*. Minneapolis: University of Minnesota Press, 1995.

Gillis, Kathy. "Talent in Action." *Billboard*. Nov. 3, 1984, 55.

Girl the Bourgeois Individualist. "Being a Little Bit Productive." *Sordid Magazine*. 2003. Accessed Oct. 19, 2010, <http://sortedmagazine.com/Sordid.php3?nID=261>.

Gold, Jonathan, and David Kendrick. "It's the Industrial Evolution." *Los Angeles Times*. Apr. 19, 1992. Calendar section: 6–7, 62.

Graham, James. "Interview with Mark Spybey of Dead Voices on Air." *Sonic Boom*. July 1996. Accessed Nov. 10, 2010, <http://www.sonic-boom.com/interview/dvoa-3.interview.html>.

Greene, Jo-Ann. "Ministry." *Goldmine* Apr. 2, 1993, 32.

Grinder, Nicholas Genital. "Greek Scene Report." *Tanz Der Rosen* no. 5 (1996), 8.

Gunn, Joshua. "Dark Admissions: Gothic Subculture and the Ambivalence of Misogyny and Resistance." *Goth: Undead Subcultures*. Eds. Lauren M. E. Goodlad and Michael Bibby. Durham, NC: Duke University Press, 2007. 41–64.

Hafler Trio. "Metanoia: Theme for 'Captured Music.'" *Tape Delay*. Ed. Charles Neal. London: SAF, 1987. 181–184.

Hanley, Jason. "'The Land of Rape and Honey': The Use of World War II Propaganda in the Music Videos of Ministry and Laibach." *American Music* vol. 22 no. 1 (Spring 2004), 158–175.

Hanley, Jason. *Metal Machine Music: Technology, Noise, and Modernism in Industrial Music, 1975–1996*. Diss., Stony Brook University, 2011.

Harris, Bon. Personal interview. May 13, 2011.

Harris, Oliver. "Cut-Up Closure: The Return to Narrative." *William S. Burroughs at the Front: Critical Reception, 1959–1989.* Eds. Jennie Skerl and Robin Lydenberg. Edwardsville: Southern Illinois University Press, 1991. 251–262.

Hegarty, Paul. "Just What Is It That Makes Today's Noise Music So Different, So Appealing?" *Organised Sound* 13/1 (2008), 13–20.

Hegarty, Paul. *Noise/Music: A History.* New York: Continuum, 2007.

Hill, Jane H. "Language, Race, and White Public Space." *American Anthropologist*, New Series vol. 100, no. 3 (Sept. 1998), 680–689.

Hillegas, Mark R. *The Future as Nightmare: H. G. Wells and Anti-Utopians.* New York: Oxford University Press, 1967.

Hobijn, Geert-Jan. Personal interview. May 12, 2011.

Hodkinson, Paul. *Goth: Identity, Style and Subculture.* New York: Oxford University Press, 2002.

Holmes, Thom. *Electronic and Experimental Music: Technology, Music, and Culture.* New York: Routledge, 2008.

Home, Stewart. *The Assault on Culture: Utopian Currents from Lettrisme to Class War.* London: Aporia Press and Unpopular Books, 1988.

Hoskyns, Barney. "Einstürzende Neubauten: Aklam Hall, Notting Hill." *New Musical Express* Aug. 20, 1983. Page numbers unavailable.

Howard, Carl. "After the Clanking's Gone (How the Cassette Culture Grows Up)." In *Cassette Mythos.* Ed. Robin James. Brooklyn: Autonomedia, 1992. 46–47.

Howard, Carl. "Hunting Lodge." *Artitude* no. 7 (Aug. 1985), 2.

Howard, Carl. "Test Dept. in New York: Breaking the Trappings of Rock." *Unsound* vol. 1 no. 5 (1984), 6–8.

Hunter, Edward. *Brainwashing in Red China: The Calculated Destruction of Men's Minds.* New York: Vanguard, 1951.

Hurley, Kelly. *The Gothic Body.* New York: Cambridge University Press, 1996.

Huxley, Martin. *Nine Inch Nails.* New York: St. Martin's Press, 1997.

Hyams, Reid. "Re: Armageddon Dildos." *RasDVA.* Apr. 29, 1994. Accessed Aug. 21, 2012, <http://www.rasdva.com/DSC03001.JPG>.

"I Am So Industrial." *Sonic Boom.* 2001. Accessed Sep. 5, 2011, <http://www.sonic-boom.com/industrial/industrial-2.html>.

I Die You Die. "Kinetik Update 2012: Ad•ver•sary's Performance." *I Die You Die.* May 17, 2012. Accessed Aug. 14, 2012, <http://www.idieyoudie.com/2012/05/kinetik-update-2012-ad·ver·sarys-performance/>.

Idelson, Karen. "Member Gives the 'Skinny' on Breakup Rumors, Album." *Arizona Daily Wildcat.* Via *rec.music.industrial.* May 1992. Accessed Aug. 22, 2012, <https://groups.google.com/forum/?fromgroups=#!topic/rec.music.industrial/OH_p9jVnCmo>.

Ivens, Dirk. Personal interview. May 18, 2011.

Jensen, Rich, and Robin James. "A Sound Mind." In *Cassette Mythos.* Ed. Robin James. Brooklyn: Autonomedia, 1992. 41–42.

Jones, Gareth. Personal interview. May 14, 2011.

Jones, Steve. "The Cassette Underground." In *Cassette Mythos.* Ed. Robin James. Brooklyn: Autonomedia, 1992. 6–7.

Kallberg, Jeffrey. "The Rhetoric of Genre: Chopin's Nocturne in G Minor." *19th-Century Music,* no. 11 (1988), 238–261.

Keenan, David. *England's Hidden Reverse: Coil, Current 93, Nurse With Wound.* London: SAF, 2003.

Key, cEvin. Facebook chat interview. Aug. 9, 2011.

King, Francis. *Sexuality, Magic and Perversion.* Secaucus, NJ: Citadel Press, 1971.

Kistner, Thomas, and Alexander Weil, dirs. *Aufbruch in die Endzeit.* Empty Records, 2005.

Kopf, Biba. "Bacillus Culture." *Tape Delay.* Ed. Charles Neal. London: SAF, 1987.

Kostelanetz, Richard. *Conversing with Cage*. London: Omnibus, 1989.

Kot, Greg. "Nightmare Rock." *Chicago Tribune* Apr. 7, 1991. Accessed Aug. 21, 2012, <http://articles.chicagotribune.com/1991-04-07/entertainment/9101310776_1_industrial-disco-wax-trax-gristle>.

Krims, Adam. *Music and Urban Geography*. New York: Routledge, 2007.

Kristeva, Julia. *The Powers of Horror*. New York: Columbia University Press, 1982.

Lanier, Jaron. *You Are Not a Gadget*. New York: Knopf, 2010.

Laurence, Alexander. "Interview with Jim Thirlwell aka Foetus." June 2002. *Perfect Sound Forever Online Music Magazine*. June 2002. Accessed Aug. 21, 2012, <http://www.furious.com/perfect/foetus.html>.

Leavitt, David. *The Man Who Knew Too Much: Alan Turing and the Invention of the Computer*. New York: Norton, 2006.

Lee, Cosmo. "Ministry." *Pitchfork*. June 17, 2008. Accessed Aug. 17, 2011, <http://pitchfork.com/features/interviews/6874-interview-ministry/>.

Lee, Stephen Clinton. *Marketing the Margins: Wax Trax Records, Alternative Music and Independent Record Labels*. Diss. University of Texas at Austin, 1993.

Leeb, Bill. Liner notes. *The Man Who Did Backwards Somersaults*. T.E.Q. Music? 1994.

Lemos, Paul. "Controlled Bleeding." *Even When It Makes No Sense* no. 1 (1985), 6–7.

Lemos, Paul. Email interview. Aug. 30, 2011.

Lena, Jennifer C., and Richard A. Peterson. "Classification as Culture: Types and Trajectories of Music Genres." *American Sociological Review* vol. 73 no. 5 (October 2008), 697–718.

Levermore, Gary. Telephone interview. Oct. 30, 2009.

Levy, William. "The New Orality." In *Cassette Mythos*. Ed. Robin James. Brooklyn: Autonomedia, 1992. 39–40.

Lewis, Scott. "Situation Industrial Music: An Avant-Garde in Popular Music." *Music on Show: Issues of Performance*. Eds. Tarja Hautamäki and Helmi Järviluoma. Tampere, Finland: Dept. of Folk Tradition, 1998. 183–196.

Lilleker, Martin. *Beats Working for a Living*. Sheffield, UK: Juma, 2005.

Lloyd, Tony. "Father Dry Lungs: A Talk with Paul Lemos of Controlled Bleeding." *H23* 1 (Spring 1989), 14–17.

Lovink, Geert. *Uncanny Networks: Dialogues with the Virtual Intelligentsia*. Cambridge: MIT Press, 2004.

Lucas, John. "Luv-A-Fair lives on in Skinny Puppy Man's Memory." *Straight.com*. May 28, 2009. Accessed Aug. 3, 2011, <http://www.straight.com/article-223414/luvafair-lives-puppy-man%3F%3Fs-memory>.

MacLuhan, Marshall. *Understanding Media*. Berkeley: Gingko Press, 2003.

Maeck, Klaus. *Hoer mit Schmerzen/Listen with Pain: Einstuerzende Neubauten 1980–1996*. Berlin: Gestalten Verlag, 1996.

Manuel, Peter. *Cassette Culture*. Chicago: University of Chicago Press, 1993.

Marinetti, F. T. "The Founding and Manifesto of Futurism." In *Manifesto: A Century of isms*. Ed. Mary Ann Caws. Lincoln: University of Nebraska Press, 2000. 185–189.

Marshall, Scott. "99 & 44/100ths Percent Pure Bullshit: The Packaging and Programming of the American Exploitation Experiment." In *Cassette Mythos*. Ed. Robin James. Brooklyn: Autonomedia, 1992. 43–44.

Masters, Marc. *No Wave*. London: Black Dog, 2007.

McCaughey, Brian F. "Skinny Puppy: A Difficult Process." *RIP Magazine* Mar. 1996. Page numbers unavailable.

McClary, Susan. *Feminine Endings*. Minneapolis: University of Minnesota Press, 1991.

McDonough, Tom, ed. *Guy Debord and the Situationist International: Texts and Documents*. Cambridge, MA: MIT Press, 2002.

McGee, Hal. "Forward." In *Cassette Mythos*. Ed. Robin James. Brooklyn: Autonomedia, 1992. vii.

McGee, Hal. Personal interview. June 17, 2011.

McKenna, Terence. "Tryptamine Hallucinogens and Consciousness." *Book of Lies*. Ed. Richard Metzger. New York: Disinformation, 2008. 62–70.

Meyer, Bill. "SPK Dokument III0 1979–1983." *The Wire* June 2008. Page numbers unavailable.

Miller, Walt, and Paul Chavez. "Who Is Dannie Flesher and Why Should I Care?" *Faqt Magazine* 3 (1997). Page numbers unavailable.

"Mindphaser.com Exclusive Michael Balch Interview." *Mindphaser*. 2004. Accessed Aug. 10, 2011, <http://www.mindphaser.com/index.php?page_id=601>.

Morley, Paul. "The Heart and Soul of Cabaret Voltaire." *New Musical Express* Nov. 29, 1980. Page numbers unavailable.

Mothersole, Dave. "Proto techno." *DJHistory.com*. Sep. 7, 2009. Accessed Aug. 26, 2011, <http://www.djhistory.com/forum/proto-techno?page=3>, <http://www.djhistory.com/forum/proto-techno?page=4>.

Müller, Andreas. "Esplendor Geométrico." *Datenverarbeitung* 8 (1982), 6–7.

Müller, Wolfgang. *Geniale Dilletanten*. Berlin: Merve Verlag, 1982.

Myer, Daniel. Personal interview. May 13, 2011.

Naked. "SPK Interviewed by Naked." *Music from the Empty Quarter* 2 (1991), 52–55.

Naremore, James, and Patrick Brantlinger. "Introduction: Six Artistic Cultures." *Modernity and Mass Culture*. Eds. James Naremore and Patrick Brantlinger. Bloomington: Indiana University Press, 1991. 1–21.

Nash, Julia. "History." *WaxTraxChicago.com*. Apr. 30, 2011. Accessed Aug. 21, 2012, <http://waxtraxchicago.com/>.

Neal, Charles. *Tape Delay*. London: SAF, 1987.

Nettwerk Records. Press release: *Last Rights*. Vancouver: Nettwerk Records, 1992.

Neville, Leigh. "Genesis P'Orridge: Pigface, Cyberspace, and Thee." *Music from the Empty Quarter* 11 (March 1995), 30–32.

Neville, Leigh. "Recall." *Music from the Empty Quarter*, 11 (1995), 20.

New Collectivism. *Neue Slowenische Kunst*. Los Angeles: Amok Books, 1991.

Newton, Adi. Personal interview. May 21, 2011.

Nine Inch Nails. Liner notes. *Broken*. TVT Records, 1992.

Noë, Alva. "What Would Disembodied Music Even Be?" *Bodily Expression in Electronic Music*. Eds. Deniz Peters, Gerhard Eckel, and Andreas Dorschel. New York: Routledge, 2012. 53–60.

Noise, Richard. "New Beat: One Nation Under a (Slowed Down) Groove." *New Musical Express*. 1991. Via *Poesie Noire*. Accessed Aug. 27, 2011, <http://www.poesienoire.com/mirrors/www.robotnik.com-synthesis/nation.html>.

"Nomeans No, too fucking wonderful for words." *Waste.org*. 1995. Accessed Aug. 21, 2012, <http://www.waste.org/~skumm/No.html>.

Novak, Jason. Personal interview. Dec. 9, 2010.

Nunes, Mark, ed. *Error: Glitch, Noise, and Jam in New Media Cultures*. New York: Continuum, 2011.

Nyman, Michael. *Experimental Music: Cage and Beyond*. New York: Cambridge University Press, 1999.

Oldanburg, Klaos. "Plagiarism, Culture, Mass Media." *Plagiarism: Art as Commodity and Strategies for Its Negation*. Ed. Stewart Home. London: Aporia Press, 1978.

Owen, Tim. "*The Culling Is Coming*." *Flowmotion* 5 (1982), 22–23.

P-Orridge, Genesis. Liner notes. *Thirst*. London: Fetish Records, 1981.

P-Orridge, Genesis Breyer. Personal interview. Mar. 10, 2011.

P-Orridge, Genesis Breyer. Email interview. Jan. 8, 2013.

P-Orridge, Genesis Breyer. *Thee Psychick Bible*. Port Townsend, WA: Feral House, 2009.

P-Orridge, Genesis Breyer. "Thee Splinter Test." *Book of Lies.* Ed. Richard Metzger. New York: Disinformation, 2003. 32–36.

Pearce, Stevo. Personal interview. May 22, 2011.

Pearson, Mike, and Michael Shanks. *Theatre/Archaeology.* London: Routledge, 2001.

Pellerin, Amanda. "Cosey Fanni Tutti." *WheelMeOut.* 2009. Accessed Dec. 15, 2011, <http://www.wheelmeout.com/4_12.php>.

Perloff, Marjorie. Review of *Fluxus Experience* (Hannah Higgins. Berkeley: University of California Press, 2002) and *Oyvind Fahlström on the Air—Manipulating the World* (Teddy Hultberg, Stockholm: Sveriges Radios Förlag / Fylkingen, 1999, with 2 CDs: *Birds in Sweden, The Holy Torsten Nilsson.*) *Modernism/Modernity,* Vol. 11, No. 3 (2004), 581–587.

Peter, 23rd. "There Are a Lot of Fools in the World." *FOPI.net.* June 2000. Accessed June 18, 2007, <http://fopi.net/inter/fred.htm>.

Peters, Deniz. Introduction. *Bodily Expression in Electronic Music.* Eds. Deniz Peters, Gerhard Eckel, and Andreas Dorschel. New York: Routledge, 2012. 1–16.

*Phosphor.* August 1993. Via *Sonic Boom.* Accessed July 1, 2012, <http://www.sonic-boom.com/mission-control/revnmind.html>.

Popson, Tom. "The WaxTrax Method of Making Records." *Chicago Tribune* July 26, 1985. Accessed Aug. 21, 2012, <http://articles.chicagotribune.com/1985-07-26/entertainment/8502190282_1_sire-records-wax-trax-records-al-jourgensen>.

"Portion Control." *Barcode Magazine.* 2004. Accessed Aug. 21, 2012, <http://www.barcodezine.com/Portion%20Control%20Interview.htm>.

Portnoy, Sean. "This Is Fascism? (Raves and the Politics of Dancing)." *Reading Rock and Roll: Authenticity, Appropriation, Aesthetics.* Eds. Kevin J. H. Dettmar and William Richey. New York: Columbia University Press, 1999. 191–207.

Rabid, Jack. "V. Vale." *The Big Takeover* 63 (2008), 100–106.

"Ramleh Interview." *Grim Humor* vol. 2 no. 2 (1992). Page numbers unavailable.

Rapp, Tobias. *Lost and Sound.* Frankfurt: Innervisions, 2010.

Ray, Robert B. *How a Film Theory Got Lost and Other Mysteries in Cultural Studies.* Bloomington: Indiana University Press, 2001.

Reed, S. Alexander. "Pig." *Interface Magazine* v 4.1 (1997), 31.

Reynolds, Simon. "Blowing Other People's Trumpets aka 2005's Bumper Book Crop." *Blissblog.* June 18, 2005. Accessed Oct. 19, 2010, <http://blissout.blogspot.com/2005/06/that-book-questionnaire-reminded-me-of.html>.

Reynolds, Simon. *Blissed Out: The Raptures of Rock.* London: Serpent's Tail, 1990.

Reynolds, Simon. "Living for Oblivion." *Village Voice.* May 23, 2000. Page numbers unavailable.

Reynolds, Simon. *Retromania.* New York: Faber and Faber, 2011.

Reynolds, Simon. *Rip It Up and Start Again.* London: Faber and Faber, 2005.

"Rhythm and Noise—Naut Humon—Z'ev." *Ear Magazine* vol. 13 no. 10 (Feb. 1989). Page numbers unavailable.

Rice, Boyd. "Boyd Rice Speaks: 'Do you Want A Total War?' from *The Fifth Path*." *Boyd Rice.* 1992. Accessed Aug. 21, 2012, <http://www.boydrice.com/interviews/fifthpath.html>.

Rice, Boyd. *No.* New York: Heartworm Press, 2009.

Rice, Boyd. Personal Interview. May 14, 2011.

"Robert Görl und Gabi Delgado—DAF—12.01.2009." *Zündfunk.* Jan. 12, 2009. Accessed Dec. 10, 2009, <http://www.podcast.at/episoden/robert-görl-und-gabi-delgado-daf-12-01-2009-5239702.html>.

Roberts, Sean. Personal interview. Mar. 13, 2011.

Ross, Alex. ". . . views expressed are not endorsed. . . ." *The Rest Is Noise.* July 2, 2004. Accessed Aug. 21, 2012, <http://www.therestisnoise.com/2004/07/views_expressed.html>.

Rudiman, Shawn. Personal interview. April 2003.

Russolo, Luigi. "The Art of Noises." In *Manifesto: A Century of isms*. Ed. Mary Ann Caws. Lincoln: University of Nebraska Press, 2000. 205–211.

"Salmon-Fishing on the Nipissiguit." *Putnam's Magazine*. vol. 6, no. 31 (July 1870), 13–22.

Samardzija, Milan. "Independent 45s Important for Chicago Groups." *Billboard* Sep. 13, 1980, 6, 76.

Savage, Jon. Introduction. *Industrial Culture Handbook*. Eds. V. Vale and Andrea Juno. San Francisco: RE/Search, 1983. 4–5.

Savage, Jon. Liner notes. *The Last Testament*. Fetish Records, 1983.

Schierbaum, Hartwig. Personal interview. May 11, 2011.

Schmelze, Peter, and Robert Schalinski. "I had twelve years of meeting a fantastic group of very talented creative people and I hope to count myself as one of them." *FOPI.net*. 2004. Dec. 6, 2009, <http://web.archive.org/web/20041220104423/http://fopi.net/inter/alaura2004.htm>.

Scott, Ridley, dir. *Blade Runner*. Warner Bros., 1982.

Seed, David. *Brainwashing: The Fictions of Mind Control: A Study of Novels and Films Since World War II*. Kent, OH: Kent State University Press, 2004.

Shear, Tom. Facebook interview. Nov. 26, 2011.

Shekhovstov, Anton. "Apoliteic Music: Neo-Folk, Martial Industrial and 'Metapolitical Fascism'." *Patterns of Prejudice* vol. 43 no. 5 (2009), 431–457.

Shekhovstov, Anton. "Apoliteic Music (Comment 1)." *Anton Shekhovstov's blog*. December 2009. Accessed Aug. 21, 2012, <http://anton-shekhovtsov.blogspot.com/2009/12/apoliteic-music -comment-1.html>.

Shore, Thomas Maxwell. Abstract. *The Western Works Project: Heterotopic Spaces and the City*. M.A. thesis. Sheffield Hallam University, 2009. Via *Thomas Maxwell Shore*. Accessed Oct. 18, 2011, <http://web.archive.org/web/20100802030751/http://thomasmaxwellshore.wordpress .com/ma-dissertation-the-western-works-project-heterotopic-spaces-and-the-city/>.

Shryane, Jennifer. *Blixa Bargeld and Einstürzende Neubauten: German Experimental Music*. Burlington: Ashgate, 2011.

Siana, Jolene. *Go Ask Ogre: Letters from a Deathrock Cutter*. Port Townsend, WA: Process, 2005.

Side-Line. "Front 242's Patrick Codenys presents workshop 'How to build an EBM track' in Lille (France)." *Side-Line*. July 25, 2011. Accessed Sep. 18, 2011, <http://www.side-line.com/news _comments.php?id=46629_0_2_0_C>.

Siegel, Carol. *Goth's Dark Empire*. Bloomington: Indiana University Press, 2005.

Smith, Nick. "The Splinter in Your Ear: Noise as the Semblance of Critique." *Culture, Theory & Critique* 46/1 (2005), 43–59.

Smith, Richard. "Obituary: John Balance." *Guardian* Dec. 11, 2004. Page numbers unavailable.

Sonst, Wilhelm. "New Beat—This Is Belgian." *Fabiola* issue 29 (November 1988). Via *New Beat*. Trans. Webmaster. Accessed Aug. 27, 2011, <http://users.skynet.be/newbeat/en/en_dit_is _belgisch.htm accessed 8/27/2011>.

Sontag, Susan. "Fascinating Fascism." *Under the Sign of Saturn*. New York: Anchor Books, 1991. 73–105.

Souvignier, Todd. "Super Chunking with the Commando Hillbillies." *Guitar* January 1994, 94–100, 110.

Star. "VNV Nation Interview." Accessed Nov. 27, 2011, <http://dancemusic.about.com/od/ artistshomepages/a/VnVNationInt_2.htm>.

Sterritt, David. *Screening the Beats*. Edwardsville: Southern Illinois University Press, 2004.

Stewart, Mark. Personal interview. May 14, 2011.

Stockhausen, Karlheinz, Aphex Twin, Scanner, and Daniel Pemberton. "Stockhausen vs. the 'Technocrats'." *Audio Culture*. Eds. Cristoph Cox and Daniel Warner. New York: Continuum Press, 2004. 381–385.

Straw, Will. "Communities and Scenes in Popular Music." *The Subcultures Reader*. Eds. Ken Gelder and Sarah Thornton. New York: Routledge, 1997. 494–505.

Strong, Martin Charles. *The Great Indie Discography*. Edinburgh: Canongate, 2003.

Stroud, Abbey. "Interview with Jurgen Engler of Die Krupps." *Sonic Boom*. Aug. 18, 1995. Accessed July 11, 2010, <http://www.aracnet.com/~jester/interview/die.krupps-2.interview.html>.

Stull, De Forest, and Roy Winthrop Hatch. *Journeys Through Many Lands: A Textbook in the New Geography*. Boston: Allyn and Bacon, 1935.

Sweers, Britta. *Electric Folk*. New York: Oxford University Press, 2005.

Sweeting, Adam. "Corridors of Power." *Melody Maker* Feb. 5, 1983, 9.

Sweeting, Adam. "Ministry of Offence." *Melody Maker* July 10, 1982. Page numbers unavailable.

Szava-Kovats, Andrew, dir. *Grindstone Redux*. True Age Media, 2009.

Tagg, Philip. "Harmony." *Continuum Encyclopedia of Popular Music of the World, Vol II: Performance and Production*. Ed. John Shepherd. New York: Continuum, 2003. Pages unavailable.

Tagg, Philip. "'Universal' Music and the Case of Death." *La Musica Come Linguaggio Universale*. Ed. Raffaele Pozzi. Florence: L. S. Olschki, 1990.

"Talking About Nothing with Trent Reznor." *Axcess* 2 (1994). Page numbers unavailable.

Théberge, Paul. "Random Access: Music, Technology, Postmodernism." *The Last Post: Music After Modernism*. Ed. Simon Miller. Manchester: Manchester University Press, 1993. 150–182.

Thompson, Dave. *Alternative Rock*. San Francisco: Miller Freeman, 2000.

Thompson, Dave. *Industrial Revolution*. Los Angeles: Cleopatra, 1993.

Thompson, Hunter S. *Fear and Loathing in Las Vegas*. New York: Vintage Books, 1971.

"Test Dept." *They're Coming to Take Me Away Ha Ha* 1 (1984), 20.

Tressler, Michael. "Interview with Bill Leeb of Front Line Assembly Live on WCRD (540 AM—Muncie Indiana), March 19, 1992." *rec.music.industrial*. Nov. 19, 1992. Accessed Nov. 27, 2011, <http://groups.google.com/group/rec.music.industrial/msg/65b859cbc1c6383c?>.

Turmel, Jean-Pierre. Liner notes. *Descending*. Trans. Malcolm Duff. Sordide Sentimental, 1985.

Tutti, Cosey Fanni. Email interview. Jan. 12, 2013.

Tutti, Cosey Fanni, and Chris Carter. Personal interview. May 13, 2011.

Twomey, Chris. "Developments from Industrial Music: Noise and Appropriation." *Sound by Artists*. Eds. Dan Lander and Micah Lexier. Toronto/Banff: Art Metropole/Walter Phillips Gallery, 1990. 267–281.

*Unsound* vol. 3 no. 2. (1987).

Urban, Hugh B. *Magia Sexualis: Sex, Magic, and Liberation in Modern Western Esotericism*. Berkeley: University of California Press, 2006.

Vale, V. Telephone interview. June 7, 2012.

Vale, V. "V. Vale on Industrial Culture Handbook." *YouTube*. Sep. 13, 2010. Accessed June 1, 2012, <http://www.youtube.com/watch?v=YwnyGT_tcGY>.

Vale, V., and Andrea Juno. *Industrial Culture Handbook*. San Francisco: RE/Search, 1983.

Vale, V., and Andrea Juno. *Pranks!* San Francisco: RE/Search, 1987.

Van Acker, Luc. Personal interview. May 18, 2011.

van den Berg, Hubert F. "Avant-garde: Some Introductory Notes on the Politics of a Label." In *Sound Commitments: Avant-garde Music and the Sixties*. Ed. Robert Adlington. New York: Oxford University Press, 2009. 15–33.

van den Troost, Guido. "New Beat: Beyond the Shame." *Fabiola* issue 31 (February 1989). Via *New Beat*. Trans. Webmaster. Accessed Aug. 27, 2011, <http://users.skynet.be/newbeat/en/en_de_schaamte_voorbij.htm>.

Van der Merwe, Peter. *Origins of the Popular Style*. New York: Oxford University Press, 1992.

van Elferen, Isabella. "'And Machine Created Music' Cybergothic Music and the Phantom Voices of the Technological Uncanny." *Digital Material: Tracing New Media in Everyday Life and Technology*. Eds. Marianne van den Boomen et al. Amsterdam: Amsterdam University Press, 2009. 121–132.

Virgin, David. "David Virgin History and Stories: Part 2." *Yahoo.com*. Oct. 21, 2007. Accessed May 31, 2012, <http://voices.yahoo.com/david-virgin-history-stories-part-2-611614.html>.

Voorvelt, Martijn. "New Sounds, Old Technology." *Organised Sound* 5/2 (2000), 67–73.

Walker, Elaine. "microtonality." *Zia*. 2012. Accessed July 2, 2012, <http://www.ziaspace.com/_microtonality/>.

Walser, Robert. *Running with the Devil*. Middletown, CT: Wesleyan University Press, 1993.

Webb, Peter. *Exploring the Networked Worlds of Popular Music*. New York: Routledge, 2007.

Whalley, Ben, dir. *Synth Britannia*. BBC 4, 2009.

Whitney, Jon. "Web Exclusive." *Brainwashed.com*. May 5, 1997. Accessed July 5, 2011, <http://brainwashed.com/coil/writings/jwint.html>.

Will, Sure. "Surgical Penis Klinik." *Slash* vol. 3 no. 5. (1980). Page numbers unavailable.

Williams, Anne. *Art of Darkness: A Poetics of Gothic*. Chicago: University of Chicago Press, 1995.

Williams, Anne. "Edifying Narratives: The Gothic Novel, 1764–1997." *Gothic: Transmutations of Horror in Late Twentieth-Century Art*. Ed. Christopher Grunenberg. Cambridge: MIT Press, 1997. 151–118 (sic).

Williams, Brian. Liner notes. *DeepNet*. Side Effects, 1996.

Wiseman-Trowse, Nathan. *Performing Class in British Popular Music*. New York: Palgrave Macmillan, 2008.

Wolanski, Coreen. "Skinny Puppy: Every Dog Has Its Day." *Exclaim.ca*. February 2002. Accessed Aug. 10, 2011, <http://exclaim.ca/Features/Timeline/skinny_puppy-every_dog_has_its_day>.

Wood, Eve, dir. *Made in Sheffield*. Plexifilm, 2001.

Woods, Bret. *Industrial Music for Industrial People*. M.A. thesis. Florida State University, 2007.

"WSKU Radio (Kent, Ohio)—Ralf Hütter—19/06/1978 American Radio Broadcasting." *Technopop-Archive*. June 19, 1978. Accessed July 20, 2011, <http://www.technopop-archive.com/interview_108.php>.

Wyman, Bill. "The Ballad of Jim and Dannie." *Chicago Reader*, Oct. 26, 1995. Page numbers unavailable.

Young, La Monte. "Lecture 1960." *Happenings and Other Acts*. Ed. Mariellen R. Sandford. New York: Routledge, 1995. 59–66.

Z'EV. "The Three-Fold Ear and the Energies of Enthusiasm." *Arcana: Musicians on Music*. Ed. John Zorn. New York: Granary Books. 170–178.

Žižek, Slavoj. *Living in the End Times*. New York: Verso Books, 2010.

Žižek, Slavoj, and Andrew Herscher. "Everything Provokes Fascism / Plečnik *avec* Laibach." *Assemblage* no. 33 (August 1997), 58–75.

Zwickel, Jonathan. "Reznor's Edge." *Ft. Lauderdale New Times* Oct. 20, 2005. Accessed Oct. 10, 2011, <http://www.browardpalmbeach.com/2005-10-20/music/reznor-s-edge>.

# Notes

### Introduction: The Front Lines

1. Levermore.
2. Butler.
3. Levermore.
4. Ibid.
5. Hanley, *Metal Machine Music* iii–iv.
6. Reynolds, "Blowing."
7. Dery 81.
8. Garcia, "Leeb."
9. Hanley, *Metal Machine Music* 17.
10. Naremore and Brantlinger 10.
11. Shryane 58.
12. Blake 123.
13. McKenna.
14. Nunes 3.
15. Rabid 100.
16. "I Am So Industrial."
17. Nettwerk.
18. Anonymous.
19. Lilleker 87.
20. Anonymous.
21. Lemos, "Controlled Bleeding" 7.
22. Boss.
23. Shryane 56.
24. Lena and Peterson 698.
25. Kallberg.
26. Lena and Peterson 701.
27. Ibid.
28. Side-Line.
29. Grinder 8.

### Part I: Technology and the Preconditions of Industrial Music

1. Densmore 611.
2. Antrim 276.
3. Ibid. 275.
4. Ibid. 279.

## Chapter 1: Italian Futurism

1. Boccioni et al. 184.
2. Ibid.
3. Marinetti 187.
4. Russolo 209.
5. Holmes 14–15.
6. Marinetti 187.
7. B. Williams.
8. Marinetti 186.


## Chapter 2: William S. Burroughs

1. Hunter 186.
2. Burroughs, *Junkie* 71.
3. Leavitt 269.
4. Seed 134.
5. MacLuhan 17.
6. Frith 26.
7. Burroughs, *Western Lands* 60.
8. Burroughs, *Naked Lunch* 94.
9. Burroughs, *Electronic Revolution* 6.
10. Friedberg 3.
11. Burroughs and Gysin, *Third Mind* 29.
12. Burroughs, *Electronic Revolution* 14–15.
13. Debord, "Detournement" 698.
14. P-Orridge, *Psychick Bible* 279.
15. Ibid.
16. Daniel 57.
17. Ibid. 58.
18. Ibid.
19. Ibid.
20. Nyman 9.
21. "Coil: Beyond the Eskaton."
22. Burroughs, *Letters* 269.
23. Burroughs and Gysin, *Colloque* 270.
24. O. Harris 256.
25. Naremore and Brantlinger 9.
26. Woods 16.
27. Hoskyns.
28. Collins 55.


## Chapter 3: Industrial Music and Art Music

1. *Phosphor.*
2. Burroughs and Odier 33.
3. Van den Berg 25.
4. Stockhausen et al. 382.

5. Ibid.
6. Gardner 29.
7. Duguid 18.
8. Owen 22.
9. J. Gill, "Forgive."
10. Morley.
11. Lilleker 10.
12. "Rhythm and Noise—Naut Humon—Z'ev."
13. Perloff 583.
14. Kostelanetz 203.
15. Cardew xiv.
16. Young 60.
17. Laurence.
18. Keenan 62.
19. Nyman xi.
20. Engels and Marx 14.

## Part II: Industrial Geography

1. Krims 7.

## Chapter 4: Northern England

1. Whalley.
2. Wood.
3. Ibid.
4. Hegarty, *Noise/Music* 108.
5. P-Orridge, "Splinter Test" 32.
6. Hafler Trio 182.
7. Wood.
8. Lilleker 12–13.
9. Ibid. 14.
10. A. Gill, "Cabaret Voltaire."
11. Lilleker 11.
12. Ibid. 10.
13. Ibid. 11.
14. Brown et al. 439.
15. Shore.
16. Reynolds, *Rip It* 168.
17. Lilleker 13, 11.
18. Morley.
19. Fish 63.
20. Lilleker 88.
21. Ibid.
22. Ibid. 90.
23. Ibid. 91.
24. Wood.
25. Lilleker 87.

26. Ibid. 48.
27. Brown et al. 439.
28. Reynolds, *Rip It* 154.
29. Lilleker 69.
30. Newton.
31. Lilleker 125.
32. Ibid.
33. D. Thompson, *Alternative* 275.
34. Lilleker 130.
35. Ibid.
36. Newton.
37. Ibid.
38. Lilleker 136.
39. Ibid.
40. Newton.
41. P-Orridge, *Thirst*.
42. Clock DVA.
43. Newton.
44. Lilleker 138.
45. Ibid. 47.
46. S. Ford 0.12.
47. Ibid. 6.32.
48. Fusco and Tutti 18.
49. S. Ford 6.33.
50. Ibid.
51. Ibid. 9.27.
52. Pellerin.
53. Tutti.
54. P-Orridge, Email.
55. Ibid.
56. Tutti.
57. P-Orridge, Interview.
58. S. Ford 1.5.
59. Ibid.
60. P-Orridge, Interview.

## Chapter 5: Berlin

1. Schierbaum.
2. Ibid.
3. Straw 494.
4. Beetz and Herdlitschke.
5. Ibid.
6. Beaumont 39.
7. Schierbaum.
8. Ibid.
9. Shryane, 14.
10. Chainsaw.
11. A. Müller 7.

12. Maeck 11.
13. Beetz and Herdlitschke.
14. W. Müller 24, author's translation.
15. Maeck 33.
16. Chung.
17. Rapp 37.
18. Esch et al.
19. Die Krupps.
20. Stroud.
21. Esch et al.
22. Die Krupps.
23. Strong.
24. Fraser and Hoffmann 268.

## Chapter 6: San Francisco

1. Vale, Interview.
2. H. S. Thompson, 67–68.
3. J. Gill, "Interview."
4. Barr, "Helios Creed."
5. Gedge.
6. Barr, "Helios Creed."
7. Esch et al.
8. Bell.
9. Vale and Juno, *Handbook* 74.
10. Vale and Juno, *Pranks!* 73.
11. Ibid.
12. Benjamin 224–225.
13. Vale and Juno, *Handbook* 110.
14. Ibid. 115.
15. Rice, Interview.
16. Ibid.
17. Vale and Juno, *Handbook* 115.
18. Ibid. 37.
19. Ibid. 27.
20. Z'EV 178.
21. Bergland and Palme.
22. Vale, YouTube.
23. Vale and Juno, *Pranks!* 14
24. Savage, Introduction 5.
25. Bergland and Palme.
26. Reynolds, *Rip It* 247.
27. Vale, Interview.
28. Ibid.
29. Ibid.

## Chapter 7: Mail Art, Tape Technology, and the Network

1. Codenys.
2. Théberge 151.
3. Levy 39.
4. Jensen and James 41.
5. Faust.
6. Jones 7.
7. Levy 40.
8. Geraci 3.
9. Manuel 19–20.
10. Corbett 98.
11. Howard, "Clanking" 46.
12. Cigéhn.
13. Rice, interview.
14. S. Ford 3.11.
15. S. Ford 1.21.
16. P-Orridge, Interview.
17. S. Ford 8.15, 12.14.
18. Carter.
19. Ibid.
20. P-Orridge, Interview.
21. Etat Brut.
22. Marshall 44-5.
23. Vale and Juno, *Handbook* 14.
24. McGee, Interview.
25. Hobijn.
26. Ibid.
27. Ayers, Interview.
28. Ferfolja.
29. Hobijn.
30. Levermore.
31. Ibid.
32. Szava-Kovats.
33. McGee, "Forward" vii.
34. Dink 107.


## Chapter 8: The Tyranny of the Beat

1. S. Ford 7.24.
2. P-Orridge, Interview.
3. 'Enthal 39.
4. Savage, *Testament*.
5. Meyer.
6. New Collectivism 21.
7. Fink, *Repeating* 3–4.
8. Daniel 21.
9. Keenan 168.
10. Lanier 10.

11. Pearce.
12. Codenys.
13. Ayers, Interview.
14. McClary 29.
15. S. Ford 6.17.
16. Savage, *Testament*.
17. Levermore.
18. Blake 115.
19. Krims 128–130.
20. Fish 150.
21. B. Harris.
22. Esch et al.


## Chapter 9: "After Cease to Exist"

1. Tutti and Carter.
2. Ibid.
3. Ibid.
4. Fish 103.
5. S. Ford 11.6.
6. Ibid. 9.18.
7. Tutti and Carter.
8. "Coil" 13.
9. Tutti and Carter.
10. Schmelze and Schalinski.
11. Whitney.
12. King 122.
13. Urban 11. Emphasis original.
14. R. Smith.
15. Pearce.
16. Chung.
17. Andrews 50.
18. Will.
19. Virgin.
20. Blake 105.
21. Chainsaw.
22. "Ramleh Interview."
23. Ibid.
24. Hegarty, "Just" 17.
25. Ibid. 20.
26. J. Gill, *Queer* 161.
27. "Test Dept." 20.
28. Allen.
29. Collins 123.
30. Neal 165.
31. Pearson and Shanks 103.
32. Neal 164.
33. "Portion Control."
34. Leeb.

35. Becu.
36. Duguid 20.
37. B. Harris.
38. di Perna 57.
39. B. Harris.
40. Ibid.
41. Ibid.
42. Ibid.
43. Ibid.
44. Codenys.
45. Noë 60.
46. Peters 1–2.
47. Turmel.

## Chapter 10: Body to Body

1.  Ivens.
2.  Genion and Meurrens.
3.  Ibid.
4.  Van Acker.
5.  Ibid.
6.  Codenys.
7.  Van Acker.
8.  Genion and Meurrens.
9.  Ibid.
10. Codenys.
11. Ibid.
12. Reynolds, *Blissed* 163. Emphasis added.
13. Codenys.
14. Ibid.
15. Ibid.
16. Kistner and Weil.
17. "WSKU Radio (Kent, Ohio)—Ralf Hütter—19/06/1978 American Radio Broadcasting."
18. Front 242.
19. Codenys.
20. Cusick 35.

## Chapter 11: Industrial Music as a Theater of Cruelty

1.  Artaud 84.
2.  Ibid. Emphasis added.
3.  Graham.
4.  Coatts 18.
5.  Howard, "Test Dept." 7.
6.  Sterritt 81.
7.  Artaud 92.
8.  Ibid.
9.  Ibid. 94.

10. Ibid. 93.
11. Ibid. 96.
12. Ibid. 95.
13. Vale and Juno, *Pranks!* 72.
14. Artaud 99.

## Chapter 12: "She's a Sleeping Beast"

1. Barclay, Jack, and Schneider 507.
2. Key.
3. Ibid.
4. Wolanski.
5. Lucas.
6. Keenan 108.
7. Naked 52.
8. Key.
9. "Mindphaser.com Exclusive Michael Balch Interview."
10. Hodkinson 48–56.
11. Key.
12. Walser; Gunn.
13. Gold and Kendrick 6.
14. Hurley 3–4.
15. Key.
16. Kopf 10.
17. Kristeva.
18. A. Williams, *Art.* 23.
19. Hurley 4.
20. Fulber.
21. Ibid.
22. Key.
23. Siana 102.
24. Ibid. 16.

## Chapter 13: Back and Forth

1. Žižek and Herscher 62.
2. FatherWithHorns.
3. Hanley, "Land" 172.
4. Ibid.
5. Ibid. 174.
6. Aspa 10.
7. Hanley, "Land" 174.
8. Ibid.
9. Freel.
10. S. Ford, *Wreckers* 9–27.
11. "Robert Görl und Gabi Delgado—DAF—12.01.2009."
12. Shekhovstov, "Apoliteic Music" 432.
13. Ibid. 436.

14. Žižek and Herscher 63.
15. Portnoy 191.
16. Shekhovstov, "Apoliteic music" 437
17. Shekhovstov, Blog.
18. Shekhovstov, "Apoliteic music" 455.
19. Ibid. 448.
20. Rice, "Speaks."
21. Ross.
22. Rice, Interview.
23. Rice, *No* 79.
24. Rice, Interview.
25. Rice, Interview.
26. Webb 85.
27. Hanley, "Land" 173.
28. English Celt.
29. Sontag 101.
30. Ibid. 105.
31. Ibid. 102.
32. Ayers, Letter 62.
33. Sontag 91–92. Emphasis added.
34. Žižek 372.
35. Ibid. 387.
36. Blake 121.
37. Carver 259.
38. Oldanburg 17.
39. Home 74.
40. Oldanburg 17–18.
41. Home 74.
42. Oldanburg 18.
43. Lovink 113.
44. I Die You Die.
45. Ibid.

## Chapter 14: White Souls in Black Suits

1. Twomey 272.
2. Holmes 61, 396.
3. Fish 93.
4. *Unsound* 112.
5. Masters 12.
6. "cEvin Key: See the Light, Feel the Heat."
7. Stewart.
8. Marshall 44.
9. P. Ford 107–108.
10. Ibid. 108.
11. Via Stull and Hatch 66.
12. Da Davo.
13. P. Ford 110.

14. Ibid.
15. Ibid. 129.
16. Hill 683.
17. Fink "ORCH5."
18. Key.
19. Savage, Introduction 5.
20. Reynolds, *Retromania* 314.
21. Lloyd 14.
22. Neville, "Recall." 20.
23. Codenys.
24. Sweers 229.
25. Van der Merwe 108.
26. de La Villemarqué.
27. "Salmon-Fishing on the Nipissiguit" 22.
28. Lemos Interview.
29. Lloyd 14.
30. Rudiman.

## Chapter 15: Wild Planet

1. G. Jones.
2. Fish 194.
3. Wyman.
4. Samardzija 76.
5. Popson.
6. Nash.
7. Roberts.
8. Gold and Kendrick 7.
9. Connelly 26–27.
10. Samardzija 76.
11. Popson.
12. Baker.
13. Brewster and Broughton, *Last Night* 298.
14. Sweeting, "Ministry."
15. Baker.
16. Sweeting, "Corridors" 9.
17. Gillis 55.
18. Connelly 22.
19. DeRogatis and Kot.
20. Freel.
21. Van Acker.
22. C. Lee.
23. S. Lee 119.
24. DeRogatis and Kot.
25. DeRogatis and Kot.
26. Dasein 28.
27. DeRogatis and Kot.
28. Van Acker.

29. Miller and Chavez.
30. S. Lee 116.
31. Nash.
32. Fulber.
33. Voorvelt 71.
34. Mothersole 3.
35. Mothersole 4.
36. D. Thompson, *Alternative* 562
37. Reynolds, "Oblivion."
38. Peter.
39. Brewster and Broughton, *Record Players* 326.
40. Noise.
41. Sonst.
42. Ibid.
43. van den Troost.
44. Elitair.
45. Barr "Young Gods."
46. Connelly 22.
47. DeRogatis 95.
48. Greene 32.
49. Souvignier 98.


## Chapter 16: Q: Why Do We Act Like Machines? A: We Do Not.

1. "Getting Down In It."
2. Huxley 74.
3. Roberts.
4. "Talking About Nothing with Trent Reznor."
5. Ibid.
6. Zwickel.
7. Roberts.
8. Nine Inch Nails.
9. Howard, "Hunting Lodge" 2.
10. Collins 415.
11. Ibid.
12. Carr 97.
13. A. Williams, "Narratives" 123.
14. Siegel 81.
15. Roberts.
16. Ibid.
17. Kot.
18. S. Lee 140.
19. Ibid.
20. Ibid. 205.
21. Kot.
22. Miller and Chavez.
23. S. Lee 141–142.
24. Ibid. 209.
25. Ibid. 206.

26. Ibid. 140.
27. Ibid. 141.
28. Connelly 173.
29. Bush, "Meat Beat Manifesto" 323.
30. S. Lee 200.
31. Ibid.
32. Connelly 195.
33. Novak.
34. Wiseman-Trowse 6.
35. Lilleker 44.

## Chapter 17: Death

1. Idelson.
2. Garcia, "Guiltman" 40.
3. Barclay, Jack, and Schneider 537.
4. Ibid. 536.
5. "Nomeans No, too fucking wonderful for words."
6. Bonner 14.
7. Bush, "Last Rights" 1019.
8. Barr, "Skinny Puppy."
9. P-Orridge personal interview.
10. D. Thompson, *Industrial Revolution* 77.
11. Hyams.
12. McCaughey.
13. Neville, "Genesis P'Orridge" 31.
14. Ibid.
15. Siana 33.
16. Ibid.
17. Myer.
18. *Culture Shock* 28.
19. Siegel 13.
20. van Elferen 126.
21. Gates.

## Chapter 18: Wonder

1. Tagg, "Harmony" 542.
2. Tagg, "Universal" 252.
3. Candey.
4. Scott.
5. Demers 106–107.
6. Girl the Bourgeois Individualist.
7. Star.
8. Shear.
9. Fulber.
10. Cyberium.

11. Hanley, *Metal Machine Music* 368.
12. Tressler.
13. Savage, Introduction 5.


## Postscript: Is There Any Escape for Noise?

1. Bohn 4.
2. Bergland and Palme.
3. McDonough xi.
4. Reed 31.
5. Lewis 195.
6. N. Smith 53.
7. Ibid. 56.
8. Ibid.
9. Ibid. 51.
10. Shryane 49.
11. Diederichsen 25.
12. Ibid. 26.
13. Ibid. 29.
14. Ibid. 31.
15. Ibid. 32.
16. Ibid. 31.
17. Ibid. 34.
18. Ibid.
19. Debord and Wolman 17.
20. Hillegas 150.
21. Bailey 22.
22. Ibid. 32.
23. Ray 75.
24. Ibid.
25. Demers 106–107.

# Index

occultism, 35–37, 100, 103, 141–144,
    193–194, 212–217, 277
    *see also* chaos magick; religious imagery
Occupy movement, 10
OFF, 247
Off-Beat Records (label), 283–284, 285
Ogilvie, Dave "Rave," 174, 274, 277
Ogre, Nivek (Kevin Ogilvie), 170, 172–182,
    274–278
Oliveros, Pauline, 99
Omnia, 225
On-U Sound Records (label), 211
Oneiroid Psychosis, 41, 169, 259, 287
Oomph, 279
*Op* (magazine), 118
Ordo Templi Orientis (OTO), 142
Orff, Carl, 264, 292
Organum, 253
Orgy, 259
Orpheus, Rodney, 281–282
Oulipo, 8
Out Out, 270

P
P-Orridge, Caresse, 141, 156
P-Orridge, Genesis [Breyer], 9, 11, 34–35,
    36–40, 52, 60, 70–83, 99, 101, 116–119,
    127, 140–145, 155, 162, 170, 200,
    245–246, 276–277
P-Orridge, Paula (Alaura O'Dell), 142, 155
P16.D4, 93, 120, 124, 173
Pailhead, 239
the Pain Machinery, 41
Pain Teens, 171, 251
Palais Schaumburg, 93
Palestine, Charlemagne, 52
Palme, Cole, 107
Pandrogyne project, 9, 11, 127, 142, 204
Panic Records and Tapes (label), 118
Pankow, 90, 139
pan-revolutionary thought, 7–12, 313,
    317–319
Parade Ground, 157
paramilitary, 29–30, 138, 141, 163
    *see also* control; violent content; World
    War II
Paris Uprising of May 1968, 9
parody, 129–131, 202
Pathak, Heman, 53
Pauline, Mark, 104–106, 108, 170

Peace, Love & Pitbulls, 216
Pearce, Douglas, 227
Pearce, Rod, 70–71, 135, 272
Pearce, Stevo, 65, 133, 138–145
Peel, John, 136, 151
Pendragon Records (label), 279
perception of reality, 35, 66, 91, 103, 142,
    146
Pere Ubu, 128
Peterson, Chris, 175, 252
Pet Shop Boys, 6
phasing, 52, 98
philosophical roots of industrial music, 7–12,
    54–55
*Phosphor* (magazine), 43
Pianvanni, Dean, 151
piercing, 142
Pig, 242, 253, 273, 306
Pigface, 256, 272, 276
Pink Floyd, 74
Plank, Conny, 95
Play It Again Sam (label), 157, 161, 164,
    241–242, 263
pleasure, 134–137
plunderphonics, 131
political content, 4–5, 16, 106, 113–115,
    129–131, 147–148, 150, 185–205
    *see also* ideology of industrial music
Polydor Records (label), 72, 231
Polyphonic Size, 157
Ponton, Ben, 48, 152
pop music, 32, 127–139, 153, 207–212,
    231–233
    *see also* dance music
Pop Will East Itself, 273
Popol Vuh, 99
Poppy, Andrew, 142
popularity of industrial music, 5–6, 12,
    127–139, 231–253
    *see also* pop music
Pornotanz, 23
Portion Control, 121, 139, 151, 173
Potter, Colin, 121
power. *see* control
power electronics, 5, 147
powernoise, 132, 296–297
Premature Ejaculation, 272
Primitive Calculators, 146
process as creative driver, 35–40, 104
Process Church of the Final Judgment, 277

Y

Young, La Monte, 45, 50–54, 100
Young Gods, 251–253, 275

Z

Z'EV, 70, 97, 103–105, 108–109, 139, 142,
    160, 169–170
Zen Paradox, 48
Zia, 46
ZickZack (label), 93–94
*ZigZag* (magazine), 69

*Zillo* (zine), 278
zines, 58, 74, 91, 101–102, 110, 116–118, 120,
    143
    *see also specific title*
Žižek, Slavoj, 11, 185, 191, 197–201
Zomba (label), 266
Zorn, John, 209
Zos Kia, 143
Zoth Ommog (label), 247, 273, 284
Zoviet France, 48, 118, 121, 152, 168
ZTT Records (label), 241